Twilight Institutions

Development and Change Book Series
As a journal, *Development and Change* distinguishes itself by its multidisciplinary approach and its breadth of coverage, publishing articles on a wide spectrum of development issues. Accommodating a deeper analysis and a more concentrated focus, it also publishes regular special issues on selected themes. *Development and Change* and Blackwell Publishing collaborate to produce these theme issues as a series of books, with the aim of bringing these pertinent resources to a wider audience.

Titles in the series include:
China's Limits to Growth: Greening State and Society
Edited by Peter Ho and Eduard B. Vermeer

Catalysing Development? A Debate on Aid
Jan Pronk et al.

State Failure, Collapse and Reconstruction
Edited by Jennifer Milliken

Forests: Nature, People, Power
Edited by Martin Doornbos, Ashwani Saith and Ben White

Gendered Poverty and Well-being
Edited by Shahra Razavi

Globalization and Identity
Edited by Birgit Meyer and Peter Geschiere

Social Futures, Global Visions
Edited by Cynthia Hewitt de Alcantara

Twilight Institutions:
Public Authority and Local Politics in Africa

Edited by

Christian Lund

First published as Volume 37, Number 4 of 'Development and Change'

BLACKWELL PUBLISHING
350 Main Street, Malden, MA 02148-5020, USA
9600 Garsington Road, Oxford OX4 2DQ, UK
550 Swanston Street, Carlton, Victoria 3053, Australia

First published in 2007 by Blackwell Publishing Ltd

1 2006

Library of Congress Cataloging-in-Publication Data

Twilight institutions: public authority and local politics in Africa / edited by Christian Lund.
p. cm.
Papers originally presented at a Ph.D. seminar at the Graduate School of International Development Studies, Roskilde University, in 2002.
Includes bibliographical references and index.
ISBN-13: 978-1-4051-5528-1 (alk. paper)
ISBN-10: 1-4051-5528-0 (alk. paper)
1. Local government—Africa, Sub-Saharan—Congresses. 2. Central-local government relations—Africa, Sub-Saharan—Congresses. 3. Law enforcement—Africa, Sub-Saharan—Congresses. 4. State, The—Congresses. 5. Africa, Sub-Saharan—Politics and government—1960—Congresses. I. Lund, Christian.

JS7525.T95 2006
320.80967—dc22

2006035612

A catalogue record for this title is available from the British Library.

Set in 11pt Times
by Techbooks, New Delhi, India
Printed and bound in the United Kingdon
by TJ International, Padstow, Cornwall

The publisher's policy is to use permanent paper from mills that operate a sustainable forestry policy, and which has been manufactured from pulp processed using acid-free and elementary chlorine-free practices. Furthermore, the publisher ensures that the text paper and cover board used have met acceptable environmental accreditation standards.

For further information on
Blackwell Publishing, visit our website:
www.blackwellpublishing.com

CONTENTS

Notes on Contributors

Giorgio Blundo is associate professor at the Ecole des Hautes Etudes en Sciences Sociales (EHESS), Marseilles (Centre de la Vieille Charité, 2 rue de la Charité 13002 Marseille, France; e-mail: blundo@univmed.fr). After his PhD research on local powers, factionalism and decentralization in Senegal, he co-ordinated (with J. P. Olivier de Sardan) a comparative anthropological research on corruption in West Africa. He is currently working on street-level bureaucracies in Senegal and Niger. His recent publications include *Monnayer les pouvoirs. Espaces, mécanismes et représentations de la corruption* (Presses Universitaires de France/IUED, 2000), and two books co-edited with J. P. Olivier de Sardan: *Pratiques de la description* (Editions de l'EHESS, 2003) and *The State and Everyday Corruption in Africa* (Zed Books, forthcoming).

Lars Buur is a Senior Researcher at the Danish Institute for International Studies in Copenhagen (lbu@diis.dk) and Research Associate at Wits Institute for Social and Economic Research, Johannesburg. He obtained his PhD in Ethnography and Social Anthropology from Aarhus University, Denmark. He has published widely on truth and reconciliation technologies, and human rights, law and order in South Africa. In 2004 he was guest editor (together with Steffen Jensen) of 'Everyday Policing in South Africa', a special issue of *African Studies*, volume 63(2). His fieldwork experience covers South Africa and Mozambique and his current work focuses on community participation in taxation and decentralization in Mozambique.

Jeremy Gould is a Fellow of the Academy of Finland based at the Institute of Development Studies, University of Helsinki (gould@valt.helsinki.fi). An anthropologist by training, his research deals with different aspects of state formation, primarily in Zambia. A related interest is the ethnographic analysis of aid relationships. An edited volume, *The New Conditionality: The Politics of Poverty Reduction Strategies* has recently been published by Zed Books.

Sten Hagberg is Associate Professor of Cultural Anthropology at Uppsala University (sten.hagberg@antro.uu.se). Since 1988 he has conducted anthropological fieldwork in Burkina Faso on various topics, such as forest perceptions, farmer–herder conflicts, ethnicity and voluntary associations, poverty and political culture. His publications include *Between Peace and Justice: Dispute Settlement between Karaboro Farmers and Fulbe Agro-pastoralists in Burkina Faso* (1998); *Poverty in Burkina Faso: Representations and Realities* (2001); the co-edited book *Bonds and Boundaries in Northern Ghana and Southern Burkina Faso* (2000); and several articles in journals and edited books.

Kristine Juul is Associate Professor at the Department of Geography and International Development Studies, Roskilde University (kristine@ruc.dk). After her PhD on the effects of drought-related migration on tenure issues and resource management among Fulani pastoralists in Northern Senegal, she has worked on decentralization and local politics in northern Senegal. She is co-editor of *Negotiating Property in Africa* (Heinemann, 2002).

Helene Maria Kyed is a PhD candidate in International Development Studies, Roskilde University Centre and is affiliated to the Danish Institute for International Studies (hmk@diis.dk). Her research areas include decentralization of government and post-conflict state formation with a specific emphasis on traditional authority and local forms of justice enforcement and policing. He fieldwork experience covers Zimbabwe and Mozambique.

Carola Lentz is Professor of Social Anthroplogy at the Department of Anthropology and African Studies, Johannes Gutenberg University of Mainz, Germany (D 55099 Mainz; lentz@uni-mainz.de). Following her doctoral research on labour migration and ethnicity in Ecuador, she has conducted research on ethnicity, elite formation and history in Northwestern Ghana. She is the author of *Ethnicity and the Making of History in Northern Ghana* (Edinburgh University Press, 2006) as well as many related articles, and is co-editor of *Ethnicity in Ghana: The Limits of Invention* (Macmillan, 2000). Her current research focuses on the history of mobility, land rights and the politics of belonging in Northern Ghana and Southern Burkina Faso, and she has recently edited the volume *Land and the Politics of Belonging in West Africa* (Brill, 2006).

Christian Lund is Professor at the Department of International Development Studies, Roskilde University (clund@ruc.dk). He has conducted research on local politics and land conflicts in West Africa. He is the author of *Law, Power and Politics in Niger: Land Struggles and the Rural Code* (LIT Verlag/Transaction Publishers, 1998) and co-editor of *Negotiating Property in Africa* (Heinemann, 2002). He is currently working on a book manuscript provisionally entitled, *Local Politics and the Dynamics of Property in Ghana*.

Pierre-Yves Le Meur is an anthropologist, programme officer at GRET (Groupe de recherche et d'échanges technologiques, Paris; e-mail: Lemeur@gret.org), and associate researcher in IRD (Institut de recherché pour le développement, Montpellier), in the research unit 'Land Regulations, Public Policy, Actors' Logics'. He is currently working on local politics, governmentality, mobility and access to natural resources in Benin. He has recently co-edited with Jean-Pierre Chauveau and Jean-Pierre Jacob *Gouverner les hommes et les ressources: dynamiques de la frontiére interne*, a special issue of *Autrepart*, 2004.

David Pratten is University Lecturer in the Social Anthropology of Africa, and Fellow of St Antony's College, Oxford; e-mail: david.pratten@sant.ox.ac.uk. He is affiliated to and teaches in the Institute of Social and Cultural Anthropology and the African Studies Centre at the University of Oxford. His research is based on Annang communities in South eastern Nigeria and he is author of a social history of this region, *The Man-Leopard Murder Mysteries: History and Society in Colonial Nigeria* (Edinburgh University Press). His recent research focuses on the ethnography of the state, vigilantism, youth and violence.

Simon Turner is Senior Researcher, Danish Institute for International Studies, Copenhagen. He has worked on politics, governance and identities in refugee camps. His publications include 'Under the Gaze of the "Big Nations": Refugees, Rumour and the International Community in Tanzania' (*African Affairs* 103[411], 2004) and 'The Tutsi are Afraid we will discover their Secrets on Secrecy and Sovereign Power in Burundi' (*Social Identities* 11[1], 2005). He is presently working on long-distance nationalism among the Burundian diaspora in Europe and East Africa.

1

Twilight Institutions: An Introduction

Christian Lund

Literature on the state in developing societies, and in particular in Africa, generally has a hard time specifying what is 'state' and what is not. It seems that the closer one gets to a particular political landscape, the more apparent it becomes that many institutions have a twilight character; they are not the state but they exercise public authority.[1] They defy clear-cut distinction. In fact, as we venture to study the political contours of public authority and the political field in which it is exercised, we are saddled with a paradox. On the one hand, actors and institutions in this field are intensely preoccupied with the state and with the distinction between state and society, but on the other hand, their practices constantly befuddle these distinctions.

In an issue of *Development and Change* entirely devoted to state collapse, Milliken and Krause (2002) question whether this phenomenon describes an actual collapse of concrete institutional forms, or whether it is our vision of a progressive, coherent and development-oriented state that has collapsed. Whereas difficult to determine, it is a useful heuristic question. Milliken and Krause argue that while full-blown state collapse remains a rare phenomenon, investigation of such cases may, as their volume proves (see for example Doornbos, 2002; Musah, 2002), provide clues for the understanding of weak and failing states which are far less exceptional.

Most of the articles in this issue of *Development and Change* were first presented at a PhD seminar at the Graduate School of International Development Studies, Roskilde University, in late 2002. The seminar produced a very stimulating debate, and as the first set of papers was circulated, others joined in with contributions to make up the issue as it is. Some of the participants in the seminar who did not deliver papers for this issue should be recognized for their important contributions to our discussions, namely Karin Barber, Simon Batterbury, Tania Murray Li, Peter Geschiere, Eric Worby and Amanda Hammar. I also wish to thank the two anonymous referees for their constructive comments and suggestions and Signe Marie Cold-Ravnkilde for assistance with the editing of the papers in Roskilde.

1. One of the questions that arose in our debate was whether 'twilight' was an appropriate metaphor to signify the phenomenon we have in mind. It was suggested that the temporal aspect of twilight would imply an expectation that these institutions should gradually disappear. In fact, none of the contributions in this collection suggest this. The metaphor simply signifies that contours and features of these institutions are hard to distinguish and discern.

This collection concentrates on Africa and essentially shares the same concern: the state and processes of state formation. However, we privilege an alternative and complementary perspective. Instead of studying collapse and failure we attempt to develop an approach to investigate *how public authority actually works* in the face of obvious state failure and impending collapse. Moreover, instead of looking at the state as an entity 'from above', we attempt to approach public authority 'from below', from the variety of concrete encounters between forms of public authority and the more or less mundane practices of ordinary people. The contributions that follow put the focus on the institutions that Bailey describes as, 'those which are partly regulated by, and partly independent of, larger encapsulating political structures; and which, so to speak, fight battles with these larger structures in a way which seldom ends in victory, rarely in dramatic defeat, but usually in a long drawn stalemate and defeat by attrition' (Bailey, 1968: 281). While sharing an interest for how public authority actually works, the contributions reflect a variety of contexts. Hence some focus on how government institutions fail to rule and other institutions of public authority emerge (Pratten, Buur, Turner, Hagberg and Blundo), while others deal with situations where government institutions to some extent rule despite the contingencies of context (Le Meur, Buur and Kyed, Juul and Gould). However, even this simple distinction is rendered precarious by the richness of the individual articles.

Thus, the ambition of this collection is not to generate general explanatory theories *à la* Chabal and Daloz (1999) where catchy statements are often purchased at the expense of nuance. Rather, the ambition is to suggest ways of investigating how public authority operates in local contexts. The first article by Lund thus suggests an analytical strategy for taking on the phenomenon of public authority in contexts where it is not the exclusive possession of government institutions, where institutional competition is intense and a range of ostensibly a-political situations become actively politicized. To zero in on the object of concern it might be useful to take a brief look at two perspectives from which we would like to distinguish ourselves. Two views on state and society in developing societies have dominated much debate since the mid-1980s; one initially focusing on economic development, the other on politics and democratization. However, both literatures contain significant gaps.

Evans, Rueschemeyer and Skocpol published *Bringing the State Back In* in 1985 in an attempt to demonstrate that effective state intervention was a prerequisite for capital accumulation (Skocpol, 1985: 4–5, 20). Two significant points issued from their work and the series of publications in its wake: not only is the state an actor in its own right with a significant degree of autonomy from particular social forces, this is true to such an extent that its structures and activities condition and configure what may appear to be socio-economic phenomena (Bratton, 1994; Chazan, 1988; Degnbol, 1999; Marenin, 1987; Migdal, 1988). While this was a welcome refocusing on the political, the conceptualization of the state treats certain central issues as given rather than problematic. First, such an approach tends to see state and society as fundamentally distinct entities. Chazan (1988: 123) is a good example, as she ventures:

> State and society are conceptualised ... as two intersecting and potentially independent variables with political processes as the dependent variable. Thus, the state entity does have an existence of its own, and its actions may have a profound bearing on social organisation and economic enterprise. Social groups, similarly, maintain an institutional and resource base which permits them to act independently as well as conjointly with structures in the political domain. These political, economic and social fields may intertwine in a multiplicity of ways.

Despite statements about the fluidity of state–society notions, the binary opposition constitutes a profound mental template (for stimulating critique see Kaviraj, 1997; Lemarchand, 1992; Mitchell, 1991; Rose and Miller, 1992). Secondly, and following from the above, this focus is pervasively state-centred, that is, it concerns itself with what is *necessary* for the state to implement policy. To the extent that the state is dis-aggregated, it is generally into various agencies (executive, legislative or judiciary), all of which are acknowledged constitutionally or otherwise legally as the state. Organizations and institutions that exercise legitimate public authority, but do not enjoy legal recognition as part of the state, are out of focus (see Migdal, 1988: 28; 2001: 15–23).

Many scholars of a state-centred inclination draw heavily on Max Weber, conceptualizing the state as an *organization* with legitimate means of coercion. However, had they turned their attention to the Weber who tried to get to grips with the 'nature and "legitimacy" of territorial political organisations' (Weber, 1922/1978: 901–4), their focus might have been less on organization and more on the *substantive activity* of competing political organizations as they exercise public authority. The main weakness in privileging organizational features of the state is that one tends to ignore the processual aspects of the formation of public authority, and in particular how it takes place in day-to-day social encounters. To paraphrase E. P. Thompson, the *state* did not rise like the sun at an appointed time. It was present at its own making. That is, one of the ways in which public authority is established is by its successful exercise as a result of struggle. When an institution authorizes, sanctions or validates certain rights, the respect or observance of these rights by people, powerful in clout or numbers, simultaneously constitutes recognition of the authority of that particular institution.

Focusing on struggle as a prime mover, Jessop proposes a definition which assumes a zoning of society into institutions, of which some are more and some less 'state'. He defines it like this: 'The core of the state apparatus comprises a distinct ensemble of institutions and organizations whose socially accepted function is to define and enforce collectively binding decisions on the members of a society in the name of their common interest or general will' (Jessop, 1990: 341). This suggests both institutional and coercive dimensions as well as elements of discourse as constituents of 'state'. Jessop hastens to qualify this by arguing for the historically-specific constitution of the 'core'; for wide variations in forms of enforcement; for common interest and general will as rhetoric and strategic statements articulating social interests and, finally, for the existence of multiple, even mutually contradictory, institutions in which various structural powers are inscribed. These social institutions constitute centres of power and develop procedures, norms, hierarchies and codes proper to themselves. This means that no institution is state as such; 'state' is, rather, the quality of an institution being able to define and enforce collectively binding decisions on members of society. We tend to reserve state qualities for government institutions, but this is more a reflection of our idea of an end result than of the messy process of state formation itself. This means that we should investigate the processes producing *institutional forms* as well as the processes that bring about the *idea* of the state.

National laws and government institutions constitute an environment for local politics and important local players within it; a structure of opportunities for the negotiation of rights and distribution of resources, and significant agents who negotiate. However, government institutions are not alone in wielding public authority. Whether labelled state or not, it seems that a wide variety of institutions constitute themselves as *de facto* public authorities, with greater or lesser success. And this is the point. Public authority can wax and wane. Institutions or groups of actors — such as mayors, district chief executives, district commissioners, magistrates, chiefs, 'strong-men', and professional associations, societies, parties, home town and youth associations, churches, revolutionary defence committees, development projects, and so forth — all take an active interest in local politics and the shaping of governance, and in defining and enforcing collectively-binding decisions and rules. Or rather, *attempting* to define and enforce them, since this capacity is rarely fully accomplished and often challenged. Consequently, while parties in dispute may go 'forum shopping', taking their claim or dispute, or issue of public concern to the institution which they deem most likely to produce a satisfactory outcome, institutions also use disputes for their own, mainly local, political ends. As Keebet von Benda-Beckmann puts it, 'besides forum-shopping disputants, there are also "shopping forums" engaged in trying to acquire and manipulate disputes from which they expect to gain political advantage, or to fend off disputes which they fear will threaten their interests. They shop for disputes as disputants shop for forums' (von Benda-Beckmann, 1981: 117). As indicated above, when an institution authorizes, sanctions or validates certain rights, the respect or observance of these rights by people constitutes recognition of the authority of that particular institution. In order to understand how political power is exercised, we therefore need to have an eye for the processual aspects of the formation of public authority, and in particular how it takes place in day-to-day social encounters. Yet, legitimate authority is not necessarily legitimate authority for good but must be vindicated and legitimated through a broad array of political practices.

In essence, such practices constitute the negotiation of public authority in a particular context.

More subtley, the state invades the field of local politics in the form of an idea (Abrams, 1988). The exercise of power and authority by local institutions alludes to the state and government policies symbolize the state and the idea of law. Hansen and Stepputat (2001a: 8) suggest that states only exist when practical and symbolic languages of governance combine. The institutionalization of law and legal discourse, and the materialization of the state in a series of permanent signs and rituals — so-called state spectacles — are integral parts of that language, and the collection of essays edited by Hansen and Stepputat (2001b) provides a range of illustrations.

Das and Poole (2004) show how the idea of the state is effectively conjured up through the production of its flipside, the 'margin'. By various forms of marginalization of regions, groups and concerns, the idea of a purposive centre develops. Work by Bierschenk and Olivier de Sardan (1997, 1998, 2003) demonstrates how the idea of a state — however seemingly distant — informs the organizing practices of everyday politics. Thus, the language of the state is not the preserve of government institutions alone, and other institutions strut in borrowed plumes. What we are witnessing is certain forms of institutionalization and formalization of the exercise of authority alluding to state, law and the bureaucracy, encoded in official language and often exercised with the paraphernalia of modern statehood. A variety of institutions may use the language of the state as well as its props in terms of contracts, deeds, attestations, stamps, stationery and declarations. The irony of such 'unstately stateliness' is that while distinctions get increasingly blurred (who is exercising state authority?), they become increasingly important (who can produce rights?).

The other major debate on state and society appears more concerned with democratization and political participation. Thus, since the early 1990s it has been difficult to talk about the state in development societies without making reference not only to society but also to civil society. However, as Mamdani (1996: 139) observes, the concept is more programmatic than analytical and more ideological than historical. The concept of civil society has travelled a long way from Scottish Enlightenment and nineteenth-century European political philosophy. It was revived after a long period of hibernation by intellectual dissidents in Eastern Europe in the 1970s and 1980s. Now, it seems to be the finest ideological export item that the West can offer the rest of the world, in particular in the light of general disillusionment with a centralized state. It has almost become a Eurocentric index of accomplishment, upon which aid and trade deals partly depend (partly, because geo-strategic considerations indeed also inform international *realpolitik* — see Comaroff and Comaroff, 1999). In political jargon, and in particular within *development speak*, a number of reductions seem to dominate. In his analysis of the debate on civil society in Africa, Karlström remarks, '[w]hile some political scientists include virtually all voluntary associations in their definition of civil society, the dominant trend among Africanists has been to narrow the concept, excluding associations that do not engage with the state in ways that enhance either the democratic character of governance or the state's capacity to carry out its policies' (Karlström, 1999: 105). In excluding the 'bad boys' from our analytical lens, we develop 'tunnel vision' and lose perspective. The unruly, the un-civil and the ones who are capricious and hard to nail down are just as significant in local politics as more angelic organizations. Moreover, such groups are generally more recalcitrant, vociferous and outright flamboyant than benign voluntary associations patronized by benevolent donors, and they lead us to identify tensions in society. They are epistemologically as well as aesthetically fascinating (see Pratten, Buur, Turner and Hagberg, this volume). However, such fascination should neither lead us to boyish celebration of violence, nor to disregard institutions that operate in less flagrant contradiction to the tenets of 'good governance'.

The state–society distinction is embedded in the idea of public–private which stands out as one of the grand dichotomies of Western thought. However, as Weintraub (1997: 2) points out, the distinction comprises not a single paired opposition, but a complex family of oppositions. Weintraub shows how various ideas and meanings are attached to private and public over time and context (see also Bobbio, 1989; Cohen and Arato, 1994; Comaroff and Comaroff, 1999; Gellner, 1996; Mamdani, 1996; Taylor, 1990). However, while the distinction between state and civil society has become a less than useful analytical tool, it has spilled over from academic to more popular political discourse with other effects. As it is 'no longer divorced from the agency of the groups of individuals it purports to describe' (Whitfield, 2003: 380), it becomes part of a dynamic process of production of popular distinctions. As a consequence, we should not refrain from studying civil society. On the contrary, we should pay careful attention to *how* concepts and distinctions are produced, instrumentalized and contested. The purpose of this collection of articles is to question the alleged lucidity of such popular distinctions.

In order to engage with the public authority, it is, nonetheless, useful to sketch out some of its elements. By *authority* is meant an instance of power which seeks at least a minimum of voluntary compliance and thus is legitimated in some way. The element of *public* should direct our attention toward two associated elements. On the one hand, public authority connotes impersonal administrative operations in a wide sense. On the other hand, it refers to public (as in 'not secret') confrontations, discussions and action in concert. Thus, we are dealing with institutions which, in the exercise of power, take on the mantle of public administrative authority (legitimated administrative operations) and in their attempts to govern articulate notions of state varying from their source of power to their antithesis. What characterizes this group of institutions is their movement in and out of a capacity to exercise public authority. They operate in the twilight between state and society, between public and private. We ought to invest our energy in an agnostic and non-normative enquiry of the hodgepodge of twilight institutions that govern daily lives in local contexts, and to problematize the distinctions we tend to accept as given. Moreover, we ought to investigate the *making* of public authority as an active and contested process of assertion, legitimization and exercise.

True to the nature of the issue at stake — state formation and transforming institutions of public authority — the contributions to this volume represent variation in empirical focus and analytical approach stretching from security and service provision, over taxation and control over space, to the definition of rule of law. However, central elements bind them together. The most conspicuous commonality is that they all deal with Africa. The ambition of this collection is not regional in a strict sense, but African history and theoretically informed empirical analysis have significant theoretical and epistemological insights to offer development studies and social science in general. Bayart's book on the politics of the belly was emblematic of much of the research on state and politics in Africa and triggered more research in that particular field (Bayart, 1989). The blurred boundary between state and non-state is often more conspicuous in Africa than in other places because of the many challenges to a grand state formation project. Empirical evidence from Africa thus clearly exposes the theoretical fragility of clear separation between state and society. Moreover, evidence from research in Africa — as demonstrated in this volume — also bespeaks the tenacity of the *idea* of a clear separation between the two. This paradox, while clearly revealed in Africa, is not reserved for this region, but could well prove significant beyond (see for example Gupta, 1995; Hansen, 2001; Nuijten, 2003).

The other common feature in the articles that follow is the focus on dynamic processes, whether in the form of conflict or more subtle negotiations. The immense variation in processes of reproduction and change of institutions of public authority calls for empirical studies which can unveil their historical, contextual and contingent construction. Socially constructed does not necessarily mean ephemeral or weak, however. While fluidity may characterize institutions and authority, it may not be of the lowest possible viscosity. Certain settlements, rights and authorities may 'stick'. Once successfully constructed, institutions of authority become markers for the future negotiation of society, and such settlements may hold for some time. The 'stickiness' of certain structured situations is related to the institutions involved in the competition and to the context of opportunities.

Local politics provides a privileged opportunity for the study of such political processes and how the capacity to regulate and control is not neatly stored within the state. The first article (by Christian Lund) aims to discuss an analytical approach to public authority in contexts where clear distinctions are rare and where ideological registers and political practices are composite and often contradictory. The article describes the phenomenon of public authority on the basis of theoretically informed empirical analyses which, though disparate, share a concern for different aspects of the phenomenon and its mercurial character. It is therefore an attempt to recover and systematize some of the insights from empirical analyses of institutions which operate between public authority and private agency in Africa. The article discusses some of the central political practices that constitute, and unravel, public authority; it also suggests a number of possible institutional ramifications of the various political practices.

The 'twin' articles by David Pratten and Lars Buur address the question of how youth in southern Nigeria and South Africa respond to disorder in the political economic and judicial spheres. Both look at vigilantes and local justice enforcement as emerging from below. While Pratten's case shows the organization set in deep vertical politics of patrimonialism, Buur's analysis shows how institutions from the struggle against apartheid search for a place in the post-apartheid political structures. Common for both is how repertoires of accountability and crime are actively employed by these institutions in order to place themselves on the side of propriety and order.

The article by Simon Turner explores how Burundian refugees in Lukole refugee camp in Tanzania negotiate public authority in a space that is at once heavily governed by international relief agencies while simultaneously marked by a collapse of the known moral order of Burundi. Thus, Turner deals with an 'exceptional situation' (though not as exceptional as one would like). The formal state is suspended, and a technical agency — UNHCR — operates as an a-political surrogate authority. Nonetheless, public authority is produced partly by the powers that UNHCR delegates to these actors and partly by the power bases that they manage to build up in the gaps in UNHCR's system. It rests partially on the respect that these brokers gain from other refugees (a respect that is earned in numerous ways, such as outwitting the international organizations) and partially on the recognition that they get from the very same organizations.

Sten Hagberg offers a 'biography' of a political entrepreneur in Burkina Faso. By studying a particular controversial 'master hunter', Hagberg reveals the intricate networks that the entrepreneur creatively appropriates in the making of public authority. He breaks state law to assert his own authority. But he also draws upon state institutions to be recognized as a legitimate political actor. Hagberg joins the other authors by locating the case in the context of the making and unmaking of public authority, and discusses its implications for understanding local political culture in contemporary Africa.

Giorgio Blundo focuses on the informalization and privatization of state services such as customs, police and local tax offices. He demonstrates how the inability of the under-staffed Senegalese administration creates opportunities for the production of institutions that undertake the day-to-day administration in increasing informality. This way, private entrepreneurs begin to undertake tasks which are normally associated with 'stateness' and thus actively remodel the distinctions. One of the central features of the state is its prerogative to tax. Kristine Juul demonstrates how the attempt to involve local councils in tax collection in the pastoral region of Senegal has not been met by great enthusiasm. Rather, payment of local taxes failed after responsibility for tax collection was transferred to the politically elected rural councils. Meanwhile, other local institutions with less clear relations to government manage to tax water, and seem to have taken over the role of providers of public services, of political representation and as suppliers of secure access or more or less formalized rights over crucial local resources. The article by Juul also broaches the aspect of space and control over spatial resources.

Helene Kyed and Lars Buur show how traditional leaders in Mozambique were formally stripped of authority during the one-party Frelimo rule. However, this did not mean that the war areas had no public authority. On the contrary, a range of non-state forms of authority filled out the socio-economic and cultural space outside the Frelimo-controlled district headquarters. The most vital of these forms of authority — traditional leaders and Renamo militants — had been forged in opposition to the Frelimo-state. While Renamo militias have by now *de jure* been converted into a political party, the government is currently trying to include and formalize chieftaincy, granting traditional leaders a dual position and double accountability as community representatives as well as agents of local state administration.

Pierre-Yves Le Meur also engages with institutional vacuums in his article on access to land in Benin. Access to and control over land is not unequivocal. Various institutional forms such as administrative chieftaincy, patron–client relationships linking migrants and autochthonous people, intra- and inter-lineage ties and alliances, religious cults and affinities, all deal with access to and control over strategic resources. Within this complex political landscape, state intervention is itself plural: besides 'classical' territorial and development services and the newly implemented political decentralization, it takes the ambiguous form of a natural resource management project funded by foreign donors and bearing a discourse of democratic participation and of power territorialization. State-making in this context is much more a product of this blurring of discursive and institutional boundaries than an evolutionary process of state construction.

Carola Lentz's article also sees the territorial ordering of space as central in state making. But state making is obviously not only the business of the state. Based on work in Ghana, Lentz engages general questions of governance at the local level: the spatial delimitation of administrative units and the social delimitation of local political communities. When civic associations, traditional rulers and other non-state institutions present their claims *vis-à-vis* the state, they often invoke some form of 'natural' solidarity that binds the local community together and legitimates its quest for a separate administrative entity. Decentralization projects therefore become arenas of debate over the boundaries of community and the relationship between 'local' and national citizenship.

In the final article, Jeremy Gould moves from the local to a national level as he undertakes a political ethnography of the 'rule of law' in a post-colonial

African context. He argues that not only are struggles over legitimacy and sovereignty played out at different scales, but that the struggles are in part about scale and whose authority is to prevail and be overarching. In the run-up to the 2001 presidential elections, the Zambian bar association was instrumental in forming an activist body of unprecedented political leverage, the Oasis Forum, which united lawyers, church leaders and the women's movement. Based on a close reading of Zambia's recent political history, Gould's contribution deals with the constitution and compelling nature of legal authority in the Zambian social imagination as authored by non-state actors with legal legitimacy, and the meaning of 'law' as a constitutive element in post-colonial state formation.

No simple pattern emerges from these contributions. Large structural transformations, such as state formation in Africa, are wrought with conflict, ambiguity and open junctures, and characterized by the presence of multiple, competing logics. However a central point can be distilled. When we approach the phenomenon of public authority and governance, it is useful not to see it as stemming from one single source, but rather to focus on how particular issues (security, justice, development, taxation and others) are governed and which actors are engaged in them. Many of the political actions in these spheres of life presuppose a state, but the state qualities of governance are not exclusively nested in government institutions. Consequently, there is an ongoing competition in society — perhaps most visibly so in African societies where governments are often under-funded, overstretched, in-capacitated and de-legitimized — to rearrange the boundaries of public authority between institutions so far unable to command enduring functional hegemony. While the twilight has an opaque character, these contributions not only show that this is when and where politics 'happens'; they also demonstrate that the twilight is certainly not beyond detailed and vivid empirical analysis.

Obviously, when trying to fill a gap in the literature on state formation by focusing on local political processes, other gaps remain and new ones emerge. Two merit mentioning here. First, this collection leaves it for others to get to grips with how public authority is constituted and contested in macro settings and could be charged with 'localism' (Mohan and Stokke, 2000). We have not dealt with how state sovereignty and international agencies and business are confronted. This is a major concern of international politics; although often seen as remote from the concerns of the present issue, there are several overlapping interests which could provide an interesting dialogue. Secondly, by selecting Africa as a critical case, we may well have privileged certain aspects of public authority and local politics. We would therefore like to see this as an invitation to others to confront our findings with empirical analyses of other contexts. This would no doubt produce complementary institutional forms and alternative ideas about the state.

REFERENCES

Abrams, P. (1988) 'Notes on the Difficulty of Studying the State', *Journal of Historical Sociology* 1(1): 58–89.

Bailey, F. G. (1968) 'Parapolitical Systems', in M. J. Swartz (ed.) *Local-Level Politics: Social and Cultural Perspectives*, pp. 281–94. London: University of London Press.

Bayart, J. F. (1989) *L'État en Afrique. La politique du ventre*. Paris: Fayard.

von Benda-Beckmann, K. (1981) 'Forum Shopping and Shopping Forums: Dispute Processing in a Minangkabau Village in West Sumatra', *Journal of Legal Pluralism* 19: 117–62.

Bierschenk, T. and J. P. de Sardan Olivier (1997) 'Local Powers and a Distant State in Rural Central African Republic', *Journal of Modern African Studies* 35(3): 441–68.

Bierschenk, T. and J. P. de Sardan Olivier (1998) 'Les arènes locales face à la décentralisation et à la démocratisation', in T. Bierschenk and J. P. Olivier de Sardan (eds) *Les pouvoirs au village. Le Bénin rural entre démocratisation et decentralisation*, pp. 11–51. Paris: Khartala.

Bierschenk, T. and J. P. de Sardan Olivier (2003) 'Powers in the Village: Rural Benin between Democratisation and Decentralisation', *Africa* 73(2): 145–73.

Bobbio, N. (1989) *Democracy and Dictatorship: The Nature and Limits of State Power*. Oxford: Polity Press.

Bratton, M. (1994) 'Peasant–State Relations in Post-colonial Africa: Patterns of Engagement and Disengagement', in J. Migdal, A. Kohli and V. Shue (eds) *State Power and Social Forces: Domination and Transformation in the Third World*, pp. 231–54. Cambridge: Cambridge University Press.

Chabal, P. and J. P. Daloz (1999) *Africa Works: Disorder as Political Instrument*. Oxford: James Currey; Bloomington, IN: International African Institute/Indiana University Press.

Chazan, N. (1988) 'Patterns of State–Society Incorporation and Disengagement in Africa', in D. Rothchild and N. Chazan (eds) *The Precarious Balance: State and Society in Africa*, pp. 121–48. Boulder, CO: Westview Press.

Cohen, J. L. and A. Arato (1994) *Civil Society and Political Theory*. Cambridge, MA: MIT Press.

Comaroff, J. and J. Comaroff (1999) 'Civil Society and Political Imagination in Africa: Introduction', in J. Comaroff and J. Comaroff (eds) *Civil Society and Political Imagination in Africa: Critical Perspectives*, pp. 1–43. Chicago, IL: Chicago University Press.

Das, V. and D. Poole (2004) 'State and its Margins. Comparative Ethnographies', in V. Das and D. Poole (eds) *Anthropology in the Margins of the State*, pp. 3–33. Santa Fe, NM: School of American Research Press; Oxford: James Currey.

Degnbol, T. (1999) 'State Bureaucracies under Pressure: A Study of the Interaction between Four Extension Agencies and Cotton-Producing Farmers in the Sikasso Region, Mali'. PhD dissertation, Roskilde University, Denmark.

Doornbos, M. (2002) 'State Collapse and Fresh Starts: Some Critical Reflections', *Development and Change* Special Issue 33(5): 797–815.

Gellner, E. (1996) *Conditions of Liberty: Civil Society and its Rivals*. London: Penguin.

Gupta, A. (1995) 'Blurred Boundaries, the Discourse of Corruption, the Culture of Politics, and the Imagined State', *American Ethnologist* 22(2): 375–402.

Hansen, T. B. (2001) 'Governance and State Mythologies in Mumbai', in T. B. Hansen and F. Stepputat (eds) *States of Imagination: Ethnographic Explorations of the Postcolonial State*, pp. 221–54. Durham, NC: Duke University Press.

Hansen, T. B. and F. Stepputat (2001a) 'Introduction: States of Imagination', in T. B. Hansen and F. Stepputat (eds) *States of Imagination: Ethnographic Explorations of the Postcolonial State*, pp. 1–38. Durham, NC: Duke University Press.

Hansen, T. B. and F. Stepputat (2001b) (eds) *States of Imagination: Ethnographic Explorations of the Postcolonial State*. Durham, NC: Duke University Press.

Jessop, B. (1990) *State Theory: Putting Capitalist States in their Place*. Oxford: Polity Press.

Karlström, M. (1999) 'Civil Society and its Presuppositions: Lessons from Uganda', in J. Comaroff and J. Comaroff (eds) *Civil Society and Political Imagination in Africa: Critical Perspectives*, pp. 104–23. Chicago, IL: Chicago University Press.
Kaviraj, S. (1997) 'The Modern State in India', in M. Doornbos and S. Kaviraj (eds) *Dynamics of State Formation: India and Europe Compared*, pp. 225–50. New Delhi: Sage Publications.
Lemarchand, R. (1992) 'Uncivil States and Civil Societies: How Illusion Became Reality', *Journal of Modern African Studies* 30(2): 177–91.
Mamdani, M. (1996) *Citizen and Subject: Contemporary Africa and the Legacy of Late Colonialism*. London: James Currey.
Marenin, O. (1987) 'The Managerial State', in Z. Ergas (ed.) *The African State in Transition*, pp. 61–85. London: MacMillan Press.
Migdal, J. (1988) *Strong States and Weak Societies: State–Society Relations and State Capabilities in the Third World*. Princeton, NJ: Princeton University Press.
Migdal, J. (2001) *State in Society: Studying how States and Societies Transform and Constitute One Another*. Cambridge: Cambridge University Press.
Milliken, J. and K. Krause (2002) 'State Failure, State Collapse, and State Reconstruction: Concepts, Lessons and Strategies', *Development and Change* Special Issue 33(5): 753–74.
Mitchell, T. (1991) 'The Limits of the State: Beyond Statist Approaches and their Critics', *American Political Science Review* 85(1): 77–96.
Mohan, G. and K. Stokke (2000) 'Participatory Development and Empowerment. The Dangers of Localism', *Third World Quarterly* 21(2): 247–68.
Musah, A. F. (2002) 'Privatization of Security, Arms Proliferation and the Process of State Collapse in Africa', *Development and Change* Special Issue 33(5): 911–33.
Nuijten, M. (2003) *Power, Community and the State: The Political Anthropology of Organisation in Mexico*. London: Pluto Press.
Rose, N. and P. Miller (1992) 'Political Power beyond the State: Problematics of Government', *British Journal of Sociology* 43(2): 173–205.
Skocpol, T. (1985) 'Bringing the State Back In', in P. Evans, D. Rueschemeyer and T. Skocpol (eds) *Bringing the Sate Back In*, pp. 3–37. Cambridge: Cambridge University Press.
Taylor, C. (1990) 'Modes of Civil Society', *Public Culture* 3(1): 95–118.
Weber, M. (1922/1978) *Economy and Society: An Outline of Interpretative Sociology*. Berkeley, CA: University of California Press.
Weintraub, J. (1997) 'The Theory and Politics of the Public/Private Distinction', in J. Weintraub and K. Kumar (eds) *Public and Private in Thought and Practice: Perspectives on a Grand Dichotomy*, pp. 1–42. Chicago, IL, and London: University of Chicago Press.
Whitfield, L. (2003) 'Civil Society as an Idea and Civil Society as Process. The Case of Ghana', *Oxford Development Studies* 31(3): 379–400.

Twilight Institutions: Public Authority and Local Politics in Africa

Christian Lund

INSTITUTIONS OF PUBLIC AUTHORITY

In his famous article on the difficulty of studying the state, Abrams makes the insightful distinction between the state system and the state as an idea. The system part is made up of tangible, mostly government, institutions, whereas the idea is what is generally expected to make up the state. As Abrams suggests, the 'relationship of the state-system and the state-idea to other forms of power should and can be central concerns of political analysis' (Abrams, 1988: 82). When approaching African political landscapes, however, two provisos seem in order. First, while government institutions are important, the state qualities of governance — that is, being able to define and enforce collectively binding decisions on members of society — are not exclusively nested in these institutions. A wider variety of institutions are at play in this enterprise. Second, while the idea of the state is powerful — Hansen and Stepputat (2001: 38) even suggest that it has become truly global and universalized — it is employed also to depict its opposite, or 'what we are not', even by institutions that effectively exercise public authority of one kind or another.

In Africa there is no shortage of institutions attempting to exercise public authority. In the first place, there are multiple layers and branches of government institutions (the judiciary, the administration, the customs service and police, the various extension agencies and so on) which are present and active to various degrees; but there are also so-called traditional institutions vying for public authority, often bolstered by government recognition. Much of the literature on African politics and its history details how governmental and chieftaincy institutions negotiate, forge alliances and compete to constitute public authority and political control (Bayart, 1989; Berry, 1993; Boone, 1998, 2003; Gluckman, 1958; Mamdani, 1996; Moore, 1986; Peel, 1983; Rathbone, 2000; van Rouveroy van Nieurwaal, 1999). In addition, associations and organizations which do not appear at first sight to be political may also exercise political power and wield public authority. Similarly, ostensibly non-political situations may reveal themselves to be active sites of political negotiation and mediation over the implementation of public goals or the distribution of public authority in which local and regional identities and power relations are reshaped and recast.[1]

In such cases it is difficult to ascribe exercised authority to the 'state' as a coherent institution; rather, public authority becomes the amalgamated result of the exercise of power by a variety of local institutions and the imposition of external institutions, conjugated with the *idea* of a state. Hence the practice of governance varies from place to place, and even from field to field such as 'security', 'citizenship', 'property', 'development' and so forth (see Bayart et al., 2001; Lemarchand, 1992). In some areas, authority may be exercised by institutions with near hegemonic competence, while at the same time their authority in other domains may be ferociously contested. This implies a certain fluidity in what Bierschenk and Olivier de Sardan (1997) call 'strategic groups'. Strategic groups defending shared interests may form or disintegrate in the course of struggle and can be seen undergoing constant reproduction and transformation. For this reason, it is often unrewarding to attempt an analytical distinction between state and civil society. Nevertheless, although analytically inert, the distinction between state and civil society has a lot going for it in the discursive and political organization of society on a grand and small scale alike. Moreover, if public authority — or 'stateness' — can wax and wane, it follows that state institutions are never definitively formed, but that a constant process of formation takes place (Olivier de Sardan, 2005: 16; Steinmetz, 1999: 9). Such institutions operate in the twilight between state and society, between public and private.

The ambition of this article is to suggest an analytical strategy for the understanding of public authority in contexts where it is not the exclusive realm of government institutions, where institutional competition is intense, and where a range of apparently a-political situations become actively politicized. In recent years anthropologists, geographers, political scientists and others have grappled with a cluster of concerns including public authority, legitimacy, belonging, citizenship and territory; naturally, they approach the topics differently and with different emphasis. This article draws on some of this research in an attempt to link into a set of exploratory questions dealing with a variety of political practices and their institutional ramifications.

Approximating Public Authority in Local Arenas

Two paths tend to be travelled in approaching public authority in local arenas. Either a rigorous universal definition of the concept is proposed, or examples representing the phenomenon are displayed. As the point of this article — and indeed of this entire collection — is to get a better understanding of something which is as yet elusive, I opt for the second possibility and offer

1. See Bierschenk et al. (2000) for West Africa; Hecht and Simone (1994) for Africa in general; Apter (1999) and Pratten and Gore (2002) for Nigeria; Cruise O'Brien (2003) on Senegal; Gilbert (1994) on Ghana; Worby (1998) on Zimbabwe.

here a handful of evocative examples which hopefully resonate with other cases with which the reader might be familiar.

Sally Falk Moore's writings demonstrate a vivid interest in the local configuration of politics and the way in which the broader socio-political field that envelops the small arenas can and does invade them, '[s]ometimes at the invitation [of] persons inside [them], sometimes at its own insistence' (Moore, 1978: 56). In her work on post-socialist micro-politics in Tanzania, she shows two dimensions of how the 'state' invades local arenas. On the one hand, it happens in the form of local public authority. The change of regime and political rhetoric made it possible for new organizations to emerge and for existing ones to change, as new opportunities arose. As she says:

> To discover what is [going on] in rural African politics, what the latest is in organisational modernities, there is nothing so revealing as contests for directing organisational milieus. Incident by incident, local designs for personal and collective futures are jockeyed around and put in place. They face a specific direction. That is the direction in which some intend the process of change to flow. (Moore, 1996: 602)

Here, local organizations in competition over resources exhibited this twilight character of being local authorities making decisions of a public nature, but in contrast to the state. They all had, in Moore's words, a 'gentle subversive purpose'. On the other hand, the state invaded these arenas in a more subtle way in the form of an idea. The exercise of power and authority by these local institutions was bolstered by references, implicit and explicit, to the state. When a lineage leader refers to himself as lineage *chairman*, it implies a certain wish for state recognition of his position (thus indicating the state's importance which he tries to emulate); when churches define themselves as NGOs, they implicitly, and in a convoluted way, bring the idea of the state to the local arena; and when a new party champions the idea of 'good governance' in World Bank speak, it also instils the idea of state in its sphere of operation. Thus, by constant reference to the (idea of the) state, these organizations manage to 'bring the state back in', but in a vastly different way from that described by Skocpol and others in the mid-1980s (Skocpol, 1985).

In my own research from Niger, comparable processes unfolded in the times of precarious democratization of the 1990s. Whether openly or indirectly, a central preoccupation seemed to be the state as a variety of local political struggles were played out. Home-town associations, chieftaincies and vigilante groups all took on the mantle of public authority in their dealings with what they considered to be their antithesis, 'the state'. Here, the state was portrayed by the various actors as distinct, removed from the 'local arena' and supposed to be in control. However, this image was called into question by *actions* in these local arenas, as territorial delimitation of districts was carried out, justice was dispensed, or 'security' was provided. The porosity of the state was demonstrated as the influence of well-placed individuals was brought to bear in vital conjunctures and changed the local outcome of things. Their ambiguous position *vis-à-vis* the state was demonstrated by the way in which these organizations searched for credibility by, on the one hand, vindicating their non-state status and yet, on the other, doing it in the formal language of the state. In one case, police matters were carried out by the vigilantes and their public authority was entrenched by the Sultan, in conspicuous contrast to the regular police which represented 'the state'. In this way, the vigilantes established a certain authority in tandem with other social and political forces as alternatives to the state. However, the syncretistic combination of ensigns of authority, derived from the police and the prefecture as well as from chieftaincy and witchcraft, testifies to the ambiguous legitimization of their operations (Lund, 2001).

Pratten and Gore (2003) demonstrate how the idioms by which youth associations, vigilante groups and area boys in southern Nigeria describe themselves are quite elastic. On the one hand, they portray themselves as resisting disorder, sticking up for ordinary people, and doing the job that the state fails to do. The youth associations 'screen' politicians before they are supported to run for office, and they control the work of contractors in the local community. Similarly, secret societies on Nigeria's university campuses operate to curb abuse and corruption by the lecturers. These are popular responses to political and economic disorder, and an exercise of accountability at the local level. On the other hand, these organizations do 'not project a revolutionary anti-state message' (Pratten and Gore, 2003: 232), and often have no qualms about being the instruments of the class of politicians and businessmen by whom they are patronized (see also Harnischfeger, 2003; Vaughan, 1995; and Ya'u, 2000). In this sense, they may come across as innovative and transforming yet conservative at the same time (see Reno, 1998, 2002). They depict the state as 'distinct' and 'distant', while simultaneously vying to establish or entrench their own public authority. Hence, paradoxically, they become part of what they depict as 'exterior'.

In a variety of ways, public authority seems to manifest itself in an ambiguous process of being and opposing the state. If we see the state as an ensemble of institutions exercising public authority (Jessop, 1990: 342), we should also be prepared to meet institutions which, in practice, are part of this ensemble but claim to be its opposite. As Moore (2001: 106) insists, distinctions must be made that identify the provenance of rules and controls. Yet the illustrations above demonstrate that rules, controls and in particular their legitimization, resist unequivocal situation in either 'state' or 'society'. The practical form of public authority is, as a result, composite and chimerical.

Obviously, it is not only institutions of public authority that provide representations of the state. Watching the evening news in many African countries, one is struck by the irony of a systematic myth of the unity and coherence of the state. An idea of a powerful state with intention, a higher rationality and a project is manifested in receptions, seminars and inaugurations, draped in the ineluctable banners with slogans of determination, designed to instil trust in its capacity to do what states are supposed to do. This is contrasted with the incoherence and incapacity of the state, the multiple parallel structures and alternative sites of authority (chiefs, vigilantes, political factions, hometown associations, neighbourhood groups) that deny any notion of unity or rationality in the singular. The irony is not merely that some parts of the state champion its unity, while being challenged by 'alternatives'; rather, it is that the idea of the state is also effectively propelled by institutions which challenge the state but depend on the idea of it to do so.

The idea of the state is formed as a combination of people's everyday encounters with representatives of the state and its representations, among other things in stories of crime and corruption, in the news and in private debates about these stories (see Blundo and Olivier de Sardan, 2001a, 2001b). Francis Nyamnjoh equally turns to the press, as he investigates the representations of citizenship and 'foreignness' in Botswana (Nyamnjoh, 2001). One of the striking observations from his research is the contrast between the traditional Tswana polity, based upon inclusion of potential members, and the contemporary discourse on citizenship — and by inference the state — which tends to feature exclusion as its constituting element. The image of the state becomes one of a 'qualifier'; endowed with juridical capital to name, nominate and qualify degrees of citizenship; that is to validate, sanction and authorize. Comaroff (2002) suggests that it was the deployment of a language of law which provided force to the *idea* of the state — metropolitan as well as colonial. The character of the state is intimately connected to the capacity to make distinctions, and this may just be the essence of public authority. The fundamental distinctions in social life may seem natural, but they are constantly (re-) produced and sanctioned, not necessarily by one single body of 'state', but by a variety of institutions which, in so doing, assume public authority and some of the character of the state. It is this operation that researchers of 'the state' should watch out for.

POLITICAL PRACTICES

The political practices undertaken to establish public authority may be coordinated or disparate, abrupt or incremental, just as efforts to challenge existing institutions' authority may unfold in a variety of ways. However, whether by conscious effort or by haphazard chance, the political practices that constitute public authority are played out on several different registers, ranging from the use of subtle idioms to more heavy handed means — often in paradoxical conjunction.

The Apparel and Orchestration of Public Authority: Questions of Protocol

These considerations lead us to questions of language and style of the state. It is important to pay attention to the reverence expressed for certain symbols in order to assess the import of the state in the local context. The ethno-political conflict over chieftaincy, land and party politics in Bawku in Northern Ghana is illustrative (Lund, 2003). Thus, when the Kusasi Youth Association conducted a raid on the Bawku Traditional Council in 1983 to oust the Mamprusi chief, looting was very selective, and the important symbols of authority of the council and its president, the Mamprusi chief, were identified. Official documents, stationery and rubber stamps, as well as registers and court books were taken, all items that signify central state recognition of the Traditional Council's public authority. They constitute the administrative regalia. Other, duller and less significant items such as furniture and fans were left untouched. The importance of stately symbols was similarly obvious when the Vice-President of Ghana visited Bawku in July 2001. A large motorcade of taxis, trucks, private cars and motorcycles awaited the Vice-President outside Bawku, and he was escorted to the town. Here, he was to pay a courtesy call on the Kusasi Chief. He was then persuaded to pay a visit to the local party headquarters. Here, another grand reception was prepared near to the house of the competing Mamprusi candidate for the chieftaincy. He was styled as a chief and all the village chiefs of Bawku district who were loyal to him gathered in their finest outfits to greet, and be greeted by him, representing not only the political party, but as Vice-President, the Republic of Ghana. This conveyed the state's approval on this faction's quest for the chieftaincy.

The looting of 'administrative regalia' and the efforts to make the Vice-President bestow the signs of official government recognition upon a gathering of chiefs with paramount aspirations illustrate Hansen and Stepputat's (2001: 8) point about the importance of the symbolic languages of governance. While the practical elements of governance — the allocation of resources, administration of rights, appointments to office, authorization of certain practices — are crucial, it is when they combine with the symbolic language and choreography of governance and its props in terms of contracts, deeds, attestations and so forth that the compound makes up the state. One group's challenge of another's grip on governance may thus be staged in terms of claiming the symbols of public authority as well, and as much as exercising the practical tasks of governance. Symbols of public authority are not moored to specific institutions, just as the 'same' institution may exercise public authority at one point and be rather insignificant in this respect at another.

Mary Douglas (1973, 1986) develops two complementary concepts that are helpful in understanding the flows of meaning and the plasticity of institutions, namely leakage of meaning and institutional bricolage. Douglas argues that for institutions (in the sense of rules) to reduce entropy, they must, somehow, be naturalized. One particularly effective (and cost-effective) naturalization is by way of analogy. 'The shared analogy is a device for legitimizing a set of fragile institutions' (Douglas, 1986: 49). Thus, people discursively draw on legitimizing symbols to cognitively anchor new institutional and social arrangements. In Douglas' words 'there needs to be an analogy by which the formal structure of a crucial set of social relations is found in the physical world, or in the supernatural world, or in eternity, anywhere so long as it is not seen as a socially contrived arrangement' (Douglas, 1986: 48).

If the idea of the state has become increasingly powerful, this is only partially matched by effective command by central government institutions, which has been limited. Concurrently, metaphors, analogies and symbols derived from this idea have served to bolster local institutions of humbler pedigree. However, this leakage of meaning is not only seeping one way; just as ideas of state and icons of modernity may be drawn upon, opposite ideas of tradition, identity and locality may equally convey legitimacy to what are essentially emerging institutions. In his work on the genealogy of the Nigerian *durbar*, Andrew Apter provides a good illustration of massive, yet well orchestrated, leakage of meaning.

The *durbar*, a large scale reception which used to be held for 'native princes' at the courts of the British viceroys of India, was mimicked by Lord Lugard, the first Viceroy of Nigeria at the beginning of the twentieth century. However, it was not re-enacted in a vacuum but grafted onto local ceremonies of celebration of local emirs, *sallah*. The *durbars* were used to invest the local rulers with the authority of the British empire by presenting them with a gown and turban from the hands of the representative of the king of England. Hence, an 'Islamic ceremony was thus reinscribed within a British cosmology, wherein the symbols of theocratic rule — the turban and gown — traced back metonymically to the English monarch' (Apter, 1999: 229). Similarly, Gilbert's studies of festivals in Ghana demonstrate that opulent rituals are 'times for the public recognition and ancestral validation of political status which people have previously manoeuvred to achieve' (Gilbert, 1994: 100).

Less conspicuous occasions than these massive manifestations of authority may exhibit essentially similar polyphony and polysemy of political symbols, icons and acts (see Cleaver, 2001, 2002; Ferme, 1999; Hecht and Simone, 1994; Lund, 2001, 2003; Worby, 1998). The point seems to be that new acts of public authority seem to fare well when they can 'piggy-back' on familiar idioms. Apter's example of a state spectacle also takes us to the concept of institutional bricolage. Social and political challenges generally change at a more rapid pace than our institutions. Thus patterns of authority and precedence basically lie around as *bric-à-brac*, ready to be pressed into service, as Douglas puts it: 'The *bricoleur* uses everything there is to make transformations within a stock repertoire of furnishings' (Douglas, 1986: 66). Hence the *sallah*, in Apter's case, proved to be an institution pliable to the needs of the *bricoleur* — *in casu* the British colonial power who turned a *durbar* into a state spectacle instrumental to indirect rule.

The concept has been employed with lucidity and further developed by Cleaver (2002) in her analyses of conflict and co-operation in Usangu, Tanzania. She uses the term institutional *bricolage* to suggest how mechanisms for resource management and collective action are borrowed or constructed from existing institutions, styles of thinking and sanctioned social relationships. Sten Hagberg's work on the hunters' associations and *syndicats d'eleveurs* in Western Burkina Faso demonstrate how institutional bricolage (transformation of traditional hunters' associations into high-strung vigilante groups) and leakage of meaning (in formalizing Fulani lineage structures according to modern requirements for state-recognized syndicates) develop new political dynamics around issues of security. Hagberg carefully shows how rights are mobilized through organizational structures that adapt themselves to broader discourses of rights and the institutional imperatives of public life in Burkina Faso (Hagberg, 1998; see also Basset, 2003). The outsourcing of security — by design or by default — constitutes a significant process for the blurring of the boundary between public and private (see Buur, 2005; Hibou, 1999; Roitman, 1999, 2004).

Another growing body of work in this vein focuses on 'development'. Development projects constitute *par excellence* arenas where institutions are harnessed to ever-changing agendas, and where the leakage of meaning is of such dimensions that social action is inundated. The deluge of meaning underscores that many institutions are multi-purpose, and different institutions with different purposes overlap, intersect and become one another in different situations (Bierschenk and Olivier de Sardan, 1998; Bierschenk et al., 2000; Ferguson, 1990; Long, 2001; Nielsen, 2000; Olivier de Sardan, 1995, 2005). Development projects not only use various institutions and *bric-à-brac* in local communities to legitimate their operations. Such projects are themselves used, willy-nilly, as institutional vehicles for political projects (in the generic sense of the term) by local political entrepreneurs. Development operators are in a particularly significant position to make 'strategic translations' of ideas about not only 'development', but public interest, authority and the state. As Ferguson argues in his book on development in Lesotho (1990), the institutionalized production of certain kinds of ideas about 'Lesotho' in the context of development projects has important effects — although not the ones anticipated. Thus, even when development interventions claim to be technical and discrete, they are often quite political and engender subtle or dramatic structural change.

The question of who invests whom with authority may well seem an endless chain of reference to 'bigger authorities' above or beyond the institutions themselves; institutions which are either more powerful or have successfully established themselves as 'natural authorities', or both. Colonialism was probably one of the largest (though definitely not the last) of such operations, and as a wealth of studies show, the very orchestration of public authority is not an epiphenomenon but its salt.

Leadership and Legitimacy, Territory and Space

If the institutional boundaries are blurred, political processes socially and spatially diffuse, and meaning not fixed to specific institutions, what are the implications for political legitimacy? The exercise of authority is intimately linked to the legitimacy of the particular institution. Not only in the sense that an institution has to be legitimate to exercise authority, but especially because the actual exercise of authority also involves a specific claim to legitimacy. As both Moore (1988) and Lentz (1998) suggest, it is not useful to see legitimacy as a fixed absolute quality against which actual conduct could be measured. It is more fruitful to investigate the processes through which various actors and institutions attempt to legitimate actions and vindications. What is legitimate varies between and within cultures and over time, and is continuously (re-) established through conflict and negotiation. Somewhat polemically, one could argue that legitimacy's most constant feature is people's practical preoccupation with it.

Different occasions make claims for legitimacy opportune and often several repertoires are engaged (see Comaroff and Roberts, 1981). As Lentz argues in a case study on Ghana, 'on closer examination we find that the ... "big men" — and this holds for Ghanaian chiefs, politicians and entrepreneurs in general — are the more powerful the better they are able to combine their stakes in different fields of action and to manoeuvre with different registers of legitimacy' (Lentz, 1998: 59; see also Turner, Hagberg, and Le Meur, this issue). Of the multitude of repertoires, two seem to be particularly popular, however, namely the 'local/non-local' tension and the reference to history. Actors and institutions often claim legitimacy with contradictory reference to 'locality'. Eligibility to leadership often, maybe even increasingly often (Geschiere and Gugler, 1998), depends on successful claims of autochtony and belonging.

Thus, the terms 'local', 'historical' or 'traditional region' are important in the political vernacular in rural and small town politics. People involved in home-town associations, chiefs and politicians, vigilante groups and their political backers freely refer to the local in contrast to the 'outside' and the 'national level'. The notion of local or regional seems to be not only a central marker but even a constituent of rural and small town politics (see for instance Berry, 1985; Bierschenk and Olivier de Sardan, 1997; Ladouceur, 1979; Lentz, 1995; Peel, 1983). Certain policies and actions are justified and legitimated with reference to the local; not necessarily always out of a considered strategy, but often with a taken-for-granted naturalness. In their deeds, on the other hand, institutions often demonstrate a variety of clearly extra-local connections, inspirations and aspirations. Local politics is clearly not confined to a local space, let alone isolated from other spheres of politics, and 'home-town' associations, elite associations, 'clubs' and strategically-placed individuals, generally with education, political office, positions in the civil administration or in commerce, are often very important to 'local development'.[2]

2. There is a large literature on this: see, for example, Barkan et al. (1991); Berry (1985, 1993); Bierschenk et al. (2000); Englund (2001); Geschiere and Gugler (1998); Honey and Okafor (1998); Ikelegbe (2001); Lentz (1995); Lucas (1994); Pratten (1996a, 1996b); Trager (1998); Woods (1994).

The term 'local' often invokes an assumed spatial mapping of 'local' in contrast to 'global' and of 'below' in contrast to 'above'. However, by imagining the primacy of certain 'levels' over others we overlook the central question of *how* this primacy is established in a social and political process. Many institutions of public authority frame their cause and *raison d'être* in terms of space and locale. The nation state is the prime example of an institution that expresses its reach in territorial terms. Borders and maps, administrative outposts and other representatives of the nation state such as schools convey a territorial representation of the state (see Miles, 1994 for Niger and Nigeria). Scott (1998) points out how the logic of the emerging modern state was to make space, people and resources legible in order to govern (see also Dean and Hindess, 1998; Ferguson and Gupta, 2002).

However, while territorial delimitation, national identity and legibility may be institutionalized to correspond to nation states, their monopolies on these processes are as precarious as their monopoly on the exercise of public authority. A wide variety of 'twilight institutions' equally manifest themselves in terms of territory and turf. The mobilization behind home-town associations and chief candidates, the memberships of the vigilante groups or religious fraternities are often based on claims of common identity, and the organizations' everyday activities often expressed in terms of space. The territorial delimitation is important in the self-image of the actors concerned as an element of contrast to 'the State', the 'centre' — the 'up-there'. Co-existence of multiple public authorities produces multiple, partly overlapping, territories, established as places as meaning is attached to otherwise rather inert spatial widths, distances and points. The same space may figure in a government development plan, be a church-sponsored development co-operative's parish of intervention, be the realm of the sultan, the home-region of intellectuals in the capital, the fief of a local politician and the turf of the area boys, *The Hooded Scorpions*. These institutions often have territorial markers in space, ranging from national flags, through signs, fences, party banners, masks and marches, to graffiti on walls (see Nunley, 1987 and Lentz, this issue). They may exercise public authority simultaneously, sometimes with complementarity, sometimes in conflict. Resurrecting historical regions, rectifying territorial mistakes, electing a canton chief, and patrolling the town by night and day, are all processes which turn space into place. Even de-territorialized organizations, such as the *Association of the Elites of the Eleventh Province* in southwestern Cameroon, play on territory in political discourse. In practical politics they are denied political representation due to their non-territorial constitution as descendants of those who were *dépaysés* due to partition between British and French Cameroon (Geschiere and Gugler, 1998; Nyamnjoh and Rowlands, 1998). Neither belonging to English-speaking Cameroon, nor accepted in the French-speaking part, the *Association of the Elites of the Eleventh Province* made a claim for recognition by invoking territorial rhetoric.

Legitimation of public authority takes many forms, but it would seem that territorialization by delimitation and assertion of control over a geographic area offers a particularly potent language. History and the past can be commemorated or commiserated with reference to space, and territorial ambitions, modest as they may be, knit together the image of state and public authority with space.

Public Revenue for Public Authorities: A Question of Tax

Exercise of public authority often comes at a cost; revenue collection is a challenging undertaking for twilight institutions, and just as varied as other political practices. In general, taxation is linked to state authority, be it national, federal or local. As Mbembe (2001: 91) points out, taxation was instrumental in the birth and development of two interrelated concepts, public authority and the common good. As Tilly (1992) argues, taxation was central to state formation in Europe and remains a central feature of state–society relations. My argument is that it is methodologically prudent not to assume an *a priori* link between taxation and our ideal typical image of the nation state. If we see tax as a form of public revenue collected in the name of a common good by a political authority, then vigilante groups who collect 'compulsory voluntary contributions' (as I once saw on a sign in a customs office on the Nigerian side of the border with Niger), political party activists in Tanzania who collect 'road tax' for the construction of secondary schools because official tax cannot be used for this purpose (Ole Therkildsen, pers. com.), and development projects that tax people's time and work in the name of participation, have something in common. In places where central government institutions do not reach at all, alternative forms of tax may emerge. The question of taxation obviously arises when development projects deliver sanitation for participation, but more fundamental relations of citizenship and authority are negotiated in terms of tax. Kristine Juul (2002) thus describes how groups of migrant herders in Senegal manoeuvre to pay (not evade!) tax since it entails a public recognition of them as citizens and their claims as rights. Needless to say, the tax paying zeal of the newcomers is vigorously opposed by the first-comers.

I do not want to stretch the analogy too far, but the broad debate on government tax systems may at least provide us with some lines of enquiry. According to Therkildsen (2001: 119), some key questions concern coercion in tax administration, reciprocity between taxation and service provision, and the economic structure and size of the taxable community. Jane Guyer (1992) observes that the institutionalization of taxation in Europe took place under non-democratic rule and through major coercion, whereas present-day states — in particular in Africa — are saddled with the task of seeking consent first, and enforcing taxation afterwards. In concrete circumstances, however, direct taxation by government often rests on potential coercion in one form or other. This seems just as true for some political authorities that represent government less clearly, or not at all.

The question of the relationship between taxation and service provision is equally relevant for institutions that are not government but still exercise authority. This is also linked to legitimacy. Thus, when farmers in eastern Niger pay local chiefs fees for a 'property certificate', they get something for their 'tax' (Lund, 2001). A particular dynamic is at play here, since 'the process of recognition of property rights by a politico-legal institution simultaneously constitutes a process of recognition of the legitimacy of this institution. . . . Hence, public authority is continually constructed in the imagination, expectation, and everyday practices of ordinary people' (Lund, 2002: 14). Taxation only compounds this. The authority of such chiefs — and hence the validity of the property certificate, and hence the reciprocity of the tax-transaction — is further secured when other important institutions recognize the validity of their acts. As Guyer argues, the increasing importance of chiefs in Nigeria 'has at least as much to do with the seriousness with which the corporate sector, both economic and political, deals with high level chieftaincy as with the people's cultural attachment to the institution' (Guyer, 1992: 58). At times, there is a fine line between a fee and a bribe for issuing a deed or certificate, and between collecting a market-place tax and running a protection racket. Obviously, this cannot be seen in isolation from questions of legitimation and recognition by people in general and by other institutions of public authority in particular. Thus, public revenue — in cash or kind — not only constitutes a significant economic dynamic for public authorities; it also entails processes of recognition of their authority, as well as of the citizenship (or membership) of the populace.

INSTITUTIONAL RAMIFICATIONS OF POLITICAL PRACTICES

Empirical research has recorded a wealth of political practices of bewildering variation. The examples above are but a minuscule selection. Indeterminacy and counter-examples abound, and evolutionary patterns are constantly shattered before our eyes. Moreover, the very richness of political life and culture makes the focus on local politics inherently interesting. However, there is a strong risk that a focus on the particular and specific produces an individualistic, voluntarist and somewhat episodic perspective on social dynamics (see Mohan and Stokke, 2000). This raises the question, what is political and the object of public authority? The easy answer is, of course, that everything is political. However, this is not entirely satisfactory. If every name of a place, every administrative operation, any participation in public events and every cup of coffee drunk with a 'big man' is political, it effectively evacuates the analytical sense from the concept. On the other hand, such issues may easily be politically significant. People die in the name of places, administrative procedures are potent instruments of exclusion, public events are ideal for the manifestation of interest and allegiance, and many a sordid deal is made over a cup of coffee. Most elements of social life can be politicized, that is, become the objects of efforts to secure interests, and may thus be significant. However, this cannot always be read from the process itself. While questions of new distinctions, of institutionalization, and of power can be asked in very particular contexts, we are tasked to assess their significance in a slightly broader perspective — beyond the event itself, so to speak — namely in terms of their institutional ramifications. This entails an 'epistemological change of gears', as it were, as we must see the political events and processes as 'diagnostic' for something broader (Moore, 1994). The institutional ramifications may be more or less enduring, more or less widespread and even mutually contradictory. The following section develops a few markers for orientation.

Institutionalization and Distinction

As we noted above, if public authority — or 'stateness' — can wax and wane, it follows that state institutions are never definitively formed, but that a constant process of formation takes places. This is not a straightforward institutionalization and homogenization of authority; indeed history abounds with examples of serious resistance to institutionalization. As Moore notes in the introduction to her seminal book, *Law as Process*, 'the making of rules and social and symbolic order is a human industry matched only by the manipulation, circumvention, remaking, replacing, and unmaking of rules and symbols in which people seem almost equally engaged' (Moore, 1978: 1). These dual processes, obviously, take many different forms and can be more or less intense, as the contributions in this particular collection amply demonstrate.

However, it is worth noting that while some institutions appear to endure and remain stable with few open conflicts, that does not mean that nothing is happening. On the contrary! Various actors, individuals and organizations are actively reproducing these institutions, although the process may at first sight seem quite inconspicuous (Juul and Lund, 2002). As hegemonic constellations of power manage to reproduce certain institutions — to 'normalize' them — such institutions will appear stable, although still depending on certain social relationships for their continued reproduction. On the other hand, less well-entrenched institutions are often dubbed transitional or temporary. Institutions such as chieftaincy, various forms of dictatorships, democracy, local particular institutions and organizations have all in various contexts been thus dismissed because of their current feeble command of the political field in which they operate.

Apart from the somewhat trite observation that everything (everyone) is temporary, it seems arrogant to dismiss the persistence of instability as if it would *eventually, in the long run* fall into some form of equilibrium. At the very least, we should spend the *meantime* studying it, as it has proved to be continuously extended. Hence, on the one hand, we should not neglect the stable institutions' inherent precariousness, nor, on the other hand, deny the potential longevity of the more unstable ones. As institutions of public authority are never definitively formed but always undergoing processes of institutionalization and its opposite, so is the distinction between state and society a moving target. To quote Mitchell, 'rather than searching for a definition that will fix the boundary, we need to examine the detailed political processes through which the uncertain yet powerful distinction between state and society is produced' (Mitchell, 1991: 78). As a corollary, political practices must be investigated for the distinctions they produce between citizen and stranger, owner and squatter, violence and punishment, acceptable and unacceptable, and so on. The articles that follow all examine such political processes and demonstrate their variation.

Institutional Congruence and Formalization

A central idea about the modern state is its internal rationality, coherence and order. While this is hardly a valid yardstick for modernity as such, institutional congruence and its opposite seem significant points of enquiry, especially if we have established that a wide variety of institutions exercise governance. Médard (1991) thus argues that a process of institutionalization and (inspired by Weber) of bureaucratic rationalization between various politico-legal institutions, is the key feature of state formation (Weber, 1922/1978). Médard also sees the reduction of the numbers of institutions as significant in this process.

In my view, it is not so much the numbers in quantitative terms but the mutual congruence or rivalry between institutions which matters. It could be argued that institutions of public authority have the appearance of several institutions only if they act as several *competing* institutions. Institutional pluralism is not, by itself, indicative of institutional incongruence. We should be prepared to see the landscape of public authorities as stretching from rule-ordered congruent relations to contradictory rivalry between institutions of public authority. Evidence does not suggest a predominantly evolutionary development from incongruence toward congruence; rather, it seems to change with historical periods and conjunctures. Moore applies a very useful distinction between two countervailing types of processes: processes of regularization and processes of situational adjustment. Processes of regularization are 'processes which produce rules and organizations and customs and symbols and rituals and categories and seek to make them durable' (Moore, 1978: 50). As she puts it, it is the result of people's efforts to fix social reality, to harden it, to give it form and predictability. Increasing predictability of the decisions made by institutions of public authority, and increasing coherence among them, thus represent processes of increasing regularization. The countervailing processes of situational adjustment are those whereby people exploit the indeterminacies in the situation or generate such indeterminacies by reinterpreting or redefining rules and relationships. Thus, manipulation of rules and manoeuvring between them impute a measure of unpredictability, inconsistency, paradox and ambiguity, and ultimately institutional incongruence. Both types of processes are generally at work simultaneously, but only by detailed examination of the outcomes of institutions' acts of governance can a broader aggregated picture be established. This is linked to the aspect of formalization.

The exercise of public authority lends itself easily to formalization. The accoutrements of the state are often intimately connected to this. However, there is no 'necessary' link between them, and we might want to look at formalization and informalization as competing forms of institutionalization. On the one hand, the political practices that borrow legitimacy from state law and bureaucratic idioms and lend credence to the idea of the potency of the state could be said to formalize practices. This contrasts with the institutionalization of informal practices more or less grounded in ideas and values embedded in institutions seen as distinct from the colonial and post-colonial state (see Benjaminsen and Lund, 2002). The competition often unfolds as one form of practice undercuts the other and offers ways of circumventing and replacing the other. The challenge is to identify these countervailing processes empirically. Often government institutions that claim to be the embodiment of the state (the judiciary, the immigration servce, the *préfecture*, the land commission, and so forth) will attempt formalization, but there is no neat dichotomy of formal/government on the one hand, and informal/non-government on the other. Reality is messier. Thus, while formalization is often propelled by government institutions and reform, formal rules and regulations are also negotiated and undone by corruption, political networks and powerful alliances with, and indeed within, the very same institutions. Moreover, formalization processes are not the state's exclusive preserve; other actors also operate in this business, as shown above.

The Question of Class

Politics is not only about politics. Beside the questions of distinction, identity and control over institutions, it has mundane effects on livelihood, opportunities to wealth, and poverty. Peters (2002) rightly points out that focusing on negotiability and fluidity of social and political relationships, on the examples that disrupt evolutionary narratives and on everyday heroes who outwit big institutions of grand design may lead to neglect of systematic, general and institutional outcomes of this unpredictable fluidity.

For example, Peters argue that poorer segments in rural Malawi tend to lose out in situations where competing public authorities determine questions of property. Plurality of institutions may open alternative avenues for some — also for poorer people — but the more affluent, the better connected, and the more knowledgeable tend to have the upper hand in such contexts. One of the institutional ramifications of the political practices sketched out above is, in short, that people are classed. Not necessarily in terms of labour and capital, but more profoundly in *haves* and *have-nots*. Distinction and formalization often systematically recognize the interests and claims of some while the plight of others remains out of focus and is effectively denied legitimate attention. Strangers, migrants, women, pastoralists and squatters are only the beginning of a long list of human beings out-classed by distinctions produced by political practices of institutions of public authority. But again, this is an empirical question rather than theoretical inference.

CONCLUSION

Attempts to exercise legitimate public authority — both successful and failed — are as much about the incoherent practices of the diverse institutions engaged in the exercise of authorizing, sanctioning and validating claims as rights, as about the image of the coherent state. The issues subject to public sanctioning are many and manifest themselves in different social arenas. Some idioms of state seem 'cross-cultural' while other idioms of legitimate power are highly context specific. To be effective, institutions must convey meaning — often by analogy — to the acts of authority. Hence, competing idioms are marshalled, along with heftier practices, by various institutions in the attempt to establish, reproduce and institutionalize a realm of jurisdiction and a legitimate authority. It is therefore important, as Mbembe (2001: 76) reminds us, to see in the confusing and often chaotic landscape of institutions, coalitions and conflict, efforts aimed at establishing new forms of legitimate order and gradually restructuring formulas of authority. Many such efforts will be kept in check while others run out of steam. But some will prosper in the constellation of structural pressure, active ingenuity and sheer chance.

The perspective on institutions outlined in this article, with its keen attention to the political activities that make (and unmake) them, allows us to see the constructive elements in apparently failing states as well as the challenges to structures apparently well consolidated. It also allows us to read broader patterns in the ways that social and political life is governed because we are not bound, hand and foot, by assumptions about state and civil society. The political practices of vastly different twilight institutions may become legible as their institutional ramifications are compared and assessed over time. Therefore, the prevalence and persistence of twilight institutional forms — resisting clear-cut and durable classification — should encourage us to re-investigate the institution and idea that we call state.

REFERENCES

Abrams, P. (1988) 'Notes on the Difficulty of Studying the State', *Journal of Historical Sociology* 1(1): 58–89.

Apter, A. (1999) 'The Subvention of Tradition: A Genealogy of the Nigerian Durbar', in G. Steinmetz (ed.) *State/Culture. State Formation after the Cultural Turn*, pp. 213–52. Ithaca, NY, and London: Cornell University Press.
Barkan, J. D., M. L. McNulty and M. A. O. Ayeni (1991) '"Hometown" Voluntary Associations, Local Development and the Emergence of Civil Society in Western Nigeria', *Journal of Modern African Studies* 29(3): 457–80.
Basset, T. J. (2003) 'Dangerous Pursuits: Hunter Associations (*Donzo Ton*) and National Politics in Côte d'Ivoire', *Africa* 73(1): 1–30.
Bayart, J. F. (1989) *L'État en Afrique. La politique du ventre*. Paris: Fayard.
Bayart, J. F., P. Geschiere and F. Nyamnjoh (2001) 'Autochtonie, démocratie et citoyenneté en Afrique', *Critique Internationale* 10: 177–94.
Benjaminsen, T. A. and C. Lund (2002) 'Formalisation and Informalisation of Land and Water Rights in Africa: An Introduction', *European Journal of Development Research* 14(2): 1–10.
Berry, S. (1985) *Fathers Work for their Sons: Accumulation, Mobility and Class Formation in an Extended Yourouba Community*. Berkeley, CA: University of California Press.
Berry, S. (1993) *No Condition is Permanent: The Social Dynamics of Agrarian Change in Sub-Saharan Africa*. Madison, WI: University of Wisconsin Press.
Bierschenk, T. and J. P. Olivier de Sardan (1997) 'Local Powers and a Distant State in Rural Central African Republic', *Journal of Modern African Studies* 35(3): 441–68.
Bierschenk, T. and J. P. Olivier de Sardan (1998) 'Les arènes locales face à la décentralisation et à la démocratisation', in T. Bierschenk and J. P. Olivier de Sardan (eds) *Les pouvoirs au village. Le Bénin rural entre démocratisation et décentralisation*, pp. 11–51. Paris: Khartala.
Bierschenk, T., J. P. Chauveau and J. P. Olivier de Sardan (2000) 'Les courtiers entre développement et État', in T. Bierschenk, J. P. Chauveau and J. P. Olivier de Sardan (eds) *Courtiers en développement. Les villages africains en quête de projets*, pp. 5–42. Paris: Karthala.
Blundo, G. and J. P. Olivier de Sardan (2001a) 'La corruption quotidienne an Afrique de l'Ouest', *Politique Africaine* 83: 8–37.
Blundo, G. and J. P. Olivier de Sardan (2001b) 'Sémiologie populaire de la corruption', *Politique Africaine* 83: 98–114.
Boone, C. (1998) 'State Building in the African Countryside: Structure and Politics at the Grass-roots', *Journal of Development Studies* 34(4): 1–31.
Boone, C. (2003) *Political Topographies of the African State: Territorial Authority and Institutional Choice*. Cambridge: Cambridge University Press.
Buur, L. (2005) 'The Sovereign Outsourced: Local Justice and Violence in Port Elisabeth', in T. B. Hansen and F. Stepputat (eds) *Sovereign Bodies: Citizeos, Migrants and States in the Postcolonial World*, pp. 192–217. Princeton, NJ: Princeton University Press.
Cleaver, F. (2001) 'Institutional Bricolage, Conflict and Cooperation in Usangu, Tanzania', *IDS Bulletin* 32(4): 26–35.
Cleaver, F. (2002) 'Reinventing Institutions: Bricolage and the Social Embeddedness of Natural Resource Management', *European Journal of Development Research* 14(2): 11–30.
Comaroff, J. (2002) 'Governmentality, Materiality, Legality, Modernity: On the Colonial State in Africa', in J. G. Deutsch, P. Probst and H. Schmict (eds) *African Modernities: Entangled Meanings in Current Debate*, pp. 107–34. Portsmouth, NH: Heinemann.
Comaroff, J. and S. Roberts (1981) *Rules and Processes: The Cultural Logic of Dispute in an African Context*. Chicago, IL: Chicago University Press.
Cruise O'Brien, D. B. (2003) *Symbolic Confrontations: Muslims Imagining the State in Africa*. London: Hurst & Company.
Dean, M. and B. Hindess (1998) 'Government, Liberalism, Society: Introduction', in M. Dean and B. Hindess (eds) *Governing Australia*, pp. 1–19. Cambridge: Cambridge University Press.
Douglas, M. (1973) *Rules and Meanings: The Anthropology of Everyday Knowledge*. Hammondsworth: Penguin.
Douglas, M. (1986) *How Institutions Think*. Syracuse, NY: Syracuse University Press.

Englund, H. (2001) 'The Making of a Home Villagers' Association in Lilongwe, Malawi', in A. Tostensen, I. Tvedted and M. Vaa (eds) *Associational Life in African Cities: Popular Responses to the Urban Crisis*, pp. 90–106. Uppsala: Nordic Africa Institute.
Ferguson, J. (1990) *The Anti-Politics Machine: 'Development', Depoliticization and Bureaucratic Power in Lesotho*. Minneapolis, MN: University of Minnesota Press.
Ferguson, J. and A. Gupta (2002) 'Spatializing States: Toward an Ethnography of Neoliberal Governmentality', *American Ethnologist* 29(4): 981–1002.
Ferme, M. (1999) 'Staging Politisi: The Dialogics of Publicity and Secrecy in Sierra Leone', in J. Comaroff and J. Comaroff (eds) *Civil Society and Political Imagination in Africa: Critical Perspectives*, pp. 160–91. Chicago, IL: Chicago University Press.
Geschiere, P. and J. Gugler (1998) 'The Urban–Rural Connection, Changing Issues of Belonging and Identification', *Africa* 68(3): 309–17.
Gilbert, M. (1994) 'Aesthetic Strategies: The Politics of a Royal Ritual', *Africa* 64(1): 99–125.
Gluckman, M. (1958) *Analysis of a Social Situation in Modern Zululand*. Manchester: Manchester University Press, on behalf of The Rhodes-Livingstone Institute.
Guyer, J. (1992) 'Representation without Taxation. An Essay on Democracy in Rural Nigeria, 1952–1990', *African Studies Review* 35(1): 41–79.
Hagberg, S. (1998) *Between Peace and Justice: Dispute Settlement between Karaboro Agriculturalists and Fulbe Pastoralists in Burkina Faso*. Uppsala: Institute for Anthropology.
Hansen, T. B. and F. Stepputat (2001) 'Introduction: States of Imagination', in T. B. Hansen and F. Stepputat (eds) *States of Imagination: Ethnographic Explorations of the Postcolonial State*, pp. 1–38. Durham, NC: Duke University Press.
Harnischfeger, J. (2003) 'The Bakassi Boys: Fighting Crime in Nigeria', *Journal of Modern African Studies* 41(1): 23–49.
Hecht, D. and M. Simone (1994) *Invisible Governance: The Art of African Micropolitics*. New York: Autonomedia.
Hibou, B. (1999) 'De la privatisation des economies à la privatisation des États', in B. Hibou (ed.) *La privatisation des États*, pp. 11–67. Paris: Karthala.
Honey, R. and S. Okafor (eds) (1998) *Hometown Associations. Indigenous Knowledge and Development in Nigeria*. London: Intermediate Technology Publications.
Ikelegbe, A. (2001) 'The Perverse Manifestation of Civil Society: Evidence from Nigeria', *Journal of Modern African Studies* 39(1): 1–24.
Jessop, B. (1990) *State Theory: Putting Capitalist States in their Place*. Oxford: Polity Press.
Juul, K. (2002) 'Post Drought Migration and the Quest for Recognition: Asserting and Securing Claims among Fulani Pastoralists in Northern Senegal', in K. Juul and C. Lund (eds) *Negotiating Property in Africa*, pp. 185–210. Portsmouth, NH: Heinemann.
Juul, K. and C. Lund (eds) (2002) *Negotiating Property in Africa*. Portsmouth, NH: Heinemann.
Ladouceur, P. A. (1979) *Chiefs and Politicians: The Politics of Regionalism in Northern Ghana*. London: Longman.
Lemarchand, R. (1992) 'Uncivil States and Civil Societies: How Illusion Became Reality', *Journal of Modern African Studies* 30(2): 177–91.
Lentz, C. (1995) '"Unity for Development": Youth Associations in North-Western Ghana', *Africa* 65(3): 395–429.
Lentz, C. (1998) 'The Chief, the Mine Captain and the Politician: Legitimating Power in Northern Ghana', *Africa* 68(1): 46–65.
Long, N. (2001) *Development Sociology: Actor Perspectives*. London: Routledge.
Lucas, J. (1994) 'The State, Civil Society and Regional Elites: A Study of Three Associations in Kano, Nigeria', *African Affairs* 93(370): 21–38.
Lund, C. (2001) 'Precarious Democratization and Local Dynamics in Niger: Micro-Politics in Zinder', *Development and Change* 32(5): 845–69.
Lund, C. (2002) 'Negotiating Property Institutions: On the Symbiosis of Property and Authority in Africa', in K. Juul and C. Lund (eds) *Negotiating Property in Africa*, pp. 11–44. Portsmouth, NH: Heinemann.

Lund, C. (2003) '"Bawku is Still Volatile!": Ethno-political Conflict and State Recognition in Northern Ghana', *Journal of Modern African Studies* 41(4): 587–610.
Mamdani, M. (1996) *Citizen and Subject: Contemporary Africa and the Legacy of Late Colonialism*. London: James Currey.
Mbembe, A. (2001) *On the Postcolony*. Berkeley, CA: University of California Press.
Médard, J. F. (1991) 'Étatisation et dé-étatisation en Afrique noire', in J. F. Médard (ed.) *États en Afrique Noire*, pp. 355–65. Paris: Karthala.
Miles, W. F. S. (1994) *Hausaland Divided: Colonialism and Independence in Nigeria and Niger*. Ithaca, NY, and London: Cornell University Press.
Mitchell, T. (1991) 'The Limits of the State: Beyond Statist Approaches and their Critics', *American Political Science Review* 85(1): 77–96.
Mohan, G. and K. Stokke (2000) 'Participatory Development and Empowerment: The Dangers of Localism', *Third World Quarterly* 21(2): 247–68.
Moore, S. F. (1978) *Law as Process*. London: Routledge and Kegan Paul.
Moore, S. F. (1986) *Social Facts and Fabrications: 'Customary' Law on Kilimanjaro 1880–1980*. Cambridge: Cambridge University Press.
Moore, S. F. (1988) 'Legitimation as a Process: The Expansion of Government and Party in Tanzania', in R. Cohen and J. D. Toland (eds) *State Formation and Political Legitimacy*, pp. 155–72. New Brunswick, NJ: Transaction Books.
Moore, S. F. (1994) 'The Ethnography of the Present and the Analysis of Process', in R. Borofsky (ed.) *Assessing Cultural Anthropology*, pp. 362–74. New York: McGraw Hill.
Moore, S. F. (1996) 'Post-socialist Micro-politics: Kilimanjaro 1993', *Africa* 66(4): 587–606.
Moore, S. F. (2001) 'Certainties Undone: Fifty Turbulent Years of Legal Anthropology, 1949–1999', *Journal of the Royal Anthropological Institute* 7: 95–116.
Nielsen, H. (2000) 'Donors and Recipients: A Critical Analysis of Development in Burkina Faso'. PhD dissertation, Roskilde University.
Nunley, J. W. (1987) *Moving with the Face of the Devil: Art and Politics in Urban West Africa*. Urbana and Chicago, IL: University of Illinois Press.
Nyamnjoh, F. (2001) 'Local Attitudes towards Citizenship and Foreigners in Botswana: An Appraisal of Recent Press Stories' (author's mimeo).
Nyamnjoh, F. and M. Rowlands (1998) 'Elite Associations and the Politics of Belonging in Cameroon', *Africa* 68(3): 320–37.
Olivier de Sardan, J. P. (1995) *Anthropologie et développement: essai en socio-anthropologie du changement social*. Paris: APAD/Karthala.
Olivier de Sardan, J. P. (2005) *Anthropology and Development: Understanding Contemporary Social Change*. London: Zed Books.
Peel, J. D. Y. (1983) *Ijeshas and Nigerians: The Incorporation of a Yourouba Kingdom 1890s–1970s*. Cambridge: Cambridge University Press.
Peters, P. (2002) 'The Limits of Negotiability: Security, Equity and Class Formation in Africa's Land Systems', in K. Juul and C. Lund (eds) *Negotiating Property in Africa*, pp. 45–66. Portsmouth, NH: Heinemann.
Pratten, D. (1996a) *Bamako Bound: The Social Organisation of Migration in Mali*. London: SOS Sahel.
Pratten, D. (1996b) *Returning to the Roots: Migration, Local Institutions and Development in Sudan*. London: SOS Sahel.
Pratten, D. and C. Gore (2003) 'The Politics of Plunder: The Rhetorics of Order and Disorder in Southern Nigeria', *African Affairs* 102: 211–40.
Rathbone, R. (2000) *Nkrumah and the Chiefs: The Politics of Chieftaincy in Ghana 1951–60*. Accra: F. Reimmer; Athens, OH: Ohio University Press; Oxford: James Currey.
Reno, W. (1998) *Warlord Politics and African States*. Boulder, CO, and London: Lynne Rienner.
Reno, W. (2002) 'Insurgencies in the Shadow of State Collapse'. Paper presented at International Development Studies Graduate School Research Seminar, Roskilde University (May).

Roitman, J. (1999) 'Le pouvoir n'est pas souverain. Nouvelles autorités réegulatrices et transformations de l'État dans le Bassin du Lac Tchad', in B. Hibou (ed.) *La privatisation des États*, pp. 163–96. Paris: Karthala.

Roitman, J. (2004) 'Productivity in the Margins: The Reconstruction of State Power in the Chad Basin', in V. Das and D. Poole (eds) *Anthropology in the Margins of the State*, pp. 191–224. Santa Fe, NM: School of American Research Press; Oxford: James Currey.

van Rouveroy van Nieurwaal, E. A. B. (1999) 'Chieftaincy in Africa: Three Facets of a Hybrid Role', in E. A. B. van Rouveroy van Nieurwaal and R. van Dijk (eds) *African Chieftaincy in a New Socio-Political Landscape*, pp. 21–48. Hamburg: LIT Verlag.

Scott, J. C. (1998) *Seeing like a State: How Certain Schemes to Improve the Human Condition Have Failed*. New Haven, CT: Yale University Press.

Skocpol, T. (1985) 'Bringing the State Back In', in P. Evans, D. Rueschemeyer and T. Skocpol (eds) *Bringing the State Back In*, pp. 3–37. Cambridge: Cambridge University Press.

Steinmetz, G. (1999) 'Introduction: Culture and the State' in G. Steinmetz (ed.) *State/Culture: State Formation after the Cultural Turn*, pp. 1–49. Durham, NC: Duke University Press.

Therkildsen, O. (2001) 'Understanding Taxation in Poor African Countries: A Critical Review of Selected Perspectives', *Forum for Development Studies* 1: 99–123.

Tilly, C. (1992) *Coercion, Capital and European States, AD 990–1992*. Oxford: Blackwell.

Trager, L. (1998) 'Home-town Linkages and Local Development in South-western Nigeria. Whose Agenda? What Impact?', *Africa* 68(3): 360–82.

Vaughan, O. (1995) 'Assessing Grassroots Politics and Community Development in Nigeria', *African Affairs* 94(377): 501–18.

Weber, M. (1922/1978) *Economy and Society: An Outline of Interpretative Sociology*. Berkeley, CA: University of California Press.

Woods, D. (1994) 'Elites, Ethnicity and "Home-town" Associations in the Côte d'Ivoire: An Historical Analysis of State–Society Linkage', *Africa* 64(4): 465–83.

Worby, E. (1998) 'Tyranny, Parody, and Ethnic Polarity: Ritual Engagements with the State in Northwestern Zimbabwe', *Journal of Southern African Studies* 24(3): 561–78.

Ya'u, Y. Z. (2000) 'The Youth, Economic Crisis and Identity Transformation: The Case of the *Yandaba* in Kano', in A. Jega (ed.) *Identity Transformation and Identity Politics under Structural Adjustment in Nigeria*, pp. 161–80. Uppsala: Nordic Africa Institute.

The Politics of Vigilance in Southeastern Nigeria

David Pratten

INTRODUCTION

It is limiting to argue that African politics can be summed up in only two concepts, rents and predation, yet these are nevertheless important features of the social and political landscape, especially in a *rentier* polity of low taxes and patronage such as Nigeria (Barber, 1982; Forrest, 1986; Watts, 2003). Rents and predation, in fact, have particular qualities that shape an inherent duality to everyday meanings of the state. Recent observations on the post-colony identify this duality in the creative tensions that emerge from a set of oppositions in which the state is both 'illusory and concrete; distant and localized; personal and impersonal; violent and destructive as well as benevolent and productive' (Hansen and Stepputat, 2001: 5). In this understanding, therefore, some forms of state intervention may be repressive and resisted while others are more benign and may be desired and demanded. The institutions of governance in contemporary Nigeria share this duality and are both instruments of political domination in local communities (predation) and means for allocating patronage (rents) (Vaughan, 1995: 502). In response, vernacular notions of governance are shaped along these two axes — by the opportunities afforded through the instrumentalization of distribution and by necessity in the face of the insecurities of instrumentalized disorder. On one axis, the politics of distribution, people organize themselves within familiar frameworks to 'capture' the state. On the other, discourses on disorder, law and order, social practices are mobilized as a response to and a protection against the state.

How political operators control or transform the post-colonial African state on behalf of specific, local economic and social groups is a question that has been framed within a number of discursive registers — the domestication and banalization of excess and largesse (Mbembe, 1992, 2001), the 'politics of the belly' (Bayart, 1993), the 'instrumentalization of disorder' (Chabal and Daloz, 1999), the 'criminalization of the state' (Bayart et al., 1999), and the 'moral matrix of family and food' (Schatzberg, 1993,

This article attempts to build on collaborative work with Charlie Gore to whom I am deeply indebted. It also draws on a paper presented at the International Development Studies, Roskilde University. My thanks to all the participants and also to John Peel, Peter Geschiere, Karin Barber, Christian Lund, Jon Mitchell, Jeff Pratt and Nigel Eltringham for their comments. I should also like to record my thanks to the Economic and Social Research Council, the British Academy and the Nuffield Foundation for research funding.

2002). Each offers powerful concepts in understanding the dynamics and positivity of personalized patrimonial modes of governmentality. These vernacular notions of governance are premised on the definition of regimes of power in an imaginative complicity between rulers and ruled, patrons and clients. Overall, these perspectives stress consumption, achievement and winning.

While the value systems and cultural codes which allow a justification of 'criminalization' and 'corruption' by those who practise it need to be explored, the focus of these works has led to an impasse in intellectual debate about the characterization of the African state. In part, attempts to understand the legitimization of 'illicit practices' within socio-cultural logics are rendered problematic because they are prone to generalization and tend to ignore the specificities of local historical narratives (Hagberg, 2002). In part also, the cultural logic of impunity represented in these recent works is dependent on highly individualist conceptions of the state and of political action, and emphasize the role of leaders and 'big men' at the expense of the lives, politics and collective actions of ordinary people (Mustapha, 2002). It is necessary, therefore, to examine the tactics of those who have yet to win and to study localized struggles against criminalization and disorder in their proper social and cultural context. Recent examples which shift the focus onto public accountability include Hagberg's (2002) analysis of the Burkinabe protest movement, *Trop c'est trop* ('Enough is Enough'), and Kelsall's (2003) comparison of cursing and financial auditing as forms of verification in northern Tanzania.

Following Mitchell's insight, it is argued that political subjects and their modes of resistance are formed within the organizational terrain of the state, rather than in some wholly exterior social space (Mitchell, 1991: 93). Modes of collective action operate within the contours and fault lines of this landscape, not outside it. Nigerian non-state groups have sought, through their claim making, to reach an accommodation and to insert themselves within patrimonial lines of state redistribution. Fears and aspirations of the state are not focused on a monolithic, bureaucratic structure, but on a set of procedures, state offices and processes through which personal power is exercised in political conflict and competition. Individuals and collective groupings therefore engage with a diverse and heterogeneous set of institutions of the Nigerian nation state, and in this context the instability of its norms, laws and institutions make it a privileged site for negotiation, bargaining and brokerage (Olivier de Sardan, 1999). The forms of social organization that concern us here do not confront or press up against the state authority from below but are rather 'contemporaries of the organs of the state — sometimes rivals, sometimes servants, sometimes watchdogs, sometimes parasites, but in every case operating on the same level' (Ferguson, 1997: 59).

To grasp these local manoeuvres we require an alternative analytic to that based on the disciplines of domination and the techniques by which governable spaces and subjects are manifested (Rose, 1999: 32; see also Ferguson and Gupta, 2002). To focus on modes of domination or the 'problematics of repression', as de Certeau refers to them, is to underplay the political agency of ordinary people:

> The privilege enjoyed by the problematics of repression in the field of research should not be surprising ... But this elucidation of the apparatus by itself has the disadvantage of not seeing practices which are heterogeneous to it and which it represses or thinks it represses. Nevertheless, they have every chance of surviving this apparatus too, and, in any case, they are also part of social life, and all the more resistant because they are more flexible and adjusted to perpetual mutation. When one examines this fleeting and permanent reality carefully, one has the impression of exploring the night-side of societies, a night longer than their day, a dark sea from which successive institutions emerge, a maritime immensity on which socioeconomic and political structures appear as ephemeral islands. (de Certeau, 1984: 41)

From this perspective it is possible to better understand the heterogeneous practices through which ordinary people survive by wit and improvisation, practices that are necessarily obscured from the glare of repressive governmental apparatus. Our attention, therefore, must focus on an analysis of what de Certeau alludes to here as the 'night-side of societies'. I take this to represent something akin, in the African context, to what Worby (1998: 564) describes as a 'gray zone' and what Lund (2001: 845) refers to as 'twilight' to describe the ambiguous, shadowy quality of institutions and individual motivations that populate the political landscape.

Michel de Certeau's insights can further illuminate the micro-political processes by which people 'make' post-colonial modes of governance and 'make do' in the face of their disorder. For this a mode of analysis is required that firstly champions the agency of ordinary people, and secondly illustrates the complexity, plurality, temporality and improvisation of their actions. It is in this context that de Certeau's theoretical framework is especially helpful in coming to terms with the practice of governance since his analysis shows how the 'weak' make use of the 'strong' and create for themselves a sphere of autonomous action and self-determination.

From the breadth of de Ceteau's work, his comments on the concept of the 'tactic' are of particular note. A 'tactic', de Certeau states, is a calculated action, an 'art of the weak' whose hallmark is vigilance:

> [A tactic] takes advantage of 'opportunities' and depends on them, being without any base where it could stockpile its winnings, build up its own position and plan raids. What it wins it cannot keep. This nowhere gives a tactic mobility, to be sure, but a mobility that must accept the chance offerings of the moment, and seize on the wing the possibilities that offer themselves at any moment. It must vigilantly make use of the cracks that particular conjunctions open in the surveillance of the proprietary powers. It poaches them. It creates surprises in them. It can be where it is least expected. It is a guileful ruse. (de Certeau, 1984: 37)

Tactics are determined by the absence of power. They must play on and within a terrain imposed upon them and therefore manoeuvre 'within the enemy's field of vision' (ibid.). An important distinction is drawn here between strategies and tactics and between their use of space and time. Unlike the strategies of those in power which concern the definition and occupation of spaces of power, tactics occupy an ambiguous space. They are defined by the absence of a 'proper locus'. Rather, tactics depend on a clever utilization of time. De Certeau therefore distinguishes between the two ways of operating, the strategies of the strong, and the tactics of the weak, according to whether they 'bet on place or on time' (ibid.: 39). Overall, the significance of this analytical framework rests on the ideas of vigilance and the monitoring of opportunities. In the context of this ethnography it is through vigilance and vigilantism that Annang youth secure niches of profit and protection within a patrimonial mode of governance in Nigeria.

This article is based on research in southern Nigeria, in Annang communities in Ukanafun Local Government Area of Akwa Ibom State. It focuses mostly on the headquarters of the local government in the village of Ikot Akpa Nkuk. Here Annang youth groups contest power through complex and ambiguous conceptions of accountability which draw on idioms of monitoring and surveillance, screening and vigilance. These repertoires of accountability operate within a framework of implied or explicit violence and at various opportunistic nodes of redistribution. Hence, within these spheres youth groups have presented various responses including vigilantism, screening political candidates, monitoring local government expenditure, checking the award of compensation payments to local chiefs, threatening contractors and parastatals to complete development programmes, and monitoring price controls. These modes of vigilance and accountability are configured by internal imperatives as much as they are by the national and transnational political economy. They are intimately associated with the elaboration of constituencies and their localized rights of political contest and action. And, above all, they are about enforcing localized cultures of accountability that are shaped epistemologically by concepts of the person — especially the patron and the thief.

Vigilance concerns the definition of cognitive, temporal and spatial boundaries. It concerns the protection and care of the community encompassed within these boundaries, and it involves maintaining surveillance and taking action against threats to this community. Vigilance is most obviously associated with vigilantes and vigilance committees, groups who take the law into their own hands, and indeed Nigerian vigilante groups will figure in this narrative. However, the actions of youth associations more generally are also configured in a wider mode of 'civic vigilance'. In this sense also, the contemporary politics of vigilance concern contests over responsibilities and functions that further blur the boundaries of the state. Several examples of this mode of 'civic vigilance' at work in Nigeria illustrate the broad range of tactics that are adopted by ordinary people as they 'make do' in the post-colony. Critically these tactics concern the deployment of 'insider' knowledge of procedures of the state, counter-surveillance, and the (re)imagining and mobilization of communities and constituencies. Crucially, these examples also illustrate that modes of accountability assume many forms, spaces and times (see also Blundo, Buur, and Kyed this issue).

Writing over a decade ago Jane Guyer (1992) analysed the local implications of the Nigerian oil boom and the political and economic centralization it fuelled on the modes of engagement between society and state. She argued that where local government had been downgraded, where resources were not generated locally from taxation, and where policy implementation at the local government level was highly dependent on central state subsidy, the material basis for 'liberal' democratic struggles for accountability and control were more or less defunct. As a result, she argued, people engaged with the state through other means:

> In a situation where the official government system does not impose a framework for thinking about — legitimating, resisting, reconceptualizing — the relevant units in, and the shifting shape of, inequality within and between communities and levels of the social hierarchy then some other moral framework and *modus vivendi* develops for dealing with wealth and power originating in the corporate sector. (Guyer, 1992: 69).

These means were especially linked to securing and making claims on public office which is seen as an imperative if unpredictable link to corporate, central sources of finance and which in turn give rise to modes of clientelism and prebendalism which dominate the Nigerian political landscape. State functions, in turn, become fractured as the functions of local government are replaced by and linked to office holders, chieftaincy and private organizations.

This process, Guyer argued, resulted in instability and a formal organizational complexity with overlap and gaps that demanded the constant vigilance and involvement of the people, especially of elites, to keep their collective as well as sectional and personal interests represented (ibid.: 69). Guyer therefore pointed to a locus of labour-intensive engagement between what she framed as the corporate and non-corporate sectors (ibid.: 68). This labouring was most pronounced among the rural elite and self-styled youth leaders, people themselves no better off than small-scale farmers or traders, many of whom were living on pensions. Combinations of these characters routinely engaged in party political mobilization and addressed 'public' issues, especially in transition periods and in the lead-up to elections.

It is the vigilance and involvement of local elite and the youth associations they lead (what Guyer refers to as 'the discrete overwork of the bourgeoisie') that more recent analyses have dealt with in the context of violence in the Niger Delta. Michael Watts, for instance, has shown how the political logic of local, ethnic claims-making serves to 'fragment, pulverise, and discredit the state and all of its forms of governance' and that in its stead factional struggles and militant particularisms have emerged, each attempting to establish order (Watts, 2003: 17–20). Illustrating this point through an example of relations between the Nembe community in the southern Delta and the Shell oil company during the 1990s, Watts shows that in order to subvert the chief's monopoly on oil company compensation payments, youth groups were established by local political figures with insider knowledge of how to manage successful claims. Their collusion with oil company liaison officers and the consequent subversion of chiefly authority was met with strategic alliances between youth and chiefs, and a growing (and armed) conflict between youth groups for access to Shell.

What emerged was a form of privatized violence, which Watts calls 'vigilante rule', involving a complex of complicities between chiefs, youth groups, local security forces and the companies. Watts refers to this process as the overthrow of pastoral chiefly power and a thickening of civil society leading to the formation of a 'governable space of civic vigilanteism [sic.]' (Watts, 2003: 20). Comparatively, therefore, this analysis appears to confirm several of the arguments outlined here concerning the mode of civic vigilance characteristic of Nigerian micro-politics — its contests over the rights of governance, its dependence on insider information, its deployment of actual and rhetorical violence, and its operations that are complicit and internal to authority.

Both these examples illustrate the politics of vigilance in southern Nigeria by focusing on the roles of youth patrons, youth groups and hometown associations. The politics of vigilance draw upon ambiguous conceptions of youth agency (Bucholtz, 2002; Durham, 2000). It is a vigilance of 'youth' in contemporary Africa that captures their political tactics, not merely as vandals but as vanguards of a public sphere whose contours are unexpected (Cruise O'Brien, 1996; Diouf, 1996; Gore and Pratten, 2003; Momoh, 2000; Ya'u, 2000). The marginality of the category of youth contributes to the dual character of its engagement in the making of patrimonial modes of governance — at once innovative and creative and yet subject to co-option as clients by patrons.

Born into the interstices of colonial rule, youth-led hometown associations have long sustained academic interest as a valuable lens on wider social and political processes. As such the literature on hometown associations spans a variety of topics and theoretical perspectives — urbanization (Banton, 1957; Gugler, 1971, 1991; Parkin, 1966, 1969; Southall, 1975); communal politics (Smock, 1971; Wolpe, 1974); rural–urban links and migration (Baker and Pedersen, 1992; Pratten, 1997, 2000; Trager, 1998); civil society and democracy (Barkan et al., 1991; Woods, 1994); indigenous knowledge and social development (Honey and Okafor, 1998; McNulty and Mark, 1996); the 'politics of belonging' (Geschiere and Gugler, 1998); and transnational resource flows (Daum, 1992; Grillo and Riccio, 2004). Each approach has stressed the continued salience of home-town identity and as such link the 'politics of improvement' (self-help projects and political representation) to the 'politics of belonging' (the constantly shifting, often fragmenting construction of meaningful constituencies). Within the analysis of the African 'crisis' they are seen sometimes as part of the solution (by liberals who see them as exponents of self-help service and infrastructure providers and as agents of political accountability); and sometimes as part of the problem (as 'tribalists'). These are the 'uncool' (Comaroff and Comaroff, 2000: 22) forms of African association, kin-based and ethnic organizations which apparently fail to enter the narrowly defined institutional arena of civil society, but which have long represented an attempt to attain some form of 'accommodation with modernity' (Smock, 1971: 9). Hence, they are ideally suited as windows on the contemporary night-side, grey zone and twilight of state–society engagement at the key interfaces of corruption and crime.

THE POLITICS OF SQUANDERMANIA

Corruption in the post-colony must be seen as a mode of deploying force and coercion with its own positivity (Mbembe, 2001: 84). It is a specific mode of active control over revenue collection and the judiciary that is not simply a matter of connivance or of exploiting bureaucratic positions. At the same time condemnations, conversations and accusations concerning corruption are neither casual nor abstract; they must be taken seriously. They appropriate culturally embedded, localized idioms of legitimacy and accountability to stake claims and assert rights; in this way 'the threat of denunciation, or in some cases the act itself, is always to be interpreted in the context of political or factional combat' (Olivier de Sardan, 1999: 49fn). Discourses of corruption therefore articulate both with the intersecting of different transnational forces and with distinctive historical trajectories (Gupta, 1995: 393).

The discourse on corruption is a discourse of accountability, and as Herzfeld argues, 'accountability is a socially produced, culturally saturated amalgam of ideas about person, presence and polity' (Herzfeld, 1993: 47). As such, 'corruption' is a marker of difference which distinguishes those with power and those without, and acts to de-legitimize the provenance of wealth and power gained from engagement with or within the bureaucratic infrastructures of the nation state. Political accountability, as John Lonsdale reminds us, is part of 'the moral calculus of power; it concerns the mutual responsibilities of inequality' (1986: 128). The rhetoric of corruption marks insiders from outsiders and maps the contours and boundaries that are drawn along ethnic, regional, religious, gender, class and rural–urban lines. The exclusionary practices of corruption and anti-corruption therefore fuel a proliferation of internal borders, whether imaginary, symbolic, in economic or power struggles (Mbembe, 2001: 87).

This discourse on corruption is highlighted in the trajectories of Annang collective action during the twentieth century in which hometown associations and their elite leaders have sought ethical probity in public office-holders. The self-styled progressive elite of the early colonial period in Annang society was partly made up of students of the first Qua Iboe Mission schools which were opened in the Annang hinterland in the early 1920s and who entered colonial service by the 1930s to become court clerks. Also 'straddling' this class were cloth traders, more successful farmers and money lenders who though illiterate had the resources to buy bicycles and therefore to travel to the District office in order to lodge petitions and protests. These were the 'A-Lights' of colonial Ukanafun, those who commissioned petition-writers and who were feared by the court sitting members who would be ousted following the A-Lights' allegations (Pratten, forthcoming). At higher echelons were the 'reading public' of the 1930s and 1940s, subscribers to the local newspapers, the audience at literary society debates (Newell, 2001) and members of organizations which engaged with the issues of political reform at provincial, regional and national levels (Udoma, 1987).

In the Annang region the dominant antecedent is the Ibibio State Union and its engagement with the provincial public sphere during the early 1940s. In 1941 and 1942 delegations of Ibibio Union members conducted 'enlightenment campaigns' in the Ibibio and Annang districts holding public lectures in council halls. Leading the 'subjects of instruction' of the Ibibio Union's campaign were exhortations to pay tax and oppose bribery. Anti-corruption, indeed, was a key plank in the progressives' attack on the Native Administration system and contributed significantly to the credibility of the educated elite's own claim to political legitimacy. It was the lawyers and journalists, therefore, who shaped the public sphere during the Second World War years when such anti-corruption campaigns were launched, when anti-bribery movements such as the League of Bribe-Scorners were formed, when the press monitored living conditions, and the colonial administration was most vigorously criticized for its under-investment despite the development and welfare legislation.

Comparatively, the end of the colonial era in Nigeria would appear to have marked less of a transition in the discourse of corruption than might be expected. Gupta, for instance, argues that nationalist as opposed to colonial regimes sought the kind of popular legitimacy that would enable them to act in the name of 'the people' (Gupta, 1995: 389). Consequently the discourse of accountability became more visible as post-colonial states vested state bureaucrats and subjects with new rights as citizens. Yet, in both the colonial and post-colonial eras the labouring of the rural Nigerian elite at the intersections of state and society has always been intensive, and as Guyer suggested vigilance has been their common watchword.

Following Sally Falk Moore's example, the following Annang case studies examine the ways in which local social action 'has its own imperatives, and its own designs' (1996: 602). Above all, the work of the rural elite, in this mode of vigilance, is twofold: defining communities and monitoring their boundaries. The rhetoric of unity is especially effective and common in delimiting these boundaries. Unity is a central feature of the idiom of progress and development deployed by youth associations and they expend a considerable proportion of their energies in 'the creation and strengthening of a community and the representation of its interests to the outside world' (Lentz, 1995: 397). By enclosing various communities within recognized associations, whether it be ethnic group, village, lineage, electoral ward, urban migrant network or committee of friends, necessarily excludes others. The rhetoric of unity is seen as a key ingredient in the cultural recipe for political progress. In the Annang context *mboho* (unity) is the principal necessity for *uforo* (progress) and the terms are bound together literally in the names of most contemporary associations. The rhetoric of unity for such unions, which is frequently couched in the language of common heritage, forms part of an investment in constructing corporate identity through discourse, symbol and ritual which often outweighs investment in social infrastructure (Lentz, 1995: 400).

For Annang communities the post-colonial politics of 'improvement' rests on the construction and tactical deployment of these constituencies. The vigilance of Annang youth associations in patrolling these various boundaries of belonging involves engagement with the institutions of governance and draws upon two related imperatives: political representation and accountability. The overt political mobilization of youth associations not only to secure power, but to engage in national distributive networks, is justified under the rubric of 'improvement' and progress based on this political representation (*ukara idem* — self-rule). At the same time, youth association strategies play on Annang conceptions of accountability. Beyond financial accounting (*ekot ibat*), the account one makes of oneself within Annang society is judged in performative terms on the basis of the 'achievements' acquired for one's people (*se enye anam* — your achievements for your people). These achievements, recounted in the obituaries of big men (*akamba owo*) are key indicators of personal progress — *ackpokpor inyene* (personal wealth). Wealth begets responsibilities and it is in these aspects that one's achievements are judged in terms of sending children to study overseas; educating poor people through sponsorship; donating in church; employing people in a company; entertaining visitors; holding the peace; and being truthful and steadfast. In short, accountability is judged in patrimonial terms (Ekeh, 1975; Smith, 2001a).

The local government reforms of 1976 and the formation of Local Government Areas mark a significant rupture in the nature of state–society engagement in the development discourse. It is possible to chart a trajectory from this point in which south-western Annang development associations shifted their focus from community development on the basis of self-help to monitoring and petitioning for state help from local government. The characteristic features of youth association engagement with the state after 1976 are captured by a union formed in the Ukanafun district at the time called Atang Anan ('Do what you say'). As its name suggests, Atang Anan, which petitioned for compensation for the land and palm plots on which the local government headquarters were built, employed a rhetoric of public accountability to ensure Ukanafun's place in the distributive process. It also drew upon local understandings of the rights and roles of youth. One of the qualities by which a young man (*akparawa*) is distinguished is public speaking *(atang iko otu* — to speak words in public). As lines of patrimonial inclusion and exclusion were reproduced, this further implied screening and counteracting the perceived excesses of successive council chairmen.

In 1985, for instance, Atang Anan's successor, the Ukanafun Youth Association, reported to the Cross River State Review Panel that, 'From 1979 to 1983, there is no evident progress in Ukanafun due to inflated contracts, kick-backs, corruption, misappropriations and gross embezzlements'.[1] In 1986, the Federal Military Government engaged in a programme to co-ordinate community development activities and to encourage the registration of development associations under the Directorate for Food, Roads and Rural Infrastructure (DFRRI). While its projects were designed to include locally mobilized inputs, the funding formula was heavily skewed towards outside investment, and in Ukanafun, as elsewhere, DFRRI funds became subject to the 'politics of plunder'. In this context the Ukanafun Youth Association again concluded that the Chairman's actions had ruined the area's development prospects: 'With ghost contracts, ghost completion certificates and ghost contract payments our Directorate for Food, Roads and Rural Infrastructure is a failure in Ukanafun. . . . We envisage an empty purse for our council at his rate of squandermania'.[2]

The pattern continued. In September 1994 the Ukanafun Youth Association called on the state military administrator to transfer 'fraudulent and dubious' senior staff of Ukanafun Local Government, including the secretary, senior technical officer (STO), and treasurer. The request was submitted, it claimed, to 'forestall impending riot and loss of life', and read as follows:

1. The STO issued fake completion certificates for unfinished jobs therefore defrauding the council of millions of Naira. The council recorded a total income of N67.65 million but had no project to show for it.
2. From 1990 the STO personally acquired 4 vehicles, 1 private car, a 12 bedroom bungalow worth N800,000, a Lister generator, an 8″ borehole with overhead tank.
3. The secretary collaborated with the Treasurer to authorise 'ghost contracts'.
4. That the group were seen at the LG treasury on Saturday and are suspected of destroying documents and preparing others for presentation to the Task Force on Recovery of Public Property by Caretaker Committee of Ukanafun Council.
5. They are now resorting to the services of wizards and demonic forces. We do not yet want to take the law into our hands but we will be forced to if these wicked and heathen fellows do not leave Ukanafun immediately.[3]

---

1. Ukanafun Youth Association to Cross River State Contract Review Panel, 25 April 1985.
2. Ukanafun Youth Association to Military Governor, Cross River State, 17 April 1987.
3. Ukanafun Youth Association to Military Administrator, Akwa Ibom State, 12 September 1994.

Such rhetoric employed by contemporary youth associations has particular features of note. The threat of violence and the invocation of non-Christian religious idioms are the poles against which notions of community 'good' are contrasted, while detailed knowledge of personal accumulation and the techniques of state bureaucracies are the bases upon which claims are legitimated. It is a rhetoric of exposé directed at patrons and redistributors in the patrimonial power webs including not only local government chairmen but also lineage heads and village chiefs. The construction of this imagined moral community is based on the language of legitimacy forged from progressive and Christian rhetoric and is expressed in the grievances of the 'concerned citizens' of communities across southern Nigeria.

Such debates about corruption further illustrate the modes of counter-surveillance through which people engage with the state; 'even members of the subaltern classes', Gupta notes, 'have a practical knowledge of the multiple levels of state authority' (1995: 382) (see also Blundo, this issue). Alongside narrative types of knowledge which frame the fortune and misfortune of local politicians in terms of witchcraft pacts and the ordeals of political rivals, an intimate knowledge of local government officials is gathered on the basis of their consumption, investment, indicators of illegitimate wealth as well as the timing and routes they take to enter and leave the village to collect the monthly budget.

Beyond the instability of the politics of 'corruption' it is important nevertheless to recognize the linkages between youth associations operating in this sphere and the state. Claim making and petition writing concerning the accountability of public office-holders are brought into the public sphere by such groups but depend on resolution through the bureaucratic procedures of the nation state. The state is appealed to as the upholder of the law and may use its sovereign power in matters of contested rights. This by definition legitimates the state and the state's means of dealing with alleged corruption irrespective of personalized patrimonialism within it. Despite the appearance of crisis, the means by which communities respond to apparent disorder contributes to a mode of governance which is dependent on validating the procedures and disciplines of the post-colonial state. Part of the way in which the state is domesticated in everyday life, therefore, is the symbolic and practical representation of the state as a locus of arbitration and adjudication. It has very little to do with dominating or restructuring the state, but rather with influencing the course of its micro-operations. The net result of the routine and regional operation of these practices in the functioning of local institutions is that governance becomes increasingly 'porous' and fragmented (Hansen and Stepputat, 2001: 32).

As Guyer suggested, times of transition, especially around elections, focus the vigilance of youth and community leaders. Electoral politics are suffused with the discourse on corruption. During the local government elections of 1997, for example, the result was challenged by local UNCP loyalists at the appeal tribunals thus confirming a familiar pattern in Ukanafun politics in which, 'every time the Council chairman is elected, instead of being allowed to sit down and design programmes to uplift the area, he is made to pass through the rigours of attending to court cases and tribunals' (*Pioneer*, 1997a). Formal legal proceedings over alleged electoral malpractices were instigated not by the party, however, but by the Ukanafun Youth Association (*Mkparawa Ikpaisong Ukanafun*). Fearing a repetition of events from 1993, when Ukanafun's vote in favour of the minority SDP party was widely seen as the reason why no commissions or pledges of amenities were made to it, the association sought to install the 'party in power'. Thus, the Ukanafun Youth Association, led by a retired army officer and former party chairman, petitioned President Abacha against the victorious NCPN candidate in language which highlighted perceptions that the election result had been a disaster for local development prospects: 'It could be recalled that since the inception of [the chairman's] administration in Ukanafun LGA no project has been embarked upon. All the council revenues and subventions are fraudulently withdrawn, while the people are in dire need of good drinking water, roads, electricity, student bursaries and other infrastructures in the area'.[4]

Ironically, the association's petition directly attributed this investment failure to the very process it had instigated, and to the fact that the council chairman was spending his time and the council's funds at the election tribunal since they went on to complain that 'For months now nothing is visible, all our funds of our council are diverted by [the council chairman] to prosecute election cases at tribunals'.[5]

Election campaigns, however, are not built around political actions or statements; a campaign is a question of 'character' and the election a calculus of patrimonial reciprocity (Lund, 2001: 857). Being represented by a member of a community with which one can identify, and 'having a chairman from the same place' is of paramount importance. It is in this context that youth associations 'screen' politicians before they are supported to stand for elected office. Such groups, as faction makers, are expressing their palpable potential to be co-opted but in the screening process are asserting their rights to be 'remembered' as clients. The Nkek Youth Development Association, for instance, examine a candidate's 'accountability' and reputation, they will assess his or her manifesto, what the candidate will offer to do for the group and the community, their parental family (whether they were 'greedy' or 'gossiping'), whether they have been 'insulting' or 'stubborn', and whether they have committed a crime. A decision on who to support for individual offices is then made within the association and the members sign a document or swear an oath that they will vote en bloc for the candidate they have decided upon.

Aspects of the ways in which a culture of impunity is restricted by the tactics of Annang youth associations are illustrated in an account of political

4. Ukanafun Youth Association to President Sani Abacha, 23 July 1997.
5. Ukanafun Youth Association to Military Administrator, Akwa Ibom State, 21 July 1997.

hustings in the village of Ikot Akpa Nkuk in the build up to the 2003 elections. A small meeting of the Youth/Vigilante group gathered one evening in February to receive the presentation of a councillorship candidate for the PRP party, a young apprentice welder who had recently returned home to the village from Port Harcourt. His manifesto centred on the proposed rehabilitation of a market, a long abandoned youth-sponsored initiative, and the provision of scholarships for youth. Where young people are unable to progress because their parents cannot pay school fees, scholarship programmes have a continued salience. They remain important also because of the long-standing idea that an educated 'alight' will be able to develop the area. The PRP councillorship candidate presented *kaikai*, a bottle of Crown 4 brandy and kola. This is a standard form of hustings and was one of a series of presentations that the aspirant had to perform in each village and to each village head and council.

While it was a rather low-key and apparently innocuous meeting (since the PRP had no recognized support in Ukanafun), it caused considerable anxiety. Under an existing zoning system operating within the urban ward, it was not Ikot Akpa Nkuk's turn to present a councillorship candidate. For the sake of peace between the villages the aspirant was asked to step down. The aspirant was also challenged on the timing of his campaign, and was asked why he wanted to stand for office at that moment since he was told in one of the many Annang electoral epithets 'politics is interest — politics is personal interest'. Why would a local candidate be desperate to upset the local balance of power if it was not for a personal agenda (to 'chop' the money) and to fail to meet campaign pledges? As night fell, the tension at the little meeting was palpable and captured much of the ambivalence felt by youth operating within political circuits at all levels. Several felt it was wrong for the village *mkparawa* to appear to be encouraging a candidate in this way because of the problems it would cause; others were encouraging the man because of the goods and money he was presenting to them. Seen in the context of a range of tactics youth employ as vehicles for inclusion the meeting represented a common dialectic in the politics of youth expressed in the discourse on corruption — they challenge clientelism and yet demand co-option.

YOUTH, TRUTH AND TRIALS

Contemporary Nigerian vigilantism concerns a range of local and global dynamics beyond informal justice. It is a lens on the politics of post-colonial Africa, the current political economy of Nigeria, and on its most intractable issues — the politics of democracy, ethnicity and religion. Vigilantism in Nigeria has recently assumed an international profile as the so-called 'ethnic militias', which emerged after the democratic transition in 1999, each assumed vigilante operations: the O'odua Peoples Congress active in cities of the south-west (Akinyele, 2001; Nolte, 2004), the *hisba* in the pro-*sharia* northern states, and the state-sanctioned Bakassi Boys of the south-east (Baker, 2002; Harnischfeger, 2003; Smith, 2004). The violence with which these vigilante groups have been linked, especially in the religious conflicts of 2000 and 2001, and in the lead-up to the 2003 elections, has earned them censure from the international human rights community (Amnesty International, 2002; Human Rights Watch, 2002, 2003), attempts at prohibition by the federal government, and ongoing contests with local authorities over the rights to judge and punish crimes. Yet, since the late 1980s, from rural lineage to urban street, the widespread growth of night guards and vigilantes has been a popular local response to theft, armed robbery and threats to village security.

The legitimation of vigilante activity has extended beyond dissatisfaction with current levels of law and order and the failings of the Nigeria Police. The way in which ordinary men and women devise and support alternate strategies to mete immediate justice or to organize vigilante groups is seen as a coping mechanism in the face of a predatory state (Chabal and Daloz, 1999). It has also been argued that a range of factors contribute to a 'political imagination' that serves to legitimate their operations. These imaginings include conceptions of the elite-status and illegitimate wealth of the criminals they target; the normalization of violence as an ethical response against disorder; and the vigilantes' symbolic status as 'superheroes' (Smith, 2004). The various regional vigilante groups are also claimed to draw legitimacy from the way in which they represent ethnic militia, ready to defend the interests of their ethnic and religious communities. Here Nigerian vigilantism and the ethnic militia have been located in the context of west Africa's 'collapsed states' and what Reno calls the politics of insurgency. In particular he situates the Nigerian ethnic militia in the militarization of patronage networks that have become an endemic feature from the Guinea Coast to the Niger Delta (Reno, 2002).

To understand the local legitimacy of vigilantism in post-colonial Nigeria, however, it is also necessary to recognize its internal imperatives. Vigilantism in this context is embedded in narratives of contested rights, in familiar everyday practices, understandings of personhood and knowledge and in alternate, older registers of governmentality. These are often dismissed as neo-traditional, reactionary or as a process of 're-traditionalisation' visible in a resurgence of ethnicity and ritualized violence (Chabal and Daloz, 1999: 45). This classification as neo-traditional often obscures the activities that take place within these associational forms and obscures the histories of localized idioms of power, knowledge and accountability in understanding popular responses to the instrumentalisation of disorder (Gore and Pratten, 2003: 213–14). As a consequence, it is important to discern how those who step into the void of disorder and de-centeredness and establish routine by knowledge and practice do so by grasping the importance of how cultural patterns are articulated to systems of political domination (Fields, 1982: 593) (see Buur and Hagberg, this issue).

The popular legitimacy of vigilantism is located in a political narrative of contests for the symbolic and economic capital derived from hearing cases. Judging cases has long been an index of power in Annang society and has been contested by its key forms of individual and collective office-holding (lineage, chieftaincy, secret societies and youth association). The ways in which thieves were apprehended and punished is most directly linked to the roles and aesthetics of various secret societies (especially the *ekpe* leopard society) and night guards. Surveillance (*ukpeme idung*, to watch village) was organized by lineage heads who picked small groups of young men to monitor paths and plots from palm-leaf constructed hides (*ufok usung*). Both the guards and societies would parade thieves they had caught around the village and the market. As Austen (1986: 385) reminds us, intolerable deviants in many African societies are those who threaten control over reproductive capacities expressed in terms of both access to food and the ability to procreate children. In Annang the protection of produce was paramount, and the theft of seed yams or cassava stems — for the following year's harvest — was considered abhorrent.

Partly because of these cultural frameworks the relationship between vigilantes and the colonial state was ambiguous and difficult. By the early 1940s the government opposed the *ufok usung* on the grounds that they had, 'developed into an organisation for demanding money with menaces'.[6] In colonial discourse the guards were thought to be a fruitful source of revenue for village chiefs who held illegal trials in which persons arrested by the *ufok usung* were forced to confess their crime. Sometimes after the thieves had been shamed by being rubbed with charcoal and paraded around the market they were taken to the Native Court, tried and sentenced again.[7] As a result of these reports *ufok usung* were banned.[8] Within a decade, however, amid persistent popular calls for their re-instatement, night guards had been accommodated as part of new 'watch committees' operating alongside the rural police patrols launched in the early 1950s.[9] While they met with an ambivalent response from the authorities it is clear from the symbols of these night guards that, as today, character was all important in the selection and symbolic repertoire of the Annang night guard. The lanterns that the guards carried became a mark of honesty that was appropriated in the imagery of post-war nationalist politics.[10] While the NCNC were represented by the symbol of the cockerel and the Action Group by the palm tree, independent

---

6. Acting Resident, Calabar to Secretary, Eastern Provinces, 19 May 1942, National Archive Enugu, CALPROF 3/1/1957.
7. Ibid.
8. Native Authority Ordinance (No 43), 1933, NAE, CALPROF 3/1/1957.
9. Annual Report, Calabar Province (C. J. Mayne), 1952, Rhodes House Library MSS Afr.S.1505.6.
10. *Qua Iboe Mission Quarterly*, January 1958 (76), Public Records Office of Northern Ireland D/3301/EA/27.

Annang political candidates used the hurricane lantern in their campaigns during the 1950s as a sign of their good character.

Fears of armed robbery in Ukanafun during the late 1990s were founded on reports of unprecedented violent crime rates. Cities across the south-east were caught in the grip of a crime-wave. Calabar was reported to be under siege by armed robbers who raided petty traders' premises by night (*Pioneer*, 1997b). A spate of 'dare-devil' armed robberies in Enugu led the state military administrator to accuse the police and traditional rulers of complicity with the criminals (*Punch*, 1997b). Owerri and Onitsha witnessed full-scale riots when ritual killers were found in possession of body parts (Smith, 2001b). And a rapid increase in the crime rate in Port Harcourt in late 1996 was crudely calculated in the deaths of armed robbers in gun-battles with police (*Tide*, 1996).

Fear of renewed crime-waves were heightened in Akwa Ibom after a spate of armed robberies in Uyo (*Pioneer*, 1997c), and as a result of renewed 'underworld activity', the Akwa Ibom State Police Commissioner criticized local government councils for failing to fund the local police effectively, and called on communities to mount vigilante patrols (*Post Express*, 1998). This request echoed that of the Paramount Ruler of Ukanafun Local Government who had proposed a resolution in the Traditional Rulers' Council in August 1996 that each village should be responsible for the formation of a vigilante committee.[11] The Akwa Ibom State Administrator's concern at the increasing rate of armed robbery in the state led him to remind traditional rulers in April 1997 to report any suspected criminals or 'strange faces' in their domains (*Punch*, 1997a). In Ikot Akpa Nkuk the youth association, *Mboho Ade Uforo Ikot Akpa Nkuk* (MUKAN — 'Unity for Progress'), for example, formed security patrols called 'vanguards' in 1988. Their responsibilities were defined as follows:

1. Every member of the Association is empowered to arrest and interrogate anybody caught stealing or suspected to have stolen and report them straight to the Police.
2. Mount routine patrols at markets to check for suspects and stolen goods.
3. Those caught buying stolen goods will be reported to the village council and to the Police.
4. Mount road blocks at night in some streets in the village to trap thieves.[12]

Despite official encouragement the relationship between vigilantes and the police is contested. Their role places vigilante groups in an ongoing conflict over judicial authority between themselves, the police and the traditional rulers. Vigilante actions, punishments and judgements, even in concert with the police and formal judicial channels, exclude the chiefs, and youth

11. Minutes of the Ukanafun Traditional Rulers Council meeting, 20 September 1996.
12. MUKAN Memorandum, 9 December 1988.

associations in some villages have deliberately avoided dispute settlement for the reason that 'This is how the chiefs "eat" and they would not permit it'. Chiefs accuse vigilantes of complicity in personal vendettas and like all parties involved in informal tribunals, they are open to allegations that criminals have bribed them for their freedom. Accommodations are reached, however, as the provision of effective justice constitutes an overriding performative criterion for contemporary Annang village chiefs.[13]

Contemporary vigilantism represents the articulation of claims to a set of rights based on the historical and spiritual legitimacy of young powerful men, 'sons of the soil', defending the community under the protection of local religious injunction. The development of *hisba* committees in northern states draws upon a religious idiom of legitimacy and discipline. Murray Last (pers. comm., 2002) argues that it is a grassroots response to the failures of the judicial system and to the inequalities experienced by those young men who invoke piety as a political act and join vigilante groups to enforce the sharia code. In southern Nigeria vigilantism draws on the pervasive idiom of the secret society. Insa Nolte's (2004) work, for instance, has shown how in Yoruba communities in south-western Nigeria the membership of the *Oro* secret society and local vigilante groups of the O'odua People's Congress overlap. Annang vigilantism draws its legitimacy from similar performative repertoires.

The various practices that Annang vigilantism embraces combine to draw cognitive and spatial boundaries. These boundaries crucially divide good from bad, insiders from strangers, and vigilantes from thieves (Heald, 1986a). For many years the vigilante force in the village of Ikot Akpa Nkuk constituted around a dozen night guards, each of whom was a man of power (*ockpochong* — having been tested). This exclusive basis for recruitment to the vigilante group has now become an inclusive principle. Now any young man who has lived in the village for at least two years should be registered as a youth/vigilante group member. Any young man who refuses to join the vigilantes falls under suspicion as being among those 'insiders' (*owo mbia*) who are thought to invite armed robbers to the village and locate their sites for ambush and routes for escape. As a result the vigilante group has grown in size with about one hundred vigilantes guarding the village each night. As such, active membership of the vigilante group itself has come to constitute the boundaries of community.

Each night at ten o'clock the vigilante patrol meets at the youth association chairman's compound to announce the beginning of the nightly curfew. De Certeau's idea that subaltern tactics must cleverly manipulate time is of

13. Heald's analysis of the relationship between chiefs, vigilantes and the police in 1960s Uganda is informative in this respect. The chieftaincy, undergoing a crisis of legitimacy and authority, co-operated with the vigilantes so that they might gain respect from both the police and their villages for handing over thieves to the authorities, thereby increasing their authority by gaining influence over a clandestine police force (Heald, 1986b).

crucial relevance here. The vigilantes and their curfew define both physical and temporal spaces. The curfew creates a niche within the police's daily routines, and it marks a time after which the character of a person who transgresses is immediately suspect. Time is important for vigilantes in other ways too. The vigilante group routinely sits as an informal tribunal, hearing domestic and land cases, and has become popular because it costs relatively little to bring a case and because unlike lineage or village meetings, which gather on particular market days, it can meet most evenings usually after work. The funding of the vigilantes is also linked, in part, to an innovative use of time. In addition to business levies, the vigilantes are funded by the commission taken from drivers operating taxi services from the village's motor park. The rights to collect commission have long been contested as the National Union of Road Transport Workers (NURTW) runs the motor park from Monday to Saturday. The village youth, however, have recently secured a time, each Sunday, when young men from each lineage take turns to access this resource.

After the curfew is announced around a dozen vigilantes dressed in black, some disguised as women, set out into the darkness in single-file to traverse the village's boundaries. The patrol encounters small groups of fellow vigilantes at various checkpoints along the main paths that run inside and around the village. The course taken maps a topography that is a physical space and a landscape of names, a genealogical history (Ferme, 2001: 23–48; McCall, 1995: 259). More than this, however, the night patrol's route marks an alternative spatiality which maps a set of resonant spatial practices whose meanings and control are beyond the grasp of the state (de Certeau, 1984: 93). Markets, crossroads and boundary paths are each traversed by the vigilantes in a practice reminiscent of the annual performances of *ekpo* (ancestral) masqueraders. During the *ekpo* season masked players march and sing along the boundary paths that defined an *ekpo* cluster thereby mapping out the political landscape of the *ekpo* leaders and the relationships between them. The most significant and dangerous of the vigilante checkpoints is at a junction on the village's boundary. As the frontier against intruders and thieves it is a potent spot especially as it was the site at which war medicines (*ibok ekong*) were prepared for the village's founders. Hushed greetings with the dozen or so guards at the junction, who are sit on felled palm trunks blocking the roads, are interrupted by the firing of guns into the air. Several of the patrol team have homemade six-shooter pistols, small and poorly machined devices that are awkward to hold, and unpredictable to use. Firing a gun not only serves as an audible deterrent and an indication of their physical protection. It also serves as a sign that the vigilantes have significant spiritual protection and are the 'rightful' persons (*unen owo*) to defend the village.

In addition to mapping temporal and spatial communities in which young men are vested with the rights to exercise justice, the legitimacy of Annang vigilantism is assessed within cultural frameworks of accountability linked to conceptions of agency, personhood and power and the oppositions this produces between vigilantes and thieves. The most distinctive interpretative clue in this context is the opposition in the character of Annang ancestors (*ekpo*) between good spirits, those who were successful, and bad ones, those who were unsuccessful or notoriously malicious. These categories were linked both to the status of the living person and the form of their death; a normal death (*mkpa*) was contrasted with a sudden or violent one (*afai*). This opposition expresses a common contrast in Annang belief between the right-hand, associated with respect, authority, truth and good character, and the left, linked to disrespect, wrong-doing and malevolence. The right/left, good/bad opposition also corresponds to the aesthetic expression of concepts of beauty (*eti*) and ugliness (*idiok*). These terms are ways of relating character (*eti ilo*, good person, *idiok ilo*, bad person) and behaviour (*eti usung*, good way, *idiok usung*, bad way). The aesthetic representations of personhood are captured at their most figurative in the ancestral masquerade (*ekpo*) and in its use of beautiful and ugly masks.

Of all the masked figures who perform at the season's end in October (*ndok*), the *ekpo ndem* masquerade is the most disfigured, ugly, anti-human, unpredictable and malevolent spirit.[14] It is a threat to security, fertility and the progress of the community. During its performance it is painted with charcoal, and is restrained by a rope tied at the waist. When apprehended a thief is handled in much the same way — they are stripped naked, painted with charcoal, a palm frond is hung around their neck and they were paraded around the village and neighbouring markets tied at the waist. The practice by which a thief is symbolically represented as a malevolent, anti-social threat to order and fertility like *ekpo ndem* points to the extent of the fear associated with thieves and armed robbers. These ideas are confirmed in other ways too. *Ekpo ndem* (of all masquerades) is associated with preparation in the bush (where initiates eat only raw food) and, as a result, with the most complete sense of spiritual embodiment (Picton, 1990: 195). Symbolically, thieves and armed robbers are also associated with dangerous, anti-social locations such as hiding in the bush, and with ambivalent, internalized forces since a thief is said to be possessed by a 'stealing spirit' (*spirit ino)* in which they enter an altered consciousness (*inam*) and 'do not know themselves again'.

Annang informal justice is popular not only because it inflects these registers of personhood, but also because it employs practices, 'rituals of verification', which establish truth, guilt and accountability through public spectacle and performance. Performance is central to Annang concepts of knowledge and oaths (*mbiam*) and ordeals (*ukang*) are the key performative devices through which people may determine truth in the retrospective attribution of cause to effect. The term for oath (*mbiam*) carries a mutable character and

14. The sight of *ekpo ndem* is relatively rare these days, but its practices are still familiar. Children's masquerades, for instance, mimic its performance in plays of their own in which young boys parade a cloth-covered figure tied at the waist to demand 'dashes' from passers-by.

its meaning varies according to context, variously oath, ordeal and poison — similarly ambivalent features as the Mende *hale* (Jedrej, 1976). In general, *mbiam* represents both an oath of innocence and a harmful charm. *Mbiam* is also sworn as an oath of secrecy, as a pact to settle a dispute between rivals and to signify the spiritual purity of title holders. In a court case *mbiam* is sworn both to prove the veracity of evidence and as an ordeal to demonstrate innocence. In all these instances swearing *mbiam*, often a stone or a phial of salt water obtained from an oath specialist (*abia mbiam*), subjected the oath-taker to a year-long ordeal during which their premature death signified guilt. Oath-swearing is far more than a guarantee of veracity, therefore; it is also an ordeal through which oath-takers live or die. As Elizabeth Tonkin (2000) says, ordeals are divinatory practices and public performances — they are dramas of truth.

Public oaths have long been a deterrent used against criminals in Annang villages. Often village-wide oaths are sworn each year to bind the village to a pledge that they will not commit crime or associate with criminal gangs. One of the most significant popular responses to the crime-waves organized by the chiefs, for instance, illustrates the continued significance of *mbiam* in the Annang judicial system, and the practice of public oath-swearing to prevent theft. This is especially relevant in relation to the discourse on armed robbery, and in Ikot Akam, for example, villagers swear at the village council in August each year. Non-Christians swear on *mbiam ikpa isong*, the spirit of the village, and Christians swear on verses from the Bible that if they should steal, associate with thieves or join armed robbery gangs then they would be killed within six months.[15]

Vigilantes are also linked to a range of practices and ordeals that establish truth and character. In the Adat Ifang clan, on *Obo* market day wives prepare food, invite their parents and friends from their natal villages, and dance for the vigilantes. This is the ordeal of cleanliness (*ukang akee sana*) and is held to test and celebrate the character of women married into the village. The type of food a woman produces proves that she works hard in the farm and has no reason to steal. The woman's innocence, cleanliness and beauty is designated by wearing a palm frond (*eyei*) on her right hand. She will sing '*mmenyong ukang, ukang akee sana*' — 'I went to ordeal, ordeal found me clean'.

The popular legitimacy of contemporary village vigilante groups is therefore derived from their role as an alternative judicial forum which, in turn, is linked to the use of a range of ordeals (*ukang*) in establishing guilt in cases of theft. In one instance in Ukanafun, a vigilante leader is himself a *ukang* ordeal specialist who investigates cases of theft with recourse to a tract from the Bible. The ordeal he administers is known as Bible Turn (Bible *akanna*). A key is placed inside the Bible and the ordeal-giver calls on the spirits of thieves in the Bible to identify the guilty party. The suspect

15. Nto Udofia Ekpuk Council Minutes, Ikot Akam, September 1989.

undergoing the test holds the loop of the key which is suspending the Bible, and if proven guilty the Bible rotates three times. Simmons (1956: 225) reported this Bible-key divination (*afia ukpohode*) being used by children in Calabar. The key is placed in Acts 5 at the story of Ananias and Sapphira. Ananias and Sapphira embezzled money from a land sale and both died instantly when Paul challenged them and announced that they had tested the 'Spirit of the Lord'. Young men wrapped their bodies and carried them away to be buried. There are a number of reasons why this passage is especially resonant in an Annang context. 'Testing' (*ndomo*) is precisely the term used to undertake an Annang investigation by ordeal. The guilt of a thief tested by Bible *akanna* is therefore a test of the spirit of dead malevolent spirits. The fact that young men were responsible for the body is also significant for young vigilantes.

Youth associations and their vigilante patrols also routinely employ the broom doctor (*ukang ujang*) or what Simmons (1956: 224) reported as 'medicine-broom divination' (*afia ifiet*). Two brooms are held with their open bristles touching one another. In this position, with no link between them, the brooms should not be able to be fastened to anything or carry any weight. First at the feet and then seven times moving up the body the specialist touches the brooms against the body of the person undergoing the ordeal. The seventh touch reaches the neck at which point the brooms will either pass by on either side thereby releasing the person and revealing that they are speaking the truth or they form a firm bind and grip the person's neck which throttles and cuts into the skin at the larynx. This is the sign of deceit and guilt.

These are not unchanging 'traditional' ordeal practices. They appropriate concepts and symbols of justice from a range of registers. A recent innovation in ordeals used by Annang vigilantes, for example, mimics an ordeal witnessed in Igbo popular videos. The video 'Issakaba', a four-part drama highlighting the role of the Bakassi Boys, resonates with images of protective charms and truth-telling ordeals readily identified and appropriated by young men in nearby Annang villages. One ordeal seen in Issakaba videos is the use of a string of cowrie shells as a 'truth-telling belt'. In response to the upsurge in armed robberies since 1999, the vigilantes of Ikot Akpa Nkuk commissioned the manufacture and empowering of a similar object in August 2000, a rope (*ikpo*) known as the 'Champion Belt.' The vigilante's Champion Belt is used by tying it around the waist of a suspected thief who will confess to their actions, their accomplices and the items they have stolen. The belt not only compels suspects to speak the truth, therefore, but as with imagery of the malevolent ancestral force (*ekpo ndem*), it symbolically confirms their representation as a deviant and anti-social spirit.

The legitimacy of Annang vigilantism is linked to a number of further factors, many of which have not been discussed here but which have to do with the way in which vigilantism is embedded in practice — in nightly routines, in relations between the generations, in bodily practice, in settling disputes, in sponsoring unemployed youth, and in scrutinizing contracts. Nevertheless it is important to stress that vigilantism above all is embedded in cultural understandings, both that it is grounded in concepts of personhood and also that it represents familiar ways of knowing and proving the truth.

CONCLUSION: TACTICS, SPACE AND TIME

The decentring of governance is one of the key features of globalization. Appadurai (2002: 24), for instance, examines these 'new geographies of governmentality' and argues that the appropriation of the means of governance by non-governmental groups has led to a crisis of 'redundancy' for the nation state. In the African context Mbembe has noted an abrupt collapse of notions of the post-colonial state's public good. Without rights or resources to redistribute, all that the post-colonial state has left to control are the forces of coercion (*commandement*). The resulting rise in the privatization of lawful violence is not an indicator of chaos, Mbembe states, but a sign of struggles aimed at establishing new forms of legitimate domination that restructure the existing formulas of authority (Mbembe, 2001: 76).

The fracturing of the state on the one hand and the increasing significance of non-state actors on the other are especially pronounced features of contemporary Nigeria. The widespread mobilization of youth in civil disorder, for instance, provides a popular counter-narrative to the legitimacy of the Nigerian nation state (Agbu, 2004; Akinyele, 2001; Ikelegbe, 2001; Watts, 2003). Here militant youth movements such as the O'odua People's Congress (OPC) in the West, the Ijaw Egbesu boys in the Niger Delta, the Bakassi Boys in the East, and the Arewa People's Congress (APC) in the North spearhead contemporary political contests between the politics of identity and citizenship. Each foregrounds contemporary social movements representing divergent imaginings of Nigeria: pro-sharia in the north, ethnic nationalism in the west, and autonomous resource control in the oil-producing south.

Neither the techniques of coercion, nor the dynamics of popular mobilization, however, capture the fine-grain of everyday ways of operating within the post-colony. In Africa, as John Peel has argued, political activity is the major mode of society's self-realization: 'It is conditioned not just by the structure of the state, but by attitudes and identities brought to the political arena by the members of local communities' (Peel, 1983: 7). The contemporary 'politics of improvement' in Nigeria is defined by access to the state since this has become a precondition for doing business successfully. As competition for access to the state has intensified so people explore a diverse array of channels of access leading to a 'restless mobility' of people and their political and economic investments (Berry, 1989: 55). This restless mobility is discussed here in the idea of a civic vigilance which points to the significance of internal imperatives and accountabilities that are employed in everyday interactions within the post-colony. The activities of the young vigilant citizens serve as a counterpoint to an analysis of cultural frameworks that emphasize instrumentalization, and contribute to work that shows how accountability assumes highly ambiguous, insurgent and surprising guises (Boyte, 1992: 341).

The mode of vigilance outlined here concerning corruption, electoral patronage and crime is a particular feature of the politics of youth. It should be stressed that the petition writers and vigilantes of Ikot Akpa Nkuk are often the same individuals. Their micro-political activities and 'invisible governances' (Hecht and Simone, 1994) appear to undermine the social cohesion necessary for the creation of meaningful institutions. They may, indeed, contribute to accounts of Nigeria that reveal 'ragged, unstable, perhaps ungovernable, spaces and analytics of government' (Watts, 2003: 26). It is not surprising, however, that use of a Foucauldian theoretical model which employs the notion of governmentality and which incorporates a focus on governable objects, governable spaces and the creation of order through discourse, disciplines and technologies of government, is found to be ill-equipped to deal with the chaotic plurality of such localized manoeuvres (Watts, 2003: 26).

In contrast, de Certeau's underemployed concept of the 'tactic' seems especially attuned to this discussion. The way in which modes of governance are fractured give rise to a complex of localized strategizing that involves encompassing space and utilizing time. Youth groups are about encompassing constituencies — youth, lineage, village, minority as marginalized groups — and hence define spatial zones as enclosures of entitlement, inclusion and exclusion (Geschiere and Nyamnjoh, 2002). They also exploit various forms of temporal opportunity, in particular elections as moments of transition, and the nocturnal frontiers policed by vigilantes. Transitions from one political regime to another are privileged contexts not only for regimes but also for ordinary people to negotiate political inclusion and exclusion (Hansen and Stepputat, 2001: 26). Equally, it is important to locate vigilantism as a frontier phenomenon not only on the physical boundaries of state control, or urban no-go areas, but in temporal frontiers — of night and day (Abrahams, 1996, 1998). The internal, cultural imperatives outlined here concerning the distributive expectations placed on patrons, and the deviant motivations inscribed on thieves, map onto political responses characterized by fear and zeal (Worby, 1998: 564). Tactics, therefore, are characterized by a watchful, opportunistic civic vigilance operating in a twilight between the predations and possibilities of the post-colony.

REFERENCES

Abrahams, R. (1996) 'Vigilantism: Order and Disorder on the Frontiers of the State', in O. Harris (ed.) *Inside and Outside the Law: Anthropological Studies of Authority and Ambiguity*, pp. 42–55. London: Routledge.

Abrahams, R. (1998) *Vigilant Citizens: Vigilantism and the State*. Cambridge: Polity Press.
Agbu, O. (2004) *Ethnic Militias and the Threat to Democracy in Post-Transition Nigeria*. Uppsala: Nordiska Afrikainstitutet.
Akinyele, R. T. (2001) 'Ethnic Militancy and National Stability in Nigeria: A Case Study of the Oodua People's Congress', *African Affairs* 100(401): 623–40.
Amnesty International (2002) 'Nigeria: Vigilante Violence in the South and South-east'. AI INDEX: AFR 44(014). Available online: http://web.amnesty.org/library/index/ENGAFR440142002
Appadurai, A. (2002) 'Deep Democracy: Urban Governmentality and the Horizon of Politics', *Public Culture* 14(1): 21–47.
Austen, R. A. (1986) 'Criminals and the African Cultural Imagination: Normative and Deviant Heroism in Pre-colonial and Modern Narratives', *Africa* 56(4): 385–98.
Baker, B. (2002) 'When the Bakassi Boys Came: Eastern Nigeria Confronts Vigilantism', *Journal of Contemporary African Studies* 20(2): 223–44.
Baker, J. P. and O. Pedersen (eds) (1992) *The Rural Urban Interface in Africa: Expansion and Adaptation*. Uppsala: The Scandinavian Institute of African Studies.
Banton, M. (1957) *West African City: A Study of Tribal Life in Freetown*. London: Oxford University Press for the International African Institute.
Barber, K. (1982) 'Popular Reactions to the Petro-Naira', *Journal of Modern African Studies* 20(3): 431–50.
Barkan, J. D., M. L. McNulty and M. A. O. Ayeni (1991) '"Hometown" Voluntary Associations, Local Development, and the Emergence of Civil Society in Western Nigeria', *The Journal of Modern African Studies* 29(3): 457–80.
Bayart, J. (1993) *The State in Africa: The Politics of the Belly*. London: Longman.
Bayart, J., S. Ellis and B. Hibou (1999) *The Criminalization of the State in Africa*. Oxford: James Currey.
Berry, S. S. (1989) 'Social Institutions and Access to Resources', *Africa* 59: 41–55.
Boyte, H. C. (1992) 'The Pragmatic Ends of Popular Politics', in C. Calhoun (ed.) *Habermas and the Public Sphere*, pp. 340–55. Cambridge, MA: MIT.
Bucholtz, M. (2002) 'Youth and Cultural Practice', *Annual Review of Anthropology* 31(1): 525–52.
Chabal, P. and J. Daloz (1999) *Africa Works: The Political Instrumentalization of Disorder*. London: James Currey.
Comaroff, J. L. and J. Comaroff (2000) 'Introduction', in J. L. Comaroff and J. Comaroff (eds) *Civil Society and the Political Imagination in Africa: Critical Perspectives*, pp. 1–43. Chicago, IL: The University of Chicago Press.
Cruise O'Brien, D. B. (1996) 'A Lost Generation? Youth Identity and State Decay in West Africa', in R. Werbner and T. Ranger (eds) *Postcolonial Identities in Africa*, pp. 55–74. London and New York: Zed Books.
Daum, C. (1992) *L'immigration Ouest-Africaine en France: Une Dynamique Nouvelle dans la Vallée du Fleuve Sénégal?* Paris: Institut Panos.
de Certeau, M. (1984) *The Practice of Everyday Life*. Berkeley, CA: University of California Press.
Diouf, M. (1996) 'Urban Youth and Senegalese Politics: Dakar 1988–1994', *Public Culture* 8(2): 225–50.
Durham, D. (2000) 'Youth and the Social Imagination in Africa: Introduction to Parts 1 and 2', *Anthropological Quarterly* 73(3): 113–20.
Ekeh, P. (1975) 'Colonialism and Two Publics in Africa: A Theoretical Statement', *Comparative Studies in Society and History* 17(1): 91–112.
Ferguson, J. (1997) 'Transnational Topographies of Power: Beyond "the State" and "Civil Society" in the Study of African Politics', in H. S. Marcussen and S. Arnfred (eds), *Concepts and Metaphors: Ideologies, Narratives and Myths in Development Discourse*, pp. 45–71. Roskilde: Roskilde University.

Ferguson, J. and A. Gupta (2002) 'Spatializing States: Toward an Ethnography of Neoliberal Governmentality', *American Ethnologist* 29(4): 981–1002.
Ferme, M. C. (2001) *The Underneath of Things: Violence, History, and the Everyday in Sierra Leone*. Berkeley, CA, and London: University of California Press.
Fields, K. (1982) 'Political Contingencies of Witchcraft in Colonial Central Africa: Culture and the State in Marxist Theory', *Canadian Journal of African Studies* 16(3): 567–93.
Forrest, T. (1986) 'The Political Economy of Civil Rule and the Economic Crisis in Nigeria (1979–84)', *Review of African Political Economy* 35: 4–26.
Geschiere, P. and J. Gugler (1998) 'The Urban–Rural Connection: Changing Issues of Belonging and Identification', *Africa* 68(3): 309–19.
Geschiere, P. and F. Nyamnjoh (2002) 'Capitalism and Autochthony: The Seesaw of Mobility and Belonging', *Public Culture* 12(2): 423–52.
Gore, C. and D. Pratten (2003) 'The Politics of Plunder: The Rhetorics of Order and Disorder in Southern Nigeria', *African Affairs* 102(407): 211–40.
Grillo, R. and B. Riccio (2004) 'Translocal Development: Italy–Senegal', *Population, Space and Place* 10: 99–111.
Gugler, J. (1971) 'Life in a Dual System: Eastern Nigerians in Town, 1961', *Cahiers d'Etudes Africaines* 11: 400–21.
Gugler, J. (1991) 'Life in a Dual System Revisited: Urban–Rural Ties in Enugu, Nigeria 1961–87', *World Development* 19(5): 399–409.
Gupta, A. (1995) 'Blurred Boundaries: The Discourse of Corruption, the Culture of Politics, and the Imagined State', *American Ethnologist* 22(2): 375–402.
Guyer, J. I. (1992) 'Representation without Taxation: An Essay on Democracy in Rural Nigeria, 1952–1990', *African Studies Review* 35(1): 41–80.
Hagberg, S. (2002) '"Enough is Enough": An Ethnography of the Struggle against Impunity in Burkina Faso', *Journal of Modern African Studies* 40(2): 217–46.
Hansen, T. B. and F. Stepputat (2001) 'Introduction', in T. B. Hansen and F. Stepputat (eds) *States of Imagination: Ethnographic Explorations of the Postcolonial State*, pp. 1–38. Durham, NC: Duke University Press.
Harnischfeger, J. (2003) 'The Bakassi Boys: Fighting Crime in Nigeria', *The Journal of Modern African Studies* 41(1): 23–49.
Heald, S. (1986a) 'Witches and Thieves: Deviant Motivations in Gisu Society', *Man* 21(1): 65–78.
Heald, S. (1986b) 'Mafias in Africa: The Rise of Drinking Companies and Vigilante Groups in Bugisu, Uganda', *Africa* 56(4): 446–67.
Hecht, D. and M. Simone (1994) *Invisible Governance: The Art of African Micropolitics*. New York: Autonomedia.
Herzfeld, M. (1993) *The Social Production of Indifference: Exploring the Symbolic Roots of Western Bureaucracy*. Chicago, IL: University of Chicago Press.
Honey, R. and S. Okafor (eds) (1998) *Hometown Associations: Indigenous Knowledge and Development in Nigeria*. London: Intermediate Technology.
Human Rights Watch (2002) 'Bakassi Boys: The Legitimization of Murder and Torture'. Report 14(5a). New York: Human Rights Watch.
Human Rights Watch (2003) 'The O'odua People's Congress: Fighting Violence with Violence'. Report 15(4). New York: Human Rights Watch.
Ikelegbe, A. (2001) 'The Perverse Manifestation of Civil Society: Evidence from Nigeria', *Journal of Modern African Studies* 39(1): 1–24.
Jedrej, M. C. (1976) 'Medicine, Fetish and Secret Society in a West African Culture', *Africa* 46: 247–57.
Kelsall, T. (2003) 'Rituals of Verification: Indigenous and Imported Accountability in Northern Tanzania', *Africa* 73(2): 174–201.
Lentz, C. (1995) 'Youth Associations in Northern Ghana: Unity for Development', *Africa* 65(3): 395–429.

Lonsdale, J. (1986) 'Political Accountability in African History', in P. Chabal (ed.) *Political Domination in Africa: Reflections on the Limits of Power*, pp. 126–57. Cambridge: Cambridge University Press.
Lund, C. (2001) 'Precarious Democratization and Local Dynamics in Niger: Micro-politics in Zinder', *Development and Change* 32(5): 845–69.
Mbembe, A. (1992) 'Provisional Notes on the Postcolony', *Africa* 62(1): 3–37.
Mbembe, A. (2001) *On the Postcolony*. Berkeley, CA: University of California Press.
McCall, J. (1995) 'Rethinking Ancestors in Africa', *Africa* 65(2): 256–70.
McNulty, M. L. and F. L. Mark (1996) 'Hometown Associations: Balancing Local and Extralocal Interests in Nigerian Communities', in B. Peter and D. M. Warren (eds) *Indigenous Organisations and Development*, pp. 21–41. London: IT Publications.
Mitchell, T. (1991) 'The Limits of the State: Beyond Statist Approaches and their Critics', *American Political Science Review* 85(1): 77–96.
Momoh, A. (2000) 'Youth Culture and Area Boys in Lagos', in A. Jega (ed.) *Identity Transformation and Identity Politics under Structural Adjustment in Nigeria*, pp. 181–203. Uppsala: Nordiska Afrikainstitutet in collaboration with the Centre for Research and Documentation, Kano.
Moore, S. F. (1996) 'Post-socialist Micro-politics: Kilimanjaro, 1993', *Africa* 66(4): 587–606.
Mustapha, A. R. (2002) 'States, Predation & Violence: Reconceptualizing Political Action and Political Community in Africa'. Paper presented at the Panel on State, Political Identity and Political Violence, 10th General Assembly of CODESRIA, Kampala, Uganda (8–12 December).
Newell, S. (2001) '"Paracolonial" Networks: Some Speculations on Local Readerships in Colonial West Africa', *Interventions: International Journal of Post-colonial Studies* 3(3): 336–54.
Nolte, I. (2004) 'Identity and Violence: The Politics of Youth in Ijebu-Remo, Nigeria', *The Journal of Modern African Studies* 42(1): 61–89.
Olivier de Sardan, J. P. (1999) 'A Moral Economy of Corruption in Africa?', *The Journal of Modern African Studies* 37(1): 25–52.
Parkin, D. (1966) 'Voluntary Associations as an Adaptive Institution', *Man New Series* 1(1): 90–95.
Parkin, D. (1969) *Neighbours and Nationals in an African City Ward*. London: Routledge and Kegan Paul.
Peel, J. D. Y. (1983) *Ijeshas and Nigerians: The Incorporation of a Yoruba Kingdom, 1880s–1970s*. Cambridge: Cambridge University Press.
Picton, J. (1990) 'What's in a Mask?', *Journal of African Languages and Culture* 2(2): 181–202.
Pioneer (1997a) 'Letter to the Editor', *Pioneer* 12–18 May (Uyo).
Pioneer (1997b) 'Calabar under Seige by Armed Robbers', *Pioneer* 12–18 May (Uyo).
Pioneer (1997c) 'Renewed Fear of Crime-waves in Uyo', *Pioneer* 12–18 May (Uyo).
Post Express (1998) 'Akwa Ibom State Police Commissioner Criticises Local Government Councils for Failing to Fund the Local Police', *Post Express* 3 November 1998 (Lagos).
Pratten, D. (1997) 'Bamako Bound: The Social Organisation of Migration in Mali'. London: SOS Sahel.
Pratten, D. (2000) *Return to the Roots? Urban Networks, Rural Development and Power in Sudan*. Edinburgh: University of Edinburgh Press.
Pratten, D. (forthcoming) *The Man-Leopard Murder Mysteries: History and Society in Colonial Nigeria*. International African Institute: Edinburgh University Press.
Punch (1997a) 'Akwa Ibom State Administrator's Concern at the Increasing Rate of Armed Robbery', *Punch* 28 April (Lagos)
Punch (1997b) '"Dare-Devil" Armed Robberies in Enugu', *Punch* 29 August (Lagos).
Reno, W. (2002) 'The Politics of Insurgency in Collapsing States', *Development and Change* 33(5): 837–58.
Rose, N. (1999) *Powers of Freedom: Reframing Political Thought*. Cambridge: Cambridge University Press.

Schatzberg, M. G. (1993) 'Power, Legitimacy and "Democratisation" in Africa', *Africa* 63(4): 445–61.
Schatzberg, M. G. (2002) *Political Legitimacy in Middle Africa: Father, Family, Food*. Bloomington, IN: Indiana University Press.
Simmons, D. C. (1956) 'Efik Divination, Ordeals and Omens', *Southwestern Journal of Anthropology* 12(2): 223–8.
Smith, D. J. (2001a) 'Kinship and Corruption in Contemporary Nigeria', *Ethnos* 66(3): 344–64.
Smith, D. J. (2001b) 'Ritual Killing, 419, and Fast Wealth: Inequality and the Popular Imagination in Southeastern Nigeria', *American Ethnologist* 28(4): 803–26.
Smith, D. J. (2004) 'The Bakassi Boys: Vigilantism, Violence and Political Imagination in Nigeria', *Current Anthropology* 19(3): 429–58.
Smock, A. C. (1971) *Ibo Politics: The Role of Ethnic Unions in Eastern Nigeria*. Harvard, MA: Harvard University Press.
Southall, A. W. (1975) 'Forms of Ethnic Linkage Between Town and Country', in P. David (ed.) *Town and Country in Central and Eastern Africa*, pp. 265–75. London: Oxford University Press for the International African Institute.
Tide (1996) 'Crime Statistics: Port Harcourt', *Tide* 17 November (Port Harcourt).
Tonkin, E. (2000) 'Autonomous Judges: African Ordeals as Dramas of Power', *Ethnos: Journal of Anthropology* 65(3): 366–86.
Trager, L. (1998) 'Home-town Linkages and Local Development in South-western Nigeria. Whose Agenda? What Impact?', *Africa* 68(3): 360–82.
Udoma, U. (1987) *The Story of the Ibibio State Union*. Ibadan: Spectrum Books.
Vaughan, O. (1995) 'Assessing Grassroots Politics and Community Development in Nigeria', *African Affairs* 94: 501–18.
Watts, M. (2003) 'Development and Governmentality', *Singapore Journal of Tropical Geography* 24(1): 6–34.
Wolpe, H. E. (1974) *Urban Politics in Nigeria: A Study of Port Harcourt*. Berkeley, CA: University of California Press.
Woods, D. (1994) 'Elites, Ethnicity, and Home Town Associations in the Cote- D'Ivoire: An Historical Analysis of State–Society Links', *Africa* 64(4): 465–83.
Worby, E. (1998) 'Tyranny, Parody, and Ethnic Polarity: Ritual Engagements with the State in Northwestern Zimbabwe', *Journal of Southern African Studies* 24(3): 561–78.
Ya'u, Y. Z. (2000) 'The Youth, Economic Crisis and Identity Transformation: The Case of the Yandaba in Kano', in A. Jega (ed.) *Identity Transformation and Identity Politics under Structural Adjustment in Nigeria*, pp. 161–80. Uppsala: Nordiska Afrikainstitutet in collaboration with the Centre for Research and Documentation, Kano.

Reordering Society: Vigilantism and Expressions of Sovereignty in Port Elizabeth's Townships

Lars Buur

INTRODUCTION

From the beginning of the 1990s, and particularly in 1994, the African National Congress (ANC) emerged as the driving force of the new democratic government of South Africa. The government embarked on a massive and, at times, profound nation-state building project, including the celebrated constitutional rewriting process, the truth and reconciliation project (Buur, 2001; Wilson, 2001) and various models for socio-economic transformation and redistribution of wealth (Nattrass and Seekings, 2001; Terreblanche, 2003). The government initiated what the ex-Speaker of Parliament, Frene Ginwala, termed a 'total overhaul of a country [intent on] re-ordering itself'. Since 1994, the parliament has laid 'the table for the country [through] 789 new pieces of legislation . . . aimed at reconfiguring South African society' (Ginwala, quoted in Madlala, 2004). This reordering was directed at undoing injustices committed under the apartheid regime. The plethora of legislation is meant to bring everybody under the same sovereign rule of law: 'One *law* for One *nation*' (as proclaimed on the first page of the new Constitution). The project has had an impact on nearly all spheres of society, concerning matters of both small and great importance.[1] In a variety of ways, the projects have included a 'nascent civil society that transcends the particularism of political organization based on identity' (Sisk, 1995: 253), that is, ethnic and racial forms of identity and/or forms of political organization characterized by violence and lack of democracy. The state has formulated a new social contract in which the legal-political order is based on the premise of people assigning their sovereign power to the state, which serves as custodian and protector of their rights (Nina, 2001; Sisk, 1995). In this Hobbesian perspective of sovereignty, the state is bequeathed the right to use violence to intervene and restore order, on behalf of individuals and for the common good. Ideally, the use of violence, an inextricable part of resistance to and application of

1. Undoing the apartheid logic of differentiated citizenship has been one aspect of nation-state building, but the project has been wider, giving order and form to the social body more generally. It includes legislating the size of condoms; the type of taxis used for 'public' transport; smoking areas; access to a certain amount of free water for poor households; redistribution of land; reshaping the local governance system and city-landscapes, and the modes of interaction to which these city-landscapes cater.

the apartheid contract, is the exclusive monopoly of state reconstructed as democratic.

The most significant single issue that has dogged the new society over the past decade is the crime that has confronted the state and ordinary people. The common perception is that crime rates are soaring and that police and government have no control over it (Institute for Security Studies, 1998). With the re-emergence of vigilantism, the limitation of the new state's pledge to secure justice for all has been exposed. Many analyses of vigilantism or non-state forms of ordering argue that vigilantism, in its benevolent form, is stimulated by the state's incapacity to police and to secure citizens' rights for them (Dixon and Johns, 2001; Schärf and Nina, 2001). Underpinning this understanding is the conviction that the new social contract has not been honoured by the state. There are many reasons for this failure. Firstly, since political transition to democracy, police have been expected to change their *modus operandi* from obtaining confessions from suspects under duress and torture to working within the law and accepting due process and human rights. Secondly, there have been and still are public and internal struggles within state structures over the redistribution of resources from privileged to formerly disadvantaged communities. This has hampered the police in concentrating on what it actually should be doing — policing. Thirdly it has been argued that the South African state serves a population whose political sensibilities have been forged in antagonism to (or in the absence of) the state (see Schärf and Nina, 2001; Tshehla, 2003).

The result is that police are perceived to be 'incompetent' and 'corrupt', interested in 'protecting the criminals' and 'non-responsive to the needs of the South African townships'.[2] Such comments reflect the perception that the state is incapable of dealing with crime in the townships or of ensuring universal citizenship rights (Buur, 2003; Buur and Jensen, 2004). Crime and capacity problems have been influential in spurring the emergence of vigilante formations all over the country. However, these factors cannot, on their own, explain why some have shown remarkable resilience and continued to function even when the officially gauged crime rate has dropped, or when the state has decided to clamp down on such formations. The reality is that intimate relationships have developed between individuals and organizations forming part of both state and vigilante groups. These relationships raise a number of questions: how is the category of criminal vigilante formation construed by the state and others; how are activities carried out and legitimized by vigilante formations; and how do vigilante formations view their activities *vis-à-vis* the state? (see also Pratten and Blundo, this issue).

To explore these questions, this article focuses on the case of the Amadlozi, a vigilante group operating in townships outside Port Elizabeth. It first describes how the Amadlozi organized crime fighting in 1999 and 2000, when

2. Common responses given during my household survey in New Brighton township outside Port Elizabeth in 2001.

crime became a matter of urgency, before investigating the ways in which institutional boundaries between criminal justice enforcement and the work of the Amadlozi came to be radically reconfigured and redrawn several times. It is possible to understand the emergence of the Amadlozi as protecting the law; this is demonstrated in the context of a consideration of the relation of discourses on crime to questions of sovereignty. The category of crime will then be examined and related to the work of the Amadlozi as the protector of the community against the criminal. Firstly, however, before probing how the Amadlozi emerged and positioned itself in the political landscape of crime fighting, some context is necessary.

FROM ALTERNATIVE SOVEREIGNS TO CRIME FIGHTERS

From 1880 until 1980, the political mobilization of African semi-urban and urban residents 'in recognizably "modern" organizational forms' (Bundy, 2000: 30) gathered momentum. It generally took two distinct forms, which in different constellations and with various twists and turns have been present ever since. The first official representative bodies, 'location committees',[3] became Advisory Boards with the introduction of the 1923 Urban Areas Legislation, while vigilante formations were termed the *iliso lomzi,* literally meaning 'eye of the house'. Early committees consisted of local notables (teachers, clerks, clergymen): these Advisory Boards represented registered municipal leaseholders (around a fifth of the male population in urban areas). *Iliso lomzi* emerged in more than fifteen urban areas in the Eastern Cape, including New Brighton, and often claimed a broader representation of a given urban community, but were generally managed by educated residents (Bundy, 2000).

Both Advisory Boards and *Iliso lomzi* manifested different forms to address the issues of security and the maintenance of peace and order that resulted from intensified urbanization. These issues included the disruption of family and community ties, depressed living standards, material deprivation, violence and social disorder. Sometimes the two forms were in competition with each other and sometimes they shared the same platform (ibid.: 34; see also Seekings, 2001: 85–6). However, where 'committees' and boards increasingly came under 'popular suspicion' (Bundy, 2000: 34) due to their 'official' status, vigilante associations attracted large followings, operating through 'mass meetings'. These organizations became the most common form of popular politics (ibid.: 35).

During the mid-1980s, the key mobilizing slogans adopted by the ANC and the United Democratic Front (UDF)[4] — 'people's power' and

3. *Location* was the name used for black urban areas until around 1960 when *township* became the dominant term.
4. Formed in 1983 as an internal umbrella movement, the UDF was an amalgamation of various civic, religious and liberation groups (see Seekings, 2000).

'making the country ungovernable' — meant that the notion of self-regulation was radicalized and adapted to the political struggle, moving 'beyond its traditional roots' (Suttner quoted in Nina, 1992: 2).[5] For some, these strategies were seen as a continuation of forms of self-regulation and community discipline that had long been a feature of rural and urban communities in South Africa (Bapela, 1987). In Port Elizabeth — where this struggle was organized by Port Elizabeth's Black Civic Organization (PEBCO) — 'people power' referred to attempts to dismantle apartheid and the security forces by displacing the authority, and to curb the reach of the state by seizing control of administrative, welfare, policing, judicial and other functions in the townships, creating an 'alternative sovereign'. The organization of residents into street and area committees (see Nina, 1992; Seekings, 2000; Schärf and Nina, 2001) was seen as a prefigurative endeavour of future democracy. The dual face of 'ungovernability and organization', as Nina phrased it in his sympathetic accounts of people's courts, created a parallel authority that 'was seen as part of a process of organizing the future society' (Nina, 1995: 7; see also Mayekiso, 1996).

From 1984 there were frequent clashes between riot police and the UDF-aligned youth, known as the Amabutho or Young Lions, as well as between youth and the Black Local Authorities (BLAs), which were primarily run by township elders. In addition, from 1985 a tense battle between the UDF and the Azanian People's Organization (AZAPO) tore Port Elizabeth townships apart.[6] Rallies by hundreds of youths at the houses of political opponents were often followed by arson attacks and sometimes by necklacing.[7] Members of the resistance movement established forums to administer civil and criminal justice through people's courts since there was no confidence in the apartheid criminal justice system.

Some commentators argue that until mid-1986, people's courts functioned in an optimal manner and were relatively well organized and politically disciplined (for further information, see Mayekiso, 1996; Nina, 1992; Seekings, 2001). However, with the declaration of the States of Emergency from 1986 onwards, the killing, imprisonment or exile of most UDF leaders, and the

5. 'Building People's Organs for People's Power' was introduced as a campaign in early 1986 following the collapse of government-created Black Local Administrations (BLAs). Residents formed alternative structures such as street committees, area committees, people's courts, school committees and residents' associations 'to liberate the people'. While the UDF emphasized that it was not officially their campaign, it was acknowledged and encouraged in publications and public speeches by UDF leaders (TRC, 1998, Vol 2: 383).
6. The UDF–AZAPO conflict had national parallels. In this region, the conflict began in 1986/7 and continued into the 1990s (Hayson, 1989: 13; TRC, 1998, Vol 3: 99–101). Elements of the conflict were related to tensions between the rival metalworker unions in the automotive industry.
7. Necklacing, or burning somebody alive with a car-tyre around the body, is widely associated with people's justice. Police statistics indicate that around 700 to 800 people were burnt to death between 1985 and 1989 (see TRC, 1998). Women were a large proportion of the victims, particularly those seen as policemen's girlfriends.

counter-insurgency strategies of the apartheid regime, discipline gave way to a more chaotic picture. People's courts became kangaroo courts that ordered severe punishment of crime and other forms of behaviour considered deviant by township activists. The construction of collaborators and *askaris* as a special target for popular justice heralded a new sanctioning of killing.[8] In the long history of popular justice in South Africa dating back to the early 1900s, execution was rare; but it became the enduring image of people's courts from the mid-1980s onward, in the form of necklacing.

Handing Sovereignty Back to the State: The CPF

The cornerstones of people's power were street and area committees. These were the most prevalent forms of local court system during the 1980s, but ceased to function in a systematic way in the early 1990s (Seekings, 2001).[9] There are several reasons for this. Firstly, there were power struggles between the ANC and various civic movements of the 1980s that gathered under the umbrella of the South African National Civic Organization (SANCO). After SANCO finally fell out with the ANC in 1996, the former largely disappeared from the picture as a well co-ordinated entity (see Cherry et al., 2000). Secondly, and related to this development, SANCO's attempts to organize justice enforcement locally were seen as a challenge to the ANC government's efforts to gain control over society. From 1991, PEBCO tried to organize and monopolize street committees in Port Elizabeth to carry on the work of people's courts in the name of Anti-Crime Committees (ACCs) (Nina, 2001: 107–14).[10] As a structured and systematic attempt to organize local justice enforcement, ACCs lost their impact through the mid- to late 1990s. In practice, more or less spontaneous initiatives emerged, with which SANCO sought to align itself. None of these formations lasted, partly because of the violence used to investigate criminal cases and partly because there was no space for organized crime-fighting efforts that might have political aspirations.

In an endeavour to regulate the relationship between the state and the wider public, the ANC-led government established Community Policing Forums (CPFs) in 1995. Anticipated from at least 1991, the concept of CPFs

8. Anybody who worked directly or indirectly for the apartheid state, including such persons' partners, were considered to be collaborators. *Askaris* were former operatives of *Umkhonto we Sizwe* (*isiXhosa* for 'The Spear of the Nation'), the ANC's military wing during the war of liberation (also known as MK) who betrayed fellow activists after being tortured. They were traitors to the anti-apartheid cause and regarded with hatred and contempt by both sides.
9. Exceptions were the Self Defence Units (SDUs) established by freedom fighters after the unbanning of the liberation movements in 1990 and the return of exiles. At times, they worked together with street committees but most often operated on their own and took on justice functions.
10. In 1993, PEBCO adopted SANCO's constitution and became SANCO-PE.

was formally introduced through the Interim Constitution of 1993 (Act 200, Section 221), was legislated through the South African Police Service Act of 1995, and remains part of law in terms of the final Constitution of 1996 (Act 106). CPF structures exist throughout the country. Every police station is required by law to have a CPF, comprising members democratically elected by the communities adjoining the police station, and a Community Police Officer. The CPFs are intended to work closely with the police, through the Community Police Officer, and are officially considered as *partners* of the police. However, the relationship can be tense, since CPFs also function as a civilian check on police negligence or abuse of power. They usually co-ordinate anti-crime initiatives from an office at the police station; they may have access to limited funding and receive different forms of training in human rights and strategic crime prevention. From the beginning, it was stipulated by the law regulating the CPF that they could form Safety and Security structures (S&S), bringing access to justice and conflict mediation at street and ward level — the lowest level in the local governance hierarchy. The S&S fall under the jurisdiction of, and are formally accountable to, CPFs.

Nina, applying the perspective of Hobbesian social contract theory, has described this development as an embryonic civil society slowly but voluntarily giving back to the state its 'traditional responsibilities', in particular the right to 'the use of physical force and physical punishment' (Nina, 2001: 107). This amounts to a reconfiguration of the sovereign space: what was constituted as an exterior sovereign is returned to the state and to the party in charge of the state. Nina concedes that this is a contradictory process in which the state is to some extent 'being modified and influenced by the community practices: popular justice re-defines state justice' (ibid.). It has indeed been a contradictory process, but whether it has taken the turn Nina hoped for — with 'positive' non-violent elements from people's courts being integrated under the sovereign of the new state — is less certain. The problem is not solely, as social contract theory would have it, that the contract has been dishonoured by the state's inability to provide sufficient security (see Tshehla, 2003), but also that the spheres or domains of civil society and state are conceived of as clearly distinguishable. The ideal constitutive separation between the two domains is, on closer scrutiny, a zone of ongoing contestation.

THE EMERGENCE OF THE AMADLOZI

The founding myth of the Amadlozi suggests that it emerged in 1999. The group was spurred into action by a group of young, armed criminals disguised in traffic police uniforms who hijacked trucks delivering furniture and refrigerators to private homes and shops in New Brighton and Kwazakele. After a tip-off from a local resident, the future Amadlozi apprehended one of the young hijackers. Instead of handing him over to the police, they gave him a bit of *patta-patta* (beating), during which he revealed where the stolen uniforms were hidden and with whom he worked. The residents traced the other members of the group and, after more *patta-patta,* discovered most of the stolen goods stored in a house, waiting to be sold. The goods were then displayed in the street so residents and delivery companies could come and collect lost items. Uniforms and recovered firearms were handed over to police. The suspects were 'put in front of the community'. They promised not to repeat their misdeeds and began working for the community as members of the Amadlozi, a development that was often emphasized.

After this initial success, residents continued to meet to deal with the criminal elements that terrorized them. More residents joined them not only from New Brighton but also from adjoining townships. SANCO-PE had approached the residents' group in order to organize it as an ACC, but the group declined the invitation. During interviews, the explanation given was 'we don't do politics'. This was a clear reference to SANCO's struggles with the ANC. Instead, the group of residents established itself under the name 'Abahlali Concerned Residents Against Crime' (CRAC). It later became known as the Amadlozi, a Zulu word meaning ancestors. In popular usage in New Brighton, it translates as 'the ones we can trust when there is nobody else'. It can be interpreted as a critique of the inability of political organizations, state agencies and the CPFs to deal with crime.[11] The name also indicates that that Amadlozi draw on the ever-present universe of powerful ancestors and the wider value system attached to it, often referred to as 'the Xhosa way'. Their first meeting place was a corner under the streetlight, but in 2000 they managed to access four classrooms at the local government school, Molefe Primary.

Over time, the group organized itself with a front and backstage leadership. The front comprised members from formerly inimical factions of the liberation struggle, including the militant, left-wing AZAPO, the UDF, and formerly exiled MK soldiers. The group also included members of other political groups such as the United Democratic Movement (UDM). The front group took charge of daily crime fighting operations and mass meetings and, over time, directed engagement with state agencies. It also hosted public, quasi-court sessions at Molefe Primary School three times a week (for further information, see Buur, 2003, 2005). Here, between 200 and 300 people (at times, as many as 400) from different sections of New Brighton and neighbouring townships gathered to present and deal with cases brought to the attention of the Amadlozi. The front group currently has an appointed chairperson, a lay priest; a chief of staff, an unemployed former AZAPO

11. People who dislike the Amadlozi use the term derogatively meaning *sperm*. In the semiotic universe of powerful ancestors, the two meanings of the term — ancestors and sperm — are not necessarily contradictory.

leader well known from township struggles of the 1980s; a second in command, a former MK soldier, also unemployed, who assists the chief of staff; and a secretary, a woman with writing skills who keeps note of incoming cases and receives any payments made.

The backstage group functions as brokers between the Amadlozi and the state structures. It is comprised of people with connections, including the director of the New Brighton Community Hall, Mr Majoli, an influential ANC member from a well-known sports family in New Brighton. Together with the chief of staff, he is one of eight people who started the concerned residents' group. Several local businessmen, including high-ranking union leaders from COSATU, belong to Amadlozi's backstage leadership. While CRAC/Amadlozi 'had been applauded by the community' (interview, 2001), they expressed bitterness that no-one from the established structures had come forward and complimented their good work, which was all voluntary. Instead, the CPF at the New Brighton police station called for their abolishment, because they operated outside the law and were not authorized by any political organization or state agency. The CPF feared that the Amadlozi would develop into an anti-state vigilante group like People Against Gangs And Drugs (PAGAD) in Cape Town.[12] The local councillor described this concern: 'If we keep letting these people operate in our communities we are going to get the same thing they have in Cape Town'. However, in spite of the disapproval of the established structures in New Brighton, people continued to attend meetings in their hundreds. Individuals from the backstage group closely aligned to the ANC did not withdraw their support for Amadlozi.

Getting the Criminals . . . At All Costs

The primary reason for Amadlozi's popularity was its extraordinarily successful anti-crime campaign. Besides public meetings, it was organized in loosely constituted working groups that conducted raids. Working groups investigated crime cases brought to their attention in public sessions or to the personal attention of one of the front or backstage members. These groups consisted of residents and usually included one or two older members and five to eight younger members, depending on the nature of the crime to be investigated. Membership usually mixed gender, but generally more men than woman participated in investigations. If transport was required, members received 'transport money' from the complainant, then drove out and conducted raids that resembled ordinary police investigations or operations: they asked questions, searched persons and property and, in instances where the person for whom they were looking was not available, he/she would be

12. PAGAD originated in Cape Town as a predominantly Muslim group targeting drug dealers and gangsters. The group drew international attention when it torched, shot and eventually killed a famous Capetonian drug dealer in August 1996 (see Dixon and Johns, 2001).

subpoenaed in writing to appear at the next open meeting. Modelled on the concept of people's courts, investigating groups would often call together a large group of residents who worked as protection when they approached suspected criminals. They also arranged rallies, summoned people who had declined to come to the open meetings and entered private premises for investigative purposes. As described to me by one of the leaders of the Amadlozi:

> When we rally in front of criminals or raid their houses, who are they going to accuse? You can't [accuse anybody] because it was a crowd of many, many people, lots of people, maybe 200. It scares the hell out of them, you can see it in their eyes, they are dammed scared. If they have guns maybe with six bullets . . . its nothing if we come with hundreds of people, so you can say it is our protection. (Interview with the leadership of the Amadlozi, May 2001)

Besides protecting the Amadlozi from criminals, this approach also protected them from being identified as culpable. Sometimes during raids, doors were broken down or furniture or other household belongings were destroyed or stolen. If somebody was identified and arrested afterwards they could always say, 'Yes I was there, but just to see what happened'.

In order to conduct raids as part of investigations, information was needed. The Amadlozi's popularity and legitimacy were intimately related to its effectiveness in recovering stolen goods. Their investigative methods were based on 'putting an ear to the ground', following clues, leads, myths and information, all primarily obtained through force, or the threat of force. The information they worked on was anything but conclusive. Yet, amazingly, Amadlozi often found the right people 'in the end'. In about 70 to 80 per cent of the cases I followed over a six-month period (Buur, 2003), there was a result. This high success rate was partly due to the fact that most of the theft cases turned out to have been committed by young relatives or neighbours, friends or family and very seldom by total strangers. If suspects were strangers, that in itself was a clue. Amadlozi investigators effectively used local forms of knowledge provided by youngsters hanging out in the area of the break-in. By following up on these leads, mainly based on suspicion, they managed to get to the right criminal, but it was an imprecise strategy: often, the wrong person was approached first and beaten in order to extract information. However, through aggressive interrogation, leads to the right person were obtained, or information that cast light on formerly unresolved cases was unearthed. The point is that in almost all cases, somebody had seen or heard something, even if it was only rumours.

Besides the open quasi-court sessions and raids, Amadlozi also held what they called in-camera sessions to hear those cases judged 'too sensitive' to be dealt with in open sessions or requiring further investigation. Such cases might involve cattle theft, rape, disputes between older members of families, certain instances of money-lending disputes, and certain disputes between neighbours.[13] In-camera sessions were usually led by a trusted male member of the Amadlozi who worked together with a younger member (male or female) who had specific information about the subject for settlement.

Interrogations involving severe physical punishment were also held 'in-camera' (see Buur, 2003, 2005), and could include the trademark technique known as 'flying': suspects thrown into the air by four grown men and then left to drop to the ground. If this did not 'get them to talk' then a few stones would be placed beneath the unfortunate individual's fall. Forms of torture learned in the exile camps of the struggle or in apartheid's torture chambers were applied. These ranged from beating and the use of various forms of water torture to electric shock. In consequence, apprehended suspects would often beg to be handed over to the police rather than receiving treatment from the Amadlozi. The fact that these forms of interrogation took place outside the immediate public eye had several functions. First, there was no doubt that the resulting screams were one of the ways that the Amadlozi played on fear to pursue their investigations and to display the consequences of crime. The screams formed part of the broader moral education going on in meetings that, during 2001, resembled community rituals (see Buur, 2005). Second, removing these interrogations from the public gaze to some extent protected members of the Amadlozi against complaints to the police, by minimizing the number of eyewitnesses. The use of force left a trail of marked and maimed suspects; few families were left without traumatized younger members. Responses from residents of the various townships where Amadlozi worked would often be: 'No it is not right with the beating . . . but it is good what they do, there is nobody else (to protect us or our interests).'

BECOMING THE STATE

In early November 2000, the Amadlozi staged a march of several hundred people to the New Brighton Police Station. A memorandum was handed over, voicing their 'concerns and grievances against the police station's style of dealing with crime'. The following day public leaders of CRAC/Amadlozi held their first meeting with the white Afrikaner police station head, Director Coetzee. At first, Coetzee had refused to acknowledge the existence of the Amadlozi, emphasizing that the police worked with the community through the CPF, as stipulated by law. He suggested that they 'go and report to their politicians in Parliament', a phrase he repeated at subsequent meetings (CRAC, 2000: 2). This was indeed what they did. First, they issued a

13. While this is the stated official norm, this is not necessarily how it functions in practice (on the relation between norms and practice, see Holy and Stuchlik, 1983). Although the leadership of the Amadlozi constantly stated that they did not deal with family matters, this position was adjusted from case to case, depending to a large degree on consent from at least one section or member of the families involved.

series of memoranda — addressed not only to the police station but also to the Provincial Department for Justice — that raised concerns regarding the 'racist attitude' of the director and the 'exclusion of black police officers' at the station of which he was in charge (ibid).

Then, on 9 November 2000, CRAC called for a mass meeting at the community hall in New Brighton. Close to a thousand people attended, with invitees from political parties alongside prominent white and black businessmen and local government officials. The police and CPF were invited too, but not to speak. Instead, CRAC/Amadlozi used the occasion to list its achievements, including the capture of criminal hijackers; the recovery of weapons, household goods and cars; assistance to the police in theft, murder and rape cases; complaints about police investigations; and the settlement of labour disputes and business contract breaches. This presentation was followed by others by prominent business leader Mkhuseli Jack, a former UDF leader in Port Elizabeth, and Jack's white business colleague. They spoke on the link between job loss and crime and on the need for positive 'role models [to hinder] the escalation of crime in our area'. They called for 'all stakeholders [to take] strong measures against criminals' and applauded CRAC/Amadlozi for reducing crime levels. Speakers from political parties raised similar themes. The last speaker was the Mayor of Port Elizabeth, Mr Nceba Faku, a former Robben Island prisoner and prominent struggle leader. According to the minutes from the meeting, his first words were: 'Crime is against revolutionary forces'. He went on to express approval of the work of CRAC/Amadlozi, and to recommend that they attend the February Annual General Meeting at which the CPF was to be elected. He ended his speech instructing CRAC/Amadlozi to provide him with a 'written report on the work they had done' (ibid.: 7).

From here on, relations between the police and CRAC/Amadlozi developed rapidly. Three days later, a meeting was called by station director Coetzee, but arranged by the CPF, at the Molefe High School to discuss CRAC's grievances. CRAC/Amadlozi suggested that the station director and the CPF had arranged the meeting in order to 'crush CRAC and defend the Director's crime-prevention strategy', the latter developed with the CPF. If this was the case, then the meeting certainly backfired. Before the meeting, front- and backstage members had met with the area commissioner of safety and security, a 'black police general' (as he was referred to by Amadlozi members), who had contacted Amadlozi after hearing about their work. At the meeting, he asked CRAC/Amadlozi to present their activities. After listening and comparing it with the work of the CPF, he stated that 'CRAC's strategy was more effective than that of the CPF'. He proposed that CRAC and the police begin to work together.

A few days later, on 13 November 2000, CRAC and the area commissioner held their first meeting with the intelligence officers and members of the detective unit at the police station (ibid: 3). The area commissioner 'instructed the Detectives to work hand in hand with CRAC'. Furthermore, he 'authorized CRAC to use police identity documents to identify themselves', as well as promising 'CRAC a police vehicle [for] their patrols with police officers' (ibid.). The final concession was his order to CRAC 'to put forward two representatives who would attend Management and Crime Meetings that discussed anti-crime strategies' at New Brighton police station (ibid.). This invitation into the very heart of police structures bypassed the CPF totally. CPF had an office at the police station, but no access to internal meetings. Furthermore, it was decided that the Amadlozi secretary should work in the CPF office during the day so that she could transfer incoming cases to the Amadlozi. This in fact made her the *de facto* liaison officer at the police station.

At the first management meeting CRAC attended (on the same day as the above mentioned meeting), they were denied access by the station director, with the strong support of the CPF who insisted that any co-operation with CRAC was illegitimate. In their view, CRAC/Amadlozi members had not been formally elected according to established protocol and had nobody to account to. However, through their brokers' access to the area commissioner, they were finally invited in. At this meeting, they managed to secure an agreement that black police officers would be invited to future meetings and they have been there since. Consequently, a form of everyday engagement with the police evolved. The Intelligence Unit noted 'they are a reliable force because of their commitment'. Amadlozi had worked with individual police officers right from their inception, sharing case numbers and information. However, these informal and *ad hoc* working relationships left no official trace in the paper work or archives — except in the form of charges against Amadlozi for the use of force.

Several charges were made at various Port Elizabeth police stations against the Amadlozi for the use of violence. Members of the group maintained that it was local residents who had been beating suspects in the name of the Amadlozi. In an attempt to distinguish themselves from other, more spontaneous rallies against suspects, they pleaded for some kind of uniform so they could be recognized by the community and the police and thus avoid the 'abuse of our good name'. This the state was not prepared to provide, but donations from a local businessman made it possible to produce an easily recognizable yellow T-shirt with the name Amadlozi written in large red letters on the front. In small print, it listed the names of nearly all the recognized political parties in New Brighton, including the ANC. After this, the T-shirt was displayed in shop fronts that hired Amadlozi members to protect their business, at a jazz festival held at the community hall where Amadlozi provided the security, and at public meetings, sport events and so on. The fees for the protection service were relatively low. The three main figures in the front group collected the fees and distributed them by seniority to other members.

However, the uniform initiative did not last long. The use of the ANC's name on the T-shirt alongside those of other political parties prompted enquiries by ANC New Brighton members close to the increasingly critical local councillor (whose family member was beaten up on suspicion of stealing cloth), asking the provincial headquarters if permission to use the ANC's name had been secured in advance. The answer was a clear 'no'. Backstage members were pressured to 'get the T-shirt off the street because it had not been authorized'. After a prolonged battle, the T-shirt slowly disappeared from the public domain. This incident indicated that there were limits to the liberties and space occupied by the Amadlozi. For the first six months of 2001, the Amadlozi continued to co-operate closely with the police and even managed to meet an officer from the Port Elizabeth Magistrates Court to discuss their concerns with regard to bail issued to suspects. They would later hold numerous other meetings with the Magistrates' Office, but this time the topic was the bail conditions for Amadlozi members arrested on charges of using excessive violence.

Redrawing the Boundary

On a short visit to New Brighton township in December 2001 and January 2002, I was enthusiastically informed by Amadlozi members that 'a lot had changed' since I was last there, three months earlier. On enquiring what had changed, I realized that they were referring to the problems they had with the police and the CPF over their 'excessive use of force and violence'. Of twenty-one cases of vigilante violence reported to the area commissioner for Port Elizabeth during a one-year period, nineteen bore the signature of the Amadlozi. In late July 2001, the area commissioner had given the station commander of New Brighton police station one month to 'close the Amadlozi down'. Central headquarters in Pretoria had begun a new emphasis on preventing vigilantism. In 2001, vigilantism spread like wild fire in townships across the country, causing embarrassment to the police and the state. Vigilantism was seen as undermining the state's work of providing justice for all. It was now emphasized that people should assist the police with information and lawful citizen arrests, but not by taking the law into their own hands by beating, flogging and burning suspects. This change in public opinion had a number of repercussions for New Brighton. Significantly, younger members of the Amadlozi were arrested for excessive use of violence and the leadership had constantly to ask for money from residents to honour bail conditions. Week after week, bail conditions became harsher, until finally it was impossible for the Amadlozi to provide bail for its members. The Amadlozi had to make several petitions to the police and to the Magistrates Court to get bail conditions relaxed and to secure separate cells for its members so they were not put in cells with suspects they had arrested.

Pressure was also put on backstage members to 'bring Amadlozi in line with official policies', in other words, under the CPF. To ignore this would be a mark of sedition. The Amadlozi refused because they could not work as an S&S structure under a CPF that was organized around ward demarcations:

Amadlozi members did not observe such demarcations and operated all over Port Elizabeth's townships. They were also told to stop using violence immediately because it would no longer be tolerated. The term 'minimal force' was coined, pointing towards forms of persuasion of a milder nature used in S&S structures in Kwazakele where no charges of vigilantism were lodged in 2001. The Amadlozi were unable to honour this demand. They claimed that they 'did what was necessary and their track record proved it'.

The station commander who first had been against the Amadlozi was ambivalent. After his initial reservations, he now saw the emergence of the Amadlozi as positive, particularly once the effects on police workloads were felt: the police crime statistics showed a reduction of 90 per cent, a figure constantly quoted in meetings with police officers and the station commander. He referred in an interview to telephone enquiries from National Intelligence in Pretoria where the Amadlozi were commended after they had managed to free the director of the parastatal Transnet within six hours after he had been hijacked. However, he finally had to give in and put his second-in-command in charge of helping the CPF take control of the Amadlozi. The backstage group could not help because the 'decision had been taken on high level and supported by the ANC that vigilantism is bad', meaning that they would put their own membership of the ANC at risk if they challenged decisions taken at a higher political level. In August 2001, a group of six Amadlozi members was arrested in a co-ordinated police action backed by CPF members. Members of the CPF and the police forced the principal of the Molefe Primary to close the school as a venue for the Amadlozi. This move was legitimized by reference to the fact that schoolteachers had on several occasions found bloodstains on the classroom walls, which was considered 'too much for the school children' (Buur, 2005).

The Amadlozi tried to secure another venue, but the CPF board had done their homework, and all possible venue holders refused the Amadlozi permission to operate from their premises. In the end, they gave in and accepted that an election would be held in the name of the CPF. In September 2001, the Amadlozi officially became a CPF structure with a constitution[14] and a democratically elected board of local residents. The meeting was held at the Molefe School, but the venue was not to be used for public sessions again. When I asked the Amadlozi leadership in 2002 whether they had changed their *modus operandi,* which often involved beating and torture, I was told that everything was the same as before: 'No, nothing has changed, we do as we have always done'. Initially, they had moved sessions 'requiring' *patta-patta* to the back yards of their own homes or the open field behind the school. The banning from Molefe School was used to explain why the Amadlozi do not have public meetings with the residents any longer.

---

14. A standard constitution was used which had been applied in thirteen other CPF structures in the neighbouring township of Kwazakele, which falls under the jurisdiction of the New Brighton police station.

In 2004, their meeting place became a 'joint' in the same street as the Molefe School run by a former MK-comrade who supported their work but never participated directly in their activities. They still focus on common grievances articulated by local residents, but concentrate most of their time and energy on high-profile cases relating to theft and murder. They charge R470, including transport in the Port Elizabeth area, to open a case. Several high-profile cases in middle to upper class formerly white and coloured residential areas have been dealt with over the last year, often with good coverage in the local press. Cases related to domestic conflicts and local grievances are today primarily dealt with by the CPF, whose office is now highly successful, with people waiting for hours for their case to be heard. However, when the CPF fails because it does not have alternative investigative tools, the problem ends up at the Amadlozi 'joint', where ill-disciplined and disrespectful suspects are perceived to need some *patta-patta* to ensure good behaviour and the return of stolen goods (which are seldom retrieved in the work of the CPF). The Amadlozi continue to provide security for public events such as the jazz festival held on 1 May 2004, where an Amadlozi group worked the whole night as bouncers and car protectors.

Their relationship with the police has also continued — caseloads are still shared with individual police officers — but today the contact is more informal than it was in 2000. When residents bring cases to the Amadlozi, they are asked to register the case with police first and to bring back the case-number. Amadlozi's services have become more specialized: a smaller group of investigators works closely together to provide information to police intelligence on high-profile cases of bank and money transport heists, car and taxi hijackings, burglaries and so on. In such instances, they are paid according to police tariffs for their services when the information they provide assists successful prosecution. They had largely avoided further charges being laid against them, until 2004 (when the first murder charge was lodged), partly because their reputation scares criminal suspects, so that just a reminder of what will follow if information is not provided 'gets them to speak the truth'; and partly because of the recognition that the successful closure of a case in a prosecution is the best short-term protection. In an act of confidence, the Amadlozi today often tell criminal suspects of their right to press charges against them before interrogation sessions. In one member's words: 'They got their rights and they should know. It is better that we tell them of their rights than they get this information from police officers who don't like us'. Many of the backstage group members seem to have stopped playing any role. Some have moved on and now 'engage in big business outside New Brighton' while others are seen from time to time with the Amadlozi.[15]

15. This information on the recent situation of the Amadlozi is based on notes and interviews from the author's fieldwork conducted in 2004.

CRIME AND THE SUSPENSION OF THE LAW

This brief account demonstrates the fragility of a state in crisis. The perception of crime — whether accurate or not — constituted a crisis in South Africa at the beginning of the twenty-first century. A variety of actors become involved in a renegotiation of boundaries between state and society. State tasks that usually fell under the police, the judiciary and CPF were, to varying degrees, shared by the Amadlozi in the name of the state. Any easy separation between state and civil society is difficult to maintain. The question of where the state stops being a state is of less interest; whether or not we agree on what the state means and what it is, '"*it*" is, nonetheless, central to all that is *not* state' (Hansen and Stepputat, 2001: 2). The state mattered for the Amadlozi. All its activities either mimicked the state's procedural forms in great detail or drew on its symbolic forms. When the Amadlozi challenged the state by issuing memoranda, the challenge confirmed the state and was directed at rectifying state practices and modes of being. Challenges were not aimed at undoing the state or establishing a different state: the aim was more state, not less state.

In this sense, the Amadlozi seem to resemble what Lund terms 'twilight institutions'. These can be defined as in-between institutions or organizations that engage in state-like performances, making it difficult to distinguish unequivocally between what is state and what is not. They challenge the state from within and from outside, using its own language of authority, and at the same time draw on, if not directly mimic, its procedural and symbolic forms of legitimacy. Lund also argues that institutions of public authority 'wax and wane' (Lund, 2001: 845, see also Lund, this issue). This account of the Amadlozi's emergence, rise to office and return to reduced prominence seems to fit this understanding of 'in-between' institutions. Stability is seldom the most profound characteristic of institutions of public authority and the challenge is to delineate the forms that materialize, the conditions under which change is undertaken, and the wider implications these institutions have for the formation of state and civil society relationships more generally.

From 1994 onwards (and as noted by Ginwala above), the ANC government attempted a profound re-ordering of society. Yet this project was suspended by the emergence of vigilante action undertaken by the Amadlozi. Although the suspension at first seemed to be only temporary, it was triggered by the development of a working relationship between the police and the Amadlozi. The actions and relationships clearly bordered on what is legally acceptable, just as the relationship between ANC-affiliated backstage members and front-stage Amadlozi members seems to have suspended the wider process of formalizing the relationship between civil society and the state in the form anticipated by the CPF process. What caused this suspension? It was *crime* or, as it has been called, the 'crime wave' (Steinberg, 2001), the spoiler of the 'telos of liberation' (Comaroff and Comaroff, 1999: 284), that hit South Africa during the late 1990s. Whether correct or not, the perception shared by the state and ordinary citizens alike was that crime challenged or undermined the gains achieved by the new democracy. In their understanding of their role, the Amadlozi did not intend the creation of a sovereign alternative, even though they clearly drew on the rhetoric and actions of 'people power' of the 1980s; nor did they attempt to undermine the new government. They saw themselves as *the* defenders of the new legal-political order; their aim was merely to assist the state and government against 'the criminal elements that terrorized us'. They framed their activities in relation to a series of speeches made by high-ranking public leaders of the government, most prominently the president of South Africa: 'We try to help them, remember what Thabo [President Thabo Mbeki] said on the radio: "people know how to deal with criminals, they have done it before and they can do it again". The government has problems and we just help them, we are not like the terrorists' [a reference to PAGAD].[16]

In the same vein, and equally discussed, the late Minister of Safety and Security Steve Tshwete made a series of tough comments in 1999 and 2000 such as, 'criminals are animals [and] we must show them no mercy'. Even more controversially, he went further, telling the police: 'When we visit criminals we will not treat them with kid gloves. We are going to make them feel like cowboys ... those who raise the dust must not complain that they cannot see. We will unleash the police force on them' (Tshwete, 2000). This implied the suspension, if necessary, of the Constitution: 'Criminals must know the South African state possesses the authority, moral and political, to ensure by all means, constitutional or unconstitutional, that the people of this country are not deprived of their human rights' (ibid.). These comments all came during the period when the government had declared 'War on Crime' (Samara, 2003) after South Africa lost its bid to host several high-profile sports competitions, including the Olympics and the Soccer World Cup,[17] and after international investments failed to materialize at the rate anticipated. All these failures were blamed on the fear of crime. Public discourses on crime in townships such as New Brighton functioned as official blueprints for action. In many ways, they resurrected the discourse of the struggle of the 1980s with ANC as the sole representative of the people. The phrase 'they have done it before and they can do it again' was constantly reiterated by Amadlozi members and residents more generally and was seen as a call for mechanisms resembling those of the 1980s to be resurrected. Now, the state and the community's interests were seen as identical in their aim of undoing injustice.

That said, it is important to recognize that public discourses on crime were mediated and tactically adopted by less high-ranking state employees in the police and the ANC. The case of the Amadlozi clearly illustrates that the

---

16. The quote does not necessarily reflect what President Mbeki actually said, but how public speeches circulate in the public domain and justify actions taken by citizens.
17. In 2004, FIFA finally granted South Africa the right to host the 2010 Soccer World Cup.

public discourse on crime intersected with local politics on various levels, for example where black police officers could use the urgency of crime to challenge the white station director's internal hierarchies. This included bringing on board the political support of the powerful area commissioner, using the crisis to alter the management system at the police station. In this sense, the discourse on crime was adopted in a fashion that defies uniformity, that seems to be blind to some of its consequences, and that plays both on instrumental calculation and on value judgements emerging from a variety of sources.

Since socially and politically situated actors use discourses to support and justify actions that fit with their own concerns, I am cautious about giving prevalence to discourse. However, as Garland has pointed out, 'Sometimes "talk" *is* action' (2001: 22), in the specific sense that political rhetoric and official representations of crime and public enemies have a symbolic weight and practical effectiveness with real consequences. The apparently widespread and invariable semantic congruence in discourses cannot be accidental; it surely reflects something in common across the spectrum of society from the highest office to the poorest shack-dweller. What do we make of it, and can we define the discourse on crime as the moment when democratic rules are suspended and another set imposed? Carl Schmitt's classic definition of the threshold of sovereignty — the 'Sovereign is he who decides on the state of exception' (Schmitt quoted in Agamben, 1998: 11) — is relevant here, because we are confronted with a paradox. Is it the congruence of discourses across different social classes that create the exception to the rule — in this case the suspension of the Constitution? The exception cannot be accounted for, as Agamben has made clear, by defining the problem of sovereignty as a 'question of who within the political order was invested with certain powers' (1998: 12). His answer is 'The state of exception, which is what the sovereign each and every time decides, takes place precisely when naked life[18] . . . is explicitly put into question and revoked as the ultimate foundation of political power' (Agamben, 2000: 5).

This formulation allows the displacement of the question of sovereignty and its foundation. 'Naked life' is what Agamben calls those '*who may be killed and yet not sacrificed*' (Agamben, 1998: 8). I understand this as meaning those whom one can with impunity treat as one wishes, without regard for their psychological and physical well-being (see Buur, 2005). If we substitute 'naked life' with the criminal suspect in the account above, he/she is the constitutive outsider of South African society because he/she defines the external limits of society, while also and simultaneously belonging to the inside. By doing away with the criminal suspect, the inside threshold of society is constituted. The criminal suspect presents him or herself both as that which needs to be excluded and at the same time as constitutive

18. This is the *homo sacer*, the sacred man, which in other texts is translated as 'bare being'.

for the included — what Agamben calls 'inclusive exclusion' (Agamben, 1998: 8).

The consequence of this understanding of sovereignty is that instead of tracing its localization in particular institutions and incumbents, sovereignty becomes a question of a *principle* defining inclusion and exclusion where one is tracing a particular threshold (ibid.: 19). This threshold cannot be localized, as shifting configurations can take many faces — the refugee, the needy, the criminal and so on — but as a principle it opens the space for determining particular political-legal orders. Formulating the question of sovereignty in this manner also carries certain risks in that the certainty associated with the figure of sovereignty vanishes. Accountability seems to be dispersed across sectors of a given society. One can easily overlook the fact that from time to time definite spatio-temporal limits can clearly be given. The fact that the actions of the Amadlozi were brought under control within a three-month period points to an internal ordering system, obedience to direction from the ANC/state, and internal discipline.[19] At the moment of the dispersion of sovereignty, when the law is not the supreme bulwark against atrocities and when violence is tolerated, what constitutes an exception depends on the respect and ethical sense of individual police officers, party officials and members of vigilante formations like the Amadlozi. If the criminal or criminal suspect is more generally viewed as public enemy number one and if this is constitutive of sovereignty, this points to a wider, uneven parallel existence, a domain of social reality constituted by different value systems. Who is the criminal and is it the same criminal that is spoken about across different spectrums of society? Are there limitations to congruence in the discourses on crime from national to local level and what are the consequences of this for our understanding of twilight institutions?

CONCLUSION

The *founding myth* that brought the Amadlozi into being referred to crime that falls within the parameters of the formal penal code. These are also other kinds of crime that members of Amadlozi prefer to allude to in interviews, news reports and public meetings, pointing toward young black males as the 'generic criminal' (Buur, 2003: 33-5; see also Samara, 2003). To use only the categories of the penal code to describe the work of the Amadlozi would, however, be a misrepresentation, because it forms only one of several competing ideas about what crime and justice are really about in their work. Most of the crime they deal with in their daily life belongs within the realm of the private or civil penal code. Crime, according to this understanding, gives shape and direction to local problems of order and disorder such as teenage

19. I am grateful to Jane Connolly from University of Cape Town for directing me towards this point.

pregnancy; violent behaviour; schooling; neighbour, generational and family disputes; theft of minor goods like clothes from washing-lines, cell phones and so on.

The nature of crime in New Brighton defies any easy continuum. Whereas crimes such as theft and murder clearly fall under penal codes, other activities such as witchcraft that have deadly consequences and are considered criminal by the community are governed by penal codes that punish attempts to identify witches (Jensen and Buur, 2004). Yet, in the understanding of crime presented here, these activities belong to the same register, that is, activities that are destructive for or challenge the community as defined by Amadlozi's version(s) of what is valued in the community. Some of these values have their origin in recollections and practices from traditional lifestyles in rural areas that have undergone changes during decades of urbanized working class life in townships. Others draw on idealized concepts of sharing and trust emerging from the hardship of the struggle against apartheid, while yet others, such as tolerance and human rights, relate more directly to the new democratic dispensation. On an abstract level, the common denominator is values which often have a strong moral content; crime refers to acts that undercut and imperil the well-being of these values. The framing of such acts as criminal allows special measures to be put in place in defence of the fairly diffuse category of the community. When one zooms in on specific instances of crime, some of these values are in contradiction with each other and have to be settled from instance to instance.

Understood in this way, the concept of crime is profoundly *polyvalent* and ranges from murder, theft, violence, conflict disputes and witchcraft accusations to particular sexual practices, all of which in contemporary township life require physical punishment not only for punishment's sake but to rectify and inculcate the norms of society. Criminal activities as defined by the Amadlozi are therefore not restricted to acts in contravention of formal law or the constitution. The state-sanctioned penal code, so important for defining *what* constitutes a crime and *how* justice is measured in the formal justice system, is important for rendering the Amadlozi visible before the state, because it legitimizes its existence as a partner in fighting crime. The polyvalent concept of crime is important because it allows for local grievances to be named and linked to broader issues. In this scenario, the ever-present criminal — and *he* is ever present because 'his' appearance seems infinite — is believed to hinder communities from accessing development funding, investments and employment initiatives.

The discrepancies in the perception of what constitutes a crime cannot be ignored. They are an important part of understanding why vigilantism emerges and why vigilante formations continue to operate. The consequence is that twilight institutions such as the Amadlozi not only engage in sovereign acts that mimic the state's monopoly on violence, but engage in sovereign acts that are constitutive of a whole range of forms of identification. These are forms of identification that ideally should be encompassed by the new

Constitution but, as we have seen, even with a concerted effort by the ANC government, such a unified socio-political reality is yet to be established.

REFERENCES

Agamben, G. (1998) *Homo Sacer: Sovereign Power and Bare Life* (translated by Daniel Heller-Roazen). Stanford, CA: Stanford University Press.

Agamben, G. (2000) *Means Without End: Notes on Politics, Vol 20*. Minnesota, MN: University of Minnesota Press.

Bapela, M. S. W. (1987) 'The People's Courts in Customary Law Perspective'. Paper presented at the Conference on New Approaches in Respect of Administration of Justice, Institute of Foreign and Contemporary Law, UNISA, South Africa.

Bundy, C. (2000) 'Survival and Resistance: Township Organization and Non-violent Direct Action in Twentieth Century South Africa', in G. Adler and J. Steinberg (eds) *From Comrades to Citizens. The South African Civics Movement and Transition to Democracy*, pp. 26–51. London: Macmillan Press.

Buur, L. (2001) 'The South African Truth and Reconciliation Commission: A Technique of Nation-State Formation', in T. B. Hansen and F. Stepputat (eds) *States of Imagination: Ethnographic Explorations of the Postcolonial State*, pp. 149–81. Durham, NC: Duke University Press.

Buur, L. (2003) 'Crime and Punishment on the Margins of the Post-Apartheid State', *Anthropology and Humanism* 28(1): 23–42.

Buur, L. (2005) 'The Sovereign Outsourced: Local Justice and Violence in Port Elizabeth', in T. B. Hansen and F. Stepputat (eds) *Sovereign Bodies: Citizens, Migrants, and States in the Postcolonial World*, pp. 192–217. Princeton, NJ: Princeton University Press.

Buur, L. and S. Jensen (2004) 'Introduction: Vigilantism and the Policing of Everyday Life in South Africa', *African Studies* 63(2): 139–52.

Cherry, J., K. Jones and J. Seekings (2000) 'Democratization and Politics in South African Townships', *International Journal of Urban and Regional Research* 24(4): 889–906.

Comaroff, J. and J. Comaroff (1999) 'Occult Economies and the Violence of Abstraction: Notes from the South African Postcolony', *American Ethnologist* 26: 297–301.

CRAC (2000) 'Abahlali Concerned Residents Against Crime (CRAC) Progress Report'. New Brighton: CRAC.

Dixon, B. and L. Johns (2001) 'Gangs, Pagad and the State: Vigilantism and Revenge Violence in the Western Cape'. Violence and Transition Series 2. Johannesburg: Centre for the Study of Violence and Reconciliation.

Garland, D. (2001) *The Culture of Control: Crime and Social Order in Contemporary Society*. Oxford and New York: Oxford University Press.

Hansen, T. B. and F. Stepputat (2001) *States of Imagination: Ethnographic Explorations of the Postcolonial State*. Durham, NC: Duke University Press.

Hayson, N. (1989) 'Vigilantes: A Contemporary Form of Repression'. Seminar Series No 4. Johannesburg: Centre for the Study of Violence and Reconciliation.

Holy, L. and M. Stuchlik (1983) *Actions, Norms and Representations*. Cambridge, New York: Cambridge University Press.

Institute for Security Studies (1998) *Crime in Cape Town: Results of a City Victim Survey*. Monograph series No 32. Pretoria, South Africa: ISS.

Jensen, S. and L. Buur (2004) 'Everyday Policing and the Occult: Notions of Witchcraft, Crime and "the People"', *African Studies* 63(2): 193–212.

Lund, C. (2001) 'Precarious Democratization and Local Dynamics in Niger: Micro-Politics in Zinder', *Development and Change* 32(5): 845–69.

Madlala, B. (2004) 'Make Judges Accountable, demands Ginwala'. *Independent Online (IOL)* (23 January). Available online: http://www.int.iol.co.za/index.php?set_id=1&click_id=13 &art_id=ct20040123212652492F650171

Mayekiso, M. (1996) *Township Politics: Civic Struggles for a New South Africa*. New York: Monthly Review Press.
Nattrass, N. and J. Seekings (2001) '"Two Nations?": Race and Economic Inequality in South Africa Today', *Dædalus* 130(1): 45–70.
Nina, D. (1992) 'Popular Justice in a New South Africa. From People's Courts to Community Courts in Alexandra', Centre for Applied Legal Studies, Occasional Paper 15. Johannesburg: University of the Witwatersrand.
Nina, D. (1995) *Rethinking Popular Justice: Self-regulation and Civil Society in South Africa*. Cape Town: Community Peace Foundation.
Nina, D. (2001) 'Popular Justice and the "Appropriation" of the State Monopoly on the Definition of Justice and Order: The Case of Anti-Crime Communities', in W. Schärf and D. Nina (eds) *The Other Law: Non-State Ordering in South Africa*, pp. 98–117. Lansdowne, Cape Town: Juta and Co.
Samara, T. R. (2003) 'State Security in Transition: The War on Crime in Post Apartheid South Africa', *Social Identities* 9(2): 277–312.
Schärf, W. and D. Nina (eds) (2001) *The Other Law: Non-State Ordering in South Africa*. Lansdowne, Cape Town: Juta and Co.
Seekings, J. (2000) *The UDF: A History of the United Democratic Front in South Africa 1983–1991*. Cape Town: David Philip.
Seekings, J. (2001) 'Social Ordering and Control in the African Townships of South Africa: An Historical Overview of Extra-state Initiatives from the 1940s to the 1990s', in W. Schärf and D. Nina (eds) *The Other Law: Non-State Ordering in South Africa*, pp. 71–97. Lansdowne, Cape Town: Juta and Co.
Sisk, T. D. (1995) *Democratization in South Africa. The Elusive Social Contract*. Princeton, NJ: Princeton University Press.
Steinberg, J. (ed.) (2001) *Crime Wave: The South Africa Underworld and its Foe*. Johannesburg: Witwatersrand University Press.
Terreblanche, S. (2003) *A History of Inequality in South Africa, 1652–2002*. Durban: University of Natal Press.
Truth and Reconciliation Commission (TRC) (1998) *Final Report of the South African Truth and Reconciliation Commission*, Volumes 1-5. Lansdowne, Cape Town: Juta & Co.
Tshehla, B. (2003) 'Filling the Justice Vacuum: The Case of the Peninsula Anti Crime Agency'. Paper presented at Wits Workshop on Law and Society, Johannesburg (25–26 September).
Tshwete, S. (2000) 'Tshwete Talks Tough' *Electronic Mail and Guardian* (10 November). Available online: http://www.mg.co.za/articledirect.aspx?articleid=215332&area=%2farchives__print_edition%2f
Wilson, R. (2001) *The Politics of Truth and Reconciliation in South Africa: Legitimizing the Post Apartheid State*. Cambridge: Cambridge University Press.

5

Negotiating Authority between UNHCR and 'The People'

Simon Turner

INTRODUCTION

Lukole refugee camp in northwest Tanzania houses almost 100,000 Burundian refugees. They are under the surveillance of the Tanzanian Ministry of Home Affairs (MHA) representative, the camp commandant, while the United Nations High Commissioner for Refugees (UNHCR) is in charge of their 'care and maintenance'. This article analyses how refugees negotiate public authority in a camp that is seen as heavily governed by international relief agencies, while simultaneously characterized by a perceived collapse of the known moral order of Burundi. It explores how certain groups of young men manage to establish public authority by relating to ideas of a Burundian moral order while at the same time relating to the 'dev-speak' of international relief operations, oscillating between these moral orders and establishing a space of their own. It is shown how party political rivalry plays a vital role in establishing public authority.[1]

It is tempting to see Lukole as an expression of Agamben's Camp as the hidden matrix and *nomos* of modern political space (Agamben, 1998: 166; Agamben, 2000: 37). It is a temporary, exceptional space, created by a sovereign Schmittean decision (Schmitt, 1985; Agamben, 1998: 168–71). Here, the Tanzanian state decides that the refugees are a threat to the nation state and puts them in this exceptional space, which is at once both inside and outside the law. In this case, the refugees are reduced to 'bare life', outside the *polis* of national citizens.[2]

However, although the concepts of bare life and the camp are compelling, Burundian refugees in Lukole are not just any kind of bare life. The camp is being subjected to a strongly moralizing and ethical biopolitical project by humanitarian agencies. Although the Tanzanian 'camp commandant' is sovereign in legal terms, UNHCR and other relief agencies take care of the day-to-day governing of the camp, as they decide the physical layout of the camp, the size and composition of food rations, the food distribution system, the kind of pit latrines to be built and procedures for defining and helping

1. This article is based on more than a year's ethnographic fieldwork in Lukole, 1997–98, including personal interviews, surveys and questionnaires.
2. For further reading on Agamben's understanding of the camp see Agamben (1998: Part 3) and Agamben (2000: 37–49). For an analysis of the various layers of sovereignty in the camp, see Turner (2005).

so-called vulnerable groups. They exert a caring biopower, concerned with the life and health of the refugee population (Turner, 2001, 2005).[3] To put it bluntly, while the Tanzanian authorities govern the camp through control and restrictions, international relief agencies — led by UNHCR — govern the camp by trying to foster life.

Whilst public authority seems to lie comfortably in the hands of UNHCR and the camp commandant — and although the camp might give the impression of order and control 'from above' — public authority is far from stable. Constant negotiations, struggles and downright fights take place inside the camp in order to establish some kind of legitimate authority that the refugees can relate to. This article explores how some of these negotiations take place and how public authority emerges in the lacunae that are produced by UNHCR and by the instability of social relations in camp life in general.

RECUPERATING POLITICS

In the exceptional biopolitical space of the camp, refugees are expected to act as victims, which in turn presupposes that they are void of political subjectivity (Turner, forthcoming). But the refugees in Burundi are not simply a kind of *tabula rasa* upon which UNHCR can create pure victims in need of help. They carry with them a bloody history and political conflicts. While political rivalry in the camp is often about establishing some kind of order and public authority at the local level, it also draws on these long historical lines in the Burundian conflict. In order to understand what goes on in the camp, we therefore have to put it in a political and historical context.

Burundi has experienced ethnic conflict between the Hutu majority and the Tutsi minority since the early 1960s. Unlike Rwanda, there was no 'Hutu revolution' around independence, and a small Tutsi elite dominated the state apparatus while officially pursuing an anti-ethnic policy, claiming ethnicity to be the invention of Belgian colonizers. In 1972 hundreds of thousands of Hutu were killed by the army in a response to a minor Hutu uprising (Lemarchand, 1996; Lemarchand and Martin, 1974). This caused hundreds of thousands of Hutu to leave the country and settle in camps in Rwanda and Tanzania, while the Hutu elite were exiled in Belgium and other European countries. It was in the camps in Tanzania that a radical Hutu opposition grew, claiming that Hutu and Tutsi were indeed different races and that the conflict was age old.[4] The *Partie pour la Libération du Peuple Hutu* (Palipehutu) was created in the camps in Tanzania where its radical ethno-nationalist liberation ideology provided answers to the desperate refugees.

---

3. This is inspired by a Foucauldian approach to government; see also Cruikshank (1999); Dean (1999); Foucault (1978).
4. Malkki (1995) vividly illustrates the obsession with history among these refugees.

In the late 1980s and early 1990s the Tutsi dominated one-party regime in Burundi gradually reformed the political system, culminating in 1993 with free multi-party elections. These elections were won by the newly established and moderate 'Hutu' party, *Front des Démocrates du Burundi* (Frodebu), and its charismatic leader, Melchior Ndadaye, became the first democratically elected Hutu president. In the new political environment in the country, Palipehutu's radical ethno-nationalist discourse became obsolete and the party lost influence.

The optimism did not last long, however; President Ndadaye was assassinated by Tutsi officers after only three months in office. This triggered massacres of Tutsi civilians by Hutu all over the country. The army hit back with predictable brutality and the country descended into violence and civil war (Lemarchand, 1996; Reyntjens, 1993). The first refugees in Lukole fled Burundi during the violence of late 1993: they were all Hutu. Some of them had been leading members of Frodebu and had fled the country because they were perceived to be particularly targeted by the army.

In 1994 an armed Hutu rebellion against the regime emerged. It was led by a faction of Frodebu that called itself *Conseil National pour la Défence de la Démocratie* (CNDD). Later, Palipehutu's armed wing also intensified its activities. In this way, the violence in Burundi evolved from ethnic massacres and counter reprisals into guerrilla warfare, with the army undertaking brutal counter-insurgency measures. This second phase of violence had a huge impact on the civilian population and resulted in large numbers of refugees arriving in Tanzania in 1995–96. In contrast to the first 'wave' of refugees, these were ordinary peasants who had not been active in Frodebu. They were often Palipehutu sympathizers.

These social and political differences obviously did not simply fade away in the camp, as camp authorities and refugee agencies might have wished. On the contrary, clandestine politics played a central role in the camp, sometimes resulting in violent conflicts between Palipehutu and Frodebu/CNDD supporters and always forcing young, male refugees to take sides. Either you are with us or you are against us, was the logic of the two rival parties. Frodebu members in the camp all supported CNDD and were actively trying to stamp out the smaller rival, Palipehutu. Palipehutu, meanwhile, enjoyed strong support in some areas of the camp and managed to force opponents to leave those areas, in effect dividing the camp spatially between the two parties. In their struggle to dominate (parts of) the camp, they needed to establish their own form of public authority among the refugee population. This was partially achieved through violence, but — and equally importantly — it was also partially based on positions within the official UNHCR structures of the camp.

Effectively, networks of 'big men' were closely linked to political networks, mutually reinforcing each other. In my first fieldwork visits to the camp, I was struck by the number of very young men who held extremely influential positions.[5] Apart from the formal street and village leaders who enjoy a great deal of respect and are important people in the camp, other categories of 'big men' are to be found in places that assure them access to public authority. This could be as businessmen or through employment with an NGO. They may even combine a job with an NGO with a small business on the side.[6] These three groups of 'big men' have different roles and are different in social composition, although they often overlap and co-operate. Whereas the leaders are the official representatives and intermediaries in charge of governing the refugees, the NGO employees carry out the everyday practices of governing. But neither are merely the instruments of the relief agencies, and they manoeuvre strategically according to very different agendas than those of the relief agencies. Businessmen have a slightly different way of establishing authority, since they generally have as little as possible to do with UNHCR. In the following analysis, we see how the three categories draw on different registers in order to establish authority (for a parallel biographical approach see Hagberg, this issue).

STEVEN: BEING WHERE THE ACTION IS

Steven is a polite, softly-spoken young man.[7] He chooses his words carefully and tries to answer all my questions as best he can. He is twenty-five years old and unmarried. He does not want to marry in exile, as he says the responsibility of a family will hinder the possibility of continuing his studies. Steven was a few months short of finishing secondary school when President Ndadaye was assassinated and he fled to Tanzania. He dreams of studying economics.

When I first met him, he was working as a primary school teacher and had done so since arriving in the camp in 1994. A few months later, he was chief security guard for Lukole A. The security guards protect public places like the food distribution centre, the market and the graveyards, and they patrol the camp night and day. They are unarmed and may arrest people for petty offences and keep them locked up for up to three days. More serious crimes are transferred to the police. In Lukole A, with a population of roughly 70,000, there are approximatey sixty security guards. In other words, Steven has been given considerable responsibility for someone of his age.

He was given the position after the UNHCR had sacked all the previous guards and 'screened' all new and old applicants to clean out the political activists among them. This followed an incident in May 1997 when the street

5. Very little has been written on refugee men. For exceptions see Brun (2000); Sommers (2001). See also Turner (1999, 2004).
6. In fact, the business often gives a higher income, while the NGO job provides the contacts and the influence.
7. In the following account, all names are fictive.

leaders had complained to the camp authorities that the chief security guard belonged to Palipehutu and was only arresting his political opponents. At the same time, the chief security guard accused the camp chairman — the overall leader of the street leaders — of being pro-CNDD and misusing his power to promote his political allies. These mutual accusations led UNHCR to employ new security guards and instigate new elections of street leaders. Ironically, Steven was deeply involved in politics, but he was pro-CNDD rather than Palipehutu and hence more in line with the camp chairman. There is no doubt that Steven is a CNDD supporter and, judging from the network of 'big men' in the camp that he knows, he is an influential member.

I was able to follow Steven for a while in the camp and have since corresponded sporadically with him. Apart from his job as chief security guard he began teaching French courses for UNHCR staff in Ngara town. He later went to Nairobi to try to study. He failed to find any sponsorship for his studies, but managed to learn some basic computer skills. He returned to Lukole and applied for resettlement in Canada. For some reason, he failed to turn up for the interview and he has now moved to a camp in Kigoma region.[8] He is married — 'after a long despair of soon regaining school', as he writes in a letter in March 2001. Both he and his wife work for international NGOs in the camp. He still hopes to go to the West and continue his studies.[9]

Steven is a typical example of a young man who held an extremely influential position in the camp. In order to see how this group differs from the camp population as a whole, it is worth examining the NGO employees in terms of social composition. (Later sections will compare NGO workers, street/village leaders and businessmen.) Humanitarian agencies employ refugees in a number of positions as security guards, primary school teachers, social workers/community mobilizers, medical assistants, nurses, laboratory technicians, hospital cooks, as members of OXFAM's Sanitation Information Teams, as loaders in food distribution centres and as construction workers.[10] Refugees employed by NGOs generally have a higher level of education than the average population.[11] Whereas only 17 per cent of the population above the age of sixteen have more than primary school education, at least 85 per cent of the NGO employees in my survey had more than primary school education.

8. Kigoma is south of Ngara district, where Lukole is situated.
9. This account is based on numerous talks with Steven, including taped interview 18 June 1997; life-story interview (taped) 24 February 1998; interviews 26 August 1997, 27 March 1998 and 28 April 1998; and letters January 1999 and March 2001.
10. NGO employees do not receive wages but so-called 'incentives', as they are already fed by WFP (World Food Programme). At the time of the fieldwork, a school teacher received 14,000 shillings (approximately US$ 20) a month, while the maximum monthly incentive for a supervisor or a doctor, for instance, was 22,000 shillings.
11. Based on a questionnaire of 464 randomly sampled refugees above the age of 16 and a questionnaire of 123 NGO employees that I conducted in April 1998.

Figure 1. Language Skills for NGO Employees and General Camp Population (by Gender)

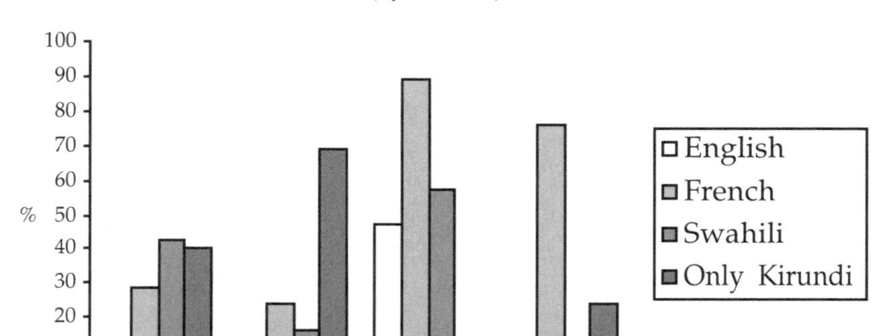

Similarly, NGO employees were significantly better at foreign languages, particularly French. French is a language that is linked to formal schooling in Burundi, and hence mastered by the educated elite of both sexes, while Swahili is learned in the public space of the camp where mostly men move. English is a mixture of the two, since the better educated have in theory been taught English in secondary school, but it is only in the camp that they actually learn to speak it. This is tentatively reflected in Figure 1 where the combination of being male and an NGO employee gives a far higher ratio of English speakers than any of the other groups.

Both English and Swahili were perceived by the refugees themselves to be the best languages to know in the camp as they allow you to 'express yourself' to the NGOs, UNHCR and the Tanzanian authorities.[12] Being able to approach the *Wazungu* (white people) or the Tanzanians was clearly seen as an asset, and people who mastered these skills were often used informally or formally (if they were street leaders, for instance) as brokers by their friends, relatives and neighbours. Language skills also allowed for upward mobility, as knowing English could give access to a job as co-ordinator or supervisor with an NGO. Here, French was not of much use, and was rather a social marker left over from Burundi. It was prestigious in the sense that it denoted a certain level of education and social position, but it was perceived to be rather anachronistic and of little use for social mobility in the present or future.

The survey also showed that the NGO employees were generally young, with an average age of twenty-nine (see Figure 2). Steven fits the profile

12. In terms of status, English was considered more prestigious than Swahili, just as European or North American agencies and staff were considered more prestigious and more honest than Tanzanian or Kenyan staff.

Figure 2. Age Distribution of NGO Employees, Camp Population, Leaders and Businessmen

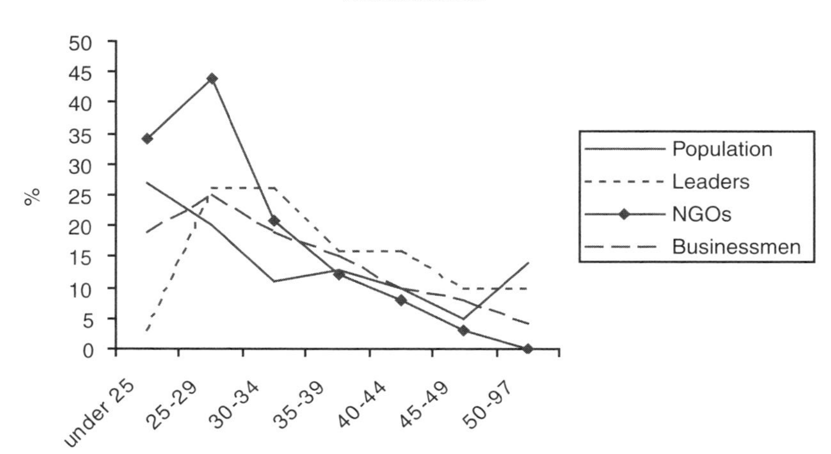

of an NGO employee that attained a pivotal role in the camp. According to their own explanations, the reasons why he and a number of other young men gained such prominent positions was in part due to their formal education (being able to 'express oneself', to read and write and to speak foreign languages), and in part due to a number of personal abilities — to cope in the camp and become a 'big man', one had to be mobile, not afraid to approach a *Muzungu* and have a certain nerve to assert oneself, they claimed. These personal abilities link up to the vague idea of being 'shy' or not. To not be shy means to dare voice one's opinion in public in front of a number of foreign and 'superior' people. It means knowing the new rules of the refugee game and knowing how to bend them to one's advantage, rather than being taken advantage of by the new rulers.

Shyness is seen as a Hutu virtue. To be shy is to show good manners. An inferior is expected to be shy towards a superior, whether that is in terms of age, gender, class or ethnicity.[13] Men and women of all ages and all social layers would express concern that these virtues were no longer being upheld in the camp, and expressed a sense of moral decay whereby women no longer obeyed their husbands and children no longer respected their parents. However, the refugees also expressed an ambiguous relation to Hutu shyness and timidity. As much as it was still praised as a virtue, it was also considered a vice. This was most clearly expressed in relation to Rwandan Hutu refugees who allegedly were not shy but 'proud'. In Lukole, people would boast of having learned 'tricks' from the Rwandans. They were, for instance, grateful

13. See Malkki (1995) for an excellent analysis of ethnic stereotypes among Hutu refugees. Lemarchand (1996, 1999) also deals with the role of myth-making in the region. Such stereotypes were also found by earlier ethnographers, although they tended to take them at face value (see Albert, 1963; Maquet, 1961; Trouwborst, 1962).

that the Rwandans had taught them to outsmart UNHCR when the agency was doing a 'head count': 'The Rwandans were very clever. They knew what medicine to use to remove ink'[14] (Diary, 27 October 1997). They believed that the longer one lived in the camp and the more one learned to shed one's shyness, the better that person would cope.

NGO employees like Steven take advantage of the fact that the old hierarchies of Burundi are no longer valid, and carve out a place for themselves by shedding their Hutu naivety and their position as inferiors. By linking up with the international agencies in the camp, they make themselves indispensable as brokers. They know the language of the humanitarian workers — not only literally Swahili and English, but also in terms of the technical NGO language of 'food rations', 'community development projects', 'hygiene sensitization programmes', and all the other codes that need deciphering in order to handle and please the new masters in the camp. Through their access to UNHCR,[15] they are able to shed their shyness; however, in order to gain respect and prove their 'intelligence' they must not merely follow the orders of UNHCR. They should preferably be seen to outsmart the omnipotent organization.

NGO employees get to function as intermediaries between the refugees and the agencies. In this sense they resemble the leaders. But whereas the leaders are the official representatives and intermediaries in charge of the refugees, the NGO employees carry out the everyday practices of governing. They give information about hygiene, they help the 'vulnerables', they teach the children, they mobilize the youth and they take care of security. This is where biopower is exercised. The employees make use of their strategic positions between donor funds and the beneficiaries. The camp population's access to essential resources — such as medical help, education and security — goes through these intermediaries. It thus becomes important to be on good terms with an NGO employee who can ask favours in return, thus creating the basis for patron–client relationships.

The jobs with NGOs are so attractive that people would pay to be allowed to work for an NGO. If an employee gets someone else a job, he or she can ask for half of the new employee's wages: 'These people who came recently don't know where to find the jobs. They don't know the mechanisms of the camp. These people who have already got jobs here in Lukole, charge them some taxes in order to get a job. And these people are very poor. They don't have shillings to pay. That's why they don't have jobs' (village leader, B3). This quote illustrates the appeal of being employed by an NGO. It also reveals a perception that the NGO employees make up a close-knit and impenetrable network. To be employed by an NGO is about more than earning extra money;

---

14. For verification purposes, each person dipped their fingers into ink that was impossible to remove.
15. For the sake of simplicity I am referring only to UNHCR, although the same applies to a number of agencies in the camp. The refugees normally also refer to UNHCR as a monolithic intentional actor and the main locus of power.

it is about becoming part of a network. These networks were often linked to the political parties. In this way, the employees could use their key positions as brokers between the refugees and the relief agencies as leverage for their political goals.

Palipehutu members would complain that they were treated badly in the clinics, because the staff was CNDD affiliated (Joseph, interview 4 May 1998). According to these rumours, the refugees working for NGOs would convince the corrupt Tanzanian staff of their version of events, thus marginalizing Palipehutu members further. As we saw in the case of the conflict between the previous chief security guard and the camp chairman, it was vital for both parties to convince the international agencies and the Tanzanian authorities of their version, demonizing the opponent as 'politically biased', while presenting themselves as politically neutral, serving the interests of the community.

JAMES: BETWEEN MOBILITY AND SEDENTARY KNOWLEDGE

Every street or village[16] had a leader, elected by the refugees. These refugee leaders attended fortnightly meetings with the UNHCR field officer or field assistant, camp commandant, and representatives from relevant NGOs. Basically, they were meant to be intermediaries between the refugee population and the agencies in control. They would voice refugees' complaints that they had lost their ration cards, that nurses treated them disrespectfully, or that OXFAM was pulling down their latrines. On the other hand, they were expected to disseminate information from the agencies to the population. This could be the field officer warning refugees to 'behave', or explaining to them why it is so important for OXFAM to make sure that they build mud brick latrines ('It is for your own good').

James is the village leader in B2 in Lukole B. The residents of B2 are people who had lived in Tanzanian villages for years and who were rounded up by the Tanzanian authorities in late 1997.[17] James had fled Burundi in 1993, and was among the first to arrive in Lukole when it was established in 1994. However, in 1996 he decided to try to earn some money and left the camp to work for a rich refugee smuggling coffee out of Burundi.[18] After a while, he moved to a Tanzanian village and worked as a builder until he, too, was rounded up and put into Lukole B. Perhaps his longer experience of camp life makes him a natural leader in a part of the camp where most of the inhabitants have only just arrived and still do not know 'the mechanisms of the camp', such as how to make the food rations last for two weeks, or what a 'community mobilizer' or a 'vulnerable' is.

16. Lukole A was organized into streets, while Lukole B was divided into villages.
17. For accounts of this brutal exercise see Human Rights Watch (1999).
18. Burundi was subject to an embargo by neighbouring countries after Buyoya's *coup d'état* in July 1996.

James is twenty-five years old. He is unmarried because he fears being forceably repatriated, and having a family would be too much of a responsibility in such a situation. He has no job and no business in the camp. He had almost finished primary school but was interrupted in his studies, in part by 'the troubles' in 1991[19] and in part because his father had left for Uganda and James had to help his mother in the fields. He went back to school in 1993, hoping to do secondary school and get a job in the administration or the army, but had to flee shortly after.

He believes that he was elected for his personality. In the intimacy of camp life, it only takes a few days to get to know somebody, he explains. People were fed up with his predecessor, who was also young but better educated, because he drank too much and was too loud mouthed. James converted to the Seventh Day Adventist Church after a close shave with death while visiting Burundi in 1995, so he does not drink at all. He also won over the other candidate, a jolly old man who had worked for UNICEF years before and who made people laugh when he presented himself for elections.

On the issue of being a good leader in Burundi, James explains: 'When they used their leadership in order to get something, these people were not respected. But there were leaders who were respected such as these ones who gave good advice or who had tried to solve problems in a good way. These people who were not shy — these people who were more proud — these people were not respected' (interview, 19 February 1998). He explains that it is important for a leader to be humble and kind. Being too 'proud' is associated with Tutsi arrogance and opposed to being shy. Although shyness can be a hindrance in the camp, it is still perceived by some to be a virtue to be kind and humble. If you also know how to solve disputes and give advice (and punish when necessary), you will be respected. James voted in the 1993 election but he assures me that he is not interested in politics. 'Politics is dealt with by these people who have been in school — who are educated', he says.

James represents quite a different 'type' than Steven. He is not as educated, he is not so keen on politics, and he does not appear to be in the limelight of international organizations. There are, however, some similarities in terms of age and in terms of the role that he plays as an intermediary between the population and the international agencies and Tanzanian authorities. Generally, James is in a more ambiguous position in terms of establishing public authority in the camp. Unlike Steven, he is not exclusively an expression of the new forces of change. Neither does he simply rely on the moral order of 'the good old days' and attempt to reinstall an idealized patriarchy and gerontocracy.

---

19. In November 1991 an abortive Hutu uprising (during which scores of civilian Tutsi were killed) resulted in thousands of Hutu being arrested and killed by the army (Lemarchand, 1996)

The leaders make up a more complex group than the NGO workers in terms of age and class, as demonstrated by the results of my survey of sixty-two street and village leaders.[20] It was, however, the youthfulness of the street leaders that surprised me when first coming to Lukole. I had expected to see only men over forty at the leaders' meetings, but as can be seen from Figure 2, 29 per cent were in their twenties, 47 per cent were in their thirties, and only 24 per cent were forty or above.

Leaders create public authority by drawing on a number of moral registers and ideals. Whereas James emphasizes being humble or 'shy', others emphasize qualities similar to those of the NGO workers, namely mobility, language and education. This is summarized in the more abstract 'not being shy'.[21] The following extract comes from an interview with the village leader from village B3:

> Yesterday we got information that today we will have a meeting with the representative of *Wilaya*.[22] Today at four o'clock. And because I am quite young, I took a megaphone and went around villages — all villages — thirteen villages — and told them that you will have a representative of *commune* who will come here to hold meeting...
> So yesterday you were told by whom?
> Camp Manager
> So you were very quick. Immediately you took a megaphone and went...
> Yeah, yeah. And because I am quite young I have to deal with many activities in a short time. But if it is an old one, he can't. That's why they have to elect someone who is very quick: someone who is very quick and who is intelligent.

Here, liaising with camp authorities and those who are in charge of resources in the camp is seen as an important role of the leader. He has to be able to react fast to any new situation. This is impossible for older men, he says. He continues that the leader has to be able to 'explain the problem fluently':

> According to Burundi customs, we usually respect elders. But ... if there is a problem, he is not fast — to go to explain the problem. It may happen that when they are going to food distribution, it may happen that some people don't have food. And the leader has to go to explain the problem — and he has to explain fluently the problem. Because when he doesn't explain the problem fluently, the people who miss the food, they don't have. They don't have it. (Village leader, B3)

Although expressing oneself fluently is not necessarily an ability exclusive to the youth, it is linked in his discourse. It goes with the same idea of not being shy and being able to express oneself openly that I found with the NGO employees. It also links with being able to speak foreign languages, especially

---

20. Unfortunately, for practical reasons, only five of the leaders in the survey are from Lukole B where roughly one third of the population live. Lukole B has quite a different history from Lukole A, resulting in a very different socio-economic and political profile.
21. The question is whether James's own success cannot be attributed to his experience of camp life and his ability to manoeuvre in the UNHCR defined space.
22. Tanzanian town council.

Swahili and English. Knowledge of languages was pointed out by the refugees themselves as an important asset for leaders, especially the young, extrovert ones; it was also mentioned by the leaders: 'Those people who are working with NGOs, different NGOs — are Tanzanians. And Tanzanians don't know how to speak French. They know how to speak Swahili and English. It is good to know Swahili language' (village leader, B3).

According to my surveys there does not seem to be a significant difference between the language skills of the leaders and the population in general. In spite of the ideal of the leader speaking Swahili (and perhaps English), in fact only about half of them do so.[23] This affirms our picture of the leaders as a mixed group, but it also shows that people choose from a variety of elements when defining an ideal leader. In the camp, they believe that mobility and language must be useful traits: to communicate with the all-powerful UNHCR is vital. But they also evaluate the leader according to other criteria, criteria which draw on the image of the ideal leader in Burundi and thus help to preserve some kind of continuity. As James emphasizes, this might be to be humble. So when electing a leader for their particular street or village, they measure the candidate partly according to his abilities at communicating with NGOs, and partly according to Burundian values and ideals.[24]

Another criterion for becoming a leader in the camp, it is claimed, is to be able to read and write: 'UNHCR told them that they had to elect someone who will know to make a report, or to represent others. Or when there is a problem, to know to explain the problem fluently' (village leader, B3). Although the leaders are not as well educated as the NGO workers, they still differ sharply from the average population in this regard: virtually all (98 per cent) have some kind of formal education while almost a third (29 per cent) of all men[25] in Lukole have no formal education.

The kind of knowledge (or 'intelligence' as they would often say in the camp) obtained from formal education is placed in opposition to the knowledge of the old men. According to this discourse, the old men's knowledge is based on experience. It is rooted in history, in a knowledge of people's lineages and their past, and it is rooted in locality; a knowledge of the land. This kind of knowledge is useless in the camp where nobody knows his neighbour, localities are new and the past is irrelevant.

The statistics on refugee leaders do not support such a drastic break as we are made to believe from the interviews with the young leaders. When I asked people what were the most important features of a good leader, the answers most certainly were more complex. As James says, it depends on

23. The leaders differ from the male population as a whole with comparatively few leaders claiming to speak either Swahili, French or English.
24. This is not to say that Burundi functioned that way. Rather, Burundi was conjured up as a kind of lost Paradise in the camp.
25. As all but one of the leaders were male, it makes more sense to compare with the male population rather than with the population as a whole.

your personality. A good leader is humble and knows how to give advice. Being able to mediate in conflicts, being able to find 'the truth' and being kind were abilities that were mentioned again and again in Lukole. To have these qualities, one obviously does not need a higher education. Neither does one need to know a lot of languages. In fact, education, language skills and not being shy may work against you. In other words, there is a risk that these well-educated, young parvenus might forget their background — their humble Hutuness — and become 'too proud', too much like the Rwandan or worse still; like the Tutsi. So while an educated young leader has the advantage of being able to express himself to camp authorities and make sure that the refugees are not tricked too much by corrupt Tanzanian staff, an older, more 'humble' man of the people may be more respected when it comes to solving problems between neighbours and when it comes to maintaining a Hutu moral order.

To sum up, the refugees are struggling between different concepts of being a 'big man' and different perceptions of how to deal with the new configuration of government in exile. Should they opt for the extrovert, mobile, young man who is not shy as the best option for achieving results in the new setting of the camp, or should they opt for the old man who symbolizes some sort of continuity and surety? In practice a leader is often a compromise between the two, like James who is young and mobile but is not well educated and not part of the NGO 'in-crowd'. He tries to live up to ideals of being a kind and humble leader, but he also knows the 'mechanisms of the camp' as they say, better than most others in his particular village, due to being an experienced refugee.

PATRICK: MINDING MY OWN BUSINESS

I first met Patrick in one of the forty medium-sized bars in Lukole A, where you sit inside a building made of mud bricks and UNHCR plastic sheeting, sometimes cut in decorative strips. There are homemade tables and benches, and often a radio playing Zairian pop music or Bob Marley highlights. Here they mainly sell *gua-gua*, banana wine that is more expensive and much preferred to the maize beer *mugorigori*. It is served in glasses that are almost clean rather than in communal plastic containers. The Tanzanians sell it at the junction outside the camp to the bar owners in Lukole.

Patrick is quite an established businessman.[26] In spite of being only twenty-two years old, he has had his own bicycle taxi business for three years,

26. Business is the term used in English (*d'affairs* in French) for any kind of income-generating activity that is not wage labour. In Swahili, the term *za shughuli*, which literally means 'of the things', nicely covers this informal wheeling and dealing. One of the wealthier refugees in the camp was nicknamed *Za Shughuli* because he worked as a school teacher, owned one of the biggest bars in the camp, worked as a photographer at weddings and the like, and generally had a lot of projects going on.

transporting people and goods on the back of his bicycle for a fee. Typically, he would transport goods to and from the junction about two kilometres outside the camp for 200 shillings. He earned enough money to buy the bicycle by working for an NGO as a watchman when he first arrived in the camp.

Patrick's parents were farmers and he only finished primary school before getting a job cleaning and cooking for a white *padre* in Burundi. His parents had fled Burundi in 1972 and he was born in Rwanda where the family stayed until 1982. He talks openly about being like a Rwandan, and claims that the Rwandans are better businessmen than Burundians:

> The reason is because Rwandese [Hutu] have been in government, have been in power. And they had chance not to be afraid of anyone. But these ones of Burundi have been ruled by Tutsi many years ago. That's why they are always afraid of some people. . . .
> But this happened before. Because now Burundese are experienced by Rwandese. Nowadays they are equal. They act at the same level. Nowadays, Burundese became more businessmen, like the Rwandese.

In Patrick's opinion, contact with Rwandans in the camp has changed the Burundians — but only for the better. He feels that he has had an advantage over other Burundians because he grew up in Rwanda and therefore has their mentality. When asked whether he would have an advantage over those who had remained in Burundi if he went back there, Patrick replies: 'Of course we will be more intelligent than those who stayed in Burundi'.

In the market in Lukole A alone, I counted forty-eight restaurants, thirty-two bars, ninety-five shops selling shoes, clothes, batteries, salt, rice, etc., ninety-four *mugorigori* outlets and 116 market stalls selling fresh fruit, vegetables and maize. Apart from this, there were hammer mills, hairdressers, radio repairers and a row of other small businesses. The businessmen are not part of the educated elite. Their level of education is not much different to that of the population in general and they seem to speak less French and English (see Figure 3). Surprisingly, they do not seem to speak much more Swahili than average. This could in part be explained by the fact that the local language, Kihangaza, is so similar to Kirundi that they understand each other, rendering Swahili superfluous for interaction with Tanzanians from neighbouring villages. It is only when communicating with NGO staff, police officers and government staff who often come from other parts of Tanzania, that Swahili becomes necessary.

Although they do not belong to the educated elite, many of the businessmen have significantly higher incomes than the NGO employees, and the wealthier among them would often be referred to as 'big men'. They are respected for their success and wield considerable authority. Even the poor businessmen demonstrate that they are not dependent on UNHCR rations, and that they do not just sit around the *blindé*, waiting to be fed but take responsibility

27. Based on a survey of seventy-nine businessmen.

Figure 3. Language Skills of Camp Population and Businessmen[27]

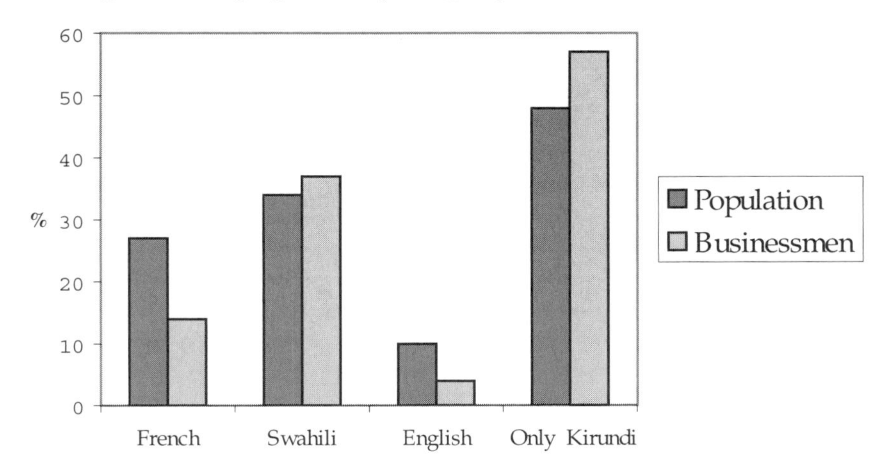

for their own lives and make a living of their own. What is more, they take responsibility for their families.[28] The owner of a *patisserie* explains that he can now afford to buy some decent food for his wife to prepare for the whole family (Diary, 1 September 1997). Being able to feed one's wife and children demonstrates an attempt to normalize life, to stabilize things as they ought to be and ideally were in Burundi where men acted as protectors and providers. It is about taking matters into one's own hands and re-establishing some sense of order.[29]

Patrick and his friends assured me that they were not interested in 'politics'. Because they work so hard, they do not have time to listen to the radio and involve themselves in such matters. And they add 'it is not good to speak about something you don't know'. A radio repairer echoes their attitude. The hardworking businessmen cannot afford the luxury of discussing politics, either here or in Burundi, he claims: 'Myself, I don't know how that problem happened in Burundi. I don't know because in [the] morning I wake up, I go to work, and [in the] evening I come back — and just it was time for eating so I didn't have time to go and discuss with others about Burundi problems' (radio repairer, 20 April 1998).

In other words, there is a self-image of a hardworking man who earns an honest living and can take care of himself. But he also minds his own business and is not interested in getting involved in politics, which is both a waste of time and potentially dangerous. This is in stark contrast to the

28. Most of the business people that I interviewed (sixty-four out of seventy-nine) were men and with a few notable exceptions, the female respondents either had small businesses selling vegetables and/or worked with their husbands.
29. As I have argued elsewhere (Turner, 1999, 2004) it is also a question of recuperating masculinity.

educated elite who work for NGOs and who constantly feel that they have to measure their personal strategies in relation to the 'common cause' of the Burundian people.

When discussing the possibilities of getting a passport in Dar-es-Salaam in order to be able to travel to Kenya for further studies, an educated refugee who worked for an NGO explained that the very rich traders often travel to Dar-es-Salaam, 'but they are not interested in politics' he said, with contempt (Albert, 1 October 1997). He clearly links politics and education, and interprets the reluctance of the businessmen to get involved as an aversion to 'politics'. So whilst there is a certain pride in minding one's own business and staying out of politics among the businessmen, this attitude is perceived very differently by the politically active, educated elite. They see the businessmen's attitude as selfish and short-sighted as opposed to their own self-sacrificing long-term strategies.

To sum up, businessmen are an important component in establishing authority in Lukole as the more successful among them have most certainly become 'big men' who command respect in the camp. However, their strategy differs from both the NGO employees and the street/village leaders. Respect is won neither through formal education and language skills nor through age, experience and knowledge of Burundi customs. Their knowledge is a third type that is very much linked to the camp context and learned neither in school nor in the Burundian hills. It is a very concrete strategy, based in the present context of the camp rather than in a nostalgic past or a utopian future.

At first sight, they do not seem to be involved in public authority, as they stay away from politics and make no pretence of representing the refugee population, just as they would rather avoid too much contact with camp authorities.[30] However, due to their success in following livelihood strategies that strengthen their independence from the relief agencies, they have become 'big men' who are respected in the camp. While NGO workers and street leaders establish themselves as brokers and gain powerful positions due to access to NGOs, businessmen gain respect and authority by proving their independence from — and defiance of — official camp authorities.

THREE WAYS OF NEGOTIATING PUBLIC AUTHORITY

In Lukole, an older order seems to have disappeared, making way for new orders to form. It is these new orders that young men like Steven, James and Patrick seek to exploit. In the de-structured space of the camp, they have been able to exploit the liberating potential of camp life and become liminal experts. They have managed to carve out a space for themselves in the camp

30. This is not completely possible, as they pay taxes to the camp commandant. The market committee also negotiates with relief agencies on how to regulate business in order to maintain certain hygiene standards, for example.

and have, to varying degrees and along different paths, managed to outmanoeuvre the old patriarchy and become the new 'big men' in the camp. No longer inhibited by Tutsi peers taking the best positions, young semi-educated men (and some women) are given important positions with relief agencies in the camp. No longer inhibited by norms and social expectations, young entrepreneurial men start up businesses of all sorts with the motto that they have nothing to lose — and some succeed and become 'big men' in the camp. And finally with knowledge of locality and history being more or less irrelevant in the camp, old men appear to be losing their grip on leadership while a number of young men are taking up the challenge of being street and village leaders.

Success in Lukole is about mobility, language skills, education and openness. There is an emphasis on youth and change and the old hierarchies are seen as archaic and useless. But this process is neither complete nor one-way. It is not a question of all the old men and all the old traditions being rejected. People are generally ambivalent about change and the status of 'big men'. They also long for the good old days. They despise the Rwandans for their rude behaviour and take pride in their distinctly Burundian behaviour as law-abiding citizens. They believe that women should respect their husbands and children their parents. In other words, there is a constant struggle between orthodox and heterodox opinion, between longing for the moral order of yesterday and striving for the opportunities created in the camp.

These 'big men' are respected for taking their future into their own hands and acting accordingly, rather than passively waiting in the camp to see what the future might bring. Whereas the businessmen take care of themselves and their nearest family in the present, the political elite are thinking of the future and of their country. In the camp, politicians are respected — even feared — as they have the courage to defy UNHCR laws and play by their own rules. In this way, they have managed to reclaim their position as men — as those who set the agenda and must be obeyed. These strategies ensure them authority in the camp. They can claim respect from other refugees. By struggling for 'the cause' of the Hutu people, Steven claims legitimacy as a big man in the camp; James claims legitimacy as a leader by being 'kind and humble'; and Patrick can claim a position as a 'man of the people' by minding his own business.

Ironically, they do not work entirely against the grain of UNHCR and MHA. In particular the political elite, employed by relief agencies or acting as official leaders, have a complex relation to camp authorities. They are employed by them; they use their access to the agencies as a means to assert their own positions *vis-à-vis* the broader population; and they also seek recognition from the international agencies. Of course there is an amount of strategic self-interest involved here, as both want to maintain their positions. But there is also an urge to be recognized by the international community as legitimately representing the refugees.

Public authority is produced partly by the powers that UNHCR delegates to these actors, and partly by the power bases that the refugees manage to build up in the gaps in UNHCR's system. Similarly it rests partly on the respect that these brokers gain from other refugees — a respect that is earned in numerous ways such as outwitting the international organizations — and partly on the recognition that they get from the very same organizations (see also Buur, this issue).

In short, this study has argued that a certain group of young men have made the best out of their positions as young and mobile, and have adapted to the new setting, the new rules and the new master. To adapt to the new master does not mean always to obey him but rather to know how to please him and how to make the best of the relationship with him. This may involve cheating him but it does not involve confronting him. The perception of UNHCR as an omnipotent other that controls their lives from above remains pervasive in the camp setting. It is the ultimate locus of power, for better or for worse. While being perceived as the agent that emasculates them and reduces them to helpless receivers of alms, it is also seen as the ultimate source of recognition. The refugees do not 'resist' it. Rather, they must relate to it and make the best of it.

This is where brokers like Steven and James and, to a lesser degree, Patrick enter the picture. Their authority is derived from both above and below. When seeking recognition from above — from UNHCR — they must prove themselves to be the true representatives of 'the refugee community'. This must be done within the language of the international agencies. Likewise, when establishing authority among 'the people', they must prove their abilities to manoeuvre in the world of international relief agencies. It is exactly from their ability to span the gap between relief agencies and the population that they derive authority. And it is in all their interests that the gap remains.

REFERENCES

Agamben, Giorgio (1998) *Homo Sacer: Sovereign Power and Bare Life*. Stanford, CA: Stanford University Press.

Agamben, Giorgio (2000) *Means Without End: Notes on Politics*. Minneapolis, MN: University of Minnesota Press.

Albert, E. (1963) 'Women of Burundi: A Study of Social Values', in D. Paulme (ed.) *Women of Tropical Africa*, pp. 179–217. London: Routledge and Kegan Paul.

Brun, C. (2000) 'Making Young Displaced Men Visible', *Forced Migration Review* 9: 10–13.

Cruikshank, B. (1999) *The Will to Empower: Democratic Citizens and Other Subjects*. Ithaca, NY: Cornell University Press.

Dean, M. (1999) *Governmentality: Power and Rule in Modern Society*. London, Thousand Oaks, CA: Sage Publications.

Foucault, M. (1978) *The History of Sexuality: An Introduction*. New York: Pantheon Books.

Human Rights Watch (1999) 'In The Name of Security: Forced Round-Ups of Refugees in Tanzania'. Human Rights Watch. Available online: http://www.hrw.org/reports/1999/tanzania/

Lemarchand, R. (1996) *Burundi: Ethnic Conflict and Genocide*. Washington, DC and Cambridge: Cambridge University Press; New York: Woodrow Wilson Center Press.

Lemarchand, R. (1999) *Ethnicity as Myth: The View from Central Africa*. Copenhagen: Centre of African Studies.
Lemarchand, R. and D. Martin (1974) *Selective Genocide in Burundi*. London: Minority Rights Group.
Malkki, L. H. (1995) *Purity and Exile: Violence, Memory, and National Cosmology among Hutu Refugees in Tanzania*. Chicago, UK: University of Chicago Press.
Maquet, J. (1961) *The Premise of Inequality in Ruanda: A Study of Political Relations in a Central African Kingdom*. London: Oxford University Press for the International African Institute.
Reyntjens, F. (1993) 'The Proof of the Pudding is in the Eating: The June 1993 Elections in Burundi', *Journal of Modern African Studies* 31(4): 563–83.
Schmitt, C. (1985) *Political Theology: Four Chapters on the Concept of Sovereignty*. Cambridge, MA: MIT Press.
Sommers, M. (2001) *Fear in Bongoland: Burundi Refugees in Urban Tanzania*. New York: Berghahn Books.
Trouwborst, A. A. (1962) 'Le Burundi', in A. A. Trouwborst, M. d'Hertefelt and J. Scherer (eds) *Les Anciens Royaumes de la Zone Interlacustre Meridionale*, pp. 117–69. London: International African Institute.
Turner, S. (1999) 'Angry Young Men in Camps: Gender, Age and Class Relations among Burundian Refugees in Tanzania'. UNHCR New Issues in Refugee Research Working Paper No 9.
Turner, S. (2001) 'The Barriers of Innocence: Humanitarian Intervention and Political Imagination in a Refugee Camp for Burundians in Tanzania'. PhD Thesis, Roskilde University.
Turner, S. (2004) 'New Opportunities: Angry Young Men in a Tanzanian Refugee Camp', in P. Essed, G. Frerks and J. Schrijvers (eds) *Refugees and the Transformation of Societies: Agency, Policies, Ethics and Politics*, pp. 94–106. New York and Oxford: Berghahn Books.
Turner, S. (2005) 'Suspended Spaces: Contesting Sovereignties in a Refugee Camp', in T. B. Hansen and F. Stepputat (eds) *Sovereign Bodies: Citizens, Migrants and States in the Post-colonial World*, pp. 312–32. Princeton, NJ: Princeton University Press.
Turner, S. (forthcoming) 'Of Victims and Troublemakers: Humanitarian Agencies and Political Activities in a Tanzanian Refugee Camp' in *Ethnos* (forthcoming).

'It was Satan that Took the People': The Making of Public Authority in Burkina Faso

Sten Hagberg

PUBLIC AUTHORITY AND POLITICAL CULTURE IN BURKINA FASO

Since the early 1990s processes of democratization and decentralization have provided a fertile ground for new political and cultural configurations in local African arenas. Local elections often incite the mobilization of political loyalties through kin, ethnicity and patrimonial networks. In particular, distinctions between 'first-comers' and 'late-comers' often carry new political meanings when political positions and resources are to be distributed. Rituals may become politically significant, and loaded with new meaning. In such contexts of experimentation and manipulation, power and authority are undergoing radical transformations.

Issues of power and authority are currently much debated in anthropology and in social sciences more generally. Power is not merely used to depict political processes, but is invoked as an explanation of different events and phenomena ranging from the power of a politician to that of a shaman or to a concept of *mana* (Cheater, 1999; Kapferer, 1997: 373–5; Seymour-Smith, 1995: 230). Anthropological descriptions of power dynamics and institutions have until recently had a Western bias in that other systems of power have been described 'as alternatives or variations of those found in Western industrial contexts' (Kapferer, 1997: 373). The issue of coercive power, especially in so-called stateless societies, has a long record in political anthropology (cf. Fortes and Evans-Pritchard, 1940; Gledhill, 1994; Horton, 1985). The shift from a Weberian distinction between power and authority to the analysis of everyday practices of power, influenced by Foucault and Bourdieu, has meant that more attention is paid to the constitutive and restructuring dynamics of power in a multitude of discourses and practices outside the institutions of government (Cheater, 1999; Kapferer, 1997: 375). The autonomy of 'the political' in modern societies is an illusion, because power rests on 'the everyday social practices which are the concrete form taken by relations

This article is based on long-term fieldwork carried out in Western Burkina. I am grateful to all informants for their hospitality and patience. I am also grateful to Jan Ovesen for commenting on an earlier draft of this article. More than anyone else, I am deeply indebted to the late Ernest Yao for the ongoing conversation on hunters and Karaboro society more generally over the years. Ernest's untimely death in March 2003 disrupted this conversation. I would therefore like to dedicate this article to the memory of Ernest Yao.

between the governing and the governed' (Gledhill, 1994: 22). Added to this shift, anthropologists have increasingly looked at the complexities of power developed through colonial and post-colonial transformations of authority and power in African societies (Goheen, 1992; Mamdani, 1996; Mbembe, 2000; Werbner and Ranger, 1996). The latest developments in terms of the invented traditional political power and authority are undoubtedly related to decentralization (Bierschenk and Olivier de Sardan, 2003; Hagberg, 2004b; Kassibo, 1997).

In this article, I am concerned with power and even more with its twin concept of authority. Who has the authority to speak on behalf of a group of people? Is the authority legitimate? Who or what makes a specific authority legitimate? How is authority constituted? To what extent is public authority constructed by individual political actors? Such questions urge us to study authority as a process in the making. If power is the result of everyday social practices, what about authority, and especially public authority? Anthropological descriptions have often come to challenge Weber's three types of authority — the traditional authority based on the legitimacy of a set of fixed and sacred norms; the rational-legal authority that is impersonal and resides in the office not in the person; and the charismatic authority, depending on the characteristics of an individual leader (Morrison, 1995).

There are important reasons to reconsider the process in which public authority is made. The making of public authority refers to intentional and unintentional actions that favour the growth of authority of an institution or an actor in the public space. We should not isolate 'the political' from the rest of society, but analyse public authority by focusing on the public life of an individual actor. By exploring what I call 'the making and unmaking of public authority' through the prism of a specific political actor, it is possible to elicit the norms, values and meanings that are embedded in local politics. In other words, the making and unmaking of public authority, at least in the case study which follows, provides a particularly fertile ground for studying local political culture.

Throughout the article I seek to explore the vague notion of local political culture in Burkina Faso. The notion of 'political culture' is not necessarily structured by tradition and culture in a classic sense, but refers to the cultural repertoires according to which people in general, and political actors in particular, give meaning to and creatively appropriate various political processes, such as the implementation of electoral laws, the formation of political movements and other public actions. Political culture is a vague notion that has come to attract many scholars, not least political scientists, attempting to grasp cultural processes and dynamics that are located outside formal politics. Trankell and Ovesen link the appeal of the notion to the combination of the 'hard' facts of politics and the 'softer' idea of culture. This definitional vagueness is felicitous, they argue, making 'political culture' 'just a notion that may cover a wide variety of interfaces between "the political" and "the cultural"' (Trankell and Ovesen, 1998: 9). To Marc Abélès, the notion of 'political culture' embraces the rituals and symbols associated with everyday political actions (Abélès, 1992).

This article explores the making of public authority through the analysis of a powerful, yet controversial political actor, a master-hunter in Western Burkina Faso whom we will call Kakre. Kakre has been breaking state law in order to assert his own authority, but he has also drawn upon state institutions in order to be recognized as a legitimate political actor. Despite the fact that Kakre lives in a rural village located off the main roads, external actors, such as civil servants, politicians and private business entrepreneurs have consulted him and asserted his public authority. Kakre is skilled in herbal medicine, and patients queue up daily at his homestead. He is also renowned for possessing the knowledge of various 'medicines' (*furaw*) to protect hunters. His public authority is thus partly grounded in these specialist skills.

However, as a political actor Kakre is generally held to be unpredictable and that is the feature that makes it particularly important to scrutinize his public authority. It could even be argued that 'unpredictability' forms part of what makes Kakre's authority and power compelling. Contrary to traditional chieftaincy institutions, where the individual is simultaneously granted, and subject to, power, the 'unpredictability' of an individual actor provides him/her with room for manoeuvre. Kakre's public authority draws upon different sources of legitimacy: he is a knowledgeable master-hunter; he is a skilled herbal specialist and diviner; he is a strong leader in the hunters' movement; he is a front figure of farmer–herder conflicts; and, finally, he is the head of a group of hunters who work as watchmen for a private enterprise in the region.

Kakre could well be seen as a descendant of a very old tradition of hunters' brotherhoods in West Africa. This tradition dates back to at least the tenth century in the regions which were to become the heart of the Mali Empire that emerged in the thirteenth century (Cissé, 1964; Thoyer, 1995). Throughout the centuries hunters have played a central role in wars and political resistance; at the end of the nineteenth century, armies were largely composed of hunters (Hagberg, 2003; Person, 1975; Şaul and Royer, 2001). Kakre is part of this tradition where the individual agency of the master-hunter is strong. This historical tradition is merged into the public action of the master-hunter Kakre. Yet there is more to the public authority of Kakre than this hunters' tradition, and I am therefore less interested in the epics and legendary narratives of hunters (see, for example, Cissé, 1964, 1985, 1994; Hellweg, 2001; Thoyer, 1995, 1997; Traoré 2000) than in the hunters' movement as a contemporary socio-political force.

The hunters' association Benkadi in Western Burkina was created on the initiative of Tiéfing Coulibaly (a much respected master-hunter in Dakoro in present-day Léraba Province) in the mid-1990s. Benkadi soon became a main actor in local politics, notably because the association recruits adult men of rural villages to ensure protection against banditry. The creation of Benkadi was motivated by increasing insecurity and criminality in rural areas.

Thieves could steal everything before the police and the gendarmerie were even informed. Hence, hunters of Benkadi do not primarily hunt game any longer; today they hunt thieves. But Benkadi is not officially recognized by the Burkinabe state. It not only challenges the state's monopoly of legitimate violence, but is also seen as a supra-ethnic armed movement of mainly Senufo farmers fighting against Fulbe agro-pastoralists.[1]

Present-day master-hunters represent simultaneously the historical tradition of *donso* hunters and the socio-political self-defence movement. According to the historical tradition of hunters there is a genealogy of hunters that is located outside kin relations. The relationship between a master-hunter and an apprentice lasts for life, and it takes the form of a father–son relationship. While initiation itself is ideally said to last seven years, in the context of Benkadi initiation only takes one day (Hagberg, 2004b). Master-hunters' straddling of these two contexts — the historical tradition of hunters and the socio-political defence movement — means that a practice approach seems to be particularly suitable for understanding master-hunters' public authority. Sherry Ortner advocates a practice approach to history that fits well to master-hunters' public authority:

> History is not simply something that happens to people, but something they make — within, of course, the very powerful constraints of the system within which they are operating. A practice approach attempts to see this making, whether in the past or in the present, whether in the creation of novelty or in the reproduction of the same old thing. Rather than fetishizing history, a practice approach offers, or at least promises, a model that implicitly unifies both historical and anthropological studies. (Ortner, 1994: 403)

Applied to Benkadi I would argue that master-hunters actively make their public authority 'within . . . the very powerful constraints of the system within which they are operating'. A practice approach suggests that less attention should be paid to legitimate institutions and that more interest should be geared towards the agent's active making of public authority. A practice approach is particularly suitable for traditional political institutions in Africa, because when studying the authority of political actors with little or no formal political power, such as the case of Kakre, public authority is construed out of the bits and pieces of history, initiation, party politics, ethnic stereotyping and money.

While it could be argued that the private sphere is equally important for understanding individual actors, the public action of a particular political actor is, together with the contexts and situations in which he finds himself, crucial for understanding the making of public authority. But this also includes the unmaking of public authority, as the political legitimacy of a particular political actor may easily erode. The public action of such an

1. For specific analyses of various aspects of Benkadi, see Hagberg (1998, 2001, 2004b 2004c, forthcoming). For a comparative analysis of hunters' movements in West Africa, see the thematic issue of *Africa Today* 51(3), Summer 2004.

actor is unpredictable in the sense that it is difficult even for political friends and allies to anticipate their actions and positions in advance. It seems that the very 'unpredictability' of specific political actors shapes their public authority. As I will demonstrate, Kakre has an authority that derives from his public action and his daily exercise of power. While he draws upon different registers of legitimacy, he is also considered to be unpredictable, even by his strongest supporters, intellectuals in Banfora. In this sense they try to take advantage of his capacity to mobilize hunters and yet they simultaneously distance themselves from him. Since Kakre's public authority is unpredictable, the temporal dimension is important. Contrary to traditional chieftaincy institutions, Kakre was not born with public authority. That is why his public authority is volatile and temporal. While traditional chieftaincy institutions often feature a mutually dependent relationship between the chief and his power — that is, the chief exercises power at the same time that he is subjected to the power itself — Kakre's unpredictability provides him with room for manoeuvre. However, this unpredictability is double-edged: when Kakre's unpredictable public action trespasses the boundaries of appropriate political behaviour, his public authority may rapidly erode.

The following section presents the story of Kakre based on interviews and fieldwork in the region. In particular, I will elaborate on two different examples of how Kakre asserts his public authority: in farmer–herder conflicts, and in the business of hired watchmen. This section will show how the authority of Kakre has become increasingly challenged. I then locate the case of Kakre in the context of the making and unmaking of public authority, and discuss its implications for understanding local political culture in contemporary Africa. I will argue that public authority is derived from a combination of different sources of legitimacy and that, therefore, public authority is shaped by the very 'unpredictability' of specific political actors.

THE STORY OF KAKRE

The story of Kakre is based on interviews conducted with him and other political actors. In additon, I rely on my long-term fieldwork in the region more generally.[2] It is of course 'my story' in the sense that I am trying to focus on the specific process by which Kakre became a public authority in the late 1990s and the early 2000s, and, more recently, how this public authority was fragmented. I therefore scrutinize Kakre's own public actions as well as the changing socio-political contexts in which he has found himself. I describe my first encounters with Kakre, and then elaborate on two different examples of how Kakre has asserted public authority. I end the section by describing the process that led to the erosion of his authority.

---

2. Since 1988 fieldwork has been carried out in Western Burkina for a total of more than 5.5 years. The research on *donso* hunters was the particular focus in 1996, 1999 and 2001 onwards.

I first met Kakre in his homestead in his village in Tiéfora district in January 1999. The village is located in what is generally held to be the core of 'Karaborola', that is, the area of Karaboro people (see Hagberg, 1998: 109–13).[3] I had learnt of Kakre from my friend the late Ernest Yao; Kakre was a powerful hunter, and since I was studying the hunters' association Benkadi in the Banfora region we decided to visit him. Kakre is famous for many skills, including divination and sorcery. When we arrived at the homestead several people were lining up for consultation with Kakre, including an urban-styled lady from Banfora. Kakre spoke loudly and laughed frequently, but at the same time he kept a certain distance, observing me with a penetrating gaze. This is an attitude I had met frequently among hunters: they generally observe and almost measure the person with whom they interact.

Kakre is known to have started the Benkadi hunters' association in Karaborola. The association was established because of high levels of plundering in the area. Kakre also stressed the importance of protecting the environment, because the hunters' association is making a strong case for hunters being those who protect nature. They work closely with the Forestry Office and have from time to time been used as collaborators with the foresters (Hagberg, 1998: 227–9). However, it was not a concern for the environment that made Benkadi attract so many people, but its role in combatting rural delinquency (Hagberg, 1998, 2004b, 2004c). Kakre explained:

> You know that we have cattle. The cattle of some people may amount to 10,000. And someone will chase the cattle and leave you with nothing. It is the same thing with sheep. And if you buy a motorbike for your son, someone will kill him to take the motorbike. The reason for starting the association is theft. But since we started the association they [the thieves] are afraid. The few cattle and sheep that remain are still here, because we do not pursue people without any reason. If you do not provoke us we have nothing to do with you. The *donsoya* [the affair of hunting] has been created to kill wild beasts, but there were too much theft.

I then asked him if they had been able to identify the thieves, knowing that many hunters tend to accuse Fulbe herders. The association has almost come to be seen as an anti-Fulbe association (Hagberg, 1998, 2004c). Kakre replied: 'We do not know [who the thieves are]. But if we pursue the thieves we most often find the Fulbe. Even if some farmers may be part of it, we have never had that case here. . . . In the area we have never arrested a Karaboro for these thefts'.

Kakre continued to assert that he had lost most of his cattle before the association started. Anybody who loses something may call the hunters and get the object back; even if it seems to have disappeared the hunters will find it, Kakre said.

> And all those that we arrest we hand them over to the authorities [that is, the police or the *gendarmerie*] and we have then nothing to do with it any more. It is sufficient to arrest

3. Karaboro is the name for an ethnic group of ancient origin in the region. 'Karaboro' is, however, a Dyula term, and in the Karaboro language, people refer to themselves as 'Kaye'.

> the person and take back the stolen object. But we bring the thieves to the authorities. The year when I was nominated there were problems. But the verdict has not yet been made. We arrested the thief who had lived in this village. We arrested him and took our things back. In addition you must pay the transport to assist in court. But what does this mean? This part of it is very disturbing and it makes us afraid. I do not think that this is normal. It is three years ago [we arrested that thief]. People say that the thief is dead but until now the verdict has not been made. We have observed that the advantage of our hunters' association is that our things finally remain. Things are not stolen any longer.

Kakre then developed his argument on why theft has proliferated in the region:

> It is as if the vital force of the game [*sogo nyama*] has caught us. Now the monkeys have been transformed to steal our wealth. Instead of targeting the object only, it happens that he kills in his field. . . . Take the case when you go to the bush to hunt and you return and find that your cattle have disappeared, yet it is not a lion, not a panther, not a hyena that has eaten it. It is the fault of the Fulbe!

Kakre thus asserted that the Fulbe are monkeys who have been transformed into thieves, conforming to the more widespread attempt to dehumanize thieves. Thieves are variously referred to as 'hyenas on two feet' and 'wild animals in town' (Hagberg, 2004c). Kakre stated that he had told the entire village that it is the fault of the Fulbe: 'All people of the district therefore accepted and became hunters'. But it was Kakre who started the association in the Tiéfora district or in Karaborola more generally:

> It is I who went in search of the association to bring it to Karaborola. It was my money and not that of the whole village. It was I who brought *donsoya* ['the affair of hunting'] here. . . . I went in search of the association by Tiéfing in Dakoro. It was 20,000 FCFA [approximately 30 Euros] of my own pocket that brought the association here.

In my attempt to narrate the story of Kakre as a political actor, the ways in which he portrayed his actions to create the association in Tiéfora are critical for understanding the making of public authority. Four observations may be made so far. First, Kakre is definitely the founder of the local group of hunters. As such he is well known in the whole region. Secondly, he was clearly identifying the Fulbe as 'thieves': he had never hidden his antipathy towards Fulbe. Thirdly, while he cautiously avoided confronting state law ('bringing the thieves to the authorities') he still criticized the lack of verdicts and the costs incurred on the victims of theft. Fourthly, Kakre asserted that the hunters' association makes a difference: there are no thefts any more, he argued, because the thieves are afraid.

In March 1999 I met Kakre at the inauguration of the hunters' clubhouse in the Sidéradougou district. Hundreds of hunters from the region and even from neighbouring countries gathered for the event (Hagberg, 2004c). The then Burkinabe Minister of Health, who originated from the region, attended the meeting together with a member of parliament from the region, and politicians and civil servants from Banfora. In contrast to our first encounter in his homestead, Kakre was in the midst of a highly significant political event. Although he did not make a public speech at the inauguration ceremony, he was shown respect as a very important master-hunter, representing the Tiéfora district. The fact that Kakre did not speak makes it even more evident that he is not to be understood as a formal political leader, but as a man of action.

The remainder of this section will elaborate on two examples of how Kakre actively contributed to the making of public authority, before turning to some recent developments that suggest that Kakre's public authority seems to have been, if not unmade, at least seriously challenged.

Farmer–Herder Conflicts

In 1999, Kakre identified Fulbe as 'thieves', and thus made some strong statements against them. Given that in the last decades the region has witnessed several outbreaks of violence between farmers and herders, leading in most cases to the killings of Fulbe, his assertion was not surprising but nonetheless outspoken. In our conversation in January 1999 he also referred implicitly to the violent conflict in Sidéradougou in December 1986 in which, after the killing of a young Fulbe herder, a Karaboro man was beaten to death by a Fulbe crowd, leading to widespread violence against Fulbe across the whole region (see Hagberg, 1998, 2001, 2005; see also Ouédraogo, 1997). The next time I met Kakre was in September 2001, about three months after an outbreak of violence between Fulbe and Karaboro in a village some 5 km from Kakre's homestead.

In June 2001, a violent conflict broke out in the village of Kankounadéni after a quarrel between Fulbe and Karaboro (*Journal du Jeudi*, 2–8 August 2001: 3–4; *L'Événement*, 25 July 2001: 10–12; *Le Pays*, 26 July 2001: 16; see also Hagberg, forthcoming). The violence started with a quarrel between a Fulbe herder and a Karaboro farmer on 6 June 2001 when the farmer and his son encountered a Fulbe herder with a cattle-herd in their field. They asked the Fulbe herder to leave and the quarrel alerted other farmers around. When the Fulbe herder was about to leave, a stone from a slingshot hit his head. The herder riposted with his firearm and shot at the son of the farmer. He was wounded on his cheek, but it was not a deadly wound. The farmers now attacked the herder, hit him and bound him, but the field-owner whose son had been wounded stopped the others who were ready to 'finish with the Fulbe' and told them to bring the herder to the village health-station. The farmers then alerted the *gendarmes* in Banfora, who sent two agents to Kankounadéni together with the member of parliament referred to earlier, and the head of the Tiéfora district. They all returned to Banfora later the same day.

However, once the *gendarmes* had left, farmers of Kankounadéni mobilized people in neighbouring villages. In the morning of 7 June, several hunters encircled the Fulbe camp and sent an emissary to ask a young Fulbe to walk out from the camp. He refused to come out and when the hunters' emissary returned, the attack began. Six Fulbe men were killed, including a man of seventy-six and a young boy of eleven; other Fulbe fled. The *gendarmerie* in Banfora was soon informed and sent two agents to the village. These two *gendarmes* succeeded in convincing the hunters to stop attacking the people, but the hunters then turned on the Fulbes' domestic animals — cattle, sheep and guinea fowls. The granaries were emptied and the houses looted. Four other *gendarmes* later came to reinforce the first two. The *gendarmes* stayed until eight o'clock in the evening. On the following morning, a group of Fulbe, escorted by four *gendarmes*, buried four of the victims; the two other corpses were found several days later. In the following weeks, the hunters continued to try to chase away the Fulbe and, indeed, many left the region. The administrative head of the Comoé Province, the High Commissioner (*Haut-Commissaire*), intervened to try to calm the situation, and the Burkinabe Minister of Security effectuated a mission in the region.

In September 2001 I interviewed Kakre. He denied any responsibility for the violent events in Kankounadéni. He argued that it was Satan that took the people. I asked him to clarify and he said:

> I heard there was a quarrel between graziers and farmers. They asked me to mediate and I did so to stop the quarrel. I do not know the cause of the quarrel. People told me that a Fulbe shot with a firearm on a farmer when he was in his field. But I did not witness this and cannot tell you why it happened. The authorities [state representatives] came to inform me and I went to stop the quarrel. I told them that it was Satan that took the people.

Kakre wanted to show that the conflict was the result of Satan and that no-one could prevent violence breaking out. But when I asked him to elaborate, he said: 'That a grazier with a firearm goes out with his cattle herd and finds a person in his field and shoots at him, if that is not the effect of Satan he should have gone to bush and let his cattle graze there'. Thus Kakre justified the actions of those hunters that he is supposed to control. He added: 'The hunters' association was not created for shooting on people. It is because of the conflict that the hunters stood up to arrange the situation to avoid that certain people were looted. That is the role of the hunters. The conflict is a problem between farmers and herders. Was it the hunters who stood up to provoke the quarrel?'.

Kakre also told me that the hunters' association had held a meeting after the outbreak of violence to explain that no hunter should start quarrelling. 'But if, however, a quarrel would start, you would find out that the instigator would neither be a farmer nor a hunter. The graziers cause the conflicts'. The blaming of Fulbe is very common among farmers in the region. Locally, there is a strong identification of the farmers as victims of the actions of Fulbe herders. Many politicians and intellectuals either openly support the claims of the hunters or remain silent over these obvious breaches of state law. One reason is that hunters count in the voting ballots; another is the resurgence of a discourse on autochthony in Banfora, where people of Banfora are contrasted with Fulbe and Mossi strangers (Hagberg, 2000). Yet Kakre locates the responsibility for the violence on the Fulbe themselves; the Fulbe are responsible for the violence inflicted upon them and, ultimately, for their own death.

In January 2002, two hunters were arrested for having participated in the killings. Relatives of the victims had identified them. In March 2002 hunters of the district formulated a written ultimatum to the *préfet* of Tiéfora. The letter demanded that their 'brothers' should be released no later than on 8 March 2002 (*Le Pays*, 20 March 2002: 20). According to the newspaper, Kakre was to be received by the High Commissioner to solve this new problem.

To conclude, the example of violent farmer–herder conflicts demonstrates the extent to which Kakre not only remained an important figure to consult, but also emerged as a political actor engaged in the conflict. However, he cautiously denied any personal responsibility. In other words, he is 'clean' himself while supporting his hunters' right to defend themselves against Fulbe's aggression. I find it highly unlikely that Kakre was not involved in the conflict or that he had not encouraged their actions. That would mean that he had no control whatsoever of the hunters supposedly under his command. Accusing Satan is a way of not falling into the trap of ethnic hatred. It is not possible to understand the action of 'the Other' (the Fulbe), the argument goes, unless one recognizes that Satan made him act immorally (entering the field of the farmer). Yet when the hunters addressed a letter of ultimatum to the *préfet*, threatening a state representative, Kakre was called in to negotiate with the High Commissioner. Kakre supported the hunters' breach of state law but was still asked to solve the problem with the highest state representative of the province. The example depicts the ways in which the public authority of Kakre was strengthened by the conflict. Although he was partly seen as responsible for what happened, the conflict made him a political actor with whom state representatives, politicians and intellectuals must deal.

Hired Watchmen

The second example of how Kakre's public authority has been asserted relates to the *Collectif d'Associations pour la Conservation et la Sauvegarde de l'Environnement* (CACOSE) and, in particular, to the role of Kakre's hunters as hired watchmen for the sugar cane company SOSUCO in the Banfora region. The CACOSE was created in 1996 to combat poaching by means of hunters patrolling. Rather than being portrayed as killers of game, hunters were presented as protectors of the environment. While the president of CACOSE is a Burkinabe living in Banfora, a local hotel-owner of

French origin was initially the driving force behind the association. To launch CACOSE a conference was organized about the protection of the environment in 1996. The conference took place in the cinema Neerwaya in Banfora and brought together some 500 hunters. A second conference was organized in 1998 in collaboration with the Global Environment Fund-supported development project *Gestion Participative des Ressources Naturelles et Fauniques* (GEPRENAF); again some 500 hunters attended. This second conference was very much centred upon how to manage the forest reserves of Bolon and Koflandé, located in Kakre's home area. The Ministry of Environment had leased the forests to the French hotel-owner as the government did not have the capacity and resources to manage them in a sustainable manner. The French hotel-owner was eager to develop safari and hunting trips for tourists and hunters from Western countries, but he needed help from local hunters to protect the areas from poachers and other people carrying out so-called illicit activities there. In that way the hunters became watchmen of the forests.

According to the president of CACOSE, it was this first experience that later turned hunters such as Kakre into hired watchmen. Although the Ministry later suspended the French hotel-owner's activities in the forests, the hunters had gained an initial experience of working as hired watchmen far outside their traditional role (Hagberg, 1998, 2004b; for a regional comparison, see Bassett, 2003, 2004; Hellweg, 2001, 2004; Ouattara, 2006). In 1999 the parastatal sugar cane company SOSUCO was privatized, accompanied by strikes and unrest. Strikers' actions soon came to include attacks on company property: sugar cane was burned and technical equipment was stolen. The strikes lasted for thirteen days and hunters were asked to protect the canes and industrial property. In an interview in 2002 the president of CACOSE explained to me: 'With the hunters we prevented a lot of thefts. I said to the director [of the SOSUCO] to sign a contract with us to protect the canes. The thefts are limited now. It is not as before. Oil disappeared, batteries etc. Now it is OK. There is no theft any more.'

The salient point is that the hunters' experience and efficiency in protecting property and combatting delinquency made them particularly suitable to become hired watchmen. Yet not all members of Benkadi hunters' association were to be hired by SOSUCO, but only those working with CACOSE. The president continued:

> It is only the hunters of CACOSE who are here [that is, who are contracted by SOSUCO]. There are 3,000 hunters with membership cards across the region. It is XX ['Kakre'] who has brought hunters to CACOSE. . . . We created CACOSE for carrying out our activities in order to allow hunters to work properly. The hunter-leaders are remunerated to give advice, but they are not in the field [that is, they do not patrol themselves].

The president exemplified how CACOSE worked with the hunters. The hunter-leaders are public authorities providing advice to young hunters, sometimes called 'new hunters' (*donsow kura kura*), who do the practical work. In April 2002, CACOSE had 128 hunters working in teams to protect the sugar canes of SOSUCO. The association takes care of recruitment and payment of those who do the work whereas SOSUCO pays to CACOSE. The president admitted that while hunters are very efficient it is a hard task to supervise them:

> The hunters shoot at thieves. They may kill, but one will never find the corpse. They kill thieves in the bush and make the corpses disappear. It is only recently that hunters bring thieves to the *gendarmerie*. A thief died at the *gendarmerie* from the wounds [he had got from the hunters]. We hold meetings with the hunters. I ask the *gendarmerie* to help me, but it is difficult. Hunters have even searched through a vehicle of *gendarmes* in the sugar fields. They think they are the equals of the *gendarmes*. Hunters are not under their authority. Thus the hunters are very efficient, but it is difficult to control them.

The president's narration of hunters' activities as watchmen is striking. This person is responsible for CACOSE's private patrolling activities for payment, and he admits the difficulty in controlling them. He insists that hunters cannot get any legal recognition in the context of Benkadi, that is, the hunters' own association founded by Tiéfing Coulibaly in the mid-1990s (Hagberg, 2004b, 2004c), but that hunters need to be controlled within the framework of a legally recognized association, such as CACOSE.

The case of CACOSE and the hunters exemplifies the outsourcing of public authority, whereby private companies and wealthy individuals contract hired watchmen. While this is nothing new, and is to some extent the logical outcome of the cutting back of government expenditures (a small number of *gendarmes* are to cover a whole region linked together by poor infrastructure), it is intriguing that hunters use their hunting skills to protect the public buildings and sugar canes against strikers. They are, in short, working for those who pay them. Hence, these hunters do not represent a youth revolution; they form a conservative armed movement composed of people who, from time to time, violently take the law in the own hands. This is further evidenced by another case. For some time, hunters were asked (by CACOSE and the Forestry Office) to control firewood entering the city of Banfora. But the experiment did not turn out well. Some hunters had, I was told, even arrested pregnant women and forced them to stay in the sun for a long time in order to discourage them from engaging in the sale of firewood.

Kakre's Eroding Public Authority

The examples of violent farmer–herder conflicts and of hunters as hired watchmen illustrate the process in which so-called traditional hunters act in political and economic contexts. The hunters are not merely remnants of the past and guardians of 'autochthonous values' (Mali, 2001) but are political actors deeply involved in contemporary politics and political violence. The participation of hunters in political campaigns is well known; as

I have demonstrated elsewhere (Hagberg, 2004c), they support the ruling majority party *Congrès pour la Démocratie et le Progrès* (CDP). Yet the case of Kakre and his political involvement is different, because many people have been critical of CACOSE in general and of Kakre's involvement in particular.

Most master-hunters of Benkadi have had difficulties because of the lack of legal recognition of the association. But Benkadi's quest for recognition is more than legal. It is a politics of recognition that crosses the law and enters the field of politics, culture and development (Hagberg 2004b; see also Englund and Nyamnjoh, 2004; Hagberg, 2004a). Hunter leaders wanted a 'birth certificate' (*wulo sebeli*) for Benkadi. Yet contrary to other master-hunters in Benkadi, Kakre skilfully used his collaboration with CACOSE to increase his power and influence. As CACOSE was recognized by the state and therefore able to sign contracts with SOSUCO, Kakre not only gained a formal status but also an income as 'advisor'. This fact was brought up in interviews with leaders of Benkadi. One leader said that CACOSE is treacherous, because the association is legally recognized. But he continued: 'CACOSE does not master the hunters. It is we who master the hunters'. Another criticism is related to money: 'CACOSE establishes a contract with SOSUCO and makes some 30,000 FCFA, but the hunters only get 10–15,000 FCFA'.

The public authority of Kakre has evolved over the years that I have been able to monitor his public actions. From his position as a knowledgeable herbalist and an outspoken master-hunter in 1999, he increasingly emerged as a controversial political actor in 2001–02 with whom others had to deal. Kakre gained power through these events, even though he was also portrayed as, at least implicitly, responsible for the violent actions (*L'Événement*, 25 July 2001: 10–12). The ways in which the president of CACOSE simultaneously depicted Kakre as a violent and unpredictable actor, and as a widely recognized public authority reveal the ambiguity that has surrounded Kakre over the years. It is as if his authority is made through this very 'unpredictability'.

This suggestion is corroborated by developments recorded in January 2004. While I did not have the opportunity to meet Kakre, I heard about some recent developments of Kakre's public authority from other political actors. Most importantly, the CACOSE had now lost its contract with the SOSUCO, following a dispute with one senior official of the company. According to the president of CACOSE, patrolling hunters had discovered that a SOSUCO senior official had stolen fertilizers from the company. The hunters told this to the General Director of the SOSUCO, but — still according to CACOSE's president — the senior official was able to tarnish CACOSE, because he was a close collaborator of the director. SOSUCO's contract with the hunters of CACOSE was therefore terminated. Another version holds that the contract was ended because CACOSE had enrolled far too many hunters and that the problematic relationship between Benkadi and CACOSE was at the heart of the conflict. While Benkadi needed CACOSE for getting access to this work, CACOSE used Benkadi's hunters and benefited from the arrangement.

In the following months a new hunters' association emerged. The new association is called Faso Donso and is supported by the same ex-MP that has appeared earlier in this narrative. 'Faso Donso' may roughly be translated as 'Hunters of the father's house/fatherland' and, like Benkadi, it organizes hunters of the Comoé Province. Faso Donso rapidly got legal recognition from the High Commissioner of the province. Hence, within a few months the impasse that had characterized Benkadi over the years — that is, the lack of official recognition (Hagberg, 1998, 2001, 2004b, 2004c) — was overcome. All hunters are now referring to 'Faso Donso' rather than to 'Benkadi', even in the countryside far from Banfora. For instance, a hunter leader in the Sidéradougou district said: 'We created Benkadi, but today it has become Faso Donso. . . . When the association got its legal recognition we opted for making Faso Donso'.

These developments indicate that hunters are continuously in a process of shape shifting (Leach, 2000). What had been referred to as 'traditional hunters' (*donso*) was transformed in the mid-1990s into a patrolling militia under the cover of a voluntary association (Benkadi). Benkadi did not receive any official state recognition, mainly due to the fact that it constitutes an armed movement that could develop into a militia outside the control of the Burkinabe State. CACOSE presented itself as an organization able to control and supervise hunters and use them as hired watchmen. With recent developments, however, Benkadi has been abandoned and CACOSE has become marginalized. The new association called Faso Donso, supported by this influential former MP, was created to overcome the legal impasse. In other words, hunters and hunters' movements have once again shifted their shapes to adjust to new political, economic and cultural circumstances. Over the years I have heard hunters variously present themselves as 'protectors of nature', 'defenders of farmers' rights' or 'vigilantes catching thieves'. Yet despite the discursive shifts there is often continuity when it comes to individual actors. Kakre has emerged as a public authority in these shifting circumstances. He has stood for outspokenness and courage; but he has also been depicted as 'stubborn' and 'savage', which has led his public authority to diminish in the course of these latest developments.

With the ending of the contract between CACOSE and SOSUCO, Kakre withdrew his hunters from the sugar canes. While his group is still part of CACOSE, they do not carry out activities as they used to do. Some actors feel that he remains the hunter leader of the Tiéfora district. Others say that as he is not member of Faso Donso and that, consequently, he is not the district representative of hunters. The public authority of Kakre has been 'unmade' or at least severely curbed in the complex process of local politics. Kakre, however, is far from being a victim of other political actors' strategies; he has himself been an agent in the erosion of his authority. First, he supported the hunters' right to attack and kill Fulbe agro-pastoralists. Secondly, he threatened the head of the Tiéfora district, telling him to release the suspected murders. Thirdly, he acted independently, without considering other master-hunters. Kakre has nonetheless made claims that are supported by many Karaboro farmers, and his refusal to compromise forms part of both the making and the unmaking of his public authority. It is this 'unpredictability' of Kakre that makes it particularly important to analyse the public actions of this specific political actor.

The case of Kakre exemplifies one pertinent way in which political actors construe public authority in Burkina Faso. It illustrates how new political actors exercise public authority at the frontier of politics and culture. It also indicates the extent to which processes of democratization and decentralization have come to complicate political games at the local level, reducing the predictability of political processes (Bierschenk and Olivier de Sardan, 2003; see also Blundo, 2001; Hagberg, 2004c; Laurent, 2001; Lentz, 1998; Lund, 2002).

CONCLUSION

The story of Kakre could be seen as merely a special case of a particularly puzzling political actor. His ambiguous public actions certainly warrant a more detailed look at his public authority than the scope of this article would allow. Yet my argument is somewhat different from the idea that Kakre is a special case. What I call the making and unmaking of Kakre's public authority indicate that time and space are central for understanding the public action of specific political actors. Kakre's public authority can fruitfully be understood through an analysis of time and space — or perhaps better, as the importance of timing and spacing in making public authority. So, rather than representing a special case, I argue that the story of Kakre gives important insights into the complicated political games at local levels in Africa. Bierschenk and Olivier de Sardan show that democratization in Benin has heightened the existing fragmentation of local political arenas and the informalization of political practices. This creates among other things 'a need for constant negotiation between political actors, thus reducing the predictability of political processes and the accountability of local political institutions' (Bierschenk and Olivier de Sardan, 2003: 147). To conclude, I would like to analyse how Kakre's timing and spacing is mediated by his very 'unpredictability'.

First, the story of Kakre has evolved over the years and as such it gives important insights into the process of making public authority. Kakre's political trajectory is clearly marked by important events, such as the second CACOSE conference in 1998, the inauguration of the hunters' clubhouse in 1999 and the outbreak of violence in 2001. Kakre's public authority has been in a constant process of negotiation. When he threatened the district head in March 2002, he was, within a few days, invited to meet the High Commissioner of the province to settle the dispute. At a time when he was benefiting from considerable support from CACOSE, he was also treated as 'rebellious' and 'savage' by its president. Over the years Kakre remained the leader for Karaboro hunters in Tiéfora district. He has no specific kin relations to traditional chieftaincy, but has emerged as a leader through his bravery and outspokenness. This kind of political actor represents one leadership model in Karaboro communities. Narrations of Karaboro uprisings before and during colonization indicate that power and authority were invested in brave individuals. According to the Karaboro informants of Jean Hébert, in times of war, the bravest warlord became the chief of the moment and for the duration of hostilities (Hébert, n.d.: 2; see also Hagberg, 1998: 124; Ouédraogo, 1997: 143–4).

Secondly, Kakre has shown a remarkable capacity to be absent while being present. When the outbreak of violence occurred he was allegedly not at home, but he returned later. He was 'informed' by people that a 'problem' between Karaboro and Fulbe had escalated. Yet he cautiously avoided telling what he had done himself, except working to 'arrange the affair'. So, Kakre was present as a strong political actor while being absent when things really went wrong and, as he put it himself, 'Satan took the people'. Once again this unpredictability makes it difficult for other political actors to ignore him. He could neither be labelled a criminal, inciting hunters to use violence, nor be dismissed as a non-influential figure.

Thirdly, Kakre's public authority has recently been challenged. The termination of SOSUCO's contract with CACOSE resulted in the withdrawal of Kakre and his hunters from the sugar canes. Moreover, the emergence of the new hunters' association Faso Donso marginalized Kakre's group further. The 'unpredictability' of Kakre was turned against him in order to assert the authority of the new association. Now Kakre is back in his village leading the hunters loyal to him; what will happen in the coming years is — yes, unpredictable.

To end this article, I would like to propose that the story of Kakre's public authority has an important theoretical implication for the more general understanding of local political culture in contemporary Africa. It moves beyond static descriptions of local politics as being either hopelessly trapped in traditional kin and ethnic loyalties or as a modern project requiring that considerable resources are invested to educate and sensitize people. Instead, the story of Kakre shows how public authority is derived from a combination of different sources of legitimacy. The public authority of a specific actor is constituted and restructured in a multitude of discourses and practices more than in rules, regulations and decrees, be they administrative, political or ritual. Such a public authority may be situated either inside or outside the state institutions, but it tends to be made out of the actor's straddling of different political and cultural contexts. Herein lies the very 'unpredictability' that plays an important role in constituting the public authority of specific political actors in local African arenas.

REFERENCES

Abèles, M. (1992) 'Anthropologie politique de la modernité', *L'Homme* 121, XXXII(1): 15–30.

Bassett, T. J. (2003) 'Dangerous Pursuits: Hunter Associations (Donzo Ton) and National Politics in Côte d'Ivoire', *Africa* 73: 1–30.

Bassett, T. J. (2004) 'Containing the Donsow: The Politics of Scale in Côte d'Ivoire', *Africa Today* 50(4): 31–49.

Bierschenk, T. and J. P. Olivier de Sardan (2003) 'Powers in the Village: Rural Benin between Democratisation and Decentralisation', *Africa* 73: 145–73.

Blundo, G. (2001) 'La corruption comme mode de gouvernance locale: trois décennies de décentralisation au Sénégal', *Afrique contemporaine* 199: 115–27.

Cheater, A. (ed.) (1999) *The Anthropology of Power: Empowerment, Disempowerment and Changing Structures*. London and New York: Routledge.

Cissé, Y. (1964) 'Notes sur les sociétés de chasseurs malinké', *Journal de la Société des Africanistes* 19: 175–226.

Cissé, Y. T. (1985) 'Les nains et l'origine des boli de chasse chez les Malinké', *Systèmes de pensée en Afrique noire* 8: 13–24.

Cissé, Y. T. (1994) *La confrérie des chasseurs Malinké et Bambara: Mythes, rites et récits intiatiques*. Ivry and Paris: Editions Nouvelles du Sud & Association ARSAN.

Englund, H. and F. B. Nyamnjoh (eds) (2004) *Rights and the Politics of Recognition in Africa*. London and New York: Zed Books.

Fortes, M. and E. E. Evans-Pritchard (eds) (1940) *African Political Systems*. London: Oxford University Press for the International African Institute.

Gledhill, J. (1994) *Power and its Disguises: Anthropological Perspectives on Politics Anthropology, Culture and Society*. London and Boulder, CO: Pluto Press.

Goheen, M. (1992) 'Chiefs, Sub-chiefs and Local Control: Negotiations over Land, Struggles over Meaning', *Africa* 62: 389–412.

Hagberg, S. (1998) *Between Peace and Justice: Dispute Settlement between Karaboro Agriculturalists and Fulbe Agro-pastoralists in Burkina Faso*. Uppsala Studies in Cultural Anthropology 25. Uppsala: Acta Universitatis Upsaliensis.

Hagberg, S. (2000) 'Strangers, Citizens, Friends: Fulbe Agro-pastoralists in Western Burkina Faso', in S. Hagberg and A. B. Tengan (eds) *Bonds and Boundaries in Northern Ghana and Southern Burkina Faso*, pp. 159–79. Uppsala Studies in Cultural Anthropology 30. Uppsala: Acta Universitatis Upsaliensis.

Hagberg, S. (2001) 'À l'ombre du conflit violent: règlement et gestion des conflit entre agriculteurs karaboro et agro-pasteurs peul au Burkina Faso', *Cahiers d'Etudes africaines* XLI-1(161): 45–72.

Hagberg, S. (2003) 'Amoro et Guimbé: histoire et religion dans la construction de l'identité tiefo', in R. Kuba, C. Lentz and C. N. Somda (eds) *Histoire du peuplement et relations inter-ethniques au Burkina Faso*, pp. 237–57. Paris: Karthala.

Hagberg, S. (2004a) 'Ethnic Identification in Voluntary Associations: The Politics of Development and Culture in Burkina Faso', in H. Englund and F. B. Nyamnjoh (eds) *Rights and the Politics of Recognition in Africa*, pp. 195–218. London and New York: Zed Books.

Hagberg, S. (2004b) 'La chasse aux voleurs! Une association des chasseurs et l'administration de l'Etat dans l'Ouest du Burkina Faso', in S. Latouche, P. J. Laurent, O. Servais and M. Singleton (eds) *Les raisons de la ruse: Une perspective anthropologique et psychanalytique*, pp. 199–219. Révue du M.A.U.S.S. Paris: La Découverte.

Hagberg, S. (2004c) 'Political Decentralization and Traditional Leadership in the Benkadi Hunters' Association of Western Burkina Faso', *Africa Today* 50(4): 51–70.

Hagberg, S. (2005) 'Dealing with Dilemmas: Violent Farmer–Pastoralist Conflicts in Burkina Faso', in P. Richards (ed.) *No Peace, No War: An Anthropology of Contemporary Armed Conflicts*, pp. 40–56. Athens, OH: Ohio University Press; Oxford: James Currey.

Hagberg, S. (forthcoming) '"Each Bird is Sitting in its Own Tree": Authority and Violence of a Hunters' Association in Burkina Faso', in B. Derman, R. Odgaard and E. Sjaastad (eds) *Citizenship and Identities in Conflicts over Land in Africa*. Oxford: James Currey.
Hébert, P. (n.d.) 'Les Karaboro'. Unpublished manuscript.
Hellweg, J. R. (2001) 'The Mande Hunters' Movement of Côte d'Ivoire: Ritual, Ethics, and Performance in the Transformation of Civil Society, 1990–1997'. PhD dissertation, University of Virginia.
Hellweg, J. R. (2004) 'Encompassing the State: Sacrifice and Security in the Hunters' Movement of Côte d'Ivoire', *Africa Today* 50(4): 3–28.
Horton, R. (1985) 'Stateless Societies in the History of West Africa', in J. F. A. Ajayi and M. Crowder (eds) *History of West Africa*, pp. 87–128. New York: Longham Inc.
Journal du Jeudi. Weekly newspaper (Ouagadougou).
Kapferer, B. (1997) 'Power', in T. Barfield (ed.) *The Dictionary of Anthropology*, pp. 373–75. Oxford: Blackwell Publishers.
Kassibo, B. (1997) 'La décentralisation au Mali: état des lieux', *APAD-Bulletin* 14: 1–20.
L'Événement. Monthly newspaper (Ouagadougou).
Laurent, P. J. (2001) 'L'espace public dans une ville émergente d'Afrique de l'ouest: aux frontières de la théorie des conventions, l'anthropologie prospective?', *Recherches Sociologiques* 32: 101–24.
Leach, M. (2000) 'New Shapes to Shift: War, Parks and the Hunting Person in Modern West Africa', *Journal of the Royal Anthropological Institute* 6: 577–95.
Lentz, C. (1998) 'The Chief, the Mine Captain and the Politician: Legitimating Power in Northern Ghana', *Africa* 68: 46–67.
Le Pays. Daily newspaper (Ouagadougou).
Lund, C. (2002) 'Negotiating Property Institutions: On the Symbiosis of Property and Authority in Africa', in K. Juul and C. Lund (eds) *Negotiating Property in Africa*, pp. 11–44. Portsmouth, NH: Heinemann.
Mali (2001) 'La chasse traditionnelle en Afrique de l'Ouest d'hier à aujourd'hui'. Actes du colloque international de Bamako (26-28 January 2001). Bamako: Ministère de la Culture du Mali.
Mamdani, M. (1996) *Citizen and Subject: Contemporary Africa and the Legacy of Late Colonialism*. Kampala: Fountain Publishers; Cape Town: David Philip; London: James Currey.
Mbembe, A. (2000) *De la postcolonie: essai sur l'imagination politique dans l'Afrique contemporaine*. Paris: Karthala.
Morrison, K. (1995) *Marx, Durkheim, Weber: Formations of Modern Social Thought*. London: Sage.
Ortner, S. B. (1994) 'Theory in Anthropology since the Sixties', in N. B. Dirks, G. Eley and S. B. Ortner (eds) *Culture, Power, History: A Reader in Contemporary Social Theory*, pp. 372–411. Princeton, NJ: Princeton University Press.
Ouattara, S. (2006) 'Deux sociétés sécrètes dans l'espace public: l'association des Dozobele (chasseurs) et des Tcholobele (Poro) en milieu Sénoufo en Côte d'Ivoire et au Mali'. Doctoral Thesis, Department of Social Anthropology, University of Gothenburg.
Ouédraogo, J. B. (1997) *Violences et communautés en Afrique Noire: La région Comoé entre règles de concurrence et logiques de destruction (Burkina Faso)*. Paris and Montréal: L'Harmattan.
Person, Y. (1975) *Samori: Une révolution dyula*. Dakar: Institut Fondamental de l'Afrique Noire (IFAN).
Şaul, M. and P. Royer (2001) *West African Challenge to Empire: Culture and History in the Volta-Bani Anticolonial War*. Athens, OH: Ohio University Press; Oxford: James Currey.
Seymour-Smith, C. (1995) *Macmillan Dictionary of Anthropology*. London: Macmillan.
Thoyer, A. (1995) *Récits épiques des chasseurs bamanan du Mali*. Paris: L'Harmattan.
Thoyer, A. (1997) *Le riche et le pauvre et autres contes bamanan du Mali*. Paris and Montréal: L'Harmattan.

Trankell, I. B. and J. Ovesen (1998) 'Introduction', in I. B. Trankell and L. Summers (eds) *Facets of Power and its Limitations: Political Culture in Southeast Asia*, pp. 9–18. Uppsala: Acta Universitatis Upsaliensis.

Traoré, K. (2000) *Le jeu et le sérieux: essai d'anthropologie littéraire sur la poésie épique des chasseurs du Mande (Afrique de l'Ouest)*. Köln: Rüdiger Köppe Verlag.

Werbner, R. and T. Ranger (eds) (1996) *Postcolonial Identities in Africa*. London: Zed Books.

Dealing with the Local State: The Informal Privatization of Street-Level Bureaucracies in Senegal

Giorgio Blundo

INTRODUCTION

How does the African state work in reality? How do public administrations function in everyday life? How are they staffed? What are their means and constraints of action, and what actual services do they provide? What forms of interaction exist between the public services and their users? Who — sociologically speaking — are the civil servants of today, and how do they perceive their functions? How do their careers evolve, and within which professional cultures do they move? The Africanist literature in social sciences posts a weird silence on these questions. While there are many studies on the African state, they have long been centred on research of the features characterizing the state in Africa — in a more or less acknowledged confrontation with its model, the Western modern state, and its historical modes of building. On the basis of an analogy with the Western state formation (cf. Mamdani, 1996), the state in Africa was defined in terms of the effectiveness of its visible structures and aims (its institutional dimension), by measuring the gap between its structures and those of its Western counterpart. The state has thus been characterized as: predatory (Darbon, 1990; Fatton, 1992), kleptocratic (Coolidge and Rose-Ackermann, 2000), under-developed (Medard, 1977), neo-patrimonial (Medard, 1991), rhizomic (Bayart, 1989) or like a shadow (Reno, 1995). Observed from the top, from the angle of the elite and of the domination processes, or from below, in terms of the 'politics' in non-official spaces, the state seems difficult to grasp when one takes an interest in the daily life of its agents, in the services at work, in the encounters between the citizens and the street-level bureaucracy (cf. Lipsky, 1980).

The current passion for 'good' or 'bad' governance may allow scope for greater attention to the interfaces at which the state administration meets and negotiates with other partners around the production of collective services. Its instrumentalization by the institutions of Bretton Woods conceals the fact that the concept of governance is neither recent, nor solely dedicated to legitimate exogenous reforms aimed at transforming dysfunctioning bureaucracies into providers of quality public services. From the 1970s onwards, public policy analysts in the North have used this notion to describe and

A previous and less elaborated version of this article has been published in French (Blundo, 2001).

analyse changes within the Western democracies, which highlight a 'governability' crisis: the emergence of actors who do not belong to the traditional governmental sphere, but yet play a part in the control of the public affairs, establishing complex relationships (of antagonism, of complementarity or simple juxtaposition) with the state.

However, studies that attempt an ethnography of governance situations are rare. In general, the current debates on governance in Africa fall schematically into two camps. The first conveys a strongly normative and instrumental concept of governance, defined, according to the popular formula, as 'the manner in which power is exercised in the management of a country's economic and social resources for development' (World Bank, 1992: 1).[1] Considered simultaneously as both the problem and as the solution to the crisis in the African states and the failure of structural adjustment policies (Schmitz, 1995), governance then becomes 'a good to strive towards, an ideal to be reached'.[2] From this perspective, the focus has primarily been on the reforms to be implemented in order to move from 'bad' to 'good' governance, synonymous with 'sound development management' (World Bank, 1992: 1): supporting a good administration; increasing the accountability of political leaders and of government officials with respect to the citizens; guaranteeing transparency; and establishing the primacy of the rule of law. That is why the literature produced by research institutes tied to the World Bank is, above all else, demonstrative and prescriptive, the aim being to show that 'governance matters' (Kaufmann et al., 2000; Schacter, 2000) with chosen 'success stories', augmented with statistics, charts and sophisticated indicators — in other words, to legitimize a new form of aid conditionality.

The second camp aims at deconstructing donors' discourses on governance, and less often at analysing practices. Authors like Ferguson (1990) suggested that the World Bank (and more generally 'the development industry') would operate as an 'anti-politics machine', providing 'neutral' technical solutions to problems, stripped beforehand of their ideological and political valence. Whilst this a-political approach to governance is undoubtedly based on the non-political mandate of the World Bank,[3] it also depends on a limited vision of the role of the state, 'as a service provider for the

1. This is not the right place to outline, even briefly, the genealogy of the use of the concept of governance by the international donors, nor to link this concept to those of democratization or political corruption. In spite of differences, notably related to the constraints of political non-interference, contained in the statutes of the World Bank, one can however acknowledge that there is a rather general consensus on the assistance and development co-operation policies inspired by the last neo-liberal paradigm.
2. See Smouts (1998: 86) for a critical analysis of the notion of governance in the sociology of international relations.
3. 'The Bank and its officers shall not interfere in the political affairs of any member; nor shall they be influenced in their decisions by the political character of the member or members concerned. Only economic considerations shall be relevant to their decisions' (Art. 10, sec. 10 of the *Articles of Agreement of the International Bank for Reconstruction and Development*, 1944, quoted in Marquette, 2001: 398).

economy, rather than as a political entity whose legitimacy is derived from the creation of identity for its citizenship and accountability toward them' (Polzer, 2001: 15).

More recently, tensions have been raised at the heart of the reforms for good governance. Firstly, the reforms have a scarcely hidden claim to universality. The calls for transparency, for accountability, for the supremacy of the rule of law so as to guarantee private property, etc., are supposedly based on principles which are desirable and applicable everywhere, regardless of local social and cultural logics, as well as the diverse trajectories of the state, and its historically constructed hybrid forms (Pagden, 1998: 9–10). Secondly, authors like Anders (2003) underlined the paradox of reforms whose ownership is allotted to governments receiving the assistance, whilst being imposed as a condition to obtain this assistance. Finally, it was suggested that the current passion for good governance cannot be dissociated from the debate on the role of the welfare state and its forms of intervention, and thus forms the central element of neo-liberal governmentality.[4] More than a pure and simple withdrawal of the state, it is undoubtedly a question of reorganizing the governmental techniques, of transferring formerly official competences to non-official, individual or collective actors, to whom the qualities of accountability and rationality are granted. Administrative participation, decentralization and transparency have thus to be understood as particular governmental technologies, endowed with their own political rationalities, their own 'govern-*mentalities*' (Ferguson and Gupta, 2002; Lemke, 2001). The stress laid upon the technical aspects of the recommended reforms of official administrations does not prevent the social and political consequences of such interventions, such as rampant or informal privatization (Blundo and Olivier de Sardan, 2001; Hibou, 1999), criminalization of some of the states of the sub-region (Bayart et al., 1997), and the increase of social inequalities.

Between normative and teleological approaches and their excessive criticism, debates on governance and on the public policies associated with it might sink or fall short. To confine oneself to an analysis of the discourses, as post-structuralists or development deconstructionists do (see Escobar, 1991, 1995, 1997), leads to scientific productions afflicted as much by an ethnographic anaemia as by an historical amnesia (Moore, 2000: 659). It is not surprising that when one systematically analyses the recent literature, the African state appears as a 'State without civil servants' (Copans, 2001), a state seized more by its desired or perceived essence than by the reality of its routine functioning. On the other hand, an empirical and comparative ethnography of the 'administrative itineraries' can enlighten the concrete mechanisms by which the African state operates in everyday life, and the social and political logics that contribute to the redeployment or to the disarticulation of public action.

---

4. A conduct that acts on other conducts, as per Foucault (1994).

In this article, I will focus on the administrative brokerage practices observed during comparative research on the mechanisms and representations of petty corruption in Benin, Niger and Senegal,[5] which was built around the relationships between public users and services (in public transport, customs administration, local taxation, public procurements, justice and public health services).[6] I will describe and analyse the role that auxiliary agents, with precarious or informal status, play in various administrative services.

Their designations, as well as their areas of intervention, are certainly varied: touts (*démarcheurs*) or *agents d'affaires*, informal customs brokers (*transitaires ambulants*), tax collectors (*juuti*), 'volunteers of justice' and civil customs personnel. Some work as volunteers or contractors for the administration, and help in collecting taxes, exposing smugglers, and dealing with bureaucratic tasks. Others, informal actors evolving on the fringe of the administration, guide the public services users through the complexities of the Senegalese bureaucracy. I will show that they possess common characteristics: all are ambiguous actors, facilitators and at the same time a 'drawn curtain' between the local state and its citizens. Created by a sometimes opaque, often under-equipped administration, given disproportionate discretionary powers and subject to little control, they contribute, as a footbridge between the civil servants and the population, to the daily functioning of the post-adjustment Senegalese state, involving negotiation, monetized powers, and the creation or adaptation of rules. More precisely, the administrative brokers facilitate the negotiation and the circumvention of the state, by its agents as well as by its users, attracting them on a common ground where the shared standards are different from those which are defined by the bureaucratic organizations.

This article has three parts. The first describes the main functioning logics of the public services observed within the justice, customs and local tax services in Senegal. Characterized by neither a culturalist nor a determinist posture, these logics operate through practices of intermediation and administrative brokerage, which will be analysed in the second section. The third and concluding section will raise more general questions about the emergence of new forms of informal privatization and the progressive institutionalization of the 'informal' as a management mode of the state in everyday life.

---

5. The research, co-ordinated by G. Blundo and J. P. Olivier de Sardan, benefited from funding by the European Commission and the Swiss Development and Co-operation Office (DDC). The persons in charge at the national level are N. Bako-Arifari for Benin, M. Tidiani Alou for Niger and G. Blundo for Senegal. Concerning Senegal, G. Blundo worked mainly on public markets, local municipalities and taxation; Ch. T. Dieye mainly collected the data on customs and P. Monteil on matters of justice. M. Mathieu investigated the fight of institutional mechanisms against corruption. The data presented here come partially from research reports of members of the team who worked on the Senegalese case.
6. For an outline of methodological aspects related to empirical research on corruption, see Blundo and Olivier de Sardan (2000).

JUSTICE, CUSTOMS AND TAX: THE EVERYDAY STATE

A number of factors, supported empirically by our research and not resulting from any cultural or social determinism, facilitate the establishment of intermediary figures within the Senegalese bureaucracy. These are to be found in most of the administrative services studied, but are not due to the government officials alone. The relations and spaces of interaction between the civil servants, the users and the intermediaries, as a whole, determine the functioning, 'for real' (Jaffré, 1999), of the public services. This section will examine these factors.

The Recourse to Voluntary and Auxiliary Personnel

Weakened by the policies of adjustment, and in competition with parallel bureaucracies generated by the develoment co-operation system,[7] government services lack motivated staff and struggle to carry out the main functions of the state. The reform of public services in Senegal started during the second phase of the economic and financial adjustment programme (1985–92), and included, from 1984, measures to freeze wage rises and a restrictive policy on recruitment and promotion. A policy promoting voluntary redundancies began in January 1990; by mid-1992 this had led to the departure of 4,300 agents. This number rises to more than 9,600 (out of a total of 68,000 public agents) if one includes the normal retirements, dismissals and departures related to the reorganization of some services. However, the reforms omitted to improve productivity and efficiency (United Nations, 1999: 31–9).

In spite of the reforms, problems such as plethoric staffs, absenteeism and under-administration persisted in certain sectors. For example, the regional customs office of Kaolack-Fatick, which covers a large area susceptible to illegal transit from Gambia, employs a total of 138 agents. For the whole of the Senegalese judiciary system, there are just sixty-four secretaries of clerks' offices and public prosecutors' departments, of which sixteen are not civil servants. The municipal tax and rates office of Kaolack (*Bureau des recettes et perception municipale*) — a town with more than 240,000 inhabitants and a commercial crossroads at the national level — officially employs only eighteen collectors for market taxes and parking fees, helped by a troop of informal collectors.

In the town of Pikine, thirty-one official collectors and ninety-five volunteers (ADM, 2000: 21) are in charge of the collection of the market

7. According to Berg, whose ten-year assessment of adjustment policies in Senegal (1980–90) highlighted certain tendencies that would worsen in the following decade, the public civil servants were the socio-economic category most affected by the structural adjustment plans (SAPs). If cut-backs spared the high administration, its purchasing power was drastically reduced. Moreover, the public office has seen its authority decline progressively with new agencies of co-ordination and application of the policies, under the aegis of international donors (Berg, 1990: 206).

taxes. To mitigate the staff shortage, recourse to voluntary help is inevitable. All of the services studied have functioned for about twenty years thanks largely to the support of non-administrative, sometimes 'voluntary' personnel — personnel who perform secretarial tasks, drive the customs vehicles, and collect the municipal taxes instead of official collectors.

Informal Privatization of the Administration

The corollary of this staff shortage is the inadequacy (or the bad allocation[8]) of the means to function,[9] generating in certain services financing strategies to complement the poor ministerial budget. Thus the customs administration, faced with the decay of its car fleet and an inadequate monthly fuel allocation (approximately 70 litres for a whole brigade), turns to private economic operators — important tradesmen or hauliers — who do not hesitate to lend them vehicles or money. These private donors will recover their investment, either when fraudulent goods are seized (profiting from auction sales particularly favourable to them, or from direct rebates on the seized goods), or in the form of significant discounts on customs duties at the time of importation procedures.

The local administration also requests the services of private operators in other contexts. It is well known, for instance, that mail from the police force, *gendarmerie*, court, prison, trade services office (*Direction du commerce*), and other offices of the administration, is distributed all over the country by chauffeurs driving vehicles intended for public transport. These same vehicles are lent to the judicial police for transporting prisoners or for raids. Also, when a policeman or a *gendarme* is relocated to another administrative district, the drivers generally move him for a special, low rate.[10] The administration must, in one way or another, return this favour to the donor or provider of informal services. These practices of evergetism,[11] by

8. The report of the national consultation on public services and good governance exposes 'how the means of the Administration are diverted to the profit of the party in power: vehicles, fuel, budget allocations, so as to ensure the life of the basic political structures and public agents (drivers, for example), at the service of the parties in power' (Concertation nationale sur le service public et la bonne gouvernance, 1999b: 10).
9. For example, the budget of the Ministry of Justice for 1998 (which represented 0.81 per cent of the total budget of the state) included 9.5 per cent for material expenditure and only 1.95 per cent for maintenance expenditure. The functioning budget of the regional Court of Tambacounda for the same year amounted to just 441,000 FCFA (about US$ 814). Under these conditions, out of stock forms slow down the delivery of certificates or the lack of file maintenance results in the degradation or the destruction of the documents (Fall, 1998).
10. According to the president of the drivers association of Kaolack, 6 January 2001.
11. Evergetism, a neologism derived from the Greek *evergesy* (act of charity), means contributing, by gifts and other generosities, to the public expenditure of the city (shows, construction of public buildings, etc). In Greek and Roman Antiquity, the figures characterized by their public generosity received the title of *evergetes* (see Veyne, 1976).

no means disinterested, contribute to an 'informal privatization'[12] of certain sectors of public services and generate symbiotic relations between the public and the private sectors: both controlled and controller, authority of the state and private provider of services, share the same places, the same normative space, the same type of activities. This practice of exchanging services and favours, this daily occurrence, creates systems of reciprocal obligation between the partners, and allows the emergence of true corruptive dyads (between customs officers, tradesmen and formal or 'travelling' forwarding agents; between government officials, civil servants and touts (or *agents d'affaires*); between lawyers, prosecutors and prison warders, and so forth).

The Unfolding of the Administration

This phenomenon is particularly observable on two levels. On the one hand there is the inanity of the formal hierarchies — municipal collectors registered as office boys or office clerks in the organization chart; drivers for the departmental court acting as interpreters at hearings; students in the sixth year of medicine writing prescriptions and medical certificates; contractual secretaries playing the role of clerks. There are abundant examples of this phenomenon. In general, one witnesses an upward shift in hierarchies and an undue enhancement of subordinates' roles, which at the same time are characterized by their polysemy.[13] The step is short, from the valorization of the volunteer officially recognized by the administration, to the tolerance of the informal broker (touts, *agent d'affaires*) in the administrative space. Thus, just as contractual workers at the level of clerks' offices have others call them *maître*, we have received reports of touts who pass themselves off as lawyers, or of stretcher-bearers or labourers who, taking advantage of the confusing uniforms of the medical staff, advise patients regarding prescriptions and forward them to parallel pharmacies. This phenomenon is the counterpart of a more general logic at the level of the civil service, where positions of responsibility are assigned not by the criteria of competence and rank, but on a purely political basis (Concertation nationale sur le service public et la bonne gouvernance, 1999b: 10).

On the other hand, the fact is that another classification — this time 'emic' — of the administrative positions superimposed on or opposed to the functional and spatial classification of bureaucratic organizations is produced by the state agents from their own everyday lives. Any customs officer, *gendarme*, treasury official (*Trésor*) or court employee can easily distinguish the lucrative or 'juicy' positions (*poste yu toy*) from the 'dry' positions

12. For a similar analysis of this phenomenon in the field of the management of hydraulics at village level in Niger, see Olivier de Sardan and Dagobi (2000).
13. See Jaffré (1999: 5–6) on health services in Mali.

(*poste yu wow*). The first, sometimes comparable with genuine mangers (*postu lekkukay*), are the positions with a strong density of transactions, those where the holder is on the ground, in direct connection with the users. They allow a very quick accumulation of a rental nature, their allocation generating rough competitions and usually following the logics of political reward. Thus we found that for any customs officer close to retirement, the Port Authority in Dakar (*Port autonome de Dakar*) represents the primary ambition, but that failing this, he would readily accept an assignment in one of the customs posts at the Gambian frontier. The 'dry' positions, with weak enrichment opportunities, are also in remote, isolated places, where the quality of life is poor and where one is likely to be quickly forgotten by the hierarchy; these are perceived as places of expiation for a fault or a chance mishap.

Slow Procedures and Bottlenecks

A shortage of qualified staff generates a work overload in the services. To quote the example of the regional work tribunal (*Tribunal du travail régional*) of Kaolack: in June 2000 the clerk was still working on cases from October 1999. However, the agents can also deliberately create bottlenecks; not to mention the traditional pretext of the file languishing at the bottom of the pile, still a common practice, as indicated by a senegalese judge: 'One has to grease palms as we say, in order to accelerate the administrative machinery to avoid sentences of this kind "there are no more forms, the act is not signed yet". . . . This is what is said everyday to the user who has not been able to decipher the access code to the benefit of the public service'.[14]

The civil services, in particular those in controlling roles like the customs, have a whole arsenal of statutory regulations to extend the waiting time of the users. There is a certain logic to the argument, for instance for the tradesmen and the taxi drivers, who must do as many journeys as possible in order to gain the amount of money they have to give periodically to the owner of the vehicle. Aware of this, the agents abuse their authority to oblige the drivers 'to give something' from their own pockets or to convince the passengers of the vehicle to do it. If they refuse, they will be kept waiting and everyone will be delayed (driver, 9 May 2000, Kaolack).

Opacity, Manipulation and Negotiation

The administrative services work on opacity. Linguistic barriers (codes and regulations written in French), weak publicity of administrative decisions, and the illiteracy of the users are all factors preventing the transparency of

14. 'Rentrée des cours et tribunaux; les facettes de la corruption qui minent la justice', *Walfadjiri* no 2293, p. 2.

administrative procedures.[15] Sometimes the rules are unknown or ignored by those who are supposed to apply them. In everyday life, the formal norms are replaced by pragmatic ones, which are in turn constantly negotiated and manipulated.

The real functioning of the public administration is made up of compromises, negotiations, invention of new rules of the game and monetized powers. Granting, controlling, sanctioning: to exert these three functions, the administrative services have a normative arsenal, sometimes insufficient (for instance in land management), sometimes overabundant (as in the customs domain). Between over-regulation and under-regulation, laws and regulations are often applied using very extensive discretionary powers.

One can punish a smuggler or close one's eyes if the value of the goods is modest. One can still decide to sanction him, and come to an agreement on the amount of the fine. In contexts where administrative laws and regulations are seldom made public but remain unknown to the citizens, the monopoly of technico-bureaucratic knowledge, combined with the weak sense of accountability of the agents with respect to their public, permits the daily negotiation of the powers of administration. This opacity and the selective application of the regulations can lead to strategies of avoidance and anticipation on behalf of the users, as well as encouraging forms of corruption.

Moreover, the system of official norms does not coincide with the system of popular norms. The border between the legal and the illicit becomes fuzzy. It can be moved according to circumstances, by the users of the administration as well as by the government officials, pulled between the duties inherent in their positions and the pressure of social, identity, and political networks: 'The character (*jikko*) of the Senegalese is bargaining (*waxaale*)! When the agents of the Domains come to evaluate the cost of the trading licence for the shop, you must discuss so that they reduce it. So, they begin to say 50,000 FCFA so that after the negotiation, you give them at least 25,000 FCFA' (shopkeeper at the central market of Kaolack, 29 September 2000).

Sometimes, the state voluntarily averts its eyes in situations of crises for which it has no solutions, and thus contributes to the creation of permissive spaces which legitimize, de facto, irregular practices without modifying the regulations. So the urban taxis of Kaolack, approved for five seats, may carry six passengers with impunity. In the same way, the obsoleteness of the carpark and the expensive prices of spare parts in Senegal, are behind a stream of illegal practices (ensuing from the gap between norms, regulations and their possible application), and feed a market of 'accommodating' technical visits.

---

15. According to a recent survey carried out by the Concertation nationale sur le service public et la bonne gouvernance, 'the populations undergo multiple harassment and rebuffs from the government officials, as well as on the level of the central administration as in the regions and departments; they are also often exploited by the civil servants, at all levels and in all services' (1999a: 17).

Embezzlement with Impunity

Both civil servants and users decry the generalized impunity with which embezzlements and other illicit practices are carried out within the administration. The public rumours, allegations and charges in the media are seldom followed by in-depth investigations, let alone by sanctions. The analysis of more than 1,500 articles in the press and certain legal sources confirm the popular perceptions.

Let us consider the 'Court against the illicit acquisition of wealth' (*Cour de répression de l'enrichissement illicite*), created with the advent of Abdou Diouf's presidency. Between September 1981 and April 1983, the special brigade of this Court investigated seventy-one cases of illicit enrichment, which resulted in just two prison sentences or fines. In most of the cases that we have been able to register, the defendants were released because of insufficient evidence.

One can have similar reservations about the work of the 'Court of budgetary discipline' (*Cour de discipline budgétaire*), incorporated in the Revenue Court (*Cour des comptes*) at the time of its creation in February 1999, which sanctions the 'faults of administrative management'. An analysis of the yearly reports of the Court reveals that the judgements seldom involve any action against the agent at fault. Where sanctions are applied, they never take the form of prison sentences, but of fines which are ridiculously low in comparison with the perpetrated embezzlements. If the administrative sanction is accompanied by a transfer (often looking curiously like a promotion), then it is more a relocation of the illicit practices, which will continue in some other place.[16]

Personalization Strategies

There is a Wolof saying: 'The one who has a spoon does not burn his fingers' (*ku am kuddu du lakk*). Contacts between the civil services and the public are marked by mistrust and uncertainty on the part of the users. The general conviction that the administration works with money and acquaintances, and that it is necessary to protect oneself against possible corrupt practices, throws the users into a ceaseless search for personal angles in the relationship.

Before addressing the civil servant behind the counter, the user will look for any real or fictitious bonds that can be evoked. In other words, the user seeks to personalize the administrative relationship. The search for protection

16. It is too early to consider the real impact of the initiatives against corruption undertaken under the new presidency of Me Abdoulaye Wade, elected in March 2000. The results of audits on public companies ordered by the new regime are long overdue. Some files have been handed over to the legal authorities, but it remains to be seen whether the accusations expected by the Senegalese people will spare the socialist caciques who 'migrated' towards the PDS when their party started to decline.

increases when the user becomes a patient or is involved in a police case, and must cross the frightening doors of a hospital or a court: 'It is seldom to see one person . . . answer to a request of the justice, who would yet not take the precaution to inform some acquaintance or a person who would really have relations at this level' (Regional Co-ordinator of the Réseau africain de développement intégré, Kaolack, 11 May 2000).

INTERMEDIATION AND BROKERAGE

In order to increase their negotiating abilities when facing an unpredictable and arbitrary administration, the users initiate themselves into the functioning of the system. Initiation at the level of the local bureaucracy is often done via genuine administrative brokers (office boys, secretaries, ushers, customs informers, volunteers and interpreters), whose personal careers and functions are studied. This strategy, a precondition to the control of non-formal codes, sometimes presupposes the development of a local know-how of corruption.

Touting for Business in the Court and the Registry Services

Provided with a portfolio and stamps, sometimes of uncertain origin, the *agent d'affaires*[17] or tout watches out at the entrance to the law courts or registry offices to intercept any users crossing the threshold. He then offers to facilitate by obtaining an act delivered by the public authority, accelerating a procedure, or advising in a lawsuit. He sometimes manages to replace the lawyer, assuring the client that he will be able 'to arrange his case' thanks to his contacts with the judge. In this latter function he is often in competition with the sworn interpreters. At the interface between the court and the defendant, and accustomed as they are to the courtroom, interpreters are believed to be important figures who can intercede in the trial. The *agent d'affaires* can demonstrate a detailed knowledge of the main procedures necessary to obtain administrative acts, combined with an insider's acquaintance with the civil servants involved. He exploits the eagerness or the ignorance of the user to make him pay for acts which are normally free.

A much sought-after service, and one which generally requires the intervention of a tout, is the issuing of birth certificates. There is a procedure for people who have not had their births registered within the legal deadline, or whose registration has been invalidated by the loss or destruction

17. The body of the *agents d'affaires* was instituted in several countries of the AOF (French Western Africa) during colonial times. In the absence of lawyers, the *agents d'affaires* assisted the parties and could even plead in front of legal institutions. There were no particular requirements for becoming an *agent d'affaires*; an admistrative agreement was sufficient. Today, this function is no longer officially recognized (Ndiaye, 1990: 141–2).

of the register, which allows them to come before a court of authorization for registration, by declaring the events of their civil status in front of the judge of the departmental court. However, this practice is frequently abused, as citizens try to be re-registered (see Madec, 1991: 116). There are multiple motivations to resort to the services of a tout in this way; for instance, if the current residence is too far away from the registry office of his or her birthplace (the only office which can provide the necessary extracts); if one is older than the regular age to go to school; to apply for a grant; to play in the *navétanes* football tournaments; or to take part in a public contest. The tout, in collusion with the registry office, 'helps people to be reborn', in the words of an old man sitting on the steps in front of the registry office of Kaolack.

The user has to address his or her request to the authority of the registry office. This request leads to an investigation at registers' level to check if the user is not already registered. However, the intervention of the *agent d'affaires* often permits a fictitious judgement, sometimes even to modify the identity of delinquents. Moreover, the ease with which it is possible to get registration acts through the *agents d'affaires* encourages the population not to declare births and deaths within the legal timeframe.

The *agent d'affaires* or the tout also plays the role of 'professional witness' in many registry matters (marriages, deaths). These testimony professionals are well known to the civil services, because they return regularly whenever a user requires a registration. Just before the presidential elections of February 2000, the press brought to light the intriguing case of a judge — transferred elsewhere after this case — who had authorized 500 registrations in a locality near to Kaolack, with the assistance of only two witnesses. The role of professional witness in lawsuits is also played by the public writers (*écrivains publics*), old men retired from the civil service who settle in the area of the court, offering to write claims or requests for illiterate people instigating legal proceedings.

Voluntary or contractual personnel can execute other brokerage functions. This is the case with the non-statutory secretaries of the court, who have relatively important positions in the various services of the law court and who contribute substantially to its functioning. These subordinate staff seek out, and find, a supplement to their meagre earning — often lower than the guaranteed minimum wage of 48,000 FCFA. Sometimes a superior acts as a patron, covering the small daily expenses, but when superiors do not provide this support, there are the small preferential treatments, 'the accelerating money' that helps to make ends meet.

These voluntary or contractual personnel use the means they have at their disposal (a typewriter and some paper in most cases) to provide paying customers with services such as the typing of documents; or they receive the 'price of the cola nut' for giving advice. In the provinces, they also work for lawyers who do not have secretaries, or they type urgent documents for *agents d'affaires*. Others are tempted to exploit their position to follow less virtuous paths:

> So at the beginning of 2000, the first magistrates' court of the regional tribunal (*1ère chambre correctionnelle du tribunal*) of Dakar had to rule on a case, implicating six 'justice volunteers', whose statute comes under that of auxiliary staff, appointed to record decisions and do the photocopying at the clerk's office of the regional court. The scandal related to the registration of the trade register and to a network fabricating false receipts. (Diarra, 2000)

The 'diverting' of printed forms, which are then resold to clients, claiming to help them out in a (fictitious) out-of-stock situation is also common.

Another current practice — although expressly prohibited by the Association of Barristers — is the touting of customers for the lawyers via the prison warders. The latter, taking advantage of the distress of the defendant and his family, offer the services of a local lawyer, whose fees are harshly negotiated, and on which they will get a commission. Especially in Dakar, the touting job (*rabattage*) of the guards favours a few lawyers, systematically present at the audiences for flagrant offences and at criminal hearings. As one informant put it: 'the defendant who has been arrested, placed in the hands of the law, meets his guard as first interlocutor, and it is he who makes him realise that his case is serious, that he needs a lawyer and that the best lawyer in his case is Mr So-and-so'. The penitentiary guards carry out the same function for some prosecutors, known in the wings of the court to have a 'tariff to be released on bail' (S. B., Kaolack, 30 April 2000).

Auxiliary Personnel in the Customs Services

The customs authorities regularly employ auxiliary staff as drivers, trackers, informers or intelligence agents. Whilst the civilians mitigate the lack of agents in the customs services, overall it is their knowledge in the field, their control of the tracks and paths in the bush, their experience of the routes that the convoys of smugglers take, that make them particularly valuable to the customs officers:

> The customs officer and civilian are complementary individuals. It is like a blind person and her guide; without the latter, the blind person can not go anywhere; the customs officer alone cannot arrest a smuggler without his help, because he does not know the bush. It happens to be us, the civilians, who are in the best position to track the smugglers. (A. G., civil driver for the customs, Kaolack, 5 January 2001).

But there is also another side to the coin:

> No head of customs brigades can manage his job efficiently without co-operating with civilians. If one would, for example, try to suppress the civil auxiliaries, the revenues would fall rapidly, because these staff would then help the smugglers by giving them all the information on the customs officers. If the civilians do not get any favours from the customs officers,

they would end up on the side of the smugglers of Touba. (A. D., customs informer, 18 June 2000).

The informers accompany the customs officers on rounds organized by the mobile brigades and lasting one or two weeks; once in the bush, they have great freedom of action. They follow the tyre tracks of vehicles transporting fraudulent goods; they are also in the front line when the load of an intercepted truck has to be checked or to negotiate with the drivers. Although mostly recruited as informal informers, they have now become real actors in the customs operations on the ground. As local people, they provide guidance in the control operations to the customs officers who are periodically transferred and relocated.

However, at the same time, they know all the smugglers of the zone. In the frontier areas of Gambia, where we carried out most of our surveys, this activity is an essential source of income for a large part of the population. Informers and trackers thus represent a kind of filter for customs interventions; they are able to negotiate payments from the smuggler to avoid the confiscation of his goods (payments which will be partly redistributed to the customs hierarchy); they can also protect drug dealers by seizing the narcotics and letting them go. An informer told us that their category 'is in perfect harmony with the smugglers: we know them personally, we go to their family ceremonies'.

The remuneration of these civilian staff is not budgeted in the customs regulations. It is left to the customs officer in charge of the operation. He can choose to register them so that they benefit from 24 per cent of the value of the litigious goods meant for the chiefs and the seizing staff. Alternatively, they are paid in kind, with part of the seized goods or in cash, depending upon the goodwill of the customs officer. For each vehicle caught, the profits for the trackers and informers can amount to 125,000 FCFA.

Local Taxation: Collectors and Assistant-Collectors

At the level of municipalities in Senegal, daily market taxes and parking fees for trucks and vehicles that transport passengers are collected by municipal agents under the control of the market's supervisor, part of the tax and rates office. Each collector (called *juuti* locally, a Wolof word derived from the English term *duty*) is helped by two or three assistants, who in turn can hire other helpers. This pyramid of delegation, in the case of the commune of Kaolack, increases the *juuti* manpower from eighteen to approximately a hundred. This phenomenon has been known to the authorities for a long time and is accepted by the treasury administration and by the municipal police as a necessary evil. It represents a clear example of the shift to the top of the hierarchies mentioned in the introduction, and it raises questions as to the means of remuneration for this troop of 'barefoot civil servants'.

On the one hand, the use of assistants — usually recruited from within the circle of the collector — reduces the need for the latter to visit the field. Generally, the collector receives the ticket books early in the morning at the tax office, which records the first serial number of each book. He then gives the books to his assistants, who share the various collection sectors (markets, main entries to the city, transport stations). The assistants immediately distribute the tickets to the traders and small stallholders, returning about noon to collect the tax. There are several reasons for this double visit: the collectors have to wait until the small shopkeepers are solvent, which is not likely to be the case at the beginning of the day, when they have not yet sold anything. But we were also told of a belief among the tradesmen that touching the ticket of a *juuti* before starting to sell compromises the business of the day. The *juuti* brings misfortune — *defay ùmmate* — therefore one must avoid him.

However, another hypothesis may explain this deferred payment. Each sector of the market is periodically tested by the municipal services in order to assess its profitability. These incursions by the market supervisor and a municipal policeman make it possible to know the value of the sector under normal conditions, that is, when everyone pays the daily tax. A collector who returns to the tax office with sums obviously lower than the fixed scale could be sanctioned. The preliminary distribution of the tickets makes it possible for the *juuti* to have an idea of the real tax revenues of the day, and then to organize his diversion strategy for a part of these receipts.

The assistant-collector does not receive any official remuneration, apart from some rebate on the productivity bonuses allotted quarterly to his boss. He must therefore make 'arrangements' with the merchants. Some will pay the official rate, and will receive a ticket, whereas others will slip half of the due taxes into the pocket of the *juuti*, and will not, of course, get any ticket. A panoply of strategies is therefore possible to circumvent the (rare) controls: tickets without dates given to several tradesmen on the same day; the use of counterfoils instead of actual tickets; forged notebooks and double accountancy, and so forth. Those who go to the field, the assistant-collectors, will have to give a part of their daily remuneration to their superiors; the question is, on which hierarchical level the redistribution of the illicit profits stops (see also Hagberg and Juul, this issue).

THE DAILY NEGOTIATION OF THE PRIVATIZED LOCAL STATE

The phenomena sketched above are nothing new in Senegal (nor in the other countries of the sub-region). These intermediary figures were already at the heart of relations between bureaucratic apparatuses and populations in the colonial government. More recently, forms of brokerage in the field of development have also been identified (Bierschenk et al., 2000; Blundo, 1995).

However, the dynamics described in this article have a new dimension. One might expect that this kind of administrative brokerage and the institutionalization of voluntary and auxiliary personnel would become more significant as a result of structural adjustment measures, which have, since the 1980s, succeeded in imposing the 'less state' dictat, without generating a 'better state'. But the *agents d'affaires* and other auxiliary staff — unlike the colonial politico-administrative brokers or the current brokers in development — do not represent the culturally different worlds of colonial enhancement and developmental co-operation. On the contrary, they share the same culture, the same behaviours, and the same attitudes as the civil servants and their public.

The generalization of administrative brokers thus represents an internal form of privatization of the state. It is not so much that the state takes the initiative (either freely or in response to external pressures) to turn to private intermediaries, delegating some of its former functions, as in the case of the partial privatization of the customs administration. Rather, the formal process of delegation of state functions to private actors is being replaced by an informal process of appropriation of the procedures and means — procedures and means that are now prerogative of the state more in appearance than in substance.

There is thus a *de facto* privatization of administrative action occurring, which has the following features: a) it is not the exclusive act of government agents, but results from the interaction between civil servants, intermediaries and users of public services; b) it relies upon arrangements made possible by the shared mobilization of practical rules, behaviours and logics that are alien to the public sphere; c) this whole group of rules, behaviours and logics brings to mind the characteristics of the so-called informal sector of the economy — an acceptance of weak profit margins, a predilection for negotiating and bargaining, and the settlement of agreements according to the principle of orality (Niane, 2000: 7).

For the civil servants, the income accrued from their lucrative positions must be shared with the one to whom they owe their public office. Their enrichment opportunities will depend upon their ability to balance constraint and accommodation, to wave the bureaucratic standard while suggesting ways to circumvent it, to excel in the art of transforming a subject without rights, or a troublesome user, into a customer worthy of attention and concern when the latter calls on the family, the Party or appeals to his pocket.

For the user, the important trick is to defend himself as well as possible against the multiple forms of corruption, and to transform them into negotiation processes borrowed from the models of current sociability. He is not so much a citizen who asserts the re-establishment of the rule of law, as an actor seeking — not without difficulty — minimum rights of access to the public services.

As for the brokers, they are just as essential to the official agents as to the customers of the civil services. Sometimes full members of the organizational chart of the institution, sometimes registered within hidden, parallel, phantom hierarchies, or sometimes at the margins of the bureaucratic apparatus, these actors have very different personal itineraries and play very different roles within the services (customs, local taxation, justice); one can, nevertheless, outline some common elements by way of conclusion.

First of all, professional experience and social capital acquired in the past constitute an essential asset. For the touts or *agents d'affaires,* for example, who are often retired civil servants, the capital of practical knowledge, but above all, the capital of relations, make it difficult to refuse them certain favours, which allows them to establish or consolidate collusions with the current civil servants. For those with no bureaucratic past, training is done 'on the job'. One acquires the necessary gestures and routines, but with restricted significance. Administrative brokers have a thorough knowledge of the various administrative and legal steps, but without sharing or knowing the ethical standards, or the meaning of the administrative procedure.

Secondly, building up years in the service, even as a simple volunteer, turns the intermediaries into guardians of the oral memory of the institution: they know its secrets, they are able to guide and advise the new chiefs. However, one also remains in place thanks to the strategic importance of the particular function. So, according to a lawyer from Dakar, the guards of the regional court of Dakar are seldom transferred elsewhere:

> They have been there for over ten years; they do not move and if they are transferred, they leave for fifteen days only and then return, God knows by which miracle because the prosecutor's office, which must give them a grade saying that 'such agent is good, we still need him here', is perhaps composed of a more or less high percentage of people practising underground with them. (Me S. B., Kaolack, 30 April 2000).

These middlemen of the administration are the object of ambivalent perceptions amongst the actors on whose behalf they mediate. Those at the service of the control and tax institutions (customs, municipal collectors) inherit the same negative popular perceptions as their employers. Just like the customs officer, the informer, the tracker or the tax collector, they are objects of avoidance and held in contempt by the population. The customs officer and the *juuti* are cursed characters, who will go to hell (*dina ñu dem safara*), because they live on others' efforts (*ñaxu jambur*), earning their living in an impure way (*ribaa*), growing rich on the backs of the weak (*dañuy lekk allalu néew doole yi*).

Sometimes the administration, although in constant touch with the brokers, denies their existence and refuses to recognize their legitimacy. The agents act as if they were ordinary users. But most of the touts are known in the services, which tolerate them because they constitute a protective shield for the misdeeds of the public agents. One may wonder, for instance, about the effectiveness of the Circular of 2000 by the former Minister for

Justice, Madior Boye, which aimed to regulate the access to the court of the *agents d'affaires* and the public writers, in order to put an end to the anarchy prevailing in the temple of Thémis.

In spite of any suspicions, these actors at the interface between the public services and their users are of great value to, and much appreciated by, the latter. They personalize the administrative procedures, while reassuring the citizen facing what he sees as an all-powerful administration. They undoubtedly contribute to speeding up procedures — to the detriment of those users who did not have recourse to them. Sometimes, they can also protect their customer, perhaps in avoiding sanctions or in improving their client's chances of winning a case or asserting his rights.

If not systematic vectors of corruption, they can nevertheless contribute to a blurring of the lines and the trivialization of illicit practices. The constant recourse to intermediaries in daily social exchanges (a marriage proposal, the loan of a field, the purchase of cattle) — the 'brokerage logic' outlined by Olivier de Sardan (1996) — makes it commonplace in all administrative steps. Yet it might be admitted that the intervention of the brokers makes it possible to 'confuse the issue' and to erase the evidence of an illicit transaction, just as it makes a corrupting exchange possible between individuals with strongly unequal statutes. Boundaries between corruption and deception are inevitably vague: the person to be tried will never know if the tout talking to the prosecutor is simply passing the time of day or if he is, in fact, interceding for him.

The ubiquitous nature of intermediation practices, whether spontaneous or sought by the administration, exemplifies the process of institutionalization of the informal, which paradoxically makes it possible to ensure the continuity of bureaucratic institutions. At the same time, the brokers, touts and *agents d'affaires* also contribute to a process of negotiation and reorientation (if not delegitimization) of the actions of the administrative services, importing new rules and new modes of circumvention.

In the current context of privatization of the local state, on the part of its agents as well as its users, representations of public office change. Careers within the administration undoubtedly take new paths and the myths of economic success are no longer exclusively dependent, in popular perceptions, on insertion into the government apparatus. It remains to be seen how the standards of public ethics will evolve, in a system in which honesty may become an exceptional quality.

REFERENCES

ADM (Agence de développement municipal) (2000) 'Diagnostic financier de la ville de Pikine'. Dakar: ADM.

Anders, G. (2003) 'An Ethnography of "Loan Arrangements" between the Bretton Woods Institutions and the Government of Malawi: Good Governance as Technology'. Paper presented at the workshop 'Order and Disjuncture: The Organisation of Aid and Development', SOAS, London (26–28 September).

Bayart, J. (1989) *L'Etat en Afrique. La politique du ventre*. Paris: Fayard.
Bayart, J., S. Ellis and B. Hibou (1997) *La criminalisation de l'Etat en Afrique*. Brussels and Paris: Ed. Complexe ('Espace international').
Berg, E. (1990) 'Adjustment Postponed: Economic Policy Reform in Senegal in the 1980s'. Report prepared for USAID, Dakar (October).
Bierschenk, T., J. P. Chauveau and J. P. Olivier de Sardan (eds) (2000) *Courtiers en développement. Les villages africains en quête de projets*. Paris: Karthala.
Blundo, G. (1995) 'Les courtiers du développement en milieu rural sénégalais', *Cahiers d'Études Africaines* 35(137): 73–99.
Blundo, G. (2001) 'Négocier l'Etat au quotidien: agents d'affaires, courtiers et rabatteurs dans les interstices de l'administration sénégalaise', *Autrepart* 20: 75–90.
Blundo, G. and J. P. Olivier de Sardan (2000) 'La corruption comme terrain. Pour une approche socio-anthropologique', in G. Blundo (ed.) *Monnayer les pouvoirs. Espaces, mécanismes et représentations de la corruption*, pp. 21–46. Paris: PUF; Genève: IUED.
Blundo, G. and J. P. Olivier de Sardan (2001) 'La corruption quotidienne en Afrique de l'Ouest', *Politique Africaine* 83(October): 8–37.
Concertation nationale sur le service public et la bonne gouvernance (1999a) 'Enquête auprès des usagers du service public. Résultats préliminaires', Dakar (July).
Concertation nationale sur le service public et la bonne gouvernance (1999b) Rapport sur le thème: 'La société face à l'administration publique', Dakar (November).
Coolidge, J. and S. Rose-Ackerman (2000) 'Kleptocracy and Reform in African Regimes: Theory and Examples', in K. R. Hope and B. C. Chikulo (eds) *Corruption and Development in Africa. Lessons from Country Case-Studies*, pp. 57–86. New York: St. Martin's Press.
Copans, J. (2001) 'Afrique noire: un État sans fonctionnaires?', *Autrepart* 20: 11–26.
Darbon, D. (1990) 'L'Etat prédateur', *Politique Africaine* 39: 37–45.
Diarra, M. (2000) 'Démarcheurs, rabatteurs au palais de justice', *Sud quotidien* 8 June.
Escobar, A. (1991) 'Anthropology and the Development Encounter: The Making and Marketing of Development Anthropology', *American Ethnologist* 18(4): 658–82.
Escobar, A. (1995) *Encountering Development. The Making and Unmaking of the Third World*. Princeton, NJ: Princeton University Press.
Escobar, A. (1997) 'Anthropologie et développement', *Revue Internationale des Sciences Sociales* 154: 539–59.
Fall, A. (1998) 'L'incidence d'une bonne distribution de la justice sur la croissance économique. Sécurité juridique et sécurité judiciaire', in *Actes de la session de formation continue sur 'Justice et transparence'*. Proceedings of CFJ/Cour de Cassation/USAID conference, Saly Portudal, Senegal (30 July – 1 August).
Fatton, R. (1992) *Predatory Rule: State and Civil Society in Africa*. Boulder, CO: Lynne Rienner Publishers.
Ferguson, J. (1990) *The Anti-Politics Machine. Development, Depolitization and Bureaucratic Power in Lesotho*. Cambridge: Cambridge University Press.
Ferguson, J. and A. Gupta (2002) 'Spatializing States: Toward an Ethnography of Neoliberal Governmentality', *American Ethnologist* 29(4): 981–1002.
Foucault, M. (1994) 'La gouvernementalité', in D. Defert, F. Ewald and J. Lagrange (eds) *Dits et Écrits* 4 vol. Text 239, t. III, pp. 635–57. Paris: Gallimard.
Hibou, B. (ed.) (1999) *La privatisation des États*. Paris: Karthala.
Jaffré, Y. (1999) 'Les services de santé "pour de vrai". Politiques sanitaires et interactions quotidiennes dans quelques centres de santé (Bamako, Dakar, Niamey)', *Bulletin de l'APAD* 17: 3–17.
Kaufman, D., A. Kraay and P. Zoido-Lobaton (2000) 'Governance Matters'. Policy Research Working Papers no 2196. Washington, DC: World Bank Institute.
Lemke, T. (2001) '"The Birth of Bio-Politics": Michel Foucault's Lecture at the Collège de France on Neo-Liberal Governmentality', *Economy and Society* 30(2): 190–207.

Lipsky, M. (1980) *Street-level Bureaucracy. Dilemmas of the Individual in Public Services*. New York: Russel Sage Foundation.
Madec, J. Y. (1991) 'Un cas concret de relations difficiles entre l'administration et le public: l'état civil et les pièces d'identité', *Revue des institutions politiques et administratives du Sénégal* 25/26(January/December): 109–120.
Mamdani, M. (1996) *Citizen and Subject: Contemporary Africa and the Legacy of Late Colonialism*. Princeton, NJ: Princeton University Press.
Marquette, H. (2001) 'Corruption, Democracy and the World Bank', *Crime, Law & Social Change* 36: 395–407.
Medard, J. F. (1977) *L'Etat sous-développé au Cameroun*. Paris: Pedone, 'L'Année africaine'.
Medard, J. F. (1991) 'L'Etat néo-patrimonial en Afrique noire', in J. F. Médard (ed.) *Etats d'Afrique noire*, pp. 323–54. Paris: Karthala.
Moore, D. S. (2000) 'The Crucible of Cultural Politics: Reworking "Development" in Zimbabwe's Eastern Highlands', *American Ethnologist* 26(3): 654–89.
Ndiaye, Y. (1990) 'Les auxiliaires de la justice', *Afrique contemporaine* 156: 140–6.
Niane, B. (2000) 'L'informel au Sénégal: un nouveau paradigme face à la crise de l'État?', communication at the colloquium 'État et acteurs émergents en Afrique', Maison des Sciences de l'Homme, Paris (16–18 November).
Olivier de Sardan, J. P. (1996) 'L'économie morale de la corruption en Afrique', *Politique Africaine* 63(October): 97–116.
Olivier de Sardan, J. P. and A. E. Dagobi (2000) 'La gestion communautaire sert-elle l'intérêt public? Le cas de l'hydraulique villageoise au Niger', *Politique Africaine* 80(December): 153–68.
Pagden, A. (1998) 'La genèse de la "gouvernance" et l'ordre mondial "cosmopolitique" selon les Lumières', *Revue Internationale des Sciences Sociales* 155: 9–17.
Polzer, T. (2001) 'Corruption: Deconstructing the World Bank Discourse'. Working Paper Series no 01-18. London: Development Studies Institute, London School of Economics.
Reno, W. (1995) *Corruption and State Politics in Sierra Leone*. Cambridge: Cambridge University Press.
Schacter, M. (2000) 'Sub-Saharan Africa: Lessons from Experience in Supporting Sound Governance'. ECD Working Paper Series No 7. Washington, DC: World Bank Operations Evaluation Department.
Schmitz, G. J. (1995) 'Democratization and Demystification: Deconstructing "Governance" as Development Paradigm', in D. B. Moore and G. J. Schmitz (eds) *Debating Development Discourse. Institutional and Popular Perspectives*, pp. 54–90. London: Macmillan Press.
Smouts, M. C. (1998) 'Du bon usage de la gouvernance en relations internationales', *Revue Internationale de Sciences Sociales* 155: 85–94.
United Nations (1999) *Monographies sur les réformes de l'administration publique de quelques pays africains. Burkina Faso, Côte d'Ivoire, Ghana, Sénégal*. New York: United Nations.
Veyne, P. (1976) *Le pain et le cirque. Sociologie historique d'un pluralisme politique*. Paris: Le Seuil.
World Bank (1992) 'Governance and Development'. Washington, DC: The World Bank.

Decentralization, Local Taxation and Citizenship in Senegal

Kristine Juul

INTRODUCTION

What makes people willing or unwilling to pay taxes, and to whom are they willing to pay? At least until recently the issue of taxation and resource mobilization has received scant attention in the African context. As indicated by Therkildsen (2001a: 99), African power holders rarely raise the issue of taxation levels or other types of resource mobilization in public debate, nor are they highlighted in party programmes. Among political scientists dealing with democratization of the African state, the issue has often remained unaddressed and poorly understood.

Through the 1990s, when economic and political liberalization were seen as going hand in hand, and decentralization became a means to promote both economic development and democracy in developing countries, more attention was given to the role of taxation, not least to its supposed role in strengthening state–society relations. Inspired by the works of Tilly (1992, 1995), who attributes an instrumental role to revenue collection in the formation of the European nation states, issues of public revenue and tax collection are now being taken up by donors and financial institutions such as the World Bank and IMF, as part of the so-called governance programme. According to these agencies, the declining economic capacity of poor African states constitutes an opportunity for local governments to start implementing tax reforms. Such reforms, it is claimed, could contribute to limiting the present gap between state and society by making state elites more dependent on public revenue and thus more accountable to taxpayers. In this way, taxation would help to strengthen democratic structures, as taxpayers are likely to meet attempts to increase tax levels with demands for either improved public services or more political representation, as was the case in Europe some hundred years ago.

The interest in taxation is also part of a general policy of decentralization aimed at increasing political and fiscal autonomy for local rural structures and, in relation to this, attempts to introduce and consolidate multiparty politics at local level. According to the new doctrine of good governance, accountability and implementation of development policy can be enhanced by politically empowering the population, as political competition between different parties is supposed to increase transparency and accountability towards the local taxpayers and hence encourage the adoption of new political strategies and new forms of representation. This in turn would alter previously clientelistic relations with the citizenry and change the neo-patrimonial nature of Senegalese society (Beck, 2001: 602). As local governments can draw on insider knowledge and generate local commitment and contributions needed for sustainable development, these institutions are seen not only as intrinsically more democratic, but also as more efficient resource managers (ibid.: 609). Public revenue and taxation obviously play a very important role in this process as a means to provide public services and hence generate legitimacy to local, decentralized bodies of the state.

The mounting pressure to introduce new taxes does not stem from local governments themselves. Nonetheless, it has become a particularly pressing issue for local governments in Africa that have benefited from the current worldwide trend towards decentralization, albeit without the financial resources to fulfil their responsibilities (ibid.: 602). Due to decreasing funds many poor African states have tended to withdraw or limit public expenditures, leaving it to local political structures to fund the infrastructural and social development projects demanded by their constituents (schools, health-care, and so forth). Now revenue targets have become major components of aid conditionality; at the same time, donors are increasingly revising their aid programmes so that matching funds are required from the local communities. This leaves local governments with little other choice than to strengthen their ability to mobilize local financial and bureaucratic resources. For, as James Manor suggests, authorities at the local level will founder if they lack the political power and resources to implement important development projects (Manor, 1999: 70).

Experiences with local taxation in the village of Barkedji in northern Senegal seem to be representative of the reaction of local Senegalese citizens to tax reforms. Since 1996 tax collection has been transferred from the state agent (the *sous-préfet*) to locally elected councillors, a process which has turned tax payment into a key issue in the local political process, if only because of the lack of its execution: revenue collection has experienced a steady decline since the transfer. By 2001 the rural councils found themselves paralysed by lack of development funds. Indeed, the situation was so bad that the rural council, unable to provide the required counterpart entry sum of 300,000 CFA (approximately 4,573 Euro) was about to miss out on a 15 million CFA health project from USAID.[1] This project, comprising the building and equipping of five primary health care centres and the purchase of an ambulance, would greatly benefit the population in an area otherwise largely deprived of any substantial health facilities.[2] As projected tax revenues amount to around 6 million CFA per year, the contribution ought to

1. 100 CFA francs = 0.152449 Euro.
2. The closest hospitals are between 30 and 100 km from the villages of Barkedji *arrondissement*.

have been achievable. However, although Barkedji is characterized by a relatively large group of well-to-do farmers and traders, tax recovery in 2001 was close to nil. Unable to raise the money among the future beneficiaries, the councillors were forced to borrow the money from the district health administration, which in turn took control of the ambulance.

This acute financial deficiency of the rural council was not a single event, but rather the culmination of a long decline through which tax recovery dropped from around 70 per cent before 1993 to around 0.5 per cent in 2001.[3] Nor is the dramatic reduction in tax revenue peculiar to Barkedji: throughout Senegal, administrators, experts and elected officials admit that taxes rarely exceed 10 per cent of the potential revenue, making the levying of taxes one of the major difficulties in the decentralization process. The situation appears to be a direct result not only of the transfer of responsibility to locally elected bodies, but also of the introduction of multiparty politics in the Senegalese countryside. In the 2000 presidential elections, the Socialist Party lost its hegemonic position in the country, leaving local inhabitants uncertain as to who was worthy of their allegiance, and hence to whom it was safe to pay a tax.

Why have Senegalese citizens developed such a reticence towards tax levying through locally elected institutions, even though the funds are, in the vast majority of cases, supposed to be used to improve much-needed services such as healthcare, water supply and so on? Is the widespread tax evasion a sign of the lack of trust in locally elected bodies due to increased political competition? Or are the attempts to create accountable and transparent institutions able to provide taxpayers with public goods and services suffering from competition with local efforts at resource mobilization carried out through other types of organizations? And what does that tell us about models of accountability and feelings of citizenry, of belonging to a community or to a nation-state?

If citizens in Senegal are reluctant to pay taxes to their local institutions (and to their national governments), it may be interesting to take a closer look at the role attributed to taxation in political theory on nation building and at the relationship between taxation and democracy (see also Blundo, this issue).

TAXING, CITIZENRY AND THE DOCTRINE OF GOOD GOVERNANCE

> 'How did citizenship come into being anyway? And what was it? If citizenship is a tie entailing mutual obligations between categorically-defined persons and a state, the identity "citizen" describes the experienced and public representation of that tie. Such an identity does not spring whole from a deliberate invention of a general principle's ineluctable implication but from the historical accumulation of continual negotiation'. (Tilly, 1995: 227)

3. The figures from 1993 are taken from the minutes of the rural council, the rest are estimates made by the *sous-préfet* and his deputy.

The positive merits ascribed to taxation in relation to state building stem in large part from the writings of Charles Tilly (1992) who conceives taxation as a key issue in explaining the emergence of nation states, citizenry and political institutions in Western Europe. Particularly the English form of democracy developed through an institutional sequence where taxation and public revenue provided the foundation for development of a central government through the creation of a corporate legal framework and the institutional mechanisms of the capitalist market. Although taxation and public revenue were institutionalized under non-democratic rule, they were struggled and negotiated over, representing an important part of 'the historical accumulation of continual negotiation' leading to citizenry as outlined by Tilly in the quotation above. The English pioneers of welfare state thinking (the Fabians) likewise saw taxation not as an obstacle to political liberalization but rather as a basis for it, through the necessary union of taxation with representation which in the end would lead to democracy. Hence, democracy, at least in the English version, 'builds its entire modus operandi on the foundation of revenue generation, control and allocation' (Guyer, 1992: 42).

According to Tilly, taxes are crucial as states cannot exercise, retain or accumulate power without financial resources. This became particularly apparent in the western European states after 1750, when mercenaries were largely replaced by regular armies drawn from the domestic populations, requiring new taxes to pay for the troops. Unlike the mercenaries, the new forms of military organization could not live by preying on their countrymen, as this was likely to undermine future possibilities for economic growth and potential taxation. Instead the state negotiated with the wealthier layers of society to pay taxes on a regular basis. In return they would gain influence on military issues and diplomatic policies and operations, which they needed in the competition with other trading nations. Key to this process was negotiation and representation:

> Ordinary people, to be sure, bore the costs of these new expensive military systems. But ordinary people and their patron fought war-impelled taxation, conscription, seizure of goods and restrictions on trade by means ranging from passive resistance to outright rebellion, put down with varying combinations of repression, persuading and bargaining. The very acts of intervening, repressing, persuading and bargaining formed wily nily institutions of direct rule. (Tilly, 1995: 230).

The crucial role of taxation in the shaping of citizenry and identity in early European states may be attributed primarily to warfare and military build-up through tax collection which, it is held, paradoxically contributed to the civilization of the state and of national politics. It is hence an ironic side-effect that this then reduced the military's autonomous political power.

Indeed, what is neutrally labelled as nation building was initially founded on the taxation of poor peasants and artisans, the forced sale of animals destined for dowry, the imprisonment of leaders as hostages to force local communities to pay taxes, and the use of military or police force to ensure tax payment (Tilly, 1992). But through a long history of resistance, struggles and negotiation, taxation became less brutal. Political struggles between power holders and capital owners over taxation led to increased political representation and to the provision of state financed services as a compensation for more stable provision of public revenue. In this way, taxation and disputes over the use of revenues stimulated the development of greater citizen rights and privileges, with democratic institutions enforcing accountability and greater transparency in expenditure (Fjeldstad, 2001: 290).

Taxation and the Anti-democratic Effects of Aid Dependency

Active revenue collection may therefore be an important means to keep the state machinery alive and active at the grassroots level. The more a state earns its income through the operation of a bureaucratic apparatus for tax collection, the more it needs to enter into reciprocal arrangements with its citizens about provision of services and representation in exchange for tax contributions. The focus on taxation as a vehicle for democracy has recently been brought into the debate about African democracy and state formations. Here particular emphasis is given to the anti-democratic effects of aid dependency: it is argued that a major reason for the failure of African states to develop greater citizen rights and privileges, as well as democratic institutions enforcing accountability and greater transparency in expenditure, is found in the replacement of taxation with development aid.

According to Moore, democracy may be regarded as 'a sub-set of a broader concept of accountability of the state to society where a polity is democratic only to the extent that there are institutionalised mechanisms through which the mass of population exercise control over the political elite in an organised fashion' (Moore, 2001, cited in Therkildsen, 2001a: 112). States which rely on a high degree of unearned income derived from aid or various forms of economic rent may therefore undermine the emergence of effective democratic governance as minimal efforts are used to raise revenues by direct forms of taxation agreed with citizens through political involvement (Therkildsen, 2001a: 112). As volumes of aid in many African countries are far more substantial than other incomes, the states have become relatively independent of their own subjects. Donors have thus contributed to undermining the values of democracy and good governance by reducing (or eradicating) the bargaining over budgets and over tax policies that would otherwise be primary ways in which state and societal goals are reconciled in democracy.

Unlike the representative governments of western Europe, which originated in political struggles between rulers and private owners of capital, the fiscal independence experienced in many African countries is therefore likely to have adverse outcomes, giving way to weak states which are heavily dependent on patrimonial and personal linkages in running government and rely more on coercion to raise revenues. Without active revenue raising, states cannot be expected to be responsive to the needs of the citizens or to consult and be accountable to them. According to donor agencies such as the World Bank and the IMF, the declining economic opportunities of the African states constitute an opportunity to implement tax reforms that can contribute to limit the present gap between state and society by making state elites more accountable to tax payers.

Formal and Informal Taxation

In spite of the merits attributed to taxation as a means to provide services and thereby legitimize local decentralized bodies of state, the collection of taxes has not been meet with any particular enthusiasm in African rural settings. Studies from many different developing countries indicate that it is not uncommon for half or more of the potential tax revenue to remain uncollected (Addison and Levin, 2004; Fjeldstad and Semboja, 2001; Moore, 2001, 2004).

In the literature on taxation in developing countries, this is usually attributed to factors such as the taxpayers' inability to pay, and a lack of clarity with respect to obligations and reasons for paying. Some suggest that the unwillingness to pay is a political protest against the degradation of public services, perceptions of unfairness over charges which do not reflect the ability to pay, or against corruption and other administrative failings (Tripp, 1997 cited in Fjeldstad and Semboja, 2001: 2060). All agree, however, that the high levels of tax non-payment in developing countries is a cause for concern, as it affects both vertical and horizontal equity and the ability of governments to provide crucial public services. There is also a moral aspect to tax evasion, as citizens' disrespect for the tax laws may go together with disrespect for other laws and thus contribute to undermining the legitimacy of government (Graetz et al., 1996 cited in Fjeldstad and Semboja, 2001: 2059).

Justifications for tax reforms are usually based on the perception highlighted above that current tax efforts in developing countries, and particularly in Africa, are weak. However, effective tax rates (including indirect taxes) can be excessively high, particularly if one adds various forms of informal taxation, such as family obligations, user charges, various self-help activities and so forth (Addison and Levin, 2004: 8). If these more invisible aspects of taxation are included, a quite different picture emerges regarding the willingness of African citizens to pay taxes. This raises other important questions: to whom are people willing to pay? What are their motives for being willing to pay in these cases?

As one of the few studies on informal taxation shows, mobilization of resources cannot be seen only in terms of revenues gathered through formal channels (Prud'homme, 1992). Prud'homme stresses that although tax collection is, normally and in principle, a highly visible and very formal activity,[4] taxation can also be invisible and informal. He defines informal taxation as 'non-formal means utilised to finance the provision of public goods and services' (ibid.: 2). In his case study from Zaire, Prud'homme found that the magnitude of taxes collected outside the formal government and tax system was five to ten times the magnitude of formal taxes recorded in the accounts of local bodies (ibid.: 16).

The types of informal taxes fell into two broad categories: public informal taxes, operated by government officials, which serve to complement the formal system; and private informal taxes, collected by private individuals, which are substitutes to the formal system. Prud'homme divides public informal taxation into 'pinch', 'extortions' and 'requisitions', carried out by civil servants in need to increase their wages. Pinch may, for example, be related to formal revenue collection, where parts of the taxes 'evaporate' in the process. In contrast, extortions are amounts paid to semi local governments in connection with authorizations and rules, either to be able to break the law, or as amounts given to obtain an authorization that should be given for free. Requisitions are situations in which semi local government authorities 'ask' households or enterprises to contribute to their activities, for example by contributing some of the good they produce or providing lorries, fuel, and so on (ibid.: 6).

Informal private taxation, on the other hand, comprises contributions, gifts and donations, the first referring to resources allocated by non-governmental agents to the provision of public good and services, for example road transportation, education and health. Enterprises in rural areas are often led to supply services necessary to the welfare of their workforce but, as Prud'homme stresses, these contributions also benefit people who are not and will never be employees of the contributing enterprises (ibid.: 7) and can therefore be categorized as having a public good nature. Prud'homme also mentions gifts made by individuals to private bodies such as citizen groups or committees, religious organizations etc., who use them to provide public services and infrastructure. Donations may have much in common with taxation, such as parent's informal contributions to schools and the like.

Prud'homme's conclusion is that informal taxes are neither economically more harmful nor more unfair than formal taxes (ibid.: 16). Rather they work as a necessary supplement to the formal tax system; the low yields within the latter make it necessary to have recourse to informal taxation, which may be the only means to provide a minimum level of much needed public services. Pinch by public servants is induced not the least by the low wages in the public sector. Pinch and extortions make it possible for civil servants to live

4. Prud'homme attributes this to the fact that tax collection is operated by government, on the basis of written law.

and work, thereby contributing to financing one of the most basic services of the state, the provision of law and order.

From the taxpayers' point of view, pinch and extortions as well as gifts and donations are just like taxes: 'transfers out of the pocket for which one does not get anything in return, at least directly' (ibid.: 16). In the long run, extortions or bribes may turn out to be a good investment for local producers or entrepreneurs, as many rules and regulations, often borrowed from developed countries, are inappropriate and inflexible and almost impossible to keep. Investment in the smoother application of these regulations can therefore save both effort and time. A further merit of informal taxation is that collection costs are normally very low, as the amount of tax is often self-estimated. Tax collectors (at least in the case of private informal taxation) are often civil leaders who are paid in social respect and self-respect.

Although Prud'homme's conclusions probably underestimate the negative elements of informal taxation, his contribution is extremely relevant when explaining the reluctance among Senegalese tax payers. As will be shown below, the population of Barkedji have considerable expenses when it comes to ensuring public services, but these funds are not always channelled through formal tax routes, or through the persons or institutions formally assigned to the task. Furthermore taxes are often paid for radically different reasons than the ones officially given.

Taxation and Citizenship: Between Control and Recognition

Whereas the good governance doctrine emphasizes what could be termed the fiscal exchange dimension of taxation, that is, the contractual relation of states providing public services in exchange for revenue collection, it tends to leave unspoken the other attributes of taxation, notably that of control. Nevertheless, taxation plays just as important a role as an instrument through which a state can extend its control over its territory and citizens: 'Tax systems . . . work in two ways. On the one hand, a tax system is potentially an instrument for political control based on information about the citizens, and on a network of tax collectors. On the other hand, it is a mechanism for generating funds to provide real services to citizens in exchange for taxation' (Therkildsen, 2001a: 114).

As part of the decentralization framework, taxation is interwoven with other political processes through which regimes attempt to create and bolster state sanctioned authority in rural areas. According to Vandergeest and Peluso (2001: 177), territorial sovereignty defines people's political identities as citizens and forms the basis on which states claim authority over the people and resources within their borders. Modern states have increasingly turned to territorial strategies to control what people can do within those boundaries. Decentralization as the establishment of territorial civil administrative units can therefore be seen as a process through which the state attempts to take over the administration of rights to land and resources (see Le Meur and Lentz, this issue).

Taxation is not only a question of citizens gaining political representation and more efficient political organizations that can counterbalance and control the state. It is just as much a question of states attempting to extend their powers through the creation of relations of reciprocity and uniform institutions such as tax collectors, a process through which local inhabitants come to accept and abide by the norms and laws of the state, as part of their creation as citizens. In the words of Fiona Wilson (1999: 96): 'States cannot assume either readymade subjects/citizens or state promoting agents, they have to strive to produce them .... Seen from the perspective of hegemony, then states need to open up channels to affiliate supporters and enrol agents who at least partially can be brought to do the work of the state'. By strengthening relations of reciprocity in state–society interaction, through what Peluso and Vandergeest have called internal territorialization, taxation therefore also has an important spatial and territorial dimension of strengthening the state in the countryside, bringing about homogeneous institutions, creating territories and local representations that can ensure compliance with state regulation.

This process, however, is not one-sided. People in local communities also attempt to retain control over local resources and try to demarcate spatial fields where they can exercise control. And here taxation also figures in the repertoire of tactics and strategies used by local people to retain or extend their control over land and resources or in their attempts to state claims of belonging or of boundaries of inclusion and exclusion (see also Kelsall, 2000).

Tax payment may, for example, be used strategically as an act of compliance with the obligations attributed to citizenry, a symbol of allegiance towards the state or other local authorities which in return are expected to yield protection of the rights and properties of the citizen. Obviously such an act of inclusion is not always very agreeable for the citizens — as when police officers in Tanzania check bus passengers at road checkpoints and ask people to show their development levy card (receipt) before continuing their journey (Fjeldstad and Semboja, 2001: 2068). Nevertheless it effectively demonstrates that the taxpayer qualifies for the degree of citizenship and for the goods and services attached to it (even if this is only the right of driving on the road). More importantly, tax payment may serve to signal membership of a certain locality or social group, for instance if a piece of land is under dispute (see below), just as non-compliance may justify exclusion not only from membership of social or spatial entities, but also from specific political representation.

As Prud'homme observes, taxation is not limited to a relation between state and citizens. Other authorities may also collect or receive taxes or tributes, for instance those paid by local farmers or herders as a sign of compliance to validate their claims over certain resources or areas. Although not necessarily recognized by public authorities, their validity and influence in the local context may often turn out to be just as weighty.

Both formal and informal tax-compliance are central themes in determining how and when someone can be regarded as a member of a community, and can be decisive for the shift from the status of foreigner to that of a 'local'. Tax payment seems to have acquired a position as one among several ways in which foreigners can signal integration and allegiance to local political leaders, acting as what Bourdieu terms 'an officializing strategy' aiming to transmute egoistic, private and particular interests into publicly avowable, disinterested collective and legitimate interests which reproduce a social, not an individualized role, with obligations as well as rights attached (Shipton and Goheen, 1992).

Given the role of tax compliance in a wide array of issues ranging from identity and belonging to rights over land and resources, it becomes clear that tax collecting institutions cannot be treated as though they have a single purpose; tax collection is undertaken by a wide variety of persons and institutions with many different tasks, by village chiefs and councillors, by local forestry agents or police forces (for example, in the case of wood-cutting permission or taxes on market stalls) as well as by user institutions such as well committees, parents associations, and so on. Collection of development levies, poll taxes or other types of revenues at the local level is not carried out in a vacuum, but is often part of a larger political game, involving a varied array of different institutions, often formally undertaking quite dissimilar tasks and with very different motivations. Taxation is not only about the extraction of public revenue for public goods. It is also an act of recognition, a sign of membership and belonging with certain rights attached to it.

The following case study from the village of Barkedji discusses how the devolution of power from central government to the local rural councils and multi-party politics have affected tax collection and the ability to finance public services. Although tax compliance is generally very low, the study shows that revenue is often collected through other channels and motivated by other interests than those highlighted by donors and policy makers.

DECENTRALIZATION, TAXES AND MULTI-PARTY POLITICS IN BARKEDJI

> 'In Barkedji, no one pays taxes. Since the reform of 1996 taxes are no longer considered an obligation. While previously a small number of the population paid, hardly anyone has paid this year. It is election year, and none of the politicians dare to bother people with tax payment'. (Sous-préfet of Barkedji, November 2001)
>
> '(Multi-party) politics has really divided people. They no longer distinguish between their own interests and the interests of the community. The principal means for development, the rural taxes, have become almost impossible to collect. Before rural taxes were compulsory,

now it is a contribution to local development'. (President CR, Barkedji, 2001)
'Today rural taxes are no longer an obligation. People feel that the councillors will only eat the money'. (Extension officer, Barkedji 2001).

The *communauté rurale* of Barkedji is located in northern Senegal in the Ferlo, a frontier region between the semi-arid north, dominated by pastoral production and a mainly Fulani population, and the south, which is characterized by slightly higher annual precipitation and occupied by a mixture of agro-pastoral Fulanis and Wolof farmers. To this mix we must add two groups of 'newcomers': the *Mouride talibe,* Wolof disciples of the Islamic Mouride brotherhood who are organized in religious farming communities *(daara's)* to clear vast tracts of land for groundnut production; and the *FuutankoBe herders*, Fulanis from the Senegal River valley who moved southwards to the Barkedji area as a result of the droughts of the 1970s and 1980s and who have now settled on a more permanent basis in the area with their large herds of sheep, goats and cattle.[5]

In spite of its remote location, some 350 km northeast of Dakar, and its dispersed and mobile population, Barkedji is renowned for its highly politicized environment and its close ties to the inner circles of the political parties. Several central politicians from the Socialist Party (PS), in power with an absolute majority until the defeat of President Abdou Diouf in March 2000, originate from the area. The most influential Fulani agro-pastoralists, especially, have counted on their kin to ensure that the interests of the Fulani population in Barkedji were defended and that infrastructural and other development projects were brought to *the communauté rurale.* The installation of a solar telephone system in Barkedji in 1993 (with a single booth set up in the shop of a local politician) and its later extension to the surrounding *communautés rurales* of the district (*arrondissement*), can probably be attributed to the efforts made by PS politicians to ensure backing in the 1993 presidential and legislative elections. The installation of electricity in the community is credited by the local population to a Socialist Party under severe threat of losing their previously secure power basis.

As in other areas of rural Senegal, the locally elected rural council of Barkedji has been dominated exclusively by the PS since its formation in the beginning of the 1980s.[6] Until 1996, the composition of the rural councils depended on a winner-takes-all election held every five years in which only nationally registered parties could present candidates. Consequently, all members of a given rural council came from the same party (PS), as it

5. Although Barkedji and the surrounding *communautés rurales* are considered their home areas, the majority of FuutankoBe herders have maintained a very mobile lifestyle, with the sheep and goats, particularly, taken southwards to the Gambian border during the dry season.
6. The rural councils were set up after the administrative reform of 1972. The creation and election of the councils took place between mid 1970 and 1984 (Vengroff and Johnston, 1987: 276).

was almost impossible for an opposition party to win representation in local government.[7]

Although significant responsibilities for matters such as land allocation, equipment, infrastructure (mainly hydraulics and health), civil protection and social assistance were formally transferred to local councils, their room for manoeuvre was restricted, as they fell under the watchful eyes of the Ministry of the Interior. Decisions were only executed after approval of the local state administrator, the *sous-prefet*, who, acting as the accountant of the rural councils, was responsible for managing all financed activities (Blundo, 1998: 5). By retaining the right of the *sous-préfet* to veto all decisions taken, the Interior Ministry retained a high degree of control over the rural councils (Beck, 2001: 608).

As the ability of the PS to absorb all opposition began to erode in the early 1990s, the political landscape in the Ferlo region began to change. Opposition parties such as Wade's liberal party (PDS) and Bathily's left wing LD-MPT acquired sporadic representation in the Ferlo, as a belated effect of the unrestricted multi-partyism in presidential elections approved in 1981. The former unquestionable solidity of the PS began to crumble and hitherto dedicated party members were forced to take sides when key political personalities such as the former Interior Minister, Djibo Ka, who holds close family ties to the ruling elites of Barkedji, broke away from the Socialist Part in the mid 1990s to form this own party (UPS). PS managed only narrowly to hold onto its control over the rural electorate in the 1993 presidential elections, although maintaining the majority of votes in 300 of Senegal's 317 rural communities, among them Barkedji. This diluted political monopoly only lasted until 2000, when the electorate chose not to re-elect the incumbent president but instead put Abdoulaye Wade from the PDS in office, the so-called *alternance* (Amundsen, 2001: 51).

The electoral reform of 1996 installed a dual system for the election of rural councillors, ending the practice of winner-takes-all by permitting members from the opposition parties to be elected from a proportional list of candidates. In the first run, the reform and the alleged devolution of power only resulted in a concentration of power within the PS. Locally elected officials remained accountable primarily to the national party hierarchy upon whom they depended for patronage resources as well as for their appointment to party electoral lists — in other words, upward accountability still prevailed over downward accountability to their constituencies.

---

7. The total domination of PS members in the rural councils should not be mistaken for a general consensus or an eradication of political competition. Although political power in Barkedji is concentrated in a few families, mainly from the SanraBe sub-clan, competition between factions within the PS has been intense. Faction or clan politics, which have been vibrantly described by Cruise O'Brien (1975: 174), are central instruments in connecting the top and bottom in clientilist politics within the PS. On several occasions this competition has been so intense that it has blocked the working of the CR and even erupted into violent conflicts.

After the transfer of power to PDS and Abdoulaye Wade in 2000, political representation within the councils also started to shift. Many locally elected councillors and *deputés* to the National Assembly switched their political allegiance overnight, in what the Senegalese newspapers described as 'political transhumance'.[8] While many, including many *préfets* and *sous-préfets*, moved over to the new ruling party, others shifted according to other priorities. In Barkedji, some followed ethnic affiliation, hoping that Djibo Ka, through his family ties to Barkedji and the Ferlo region, would defend the rights and interests of Fulani herders in an otherwise Wolof dominated government. A small minority chose to join the tiny LD-MPT of Abdoulaye Bathily, who although a descendant of the Soninke aristocracy, comes from the Senegal River Valley and hence would be liable to defend the interests of northern Senegal. Political transhumance had direct repercussions on the rural council of Barkedji. The councillors, who had all been elected in 1996 as members of the PS, now represented three different parties, and although the President remained a member of PS, his party no longer held a majority among the twenty-eight councillors.

The question is now whether this political competition has opened up the path to transparency and accountability, notwithstanding the reciprocity and closer state–society relations considered crucial for the formation of the citizenry.

Multi-party Politics and Tax Collection

As elsewhere in Africa (see Therkildsen, 2001b), taxes in rural Senegal are collected as poll taxes, a fixed amount imposed by the state at a flat, low rate, bearing no relationship to property or income. For many years, rates have been fixed at 1000 CFA francs (approximately 1.5 euro) per head per year. Expected tax revenues for the *communauté rurale* of Barkedji thus amount to a limited sum of money of around 3 million CFA francs.[9]

Taxes are not collected by professional tax collectors but by the village chiefs, who receive an indemnity (7–10 per cent of the taxes collected[10]) for their efforts. The village chief then transfers the funds collected to the treasurer of the Rural Council. An administrative census, necessary to determine the number of taxpayers, usually takes place in the rainy season (between July and October) when most inhabitants are present in the village, while taxes are to be paid in January, when groundnuts and cotton have been sold and farmers are expected to be solvent (Blundo, 1998: 7). Long distances and

8. Borrowing a term taken from pastoral production systems describing the movement of herders between dry season and rainy season pastures.
9. For example, tax incomes for 1997 were expected to amount to 3,198,000 CFA francs; data from the minutes of the Rural Council of Barkedji.
10. The indemnity depends on the rate of collection, whether below or equal to 100 per cent (Blundo, 1998: 6).

complicated bureaucratic measures contribute to making illicit appropriation of a part of the local fiscal resources a common complaint (see Blundo, 1998 and this issue).

Poll taxes are not, however, the only form of revenue collected by the Rural Council. Taxes are also levied on market stalls at the weekly rural market, on commercial businesses (retail shops and commercialization of livestock), on permissions for wood-cutting or gum arabic extraction, and so forth, just as incomes are generated through fines for illegal felling, for animals trespassing into fields, for setting of bush fires and other 'offences'. A number of public services are also subject to user fees, such as schools, healthcare and water supply. There are, however, no taxes on agricultural production, on landed property or on livestock.

While tax collection until the reform of 1990 was under the supervision of the *sous-préfet*, the local representative of the Ministry of the Interior, who could count on help from the local police officers if village chiefs were unable to gather the expected funds, revenue collection is now entirely the responsibility of the Rural Council (Beck, 2001: 609). From 1990 Rural Councils have been responsible for their own development plans, although the state contributes to local development through a fund, the *Fond National de Solidarité* (Barkedji, for example, received a little more than 1 million CFAF).

However, as the quotations at the beginning of this section suggest, this increased opportunity for taxpayers to control the use of locally collected funds has not translated into any observable zest for tax payment. According to the minutes of the Rural Council of Barkedji, the immediate result of the 1990 changes was that only 900,000 CFA francs were collected of a projected 5.6 million CFA francs. Councillors explained that this was because they could no longer draw on the services of the police force to help them enforce tax levying. As coercion decreased, so did the financial basis of the Rural Council.

Since then tax revenues have been steadily decreasing. After the 1996 reform, the discourse on taxation has also changed as taxes are no longer to be considered an obligation, but rather as a 'contribution' to local development, suggesting something more or less voluntary. This change could be seen as an attempt to minimize the cost of enforcement by creating a higher degree of voluntary compliance (see Fjeldstad, 2001: 293 on similar experience from Tanzania). These efforts seem to have been in vain: according to different sources, tax revenues actually collected in Barkedji are now between 0 and 5 per cent of projected totals.[11]

11. According to the *sous-préfet*, tax revenue levels were 70 per cent in 1999, 10 per cent in 2000 and 0 per cent in 2001, an election year. While the figures from 2000 and 2001 appear reasonable, it is more doubtful whether tax compliance in 1999 was as high as 70 per cent, notably if one compares with data from 1993 (see above). According to his assistant, tax receipts in the last few years have varied between 3 per cent and 5 per cent, the best record found in the neighbouring *communauté rurale* of Gassane where 10 per cent of the potential revenue was recovered.

As a result of the shortfall in financial resources, none of the anticipated development projects are being carried out and no investments made. The *communauté rurale* is unable to finance repair of local infrastructure such as wells, health clinics, borehole pumps and so on. Instead, politicians concentrate on trying to mobilize donor agencies to provide the missing funding, or draw on their clientilist relations to finance repairs of crucial borehole machinery and the like (see below). However, the task is becoming increasingly difficult as many donor agencies are opting for new strategies which aim to increase the efficiency of their projects by increasing local involvement. As in the case of the Barkedji USAID health project, donors increasingly require a matching contribution from local governments before engaging in development projects (Fjeldstad, 2001: 290).

In this stalemate situation, politicians have few other possibilities than to take recourse to their old clientelistic networks to finance pressing infrastructural projects. For example, councillors from the LD-MPT managed to end several weeks of water shortages through the intervention of their party leader, Abdoulaye Bathily: Bathily was at that time Minister of the Environment and of Waterworks, a position which enabled him to donate a brand new motor for the borehole pump to the community. While this resolved an acute problem for the local population, the solution was hardly conducive to fostering a spirit of negotiation between state and society over taxation and public services. Contrary to the assumptions of the good governance framework, the immediate effects of the transfer of responsibility seem to be that clientelism and neo-patrimonial bonds have been reinforced (see also Lentz, this issue).

The assumption made by USAID and other donors that co-financing by the rural communities should motivate the population to contribute to their own development obviously does not hold true — or rather it is hindered by problems related to lack of trust regarding the workings of multi-party politics at the local level. People do not feel any obligation to contribute to the development of the village, and argue that they are still awaiting any tangible benefits from the previous tax payment. Rather the inability of the councillors to meet the terms of the health care project and the taking of the ambulance (mentioned above) are regarded as problems for the President of the *communauté rurale* to deal with.

The reasons given for tax non-compliance are many, but they tend to circle around the lack of service provision, and the fear that councillors would 'eat' the money. Obviously the political cleavages — spurred by successive elections and electoral campaigns over recent years —together with general political rivalry, divisions between villages, and so forth, have all contributed to the present situation. Far from bringing transparency and downward accountability to rural communities, this has brought forth some of the darker sides of political competition. In the words of a member of the *communauté rurale* of Wassadou, in the south-eastern part of Senegal, tax collection also plays a major part in the electoral campaigns: 'Village chiefs entertain themselves by collecting taxes among their political opponents, while others are not disturbed' (Echos, 2001: 10). The difficult relation between levying taxes and gaining electoral support is also highlighted by a *sous-prefét*, who indicated that no taxes were collected by the councillors in the election year of 2000 for fear of losing political support.

Indeed multi-partyism does not seem to have contributed to increased political accountability nor to have furthered greater transparency in the activities of rural councils. Instead the defeat of the Socialist Party in 2000 and the massive 'political transhumance' which ensued has led to a freeze of political activities. Multi-party politics has proved to be a painful experience for many of the central political families of Barkedji as family members have placed their political allegiance with different patrons and party leaders, with the effect, according to villagers, that brothers and sisters no longer communicate.

Contrary to popular wisdom, then, the establishment of multi-party politics and the switches in allegiance which have accompanied it do not seem to have transformed the character of upward accountability but merely transferred it from one party to another. As Beck argues, PDS does not represent an alternative to the ethno-clientelism of PS: even as an opposition party, PDS created alliances with customary leaders whenever possible, and now that it is in power, it is either extending its own networks to customary leaders, or absorbing those of the PS (Beck, 2001: 611).

In Barkedji, the Rural Council is unable to perform its duties. The President, who remain affiliated to the PS, has lost his legitimacy as he no longer holds a majority. As a concrete effect of this, it is difficult to attain a quorum and hence decisions cannot be taken.[12] The deliberate abstention of some members from participating in meetings is a purely political act, part of a neo-patrimonial game in which political support is gained not least through the failures of one's opponent. The obvious result of this is that the chance for councillors to show taxpayers that their taxes are used to improve public services is effectively curtailed.

Moore has argued that aid undermines the development of accountable institutions. This seems to some extent to turn the problem on its head. *Communautés rurales* seem to be caught in a vicious circle, with hardly any funds for carrying out prospected development plans — a situation which inevitably carries the seeds of dissatisfaction.

Tax in the Twilight Zone

So far, this article has dealt only with people trying to avoid paying taxes and the resulting 'missing link' in the establishment of firm state–society relations. Such a focus on the general reluctance of rural people to participate in state–society relations could easily be interpreted as yet another indicator

12. For a quorum half of the assembly + one (in this case fifteen members) must be present.

of peasant withdrawal from the state, as a popular protest against the lack of accountability of state elites and local politicians, a defence against the generalized practice of diverting private funds for private use.

However, instead of focusing solely on those avoiding paying taxes it may be revelatory to look at another group, which receives little or no attention in the debate — those who try to pay taxes but who are constrained in doing so. By shifting the focus to this group, it becomes clear that problems related to taxation cannot be interpreted only as a democratic struggle for accountability and control or as a case of withdrawal from the state.

People have many and varied reasons for either paying, or avoiding paying, taxes. It is often assumed that people engage with the state because they cannot avoid it. However, there are also those who do not want to avoid it. The payment of taxes can be a symbolic act of connecting to the state, a means of gaining legitimacy and of validating one claims *vis-à-vis* state and local authorities. This is illustrated by the attempts among local politicians and village chiefs in Barkedji to stop newcomers from paying taxes in the area.

As mentioned above, there is in the village of Barkedji a marked divide between a settled majority of agro-pastoralists Fulani, predominantly from the SanraBe clan group, and a minority group of newcomers, who arrived in the area after the droughts of the 1970s and 1980s. These so-called FuutankoBe herders, Fulanis from the Fuuta region along the Senegal River valley, are settled on a more or less permanent basis around Barkedji, where they have set up an extremely efficient system of herd management based on the labour-intensive and mobile rearing of sheep, goats and cattle (see Juul, 1999). As a result of this specialized system of production, most of these former drought refugees have become very rich and therefore subject to suspicion and jealousy from the autochtonous population, who have tried to limit their access to pastures and water. Since the late 1990s, payment of taxes has turned into a major struggle about difference and belonging.

In the early 1990s settled agro-pastoralists often expressed their discontent with the 'foreign herders' by referring to the fact that they did not pay taxes in the Barkedji area but only pretended to do so in their villages of origin in the Fuuta. The argument followed that, as they did not pay taxes in their present area of residence, this signified that they were not really settled but only awaited the opportunity to move back to their area of origin; hence they could not make claims on a more long-term basis to crucial resources such as water and pastures.

The claim that tax evasion was widespread among these very mobile herders is likely to contain elements of truth, as many of the FuutankoBe herders did not have the time, energy or motivation to travel back to their village of origin at times of tax collection. This situation was, however, not substantially different from that of many indigenous herders who (as shown above) also have considerable experience when it comes to different strategies to escape tax collection.

On closer inspection, the issue proved to be far more complicated than it appeared at first sight. In fact, as the quotations below demonstrate, a number of newcomers had tried to act as citizens and responsible taxpayers. But this act of allegiance was often not well taken by local politicians and administrators:

> Here the population is not very friendly. But we pay our taxes and make sure to have our vaccination papers in order, so that we can prove that our animals are not ill. Then they can't chase us away, even if they try. (FuutankoBe herder, Thiargny, February 1993)

> When I first arrived, the people of the neighbouring village were very much against us, but they couldn't really do anything against us. Two years after we had settled I started paying taxes in Barkedji. Several of my relatives had settled in the vicinities and we decided to form a village. This was authorized by the *sous-préfet*, but the villagers complained and in the end, the *sous-préfet* was removed. Several other FutankoBe villages also tried to get recognized but it worked out only for three of us. The reason that we were recognized was that we could show the receipts. It was very fortunate that I had kept the receipts for the councillors had hidden away the book in which payments were registered.

Clearly, tax compliance has acquired some sort of symbolic meaning; it is often referred to both by FuutankoBe herders present in the area on a more permanent basis and by local leaders as a sign of political allegiance, a tribute paid to the local notables. Tax payment is expected, in the short or long run, to guarantee some sort of protection of use rights. In short, payment of taxes represented a way to make the newcomer's presence in the area official, a way of being recognized as a citizen with rights and obligations. And it was particularly because of these attributes that certain autochthonous herders found it necessary to avoid its proliferation.

The various political agendas involved in the simple act of tax payment are reflected in the account of the Fuutankobe treasurer of a neighbouring well committee:

> It's true that conflicts are increasing. There are more people now and more animals, more and more people arrive from the north. The indigenous population fear that these newcomers will also decide to settle here for good. They fear that as the FuutankoBe population will grow, they will also claim representation in the rural council. But this goes only for those who pay their taxes here. This is why it is sometimes very difficult to get to pay your taxes. This has caused many transhumant herders to give up paying. (Treasurer, Borehole of Yonofere, 1993)

A principal means to restrict tax payment is by limiting the number of 'foreign' village chiefs. This is done with reference to the 'illicit character of the villages', that they are either too small, located in the gazetted forest or that their inhabitants are not fixed (see Juul, 1999). With the newcomers having problems finding a village chief to whom they could pay their taxes, a paradoxical situation was created whereby newcomers were condemned for not paying taxes, while tax collection among newcomers was indirectly constrained and prevented.

Increasingly, newcomers have understood the importance of linking up to public authority and many have now found ways to comply with formal exigencies such as taxes and other types of obligations. Meanwhile, the large majority of the so-called autochtonous inhabitants have given up paying taxes (due to a combination of lack of motivation and lack of trust) leading to an interesting situation in which the small amounts of taxes that are collected come primarily from newcomers and external agents trying to validate their claims and increase their rights.

Private Entrepreneurs in No-man's Land

FuutankoBe herders have thus used formal taxation and the official status derived from it as a vehicle in their quest to be recognized as citizens of Barkedji. By active manoeuvring to become taxpayers, they managed to block attempts by local elites to deny them their civil rights. This does not necessarily mean that in practice they now enjoy equal rights to the first comers with regard to political representation, but it does imply a formal recognition on the side of the state that can be useful in times of conflicts when their user rights or rights of settlement are being questioned.

Among the group of would-be taxpayers another type of stakeholder can be identified, whose beneficial role within the local community is often invoked, although their contribution to the local economy is seldom well assessed — private companies and entrepreneurs. Contrary to the common belief that private businessmen provide funding to local government, these entrepreneurs do not contribute substantially to local revenues, as taxes are not based on property. And, as Guyer notes, with no property taxes, there is no basis for the growing outside interests in the area to support its development (Guyer, 1992: 57).

In reality, Rural Councils are in something of a dilemma when it comes to enhancing resource mobilization and hence possibilities of improving public services in their constituencies. Many services provided by the councils, such as the attribution of agricultural land or constructions sites, the right to use common pastures, or the right to dig a well, are not subject to any form of charge or taxation. When large pieces of land are leased to private companies with productive aspirations, the land remains the property of the state and is handed over free of charge in the faint hope that the investments will bear fruit and the state will be able to collect VAT on the future revenue.

Obviously, these simple procedures bring significant advantages for private entrepreneurs who can launch investment projects at reduced risk. On the other hand the few larger companies which have ventured into productive businesses in the difficult conditions of the remote savannas of the Ferlo have also struggled with problems of being recognized and accepted by the local population, with whom they are forced to build up a tolerable working relation if costs of control, guarding, etc. are not to become insurmountable.

The difficulty of gaining legitimacy in a non-taxpaying environment is illustrated by the case of the large gum arabic project. This project was launched in the neighbouring arrondissement of Doli in 1999 by a large Saudi Arabian investor with ambitions of becoming the world's largest producer of gum arabic, a natural starch extracted from the *Acacia senegal* tree, which is used in products as diverse as ice cream, pharmaceuticals, paint and fine red wines (Freudenberger, 1992: 10–12). In 1999, the company started clearing large tracts of land in different *communauté rurales* in order to plant stands of *Acacia senegal* for gum production. By June 2002 more than 17,000 hectares of land had been cleared and planted, the total target being 50,000 hectares of land.

From the perspective of the councillors, this attribution of land constituted a development project which would provide employment opportunities for young people who could be hired to clear the land and plant cuttings of the gum-producing trees. The project also involved various so-called development activities, as the company promised to provide the communities affected by the project with healthcare facilities as well as nurses and medicine. This gesture may be seen as a form of informal taxation similar to Proud'homme's 'contributions', where private companies 'voluntarily' provide services of a public good nature.

For local users the allocation of their land came as a complete surprise, of which they learnt only when they interrogated the hired labourers in charge of delineating the prospected clearings. The herders and farmers who had hitherto used the land for grazing and cultivation perceived this handing over of several hundred hectares of their village land to a private investor as another example of fraudulent and incompetent administration by their elected leaders. This sentiment was further reinforced when it was revealed that the generous Saudi investor had provided a fare to Mecca to a number of councillors and high-ranking civil servants in the *Prefecture*. In next to no time, the affected farmers and herders got together to dispatch a letter of protest to the President of the Republic as well as to local and national politicians, complaining that their elected leaders were giving away their land without any notice or prior consultation with the affected user groups.

The obvious blunder in the participatory approach of the rural councillors aside, this case illustrates some of the difficulties encountered by local governments and private investors in terms of gaining legitimacy and recognition for such private initiatives. The story highlights a vast institutional void that exists in formulating and implementing collective endeavours. The dilemma for the rural councils is that many important services which they provide are not subject to any form of taxation.[13] However, when rights over land, for instance, are given free of charge, this dilutes the level of formal recognition implied by the action, leaving an opening for local populations

13. In some cases, such as formal attribution of land or construction sites, a small fee is charged to cover the administration costs.

to question the legitimacy of the decision. Seen in this perspective, the gifts and the travels to Mecca given by the private company can be interpreted not so much as an attempt to bribe the councillors, but rather as recognition of the value, or cost, of such services, which is expressed in the form of a personalized tribute or an informal tax. In the absence of legitimate tools for gaining recognition and validating their claims, private investors instead seek to gain legitimacy through illicit means, through personalized and collective tributes in the form of health projects, schooling facilities and the provision of diesel, a form of unofficial taxation by officials for the mobilization of resources. The validity of such informal taxation is less indisputable than that acquired through more formal channels, but in many instances it is the only type available.

Validating Claims through Informal Taxation: Bribes and Extortions

Validating claims also take place through other channels than the formal political-administrative. Bearing in mind the difficulties encountered by the FuutankoBe herders — still considered foreigners after more than twenty-five years in the area and more than ten years of tax compliance — it is not surprising that other means are employed to gain more secure rights to common assets such as rangeland and water.

One such method, which has gained considerable popularity in recent years, consists of building permanent infrastructure in order to signal rights of belonging. During fieldwork in 2001, a large number of brick houses and schoolrooms were suddenly found in camps inhabited by FuutankoBe herders. Several cases were observed in which individual herders had invested considerable funds into the excavation of private wells. This was surprising not only because the building of permanent housing and digging of wells is prohibited within the limits of the gazetted forests, but also because these herders are generally involved in systems of herd management based on high degrees of mobility. Considering the important investments involved and their limited yield (in the case of the wells, a diminutive amount of water was provided when compared with the quantities needed for the large herds owned by these households), this new strategy signalling sedentarity and sense of place seemed bewildering.

When I started asking questions about this new practice, it appeared that the buildings were erected and wells dug in response to rumours that the Forestry Department was planning a large campaign to evict all inhabitants from gazetted forest areas (which include most of the pasture lands of the *arrondissement* of Barkedji). Through bribery and extortion of relevant civil servants, individual FuutankoBe herders had obtained licence to break the law, and build or dig in the gazetted areas. That these construction activities involved schools and wells was interesting: since few pupils attended the school and the wells provided a very limited amount of water, their role seemed primarily to be that of symbols of sedentarity and belonging. Apparently, semi-public institutions such as wells and schools were selected as the symbols that could best communicate the message of permanent occupancy, integration and engagement in the role as citizens.

User Fees or Informal Taxation: The Role of Well Committees

The constraints faced by the newcomers in terms of paying taxes does not mean that they have not contributed to the local economy in the years since their arrival. Quite the contrary: the influx of the FuutankoBe herders in the aftermath of the droughts gave a significant boost to local economies, first and foremost through the excessive taxing of foreign animals at the public boreholes. As the number of animals using a particular borehole doubled or tripled due to the combined effects of an increased user group and their successful herd management strategies, the well committees, previously in chronic financial deficit, began to see a turn around in their fortunes. Although intended to be non-profit institutions, these water management committees have turned into big businesses, as the newcomers, be they temporary or more permanent, are made to pay exorbitant fees for their herds, far exceeding the fees envisaged by the state (see Juul, 1999, 2001).

In contrast to the indigenous herders who can limit their contributions to the well committees by making informal agreements with tax collectors, newcomers have contributed significantly to ensuring reliable water provision, both by way of the informal and excessive tax rates, and in some cases by investing in spare parts in the event of mechanical problems with the borehole pump. In this way, they are active contributors to the provision of public services. Recalling Prud'homme's categories, watering fees are clearly a form of private informal taxation utilized to finance public goods and services.

However, in contrast to the incidences of formal and informal taxation listed above, taxation through watering fees also constitutes a significant battlefield in terms of political representation. Dry-season grazing in the Ferlo is impossible if access to watering facilities is denied. Well committees have therefore become vital institutions not only in the management of water and the adjacent pastures but also as key institutions in local politics. Given their economic and strategic importance, these committees have become wealthy institutions in an area largely deprived of other important projects or funds for appropriation. Considerable effort is put into maintaining this source of capital for clientelistic redistribution, for apart from constituting a basis for profit, they are also important sources of legitimacy for those who control them. As noted by Shipton and Goheen (1992), people use resources such as water and land not only for enrichment and survival but also to gain control over others and to define personal and social identities. The well committee and the taxation involved are of particular interest for those members of the political elite who have aspirations for a wider political career, as a person's status and influence hinges on his ability to mobilize supporters.

Seen in this perspective, the limited contribution of the autochthonous population to the running costs of the boreholes has become a key point of vulnerability for them in the local division of power. The heavy fees paid by 'foreign' herders have proved to be an important platform from which they can negotiate political representation on the well committee board. Increasingly, foreign herders are demanding representation in exchange for taxation, arguing that in return for continuing to finance minor repair, spare parts and the bulk of the running costs, they also want to have representation on the board, a demand which in many ways has improved transparency of accounts and efficiency in the management of the well.

At election times, FuutankoBe herders, who constitute an important source of backing for some of the local candidates, have also refused to contribute economically to the national electoral campaigns until the post of treasurer or president of the well committee is promised to a representative of the FuutankoBe population. In this case representation and taxation do seem to go hand in hand, as envisaged by Tilly and by the governance framework, at least partially.

CONCLUSION

In the case of Barkedji, the reasons for compliance or non-compliance among the tax-eligible citizens do not sit easily with the arguments of Tilly and Moore. In general transfer of taxation to the local level has neither been met with demands for increased public services nor with demands for political representation. From fear of not being re-elected, local leaders seldom raise the issue of tax policy and often depend on indirect taxes for a large proportion of state revenue — with the unfortunate result that there are no discussions of how revenues are collected and used and no taxpayers to hold officials accountable. Once the former ties of coercion were loosened with the transfer of responsibility from the *sous-préfet* to the rural councillors, people no longer felt any obligation to pay their taxes at all. So although Moore may be correct to stress the importance of non-coercive methods to mobilize resources in ways which are conducive to political stability and state citizen accountability, it may be difficult to see any alternative ways to increase the rates of direct taxation.

In rural areas of West Africa, people seldom make substantial requests for specific services in return for the taxes paid. Rather, the expectation is that such services will be provided through political patrons at local or national level. As seen in Barkedji, financial management is generally a poor basis from which to demand public accountability, as the low tax contributions force the elected representatives to turn to their clientelistic networks to finance projects such as infrastructure repairs, notwithstanding development initiatives. Indeed, the motivation for the generalized non-payment of taxes seems to be less a question of lack of accountability and rather a matter of excessive politicization.

In the transfer of financial responsibility, local politicians have not been given any impetus to transform the clientelistic relationship between state and society. With no graduation of taxes, except between insiders and outsiders, there is, as Guyer points out, no official theory of inequality and no way for the poorer segments to demand higher contributions from their wealthy neighbours. With no property tax there is no basis for the growing outside business interests in the area to support local economic development. And with no real policy about, or financial instruments for development of, locally defined projects within the government system, the extension of national plans to local areas fails because the necessary financing bears no relation to the population affected by it.

This brings us back to our initial question: why then, do people pay taxes and to whom are they willing to pay? In general people are less willing to invest in development of the community through rural councils and prefer to invest in networks and relations that can improve their personal situation (as is the case of extortions, gifts and bribes). As Prud'homme argues, such levies may be considered as informal taxation, which contributes to the provision of certain services of a public good nature. And as both Prud'homme and Guyer have shown, the value of resources devoted by ordinary citizens to issues that, in other systems, would fall under the purview of the local government, is far in excess of the official tax rate.

At the same time, formal taxation is also used to serve wider purposes in the local struggles for recognition and is therefore not totally disregarded by the taxpayers. In the case of Barkedji, where struggles over difference and belonging tend to dominate the political agenda, formal taxation can play a significant role as it carries with it some degree of recognition of the taxpayer's rights as a citizen. In such situations, the state may act as the 'qualifier' endowed with the political capital to nominate and qualify degrees of citizenship. Hence, although paid at the local level, tax bears an official stamp which, paradoxically, may increase the rights of the individual taxpayer *vis-à-vis* the local councillors in those cases where newcomers' rights are threatened by local political leaders.

Nonetheless, in Barkedji formal taxation bears only scant relation to any particular form of representation or control over the elite, of the kind suggested by Moore. Perhaps surprisingly, the informal taxation carried out by the borehole committees was the only instance which supported the anticipated connection between taxation and representation. Here, newcomers were willing to pay excessive taxes in exchange for gaining access to crucial resources; but as they realized that through their contributions they held the key to a major asset in local political life, they were able to use their strength as taxpayers to also gain representation.

REFERENCES

Addison, T. and J. Levin (2004) 'Tax Policy Reform in Developing Countries'. Paper presented at DANIDA Seminar on taxation policies and tax reforms in Third World countries, the Royal Danish Ministry of Foreign Affairs, Copenhagen (22 June).

Amundsen, I. (2001) 'The Limits of Clientelism: Multi-party Politics in Sub-Saharan Africa', *Forum for Development Studies* 28(1): 43–57.

Beck, L. J. (2001) 'Reining in the Marabouts? Democratization and Local Governance in Senegal', *African Affairs* 100(401): 601–21.

Blundo, G. (1998) 'Decentralisation, Participation and Corruption in Senegal'. Paper presented at the 14th congress of Anthropological and Ethnological Science, Williamsburg, Virginia (26 July–1 August).

Cruise O' Brien, D. (1975) *Saints and Politicians: Essays in the Organization of Senegalese Peasant Society*. Cambridge: Cambridge University Press.

Echos (2001) 'Echos des Collectivités Locales', No 1 (October/December), pp. 9–17. Dakar: DGL Felo, for USAID.

Fjeldstad, O. H. (2001) 'Taxation, Coercion and Donors: Local Government Tax Enforcement in Tanzania', *The Journal of Modern African Studies* 39(2): 289–97.

Fjeldstad, O. H. and J. Semboja (2001) 'Why People Pay Taxes: The Case of the Development Levy in Tanzania', *World Development* 29(12): 2059–74.

Freudenberger, M. S. (1992) 'The Great Gum Gamble: A Planning Perspective on Environmental Change in Northern Senegal'. PhD dissertation, University of California, Los Angeles.

Graetz, M. J., J. F. Reinganum and L. L. Wilde (1986) 'The Tax Compliance Game: Towards an Interactive Theory of Law Enforcement', *Journal of Law, Economics and Organization* 38: 1–32.

Guyer, J. (1992) 'Representation without Taxation: An Essay on Democracy in Rural Nigeria 1952–1990', *African Studies Review* 35(1): 41–79.

Juul, K. (1999) 'Tubes, Tenure and Turbulence: The Effects of Drought Related Migration on Tenure Issues and Resource Management in Northern Senegal'. PhD dissertation, University of Roskilde, Denmark.

Juul, K. (2001) 'Power, Pastures and Politics: Boreholes and Decentralisation of Local Resource Management in Northern Senegal', in T. Benjaminsen and C. Lund (eds) *Politics, Property and Production in the West African Sahel: Understanding Natural Resource Management*, pp. 57–74. Uppsala: Nordiska Afrikainstitutet.

Kelsall, T. (2000) 'Governance Politics and Districtisation in Tanzania: The 1998 Arumeru Tax Revolt', *African Affairs* 99(397): 533–51.

Manor, J. (1999) *The Political Economy of Democratic Decentralization: Directions in Development*. Washington, DC: The World Bank.

Moore, M. (2001) 'Politisk underudvikling', *Den Ny Verden* 34(4): 27–54.

Moore, M. (2004) 'Taxation and the Political Agenda, North and South', *Forum for Development Studies* 1(4): 7–32. Available online: http://www.nupi.no/English/

Prud'homme, R. (1992) 'Informal Local Taxation in Developing Countries', *Environment and Planning C: Government and Policy* 10: 1–17.

Shipton, P. and M. Goheen (1992) 'Understanding African Landholding: Power, Wealth and Meaning', *Africa* 62(3): 307–25.

Therkildsen, O. (2001a) 'Understanding Taxation in Poor African Countries: A Critical Review of Selected Perspectives', *Forum for Development Studies* 28(1): 99–123.

Therkildsen, O. (2001b) 'Tre påstande om skat, demokrati og bistand', *Den Ny Verden* 34(4): 13–26.

Tilly, C. (1992) *Coercion, Capital and European States AD 990–1992*. Cambridge: Blackwell Publishers.

Tilly, C. (1995) 'The Emergence of Citizenship in France and Elsewhere', in C. Tilly (ed.) *Citizenship, Identity and Social History*, pp. 223–36. Cambridge: Cambridge University Press.

Tripp, A. M. (1997) *Changing the Rules: The Politics of Liberalization and the Urban Informal Economy in Tanzania*. Berkeley, CA: California University Press.
Vandergeest, P. and N. Peluso (2001) 'Territorialization and State Power in Thailand', in N. Blomley, D. Delaney and R. T. Fox (eds) *The Legal Geographies Reader*, pp. 177–86. Oxford Blackwell Publishers.
Vengroff, R. and A. Johnston (1987) 'Decentralization and the Implementation of Rural Development in Senegal: The Role of the Rural Councils', *Public Administration and Development* 7: 273–88.
Wilson, F. (1999) 'Stating the Borders: A Discussion of Territoriality and State in the Peruvian Andes', in *External and Internal Constraints on Policy Making: How Autonomous are the States?*, pp. 95–120. Occasional Paper No 20. Roskilde: International Development Studies, University of Roskilde.

9

Contested Sources of Authority: Re-claiming State Sovereignty by Formalizing Traditional Authority in Mozambique

Lars Buur and Helene Maria Kyed

INTRODUCTION

In post-war Mozambique, decentralization and the delegation of administrative tasks to non-state actors have increasingly been seen as the means to make the state more efficient and responsive to local needs. The shift of the 1990 Constitution from a one-party Marxist–Leninist state to a liberal and political pluralist model has resulted in novel imaginings of rural local governance. Formally, governance has moved from a Marxist preoccupation with class and party structures to a focus on chieftaincy, culture and civil society. Post-war constitutional commitments to democratic decentralization led in 1997 to the institution of a system of elected local governments. Unlike reform initiatives in other Southern African states, the Municipal Law 2/1997 only made provision for elected local governments in thirty-three urban municipalities (*autarquias*) and not in any rural areas. As a consequence, no elected organs are in place outside urban centres.

In rural districts, a three-tiered local state administrative structure enacts local governance; since 2000 this has been supplemented by Decree 15/2000. Mirroring the processes of re-traditionalization across sub-Saharan Africa since the 1990s (Englebert, 2002; Oomen, 2002), Decree 15/2000 is the first piece of post-colonial legislation to officially recognize 'traditional authority' in Mozambique. The Decree includes three categories of 'community authorities' that can be legally recognized by the state on the basis of local community legitimization: 'traditional chiefs', former Frelimo 'secretaries of suburban-quarters or villages', and 'other leaders legitimized as such by the respective local communities' (Republica de Moçambique, 2000a: Art. 1). Recognized authorities are envisaged as performing the double role of representatives of rural communities and assistants of the state. They are delegated a range of key state-administrative tasks that include, *inter alia,* policing, taxation, population registration, justice enforcement, land allocation and rural development. Besides administrative tasks, they are expected to perform various elements of civic education in their communities, for example, fostering a patriotic spirit, supporting the celebration of national days, promoting environmental sustainability, encouraging payment of taxes, and preventing crime, epidemics, HIV/AIDS, and premature pregnancy and marriage (Republica de Moçambique, 2000a: Art. 5). Since 2002, around 4,000 former Frelimo secretaries and traditional leaders have been officially recognized, have signed a contract with the state and have received emblems of the republic to wear and a national flag to place at their homestead. No persons falling within the category of 'other leaders' have been recognized (MAE, 2004).

In this article, we explore the process of legitimizing community authorities in the rural areas of Sussundenga District where traditional chiefs were the first authorities to be recognized. Avenues to legal recognition based on various, highly negotiable claims to traditional legitimacy did not fit neatly within the understanding of traditional authority at the heart of the Decree. Publications by the Ministry of State Administration (Ministério de Administração Estatal, or MAE), which provided the basis of the Decree, set out to prove the existence of truly traditional authority, stating that: 'This institution of the community is a reality that manifests itself before the state and its juridical system. They are not created by the Law, but are generated by the respective communities' (Lundin and Machava, 1995: 151; see also MAE, 1996: 24.). Traditional authority was thus distanced both from its colonial past and from party politics, in answer to various critics who claim that today's traditional authority has been corrupted by externally imposed regimes (Artur and Weimer, 1998: 19). Despite the acknowledgement of the chief's role in shifting political arrangements, it was nonetheless established that 'true' traditional authority exists and is legitimized by pre-colonial practices and beliefs. As West and Kloeck-Jenson have illustrated, the tag 'traditional' in the work of the MAE marked both the institution and its office holders as anachronisms (1999: 457). The reified and timeless notion of community and traditional authority in this understanding of tradition or the traditional is not new. Weber's ideal-typical model of different forms of legitimacy presents tradition as 'that which has always been' (Weber, 1978: 36). Present articulations of traditional forms of authority and legitimacy then become a question of simple continuity and not, as Handler and Linnekin (1984) have pointed out, symbolic processes that take past symbolisms for granted and productively render them present anew by reinterpreting them according to current requirements. As the process of legitimizing traditional authority shows, kin-based authorities are not alone in deriving 'influence and/or power from positions held within institutions built upon the organizing principles of kinship' (West and Kloeck-Jenson, 1999: 457). Influence, status and legitimacy also derive from the symbols and performative skills related to the domain of state-administration that to a large extent has its origin in colonial governance.

Based on ethnographic material from Sussundenga District, the article explores how the implementation of Decree 15/2000 has involved a contested process of stabilizing traditional authority and territorially-bounded communities as a prerequisite for state recognition.[1] In competing claims to leadership, the traditional was internally contested and its practical manifestations and procedures of instalment were the outcome of both redefinition and reproduction. Sources used to settle the legitimacy of community authorities had multiple origins: some derived from the colonial register and others from interpretations of the Decree or fragmented recollections of historical material scattered in time and space; others derived from different abilities to perform and engage with the state and pragmatic requirements arising from present needs and challenges. Implementation is explored in the context of struggles over legitimate leadership in three different arenas in the Mathica, Mouha and Dombe administrative areas. The first example shows a failed attempt by a state functionary to get a sub-chief recognized as a community authority in his area of jurisdiction; the second shows the competition within a chiefly family over the position of chief; the third illustrates the struggles between two sub-chiefs over their ranking in the chiefly hierarchy. Conflicts varied in intensity, scope and make-up. Common among the case studies was the tension between different sources of legitimacy in the quest for state recognition. Some appealed to needs and requirements arising from public administration and others to ideas about ascribed status based on succession lines and spiritual power. The Decree underscores the twilight character of traditional institutions, through the dual position granted to the recognized leaders as both community representatives and agents of state administration. Before examining the three cases in greater detail, a brief note on the historical background of traditional authority and the Decree is necessary to provide some context.

FROM BANNING TO RECOGNITION

The strong position held by traditional chiefs or *régulos* (small kings) during Portuguese colonial rule came to an official end at Independence in 1975. As part of attempts to break with the colonial bifurcated system of governance and to build a single-party state along Marxist–Leninist lines, the new Frelimo (*Frente de Libertação de Moçambique*) government replaced the chieftainship system with *grupos dinamizadores* (dynamizing groups) led by party secretaries. Chiefs were formally excluded from participation in Frelimo's new party-state hierarchies (O'Laughlin, 2000: 26–30). They were portrayed as collaborators of the Portuguese colonial state and their practices were branded detrimental to the modernization of society and the production of national unity (see Artur and Weimer, 1998: 4). Since 1992, when the General Peace Agreement (GPA) was signed by Frelimo and Renamo (*Resistência Nacional Moçambicana*), the rise of traditional authority in local governance gained momentum in national political circles. The increasing

1. This article is based on fieldwork conducted between May and November 2002.

impetus for formalizing kin-based institutions was influenced by a complex interplay between political and academic agendas, the vision of donor agencies and actual, on-the-ground conditions in the rural areas following the war. The academic celebration of the democratic potential of traditional African forms of governance coupled with donor agencies' calls for decentralization and localization of governance were profound. Unable to identify a civil society that could democratically and effectively represent community interests in rural Mozambique, Western donors and NGOs increasingly looked to 'traditional authority' as a site for local or community-based governance (West and Kloeck-Jenson, 1999: 461). For the Frelimo government, the prime impetus for formalizing traditional authority has been overwhelmingly political and administrative. This must be seen against the background of what Alexander (1997: 20) refers to as a 'profound crises of authority' in the post-war rural areas. As in other post-conflict countries, one of the key concerns facing the central government and policy designers was contestation over state sovereignty and state institutions. Both held very meagre sway in formerly war-torn areas like Sussundenga District.

This did not mean a *terra nullius* of *de facto* public authority. During and immediately after the war, non-state forms of authority competed for the socio-economic and cultural space outside the primarily urban and semi-urban areas controlled by Frelimo and state institutions. Apart from the dispersed presence of emergency relief NGOs and the fragile Frelimo party structures, these actors mainly comprised institutions forged in opposition to and operating outside the sovereign power of the Frelimo-state (Alexander, 1997; Artur and Weimer, 1998). Renamo's strategic links with those chiefs that had operated during colonial rule and/or with newly imposed ones, made the question of traditional authority in post-war local governance not merely one of administrative effectiveness, but also one of political alliance.

Arguments such as Geffray's (1990), which held that Frelimo's banning of the chieftainship system was one of the prime reasons for Renamo's support during the civil war and for the state's loss of legitimacy, increasingly won support within Frelimo and the donor community (West and Kloeck-Jenson, 1999: 460–1). Following the war, Renamo's electoral victory (1994/99) in the rural areas and media-documented acts of chiefs' hostility towards the re-establishment of state institutions contributed further to this interpretation (for Dombe in Sussundenga, see articles in the newspaper *Noticias*, 1995a; 1995b). At the national level it was increasingly believed that Frelimo's attempt to substitute traditional leadership with new local party-based institutions at Independence had proven detrimental to the legitimacy of the Frelimo state. At the local level, the fragmented kin-based institutions had continued to exercise public authority. The authority of chiefs had been interwoven directly in Renamo strongholds but also unofficially with Frelimo party state structures. As documented by Alexander (1997) and West and Kloeck-Jenson (1999), local state officials in some areas relied more on informal day-to-day collaboration with chiefs than on the new Frelimo secretaries. In other areas they punished chiefs caught solving community problems.

Decree 15/2000 hence emerged from a complex history of shifting roles and allegiances and can be seen as an attempt to bring these *de facto,* loosely organized forms of traditional authority and their subject populations under state control. The Decree combines the objective of re-claiming state sovereignty by extending administrative and territorial reach to rural authorities with the recognition of local forms of organization. This has been loosely formulated in the Decree as instituting an articulation between local state organs and community authorities: 'For the process of administrative decentralization, for the valuation of the social organization of communities and for the improvement of the conditions of their participation in public administration for the socio-economic and cultural development of the country, it is necessary to establish forms of articulation between the local state organs and those of the community authorities' (Republica de Moçambique, 2000b: Introduction; authors' translation).[2]

The key objective of the 'participation of local communities' meets potential contradictions in the remaining articles of the Decree, its regulation and in practice. Leaders to be recognized as community authorities within the category of traditional are to be chosen according to 'traditional rules of the respective community' (Republica de Moçambique, 2000a: Art.1.a). In practice, no precise criteria for 'traditional rules' could be specified. This is not surprising when we note existing divisions within local populations and the shifting historical-political contexts in which 'traditional chiefs' have operated (West and Kloeck-Jenson, 1999: 455). The Decree's definition of community as 'the collective of people comprised in a unified territorial organization' (Republica de Moçambique, 2000a: Art. 8) takes for granted the existence of consensual traditional communities and, perhaps for that reason, provides no legal mechanisms to ensure broad-based participation. This ethos followed the results of a series of donor-funded studies on traditional authority conducted by the MAE in the period 1991–97. Here it was asserted that traditional leaders 'represent the whole community, beyond political differences, embodying the will of all people and not excluding anyone' (MAE, 1996: 11).

Another ambiguity is the relationship between state and community authority. The recognition of community authority is aimed at forging a new partnership, but the Decree insists that the two structures should remain

2. Local state organs cover the three-tiered hierarchy of district, administrative post and *localidade*. The law on local organs of the state (*Lei dos órgãos locais do Estado*) was only approved at the beginning of 2003 by parliament, in other words, after the passing of the Decree. It was supposed to have included the institution of consultative forums comprising elected people's representatives (*consehlos consultativos*) at *localidade* level. In October 2002 these were erased from the law, with the argument by the MAE that Decree 15/2000 catered for community participation in local government and development.

separate. Maintaining that the state cannot intervene in community matters, the Decree at the same time obligates the community authorities to fulfil a long list of state-administrative functions in 'concord with the consolidation of national unity' (ibid.) and 'within the limits of the law' (Republica de Moçambique, 2000a: Art. 5). In fact, the first item on the list of 'obligations' of community authorities is to 'divulge the laws and deliberations of state organs' (ibid.). The ideal separation between state and community authority, as we will illustrate in the following sections, also proved highly unrealistic in the actual acts of legitimization and recognition. In Sussundenga District, the conceptual distinctions of state and non-state appeared to converge, as did those of the traditional and state/modern/party. Practice highlighted the unfixed character of these domains.

Implementation of the Decree at *localidade* level began in most areas of the country in 2001. However, the process was characterized by an increase in conflict. This was influenced by the diverse local political landscapes across the country, by tense struggles over positions and by local state officials' interpretations of the Decree in line with different ideas about rural authority and pragmatic strategies of governance (Dava et al., 2003). Although the new term 'community authority' opens space for the recognition of any leader that a designated group of people finds fit to represent them, only former Frelimo secretaries and traditional leaders have been recognized. In the Frelimo-dominated south and in Capo Delgado in the North, former Frelimo secretaries have won most seats. In the Renamo strongholds of Manica and Sofala Provinces, traditional leaders took close to 100 per cent of the seats (MAE, 2004).

The absence of any persons falling within the category of 'other leaders' or 'secretaries' in the Sussundenga District, in Manica Province, was determined largely by local state officials' interpretation of 'community authority' as being traditional chiefs or rather those bearing the name of an already registered *régulo* area. No space was opened and no awareness was raised of the possibility for actors who could not define themselves as traditional (such as NGO workers, teachers, religious leaders or businessmen) to stand as candidates for the post of community authority. Although nine secretaries were in fact recognized in 2004, two years after the traditional leaders, this was exclusively done in areas around administrative heads.[3] To have recognized secretaries in rural Renamo strongholds would in any case not have been a strategic choice. Here, secretaries have a history as Frelimo partisans, as former implementers of unpopular policies and as a threat to the position of *régulos* (Alexander, 1997). The conviction of state officials that traditional leaders have 'a lot of power' (interview, DA, September 2002)

3. The recognition of secretaries in Sussundenga District was widely considered to be part of Frelimo's mobilization of its constituencies before the elections held in December 2004. It spurred a new wave of discontent amongst sub-chiefs who considered themselves superior to secretaries, but who now held an inferior position in the state register.

was a significant factor in focusing on their recognition. This was not only a calculated means to ease the execution of administrative tasks: many state officials were also guided by belief in the spiritual power of chiefs and their ability to use witchcraft against oppositional forces. Despite the exclusive focus on the category of traditional leaders while implementing the Decree, there was space for manoeuvrability.

MATHICA: WHEN THE *RÉGULO* IS NOT A *RÉGULO*

Mathica, a *localidade* of Sussundenga Sede in the north, is surrounded by fallow agricultural fields that used to belong to a post-independence agricultural co-operative. During the colonial era, this land was privately owned, yielding high agricultural outputs and employing hundreds of workers. During the war, the population increased dramatically as internally displaced people settled on or at the fringes of the co-op. They had come from Dombe in the south and from the nearby mountains where bloody battles had been fought. Today, Mathica has a donor-funded state school, a privately-owned mill and an influx of private investors, NGOs and white Zimbabwean and South African farmers looking for land and business opportunities.

In July 2002, a 'recognition ceremony' was staged for *régulo* Ganda, who was to be the community authority for Mathica *localidade*. At the time of 'identification and formal registration of community authority', the assistant of the district administrator called out for the person to be recognized. Ganda stepped forward onto the raised platform where state representatives were seated. The assistant asked: 'Are you *régulo* Ganda?'. Before he could answer, another person moved forward. The assistant burst out: 'Who are you?' to which the person answered: 'I am *régulo* Buapua'. After moments of silence the district administrator went forward. Looking at the audience, he asked 'Which of them is the *régulo*?'. Ganda looked down and said nothing. Buapua looked straight at the administrator, and repeated, 'I am *régulo* Buapua'. The administrator shook his head in disbelief. After a while, comments slowly started to flow from the audience, some supporting Buapua, others supporting Ganda. The *chefe da localidade*, who was in charge of the ceremony, retreated to his office together with the district administrator.[4] When they returned, the first secretary of Frelimo stood up, asked people to be quiet and then began to question Buapua, Ganda and the audience in the Shona vernacular. A heated discussion followed. From the audience, the name Zixixi came up several times. It emerged that neither Buapua nor Ganda was the *Régulo Grande* (the paramount chief). The real *régulo* was Zixixi who lived on the western side of the mountains in an area belonging to Mouha administrative post. Buapua and Ganda were sub-chiefs (*chefes do grupo*) under Zixixi. In

4. The title *chefe da localidade* designates state officials in charge of localities, the lowest level of the state administration.

the end, the district administrator, clearly shocked, stated loudly: 'I have to consult the register, so we know who the *régulo* is'. The signing of 'the Act of Recognition' was postponed. Two weeks later, Zixixi was recognized as *régulo* with both Ganda and Buapua at his side. They were now formally established as sub-chiefs.

Governmental Considerations

The crux of the matter was that the *chefe da localidade* had managed to get Ganda registered as *régulo* for the area of Mathica. This had happened during the process of identification, which provided the initial step of implementing the Decree in Sussundenga District, and was followed by the registration of the *régulo verdadeiro* — true *régulo* — in the official register of *régulos*. These two steps were to have taken place at so-called 'legitimization meetings' where local communities should formally appoint their leader. In practice, state officials had gone out to communities only after registration to verify that the person inscribed in the official register was indeed considered legitimate by the community. These meetings took place at a venue close to the homestead of an already registered chief and in all cases included the participation of between 100 and 200 people (against the 1997 census figures, this meant never more than 10 per cent of the population registered within a *regulado*). Approximately a year later, the 'recognition ceremonies' were held and the final contract between community authorities and the state signed (July–August 2002).[5]

State officials expended considerable energy on creating the register, as it formed part of the process of re-establishing the presence of the state in formerly hostile Renamo territories. Part of identifying *régulos* involved indexing the wider hierarchical system of sub-chiefs — *chefe do grupo* [second sub-chief] and *chefe da povoação* [third sub-chief]. *Régulos* had also been told to produce 'registers of the population' with 'the number of families and inhabitants according to sex', so that the tax base could be measured and health services and school buildings planned.[6] The register was not created from scratch. It had slowly been established against the old colonial registers' three-tiered hierarchy of *autoridades gentilicas,* which had incorporated pre-existing hierarchies as well as imposing new ones (see West and Kloeck-Jenson, 1999: 471). The MAE studies had also used the colonial register as a point of reference. Names had been either changed or confirmed during the registration for food relief after the GPA and again during the 2000 floods, and the register had been consulted during the workshops held by the administration as part of preparing for the implementation of the Decree. For lower level state officials, the emic name for the register was *O Livro*. Its

5. For a detailed description of the recognition ceremonies, see Buur and Kyed (2003).
6. Interview, *Chefe do Posto* Dombe, September 2002.

name in local dialect was *Ma-Bhuku*, which had also been the name used for its colonial version.

When the administrator went to consult the register in order to clarify the status of Ganda, he had to go further than the new register. This register would merely have confirmed the status of Ganda due to the *chefe da localidade's* manipulation. Against the colonial register it was declared that by 'mistake Ganda had been registered as a *régulo* in *O Livro*. The real *régulo* was Zixixi'.[7] The *chefe da localidade* was aware of this. He knew the kin-based hierarchy from working in Mathica for several years. Concerns for the future status of his *localidade* had made him manipulate the new register, as he later confessed: 'Now we are going to lose out on development, now there is no community leader when the NGOs come'.[8] That he could have personal interest in getting Ganda recognized should not make us lose sight of government considerations that recognition of traditional leaders attempts to address. His comment reflects a specific understanding of the Decree, that development provisions by state and aid agencies would be channelled through the new governmental grid of a *régulo* in charge of a territorially defined unit. Rightly or wrongly, he assumed that his *localidade* would not benefit from recognition of community authorities, because the individual to be recognized belonged to a different administrative post. However, this was not the only problem.

From the perspective of the kin-based hierarchy, the status of *régulo* Zixixi was undisputed. He has power (*têm papel*), as people living in the area framed it, but from a public administrative point of view he was a disaster. Zixixi was not interested in any engagement with public administrative tasks, because he did not trust 'them' (the Frelimo government). He lived 74 km away from the *Posto* of Mouha where he formally reported. There was no road into his homestead and when he was told to build one he simply declined. Two years after recognition, the flag post had still not been set up to mark his 'articulation with the state'. He did not enforce any tax collection nor draft manpower for maintenance of the school even though a young assistant was keen to do so. Without Zixixi's input, nobody would take the initiative and when the young assistant did, the population lambasted him for 'thinking he was something' and for 'not respecting the hierarchy'.[9] Seen from the perspective of the *chefe da localidade*, the fact that Zixixi was not interested in engagement with the state and belonged to a different administrative area of jurisdiction would not help him in his administrative tasks. *Ma-Bhuku* had spoken and there was not much the *chefe* could do. If to govern was, for the state and its officials, to seek an authoritative figure for their own authority, by converting the authority in one field into another, then governing could run into problems. Such problems emerged partly because the use of a

---

7. Interview, district administrator, Sussundenga, August 2002.
8. Interview, *Chefe da Localidade* Mathica, August 2002.
9. Interview, Jorge, September 2002.

mediating leader in charge of a territorially-defined unit did not necessarily fit well within the kin-based institution's hierarchy of territorial space and partly because legitimacy based on ascribed status does not necessarily follow legitimacy based on performance. The potential conflict between administrative concerns for adequate performance and justification of leadership against non-performative criteria also appeared in the Gudza area.

GUDZA: BETWEEN TRADITION AND ADMINISTRATIVE APTITUDE

The *regulado* of Gudza is situated in Javela *localidade*, a few kilometres west of Lucite River where the Dombe administration is located. During the war it functioned as a combat frontier between Renamo, which controlled the rural parts, and Frelimo, which managed to hold on to the Dombe administrative head until the last year of the war, when Renamo successfully captured the entire territory. Renamo control of Javela was only gradually eroded from 1996 when the administrative head came under state control. The western part was not reached by state and police officials until 2001. This coincided with the implementation of the Decree. The 'legitimization meetings' marked the first visit of a post-colonial state official to all of the chieftaincy homes. In Javela, three *regulados* — Gudza, Chibue and Cóa — were recognized in 2002. While there were no disputes in the Chibue and Cóa areas, the Gudza *regulado* was fraught with conflicts over leadership between sub-chiefs and within the main *régulo* lineage.

Benjamin, who had been pointed out at the 'legitimization meeting' in the Gudza *regulado* a year previously, did not turn up for his recognition. The reason given was that he had 'fallen sick'. It later emerged that his 'sickness' was due to a conflict between him and his uncle, João, who had previously acted as *régulo*. The *chefe do posto*, who needed to pursue the recognition ceremonies within the MAE timeframe, reacted by instructing the members of the Gudza lineage to solve the matter quickly. Within six days a new ceremony was completed. Much to the surprise of people outside the chiefly organization, Benjamin's 27-year-old half-sister, Concessão, signed the contract with the state. She was inaugurated as *régulo*-queen. João and Benjamin were stripped of any kind of formal power and Mateus, a second uncle, was made her assistant.

The moment of state recognition became, in the Gudza area, one of internal stabilization of tradition. One particular story was established as the official genesis of the Gudza *regulado*. It justified the young woman's legitimacy as an indisputable resurrection of the tradition, articulated as 'this is how it has always been'. Perhaps not surprisingly, it was a story agreed upon by the group of people who comprised the core of the governing organization of the *regulado*: the council of (male) elders (*madotas*) and the closest family members of the Gudza lineage. The basis of justification was the true succession line which, despite ardent claims to the contrary, was in fact only reconstructed during the six days between the two ceremonies. Joachim, the only member of the *madotas* who had a long formal education, stated: 'No one knew that Concessão would be recognized. This we found out through a study when the ancestral spirits were consulted'.[10] Despite disparities produced through the collective memory, the following account was given.

For more than four hundred years, a queen with supreme spiritual power (*nhacuaua)* had ruled the Gudza *regulado*. She was always assisted by a man of her lineage to take care of non-spiritual tasks such as tax-collection, policing and forced labour recruitment. The latest queen they could recall was referred to as Mumera, who was assisted by Ofisse, the father of João and Mateus. After him came Jemusse, Ofisse's oldest son and Benjamin and Concessão's father. He reigned from the last years of Portuguese rule until his death in 1989. During the war he was in exile in the mountains near Zimbabwe. No queen ruled during this time. The war and Concessão's infancy were given as reasons. The course of events from Jemusse's death to the present was a story of conflict and instability. Mateus, who was the full younger brother of Jemusse (both were sons of Ofisse's first wife), had been appointed as successor and as assistant of Concessão, but Mateus had been captured by Renamo troops and the twenty-five year old Benjamin was chosen as replacement. He ruled from 1989 until 1996 when he took up migrant work in South Africa. João, also a brother of Jemusse, but the son of Ofisse's second wife, who was working in Beira at the time, was called to assume the position in the meantime. The choice fell on him because he was the eldest of the lineage. When Benjamin returned in 2000 he was not reinstated until a year later when the state-arranged legitimization meeting was held. Although some of the elders referred to João's 'selfish ambition for power' as an obstacle to Benjamin's reassertion of rule, this was not given as the reason why Benjamin did not turn up at the recognition ceremony. The true cause was the ferocity of the ancestral spirits. Speaking through the *curandeiros* (healers and spirit mediums), the spirits had explained that Benjamin fell sick because it was Concessão who was the true leader. Not only was she the eldest living daughter of Jemusse's first wife, she was also imbued with the spiritual power, *nhacuaua*. Upholding the indisputability of this (female) spiritual basis of legitimacy, Concessão's enthronement was presented as a return to normalcy. It was justified by the notion that 'if the spirits are not kept happy everything will ultimately go wrong'.[11] In a rather tautological line of argument, the disruptions of the tradition that had occurred over time were both ascribed to, and blamed for, the ills that had inflicted the *regulado* — namely floods, war, sickness and lack of prosperity.

---

10. Interview, Joachim, September 2002.
11. Interview, Joachim, September 2002.

Tradition Revisited

The official colonial register challenges the historical justification for Concessão's enthronement. No queen is mentioned in the 1969 register outlining the names of Gudza *régulos* six generations back.[12] The name 'Umera' does figure, but here as the elder brother of Ofisse. This does not necessarily falsify the reconstructed succession line, as the colonial powers were known to remove or deny recognition of locally supported leaders (Artur, 1999). It does, however, negate the claim that a queen was officially the Gudza *régulo* under colonial rule. Interestingly, under the *regulado* of Ingomane, 100 km north of Gudza, a queen of the name 'Numera' figures in the register two generations prior to the queen ruling in 1969. Oral history collected by Artur (1999) also suggests that the Murivane predecessors of the Gudza *regulado*, arriving from M'bire in central Zimbabwe, installed female chiefs as a strategy of expansion due to lack of sons. This suggests that the *madotas* drew on memories of other areas prior to Portuguese rule. That such a conglomeration of historical 'facts' was a strategic means for contemporary ends is suggested by alternative stories of why Concessão was recognized.

The official version was challenged by people who did not hold a position in the Gudza organization, not least by those supportive of Benjamin. A teacher and a Red Cross worker of the area suggested that Concessão's appointment should not be understood as an inevitable outcome of traditional resurgence or as a matter of spiritual belief *per se*. It was also a pragmatic solution to long-standing power conflicts within the Gudza family. Emphasizing the possibility of other sources of justification, among which performative skills were significant, they were convinced that the outcome could have been otherwise. They stressed that when Benjamin arrived from the family's place of exile after the war, Jemusse's nephew had asserted the position as *régulo* and refused to resign. To solve the problem Benjamin called João 'because he knows about the *botanica*' [a word used to describe plants applied in witchcraft]. Soon after João's advent, the nephew suspiciously died. João ruled when Benjamin was in South Africa.

Troubles over leadership arose again when João declined to resign on Benjamin's return. He used witchcraft to keep Benjamin at bay. When explaining how Benjamin succeeded in becoming legitimized at the state meeting, neither succession line nor spiritual indication was presented as a significant basis of legitimacy. Rather, the case was made that João had ruled shoddily. Besides being a heavy drinker, he was inconsiderate of the needs of the wider population. The most frequent example recounted was that João had not turned up at meetings with donors when food relief was given out

12. The register emanates from a study made by the Portuguese in the 1960s of local political organization in the Manica and Sofala areas (*Secreto, Portugal: Serviços de centralização e coordinação de informacões. Prospecção das forces tradicional. Manica e Sofala, Provincia de Moçambique 1969*).

after the 2000 floods, resulting in the loss of emergency packages for the Gudza population. As a leader he was also deemed highly immoral, seen as an ambitious person who wanted all the power, at any cost, and as one ruled by fear. He used his status as elder and his capacity to engage in witchcraft for his own ends. Many believed he had killed Benjamin's mother with poison as an act of revenge following the legitimization meeting. In contrast, Benjamin was characterized by all informants as an excellent performer. Notably consistent with criteria conducive to state assistance, he was described as good at collecting taxes, at speaking with NGOs and state officials, and at holding court sessions. Benjamin was also regarded as a good leader on moral grounds: he was portrayed as neither egotistical nor greedy for power, but as an open-minded, generous and consultative person.

According to unofficial stories, constant fear of João and the inability to deal with him within the timeframe set by the state had been the primary reasons for why Benjamin was never recognized. The choice had fallen on Concessão because the *madotas* believed that she would be immune to witchcraft given her spiritual power. Accentuating João's status as the eldest in the lineage, it was accepted that he could have succeeded in being recognized had he performed well. The performative aspect of achieved authority differed noticeably from the ascribed status of Concessão. The various stories that we were told suggest that the state-organized legitimization meeting opened a space for replacing a 'bad' (João) with a 'good' performing ruler (Benjamin), although still from within the lineage registered in *O Livro*. Legitimacy according to authentic spiritual power and succession line, as used for recognizing Concessão, apparently sacrificed the bureaucratic outcome and popular supportive aspect of the legitimization meeting.

The choice of Concessão was a compromise. Her lack of aptitude not only applied to the delegated tasks of the Decree, but also to what were defined as traditional functions — court sessions (*banjas*), annual rainmaking ceremonies and smaller rites of consulting ancestral spirits. Concessão completely lacked the performative skills and knowledge that were required for practical rule. She explicitly stated to us that she was not interested in doing the job of men or of 'talk(ing) politics', as she termed those tasks that lay outside domestic work.[13] The rather pragmatic reasons behind Concessão's enthronement were however, according to critics of her appointment, kept 'secret' by the family and the elders in order to cover up for their inability to keep the popular Benjamin in power.

While not rejecting the significance of spiritual belief behind Concessão's inauguration, it does seem probable that such secrecy also had to do with the interests of those organized around the *regulado* in stabilizing an undisputable order. Not only did their own position depend on such an order, it was a necessary prerequisite for state recognition and its possible benefits. The impetus for stabilizing leadership was in fact broadly shared. Even the critical

13. Interview, Concessão, August 2002.

NGO workers and school teachers referred to above expressed support for the pragmatic stand. Their work too depended on the stability of the *regulado*. For state functionaries it was important that the conflict was settled so that administrative work could begin. The negative effects of recognizing less able leaders from within the Gudza *regulado* could always be taken up at a later stage and changes made if necessary. Exactly how this would be done was a contentious issue. The revised state register — intriguingly enough — verified the official version. In the MAE list of persons legitimized and recognized at district level in 2003, Concessão's name also appears on the date of legitimization in 2001, although it had in fact been Benjamin on that date (MAE, 2004). This clearly points to attempts by local state officials to downplay discrepancies that had occurred in the process of recognition, adding to the idea that the Decree was simply an act of recognizing 'what already exists'.[14]

SUB-CHIEFS: STRUGGLES OVER 'SMALL' BIGNESS

Implementation of the Decree went beyond recognizing the paramount *régulos*. It also attempted to fix the three-tiered hierarchy beneath a *régulo*. The most significant of sub-chiefs is the *chefe do grupo* who holds sway over a designated area within the larger territory of a *regulado*. During the implementation process these sub-chiefs were promised official recognition and a uniform different from the community authorities. Although this is not legally borne out by the Decree, the MAE was planning in 2004 to go ahead with these promises.[15] It is in this context that the power-struggle between the two Gudza sub-chiefs, Jossias and Struba, should be situated. Although the dispute went back some years, and was extensively prolonged by shifting positions within the main lineage, it was intensified and given new content by the implementation of Decree 15/2000. The primary point of dispute was identifying the number one *chefe do grupo* below the new queen. The strategies and criteria of legitimacy invoked in claims to this position were complex. They included disagreements over areas of jurisdiction, spiritual power, performative skills, popular legitimization at state-arranged meetings and the name in the state 'book'. Finally, claims also began to be raised in relation to the newly established succession line of the Gudza Queen.

Spirits, 'Feeding' and Performance

At Benjamin's aborted recognition ceremony at Chibue's homestead, we met Struba, a middle-aged, strong, well-dressed man who spoke some Portuguese.

14. Interview, District Administrator, Sussundenga, August 2002.
15. Interview, Director of rural development and planning, MAE, April 2004.

He told us that he had come to represent the Gudza *regulado* as the '*chefe de grupo* number one' and to bring the message that 'Benjamin had fallen sick'. His status as '*chefe de grupo* number one' was confirmed not only in the state register from 2001, but also by Concessão's recognition ceremony. Here, Struba took a leading role in organizing the ceremonial venue together with the local state official and in escorting and supporting Concessão during all steps of the ceremony. We were quickly convinced that he was a well-esteemed sub-chief, which the state officials also constantly confirmed in speech and actions. Despite these observable acts and his name in *O Livro*, we found that Struba was not recognized as such by the Gudza *regulado*. Reflecting the opinion of this group, the queen's assistant, Mateus, stated: 'He is nothing; he is just a small *Saguta* [lowest sub-chief with no area of jurisdiction]. He just likes to be in the front of things, but he does not have spiritual power and cannot make ceremonies. Jossias is the real *chefe do grupo* number one'.[16] While recognized by the *regulado* as *Sabuko*, Jossias' family name was not mentioned in the register. Different explanations of this discrepancy between the truth of *O Livro* and that of the *regulado* were proffered.

The version agreed upon by Jossias, Mateus and the *madotas* emphasized that according to the Gudza tradition, Struba could only be *Saguta*, because that position was given to his forefathers by the old queen as a reward for 'sacrificing' a son to the Portuguese army. Given that this position was purely 'achieved', it had never been invested with spiritual power. Jossias, who was a timid person, drew up a succession line with some difficulty to illustrate his ancestry from the first queen's number one *chefe do grupo*. He evoked the spiritual power attached to this position: 'My lineage has always had the honourable task of going up in the mountains for annual offerings to *Zviquiro* [the supreme spirit medium] on behalf of the whole *regulado*. This is to ensure rain and the well-being of the population'.[17]

His position came under threat just after the end of the war when the government needed the numbers of people in each area of the *regulado* for distribution of relief-packages. At this point, Struba had seized the opportunity to 'steal land' from Jossias by registering under his own name people residing within the area belonging to Jossias' lineage. This had repeated itself after the floods in 2000 when Jossias' family name was removed from the 'book'. João was blamed. He had secured Struba's lineage by registering him when the administration called for lists of sub-chiefs. Jossias and Mateus were convinced that Struba had 'corrupted' João with good food and drink. This notion of 'feeding' should be understood not only literally, but also metaphorically as a common way of describing the achievement and consumption of the fruits of power in Mozambique (and elsewhere on the continent) (Mbembe, 2001). In light of Struba's lack of spiritual legitimacy,

16. Interview, Mateus, August 2002.
17. Interview, Jossias, September 2002.

his opponents presented this notion of 'feeding' as a clever strategy, but also as an immoral means of achieving, enlarging and sustaining power. According to several members of the *regulado,* the 'feeding' had been extended to the state officials whom, they believed, had been fed with good food by Struba. The latter's presumed conversion from Renamo to Frelimo was also recounted as one of his clever ways of being in good favour with the government people. One sub-chief explained it as follows: 'Struba is only *chefe de grupo* because he is clever. He always stands in front when the state officials come. And he gives them good food . . . Do you know if I am lying? No? Well Struba lies to the state officials and they believe him because he is always the first to tell them the story'.[18]

Merging the Spirits and the Book

Struba's energy and performative skills were undeniable and he fed state officials and other visitors significant food such as meat and local liquor. He was popular outside the Gudza *regulado* and was much better equipped to meet the expectations of the Decree than any other person we met. He had collected the highest amount of tax during 2001 and 2002 and was one of the few people speaking at all the public meetings arranged by state employees and NGOs. By making frequent visits to the administration in Dombe and by turning up on time for meetings he also differed from the other chiefs. He had succeeded in attracting smaller income-generating projects and food relief to his area so the general population were gaining from his success. Beyond his performative skills, Struba also stood out as one of the wealthiest persons that we met outside the administrative headquarters. He had seven wives and a large area of extremely fertile land that was extensively cultivated. The types and quantities of material items that he owned far exceeded any other chief — items that he had acquired through migrant work in South Africa. He was also well-organized. Struba had four police assistants, six *sagutas* (two more than the Gudza queen) and he held well-attended weekly court sessions (*banjas*).

From this, we may conclude that Struba's avenue to the position that he claimed lay outside the spiritual domain and, rather, within the sphere of achieved status — in other words, through performative skills, wealth and popularity. According to Struba's own justification of leadership, this was not entirely the case. In fact, he emphasized his historical relation to the old queen and to spiritual power as the most significant basis of his legitimacy. The noteworthy difference from Jossias was that he combined this set of justifications with other registers of power. According to Struba's version of his lineage history, the old queen had given his grandfather the title of 'number one *chefe do grupo*' after he had served in the army. Subsequently,

18. Interview, Magheba, August 2002.

he was registered in the colonial book and given land, people and spiritual power. As a piece of evidence, Struba showed us a wooden copy of the gun that his grandfather had been given by the colonial army. It was now kept safely in the house of ancestral spirits as a token of his lineage's powerful position in the *regulado*. Frelimo had taken the gun after Independence so he had made a copy for the house of spirits to symbolize the double foundation of his legitimacy. To further legitimize his position, he ensured that Jemusse Gudza had supported his enthronement as superior sub-chief in 1978.

For Struba, the current conflict began after the war when people had lost a sense of who the right leaders were. Matters had been complicated when people like Jossias and João manipulated the true tradition. Struba was nonetheless certain that his success at the legitimization meeting, where he had managed to remain in *O Livro*, was sufficient to win the case against Jossias. *O Livro*, Struba insisted, 'is the thing that identifies [leaders], because if one is lying and the other is telling the truth, the book is what can tell you the truth'. Particularly illustrative of Struba's ability to merge different sources of legitimacy was the way in which he held out the state register not as secondary evidence, but as actual testimony of his traditional, spiritual status. Combined with active performance and strategic alliances across the spectrum of officials, such a merger became momentous in the actual upshot of the conflict.

While Jossias and Mateus held on to the idea that it was the Gudza queen who had the authority to make the final judgment, no actions were taken in that regard. Struba, by contrast, went directly to the *chefe da localidade*, Raul, and demanded a public hearing. Drawing on the legal language of the state, he assured Raul that he would take the case to Sussundenga and even to Maputo if anyone changed the register. He reminded him that falsification of names would bring the lawbreaker to prison. Shortly hereafter, a public meeting was held at the Gudza School. Since it is not legally permissible for state officials to intervene in conflicts within the traditional organization, the event was launched as a 'tax-collection meeting', spearheaded by Raul and the local Frelimo secretary. After discussing the case, the meeting's protagonists — Struba, Jossias, Raul and Mateus — decided that the school director should travel to Dombe, make a written copy of the register and bring it back to the *regulado*.

According to Struba and Raul, the case was solved when the director came back and read aloud the names in the register. For them, *O Livro* became the final arbitrator, which naturally suited Struba as it left Jossias with no *de jure* position. Jossias and Mateus still maintained that the case was unsolved. Surprisingly, this was not because they awaited the judgment of Concessão or the ancestral spirits. Rather, they expected Raul to return and make the final judgment in their favour. This reliance on a state official contradicted not only the principle of spiritual judgment, held as supreme in the appointment of Concessão, but also the state's legal mandate. It nonetheless illustrates how the advent of state recognition may in practice lead to a convergence of two ideally separate spheres of leadership arbitration. Despite no direct appointment of leaders by state officials, conflicts over positions cannot be understood independently of more or less direct actions taken by and in the name of the state: registration of the population for food relief, names in the state register, legitimization meetings and promises of recognition, regalia and subsidies. In addition, strategies of legitimization were usurped as well as interpreted and evaluated in relation to what was regarded as favourable to the state or to government. In Struba's case, the ability to perform the tasks of the Decree, popular support and the ability to convince state officials about traditional status vested in the past served to secure his authority.

Struba's success should be seen against the background of his ability to manoeuvre within different registers of legitimacy that straddled across any ideal boundary between traditional, modern/bureaucratic and democratic/ community types of legitimacy of political office. While Struba held out his ancestors and *O Livro* as the basis of traditional status, he recognized the pragmatic strategies of being 'known by the government people', working hard and showing respect, in public, for the order of the state. Yet, Struba's on-stage compliance with the state and Frelimo representatives did not mean straightforward support for the government. Off-stage, he was much more critical than his opponents believed, and in fact more so than any of the other chiefs we met. Interpreting the Decree as driven by political interests, Struba was convinced that state recognition was aimed at *ganhar as pessoas* (winning the people):

> We can see that it is politics . . . All that [recognition] is to win the people. They hope that to gain the *régulo* is to win the people, because the *régulo* can mobilize the people. We know that this is what it is about. But we have to be quiet because we know that it is them who are in the government. If I speak tomorrow, I will go to prison or be killed.[19]

CONCLUDING DISCUSSION

With its incorporation into the universal order of the state and in partnership in public administration, one might expect a homogenization or fixing of 'traditional authority'. Granting to community authorities the right to display the national flag and wear national emblems along with a universal set of state-defined tasks to pursue seems to indicate that homogenization was indeed an objective of Decree 15/2000. To simply assume such a result would be to overlook the fact that different brokers and intermediaries — state as well as non-state — translated the Decree in the course of its implementation (Wilson, 2001: 313–18). While *de jure* recognition by the state is expected to influence local politics beyond the initial acts of putting the Decree into practice, we cannot assume that legalization *per se* assures the kind of public authority envisaged in the Decree (Lund, 2001). Equally, the legitimacy of community authority that is now inscribed in *O Livro* and displayed by

19. Interview, Struba, October 2002.

'the flag' does not guarantee *de facto* broad-based legitimacy of either the institution or its office holder. The meagre participation in state-convened legitimization meetings, the negotiability of and disagreement on what counts as *the* tradition and the shifting positioning and vigour of chieftaincy over time all make it tricky to equate *de jure* with *de facto* authority. Whether local populations and external agents are practically able to use the institution and whether newly recognized leaders are able to effectively enforce collective decisions remains to be seen. Divisions within those communities defined in the Decree as 'the collective of people comprised in a unified territorial organization' (Republica de Moçambique, 2000a: Art. 8) will influence the recognized leaders' ability to entrench and maintain the kind of public authority that is envisaged.

So far, the process of legitimization and recognition suggests a (re)production of both complementary and conflicting notions of legitimate authority. While all protagonists in the cases analysed drew on tradition as essential to their legitimacy, the question of what comprises the truly or most significantly traditional rules of appointment and basis of authority were negotiable and situation-specific. As we have noted, these could range from *ascribed* assets — spiritual power and succession line — to *performative* abilities regarded as qualities of a good traditional leader, such as knowledge of practices defined as traditional and the ability to perform them (court sessions, annual rainmaking ceremonies and spiritual consultation). Personal capital such as hard work, administrative skills, ability to consult state officials and NGOs, a generous personality and popularity amongst the residents of the area were also important. This suggests that legitimacy may be understood not as a fixed quality, but as 'a conflict-ridden and open process' in which different local power holders and their judges or 'audiences' intervene (Lentz, 1998: 47).

In Sussundenga, broad-based community legitimization included identifying persons from within an already state-registered lineage. Authorization by a designated group of elders and confirmation/disconfirmation of the register influenced the final recognition. How tradition was successfully defined defied any generalized Weberian dichotomy between 'traditional' and 'modern/state' types of authority and forms of legitimization. This is not surprising when we understand the shifting historical-political contexts in which traditional chiefs have operated, and how these inform contemporary images of authority, power and adequate performance (West and Kloeck-Jenson, 1999: 455). Struba's merger of the 'book' and 'the spirits' is a case in point. The ahistorical portrait of the 'truly traditional' that forms the basis of the Decree was only momentarily enacted in legitimacy claims. In this, we share Moore's (1986) view of the traditional as internally contested and its manifestation in any given historical moment as the outcome of processes of invention, redefinition and reproduction.

Following Pierre Bourdieu´s (1986) work on forms of capital produced and reproduced within different social fields, it is clear that kin-based legitimacy can be (and often is) articulated alongside other forms of capital, not least when kin-based institutions are expected to operate (and have historically operated) within different fields of action. To assume that these fields of action, structured by different sources and types of capital, are easy to distinguish in practice would be foolish. Equally, it would be unwise to assume any simple conversion between what counts as legitimate forms of capital in traditional and state-administrative fields. Lentz (1998) and Oomen's (2002) studies in Ghana and South Africa suggest a distinction between the *basis of legitimacy* — a common denominator here being some version of *the* tradition — and *pragmatic strategies* of achieving and enlarging the scope of authority within different fields of action. Not only the Decree, but also state and non-state actors in Sussundenga District draw an ideal and often morally grounded separation between 'state/party/government' and 'traditional' types of office. However, this should not make us overlook the fact that, on a pragmatic level, there are (and have been) multiple links between party politics, government policies/actions and traditional office. Perhaps the most powerful image of this was the common reliance on *O Livro* to legitimate authority. *O Livro* itself was derived from colonial and post-colonial administrative work. This concrete 'reality' when merged with the fragmented 'reality' of multiple personal memories, each with a political agenda, impacted on the previously created concrete 'reality'. As the Gudza case illustrates, the 'book' could be corrected to reflect the outcome desired by the more powerful party.

The domains of state and tradition are not isolated entities in everyday practice, but part of a particular local political context where different imaginings and practices of power and authority mingle (see Le Meur, this issue). This was reflected in the ways in which state officials translated the Decree. The exclusive encouragement of the recognition of *régulos* in Sussundenga's rural areas seems partly due to the legal basis on which legitimization rested — 'the traditional rules of the respective community'. State officials were cautious to impose candidates who could not fulfil such requirements. Even though subversion was attempted — as for example in the Mathica case — the recognition of leaders remained within the wider traditional system. The regional differences suggest cautiousness on the part of state officials operating in Renamo strongholds. In this context, the appeal of *the* traditional has, as we have illustrated in different ways, clear government objectives. Some kind of articulation is needed between rural constituencies and the state. Beyond the urban or semi-urban areas of Sussundenga District, Renamo control and war insurgence were intense. Where the guardian of tradition contradicted the performative capacity and/or the *de facto* authority presumed in the Decree, compromise was reached — as in the case of Concessão and Zixixi. In the Gudza *regulado* the main objective was to stabilize leadership in order to end destructive internal conflicts which, it is alleged, had led to two murders within the *régulo* family. In the Zixixi case, tradition was what state officials had to rely on in order to keep the peace even when it made little administrative sense.

Despite the fault lines, state officials' strong conviction that traditional leaders have 'a lot of power' was significant for the implementation of the Decree. The role of chiefs as effective performers of state-administrative tasks during colonial rule was frequently reiterated, if not envied. Likewise, former alliances with Renamo were interpreted as causing hostility towards state institutions after the war, extremely low tax-payment and distancing from donor/government-launched development projects. Overall, the chiefs' sway over the population was seen as contributing toward these difficulties. Seeing the impetus for recognizing *régulos* as a pragmatic means to ease administrative tasks and government programmes should not lead us to underestimate state officials' own ideas about the spiritual power of chiefs and their ability to use witchcraft against oppositional forces. In this regard, it is important to note that the blurring of the ideal boundaries between 'traditional' and 'modern' domains of power and authority is not limited to the sphere of chieftaincy, but also permeates the state.

In rural as well as urban areas, it is common to explain the power of state officials, just like that of chiefs, as deriving from supernatural means and/or materials acquired from *curandeiros*.[20] National leaders and high-ranking civil servants are often believed to have specific spiritual power. Some are even regarded as being *feiticeiros* (people capable of witchcraft). Beliefs and imaginings about power succession are also important. In speeches by state officials at public events such as national days, the Frelimo leadership since the liberation war would often be presented as a 'lineage'. The message was: just as the *régulo* of a certain lineage always ruled in his area, members of the Frelimo family have ruled and will always rule in Mozambique. The *regulado* thereby became a metonymical expression for a general understanding of the succession of power holding (Kyed and Buur, 2006 forthcoming).

As state agents and representatives of local communities, traditional leaders merge the ideally separate domains of the 'traditional' and the 'modern-state', adding further shades to the 'twilight' character of current state formation processes in post-war Mozambique. The potential contradictions that emerge with regard to the objectives of Decree 15/2000 will depend on how it continues to be mediated and interpreted locally. If we begin with the agreement by all informants — state and non-state — that entrenchment and maintenance of authority will depend on the community leaders' ability to 'show results', the question still remains: what results and for whom? The Decree itself provides no ready-made answers.

REFERENCES

Alexander, J. (1997) 'The Local State in Post-war Mozambique: Political Practices and Ideas about Authority', *Africa* 67(1): 1–26.

20. Sanders (2001) makes a similar point for Tanzania, as do Geschiere (1997) and Mbembe (2001) for Cameroon.

Artur, D. do R. (1999) 'Estudo de Caso Provincia de Manica', in D. do R. Artur, J. C. Cafuquiza and A. Z. Ivala (eds) *Tradição e Modernidade. Que Lugar para a Tradição Africana na Governação Descentralizada de Moçambique?*, pp. 49–139. Maputo: PDD (GTZ) and Ministerio da Administração Estatal.

Artur, D. do R. and B. Weimer (1998) 'Decentralisation and Democratisation in Post-war Mozambique: What Role of Traditional African Authority in Local Government Reform?'. Paper presented at the 14th Congress of the International Union of Anthropological and Ethnological Sciences, Williamsburg, VA (25 July–1 August).

Bourdieu, P. (1986) 'The Forms of Capital', in J. G. Richardson (ed.) *Handbook of Theory and Research for the Sociology of Education*, pp. 241–58. New York, Westport, CT, and London: Greenwood Press.

Buur, L. and H. M. Kyed (2003) 'Implementation of Decree 15/2000 in Mozambique: The Consequences of State Recognition of Traditional Authority in Sussundenga'. Report. Copenhagen: Institute for International Studies; Aarhus: University of Aarhus.

Dava, F., M. Macia and R. Dove (2003) *Reconhecimento e Legitimação das Autoridades Comunitárias à Luz do Decreto 15/2000. O caso de grupo etnolinguístico Ndau*. Colecção Embondeito, 24. Maputo: ARPAC.

Englebert, P. (2002) 'Patterns and Theories of Traditional Resurgence in Tropical Africa', *Mondes en Development* 30: 118–51.

Geffray, C. (1990) *A Causa das Armas. Antropologia da Guerra Contemporânea em Moçambique*. Porto: Edições Afrontamento.

Geschiere, P. (1997) *The Modernity of Witchcraft. Politics and the Occult in Postcolonial Africa*. Charlottesville, VA, and London: University of Virginia Press.

Handler, R. and J. Linnekin (1984) 'Tradition, Genuine or Spurious', *Journal of American Folklore* 97: 273–89.

Kyed, H. M. and L. Buur (2006 forthcoming) 'New Sites of Citizenship: Recognition of Traditional Authority and Group-based Citizenship in Mozambique', *Journal of Southern African Studies* 32(3).

Lentz, C. (1998) 'The Chief, the Mine Captain and the Politician: Legitimating Power in Northern Ghana', *Africa* 68(1): 46–67.

Lund, C. (2001) 'Precarious Democratization and Local Dynamics in Niger: Cases of Local Politics in Zinder', *Development and Change* 32(5): 845–69.

Lundin, I. B. and J. Machava (1995) 'Quadro de Conclusoes Gerais sobre o debate das Autoridades tradicionais', in I. B. Lundin and J. Machava (eds) *Autoridade e Poder Tradicional Vol. 1*, pp. 151–2. Maputo: Ministério da Administração Estatal/Núcleo de Desenvolvimento Administrativo.

Mbembe, A. (2001) *On the Postcolony*. Berkeley, CA, and London: University of California Press.

MAE (1996) *Autoridade Tradicional em Moçambique. Autoridade Tradicional Brochura 1*. Maputo: Ministério da Administração Estatal.

MAE (2004) *Mapas de autoridades Comunitárias legitimadas e reconhecidas poer provincial*. Maputo: Ministério da Administração Estatal.

Moore, S. F. (1986) *Social Facts and Fabrications: 'Customary' Law on Kilimanjaro 1880–1980*. Cambridge: Cambridge University Press.

Noticias (1995a) 'Régulos explusam agents the PRM em Dombe', *Noticias* 29 June (Maputo).

Noticias (1995b) 'Problemas dos Régulos em Dombe requerem medidas urgentes', *Noticias* 4 July (Maputo).

O'Laughlin, B. (2000) 'Class and the Customary: The Ambiguous Legacy of the Indigenato in Mozambique', *African Affairs* 99: 5–42.

Oomen, B. M. (2002) 'Chiefs! Law, Power and Culture in Contemporary South Africa'. PhD Dissertation, University of Leiden, Netherlands.

Republica de Moçambique (2000a) 'Diploma Ministerial no. 107-a/2000', Ministério de Administração Estatal (27 August). Maputo: Imprensa Nacional.

Republica de Moçambique (2000b) 'Decreto no. 15/2000', Conselho de Ministros (20 June). Maputo: Imprensa Nacional.

Sanders, Todd (2001) 'Save our Skins: Structural Adjustment, Morality and the Occult in Tanzania', in H. L. Moore and Todd Sanders (eds) *Magical Interpretations, Material Realities. Modernity, Witchcraft and the Occult in Postcolonial Africa*, pp. 160–83. London and New York: Routledge.

Weber, M. (1978) *Economy and Society*, G. Roth and C. Wittich (eds). Berkeley, CA, and London: University of California Press.

West, H. G. and S. Kloeck-Jenson (1999) 'Betwixt and Between: "Traditional Authority" and Democratic Decentralization in Post-War Mozambique', *African Affairs* 98: 455–84.

Wilson, F. (2001) 'In the Name of the State? Schools and Teachers in an Andean Province', in T. B. Hansen and F. Stepputat (eds) *States of Imagination: Ethnographic Explorations of the Postcolonial State*, pp. 313–44. Durham, NC: Duke University Press.

State Making and the Politics of the Frontier in Central Benin

Pierre-Yves Le Meur

Igor Kopytoff's internal frontier thesis has opened room for renewed approaches to settlement history, ethnicity and cultural reproduction in pre-colonial Africa. In his seminal book *The African Frontier* (1987), he proposes a general interpretative model placing mobility at the centre stage as a structural feature in the production of the social and political order. 'The African frontier we focus on consists of politically open areas nestling between organized societies but "internal" to the larger regions in which they are found — what might be called an "internal" or "interstitial frontier"' (ibid.: 9). This genetic approach to the frontier is based on a continued sequence of fragmentation (production of frontiersmen ejected from their original society) and aggregation (production of adherents as kinsmen and later subjects) (ibid.: 16–17). One crucial point lies in the construction of an 'institutional vacuum':

> [T]he frontier also arises out of subjective definitions of reality: societies often define neighboring areas as lacking any legitimate political institutions and as being open to legitimate intrusion and settlement — this even if the areas are in fact occupied by organized polities. In brief, the frontier is above all a political fact, a matter of a political definition of geographical space. (ibid.: 11)

Another important aspect of Kopytoff's model rests upon the idea of 'institutional bricolage' (in Mary Douglas's sense: he does not use the expression). Frontiersmen and their followers resort to the existing stock of cultural and normative patterns in order to build a new polity. This would explain the elements of continuity and reproduction underlying the whole process. 'Our analysis has tried to take a shorter step — from the political ecology of the frontier and its constraints to the structural setting in which African political culture was perpetuated and to the shaping in this setting of certain fundamental and very often contradictory features of that political culture' (ibid.: 76).

As we will briefly see below, Kopytoff's explanatory framework applies quite well to the pre-colonial history of central Benin, as far as the structuring position of segmentation and mobility in the (re)production of social and political order are concerned. One could thus ask if the model validly expands beyond the rupture of the colonial conquest and if it has 'something to say' about the trajectory of colonial and post-colonial states in Africa.

I would like to thank Jean-Pierre Jacob warmly for his comments, as astute and stimulating as usual, and Lara Colo for her careful proofreading.

Drawing on the case of Central Benin,[1] I will argue that one can interpret the colonial intrusion, at least partly, in terms of frontier dynamics. First, its conceptual (ideological) basis is about filling in — actually constructing — an institutional and moral vacuum, the latter (absent from Kopytoff's framework) working as a justifying principle for the whole. Second, despite the objective of territorializing domination through coercive and administrative procedures, colonial governmentality (Pels, 1997) has allowed new patterns of mobility to emerge that have strongly influenced the local politics of belonging and resource control in central Benin. In- and out-migration flows have transformed the conditions of access to land and control over labour, giving the frontier institution of *tutorat* (sponsorship) a central position organizing relations between autochthonous landholders and migrants along a patron–client pattern (Chauveau, 2006). This link has ruled access to land in close connection with service and labour exchanges. Beyond its dyadic form, it has up to now constituted the core unit of the government of people and resources in this frontier context, interacting with politico-legal bodies (chieftaincy, hometown associations, village councils), and state and development interventions.

I will further argue that the political frontier metaphor provides us with a useful heuristic device to capture the logic of state making in post-colonial Benin. State making is here conceived as the unpredictable (and often rather unstable) outcome of organizing practices (Nuijten, 2003: 10–12) taking place inside and outside state and non-state organizations and arenas.[2] In this respect, the development aid apparatus has been playing an increasing role since the late 1980s in Benin, as a structural feature of the national political economy (or as 'development rent'; see Bierschenk, 1993; Le Meur, 2000) and as part and parcel of the state-making processes.

---

1. I first came to Gbanlin (an administrative village in the commune of Ouesse, *Département des Collines*) in 1993 for a short collective inquiry within the framework of a programme on democratization and local powers in rural Benin (Bierschenk and Olivier de Sardan, 1998, 2003). I carried out individual fieldwork within the same programme in 1995, taking over from the rural sociologist Cyriaque Adjinacou who did fieldwork in 1993 before beginning to work with PGRN in Ouessè (Adjinacou, 1995; Le Meur, 1998; Le Meur and Adjinacou, 1998). I returned to Gbanlin in 2002 and 2004, this time for an INCO project funded by the European Union on 'changes in land access, institutions and markets in West Africa' (CLAIMS). The work is still in progress (see Le Meur, forthcoming, on delayed decentralization viewed from the local level). Julien Barbier, an MSc student from CNEARC (National Centre for Agronomy in the Tropics, Montpellier) did fieldwork under my supervision in 2003/04 (and together with me in January and February 2004; see Barbier, 2005). In this article, use is made of documents from the National Archives of Benin (ANB); unless otherwise stated, translations from the original are my own.
2. My argument is thus situated, as it were, 'beyond' Berman and Lonsdale's distinction (1992: 5) 'between *state-building*, as a conscious effort of creating an apparatus of control, and *state-formation*, as an historical process of conflicts, negotiations and compromises between diverse groups whose self-serving actions and trade-offs constitute the "vulgarisation of power"'.

Resorting to the interstitial frontier approach is productive here, especially as regards the discursive practices inherent in development as both an exogenous intervention and a set of institutions. As we will see in the example of an externally funded natural resource management project, some of the main frontier features, such as the conquest of areas imagined to be 'institutional vacuums', are filled in by standardized committees and give room for entrepreneurs' and brokers' strategies. Segmentary tendencies and cultural conservatism (see Kopytoff, 1999) underlie the functioning of projects as the co-existence of diverging stories about their arrival and implementation, stories fuelled by the combination of different narratives and ideologies (of modernization, of democratic participation, of autochthony, of territory and village, of kinship, and so on).[3] Denying the relevance or the very existence of alternative local stories (that is: of actions and knowledge too) constitutes a factor (among others) that contributes to the political creation of an institutional and cognitive vacuum (see for example Bierschenk, 1988; van der Ploeg, 1993). These effects are strengthened by the non-systematic nature of development, selecting intervention areas according to obfuscating criteria and favouring the weakly reflected notion of pilot-project.[4] Generating and bearing complex flows of resources, techniques and ideas (Appadurai, 1996), development works as a 'global internal frontier' (Chauveau et al., 2004) interacting at all levels with state and non-state actors and authorities and contributing to a normative and institutional production shaping state-making processes in a specific way.

State making, as a loose set of organizing practices, is 'fundamentally about defining the forms and legitimations of government and governmentality' (Sivaramakrishnan, 2000: 433). Accordingly, it draws cognitive and politico-administrative boundaries regarding territory, natural resources, ethnicity, citizenship, public/private, and knowledge, as well as development, as part of the process. They are embedded in the specific trajectory of a frontier society — or rather a frontier situation[5] — and contribute to reproducing and reshaping this specific configuration. A focus and result of this interplay is the village as a form of locality. A specific moment in the course of mobile trajectories before the colonial conquest, villages were transformed into entry-gates for state penetration under colonial rule. Political and administrative village government has changed over time, especially in the last fifteen years under the pressure of three interconnected factors: democratization (1989–91), development projects (here mainly a natural resource

---

3. Here I follow Sivaramakrishnan (2000: 432) who writes that '*development* — as it is imagined, practised, and re-created — is best described as stories that can change in their telling, as they are pieced together into contingently coherent narratives. Development's stories are rife with a micropolitics often obscured by the consistency or more orderly progression implied by the terms *discourse* or *narrative*'.
4. See Scott (1998: 257–61) on the idea of miniaturization in development intervention.
5. See Ingold (1996) for a contradictory debate on the heuristic productivity of the concept of 'society', especially J. Peel's and M. Strathern's contradictory thesis.

management project 1993–2003[6]), and decentralization (2002–03). The production of locality (Appadurai, 1996: 178 ff.) stands at the centre of these processes and PGRN/PGTRN has been playing a very specific role in this respect, by promoting a paradoxical modality of 'villagization'. It does not rely anymore on the resettlement of scattered populations in core villages concentrating state services and making political and administrative control easier.[7] The notion of *terroir* (the T of PGTRN) is used here as the conceptual operator of the villagization, conflating different layers: the village as administrative level, residential unit, bounded territory and farmed area. As a PGRN/PGTRN component, land operations (the Rural Land Plan, PFR) identify and recognize so-called customary land rights. It is implemented at village level too, reinforcing the process of village production.[8]

As we will see in this text, the production of the village, as resulting from the interplay between moral community building and localizing state (von Oppen, 1999: 50), is in no way a smooth and linear process. Firstly, the local political arena is highly conflictive and polycentric (see Le Meur and Adjinacou, 1998 for detailed case studies). Secondly, viewed from a perspective including its relations to neighbouring localities and exogenous interventions, local political life seems to work along (irregular) cycles of fission and fusion, as if the segmentary logic of the frontier were imprisoned in the village cage. Finally, the efficiency of projects (project in a broad meaning: PFR/PGRTN/decentralization) in creating democratic and governable spaces — or villages — remains highly questionable.[9]

THE PRE-COLONIAL POLITICAL FRONTIER AND COLONIAL PENETRATION: GOVERNING MOBILITY

Over the long term, mobility is a structural feature of central Benin's social history, from pre-colonial times onwards. Movements of people, resources, norms and values have been crucial in the production and reproduction of the social and political order.

---

6. PGRN (*Projet de gestion des ressources naturelles*, 1993–8), later PGTRN (*Projet de gestion des terroirs et des ressources naturelles*, 1999–2003).
7. Cf. Scott (1998: ch. 7), von Oppen (1999, 2002) for colonial Zambia and post-colonial Tanzania, and Moore (2000) for Zimbabwe. Dahomey saw a brief (but with enduring effects) phase of villagization under President Maga (1960–63) mainly in the north of the country; see Bako-Arifari (1998: 59–60) for a case study. See Woost (1994) for a complementary perspective on the place of the village in nation-building processes.
8. The Benin Rural Land Plan (*Plan foncier rural*, PFR) experience is detailed in Le Meur (2006). See Colin et al. (forthcoming) on customary land rights recording in a comparative perspective.
9. See Rose's discussion on the making of 'governable spaces' (1999: 31 ff.).

Pre-Colonial Mobility of Lineages, Localities and Boundaries

From the seventeenth century, central Benin was a buffer and refuge area between the slave raider states of Danhome in the south and Oyo in the east, and Wasangari chiefships of pre-colonial Borgu to the north. The Mahi 'ethnic group', to which the founders of Gbanlin and most other villages located west of Ouessè (the study area) belong, can be seen as a by-product of this history. The Mahi belong to the Gbe-speaking group like the Fon, the dominant ethnic group in south Benin and, together with various Yoruba subgroups (Sabe, Idasa and others), are considered to be the 'autochthons' of central Benin. The Mahi ethnogenesis is a long-term process made of mobility and shifting identities and political allegiances. The earliest written recordings of the denomination trace back to the 1730s (Law, 1991: 19n), but this does not mean that the term did not exist before. The various Mahi groups would have actually emerged in the sixteenth and seventeenth centuries (see Lespinay's synthesis, 1994). As an ethnic group, it would have resulted from the slow merging of 'Yoruba' autochthonous peoples[10] and latecomers with Adja-Fon groups (and probably other groups, through slavery) from the south (the Abomey plateau but also the Ouemè river region and Adjaland, Aheme Lake for the Dovi founders of the Kingdom of Savalou) escaping the Dahomean expansion — or internal political rivalries — to the north (Bergé, 1928; Mulira, 1984). This common history does not mean that the Mahi had already formed a well-defined we-group by the eighteenth century. In fact, the ethnic denomination 'Mahi' seems to be an exogenous name (which does not mean that the very group is an 'artificial' or merely exogenous creation). Even though its etymology is still contested, most historians agree upon a Dahomean origin, stressing for some of them the independent and wild character of these populations (Anignikin, 2001: 253–6; Mulira, 1984: 10–13).

The ethnic denomination tends to conflate with a geographical meaning, Mahiland, seemingly devoid of ethnic connotation. It encompasses territories located north of Danhomē kingdom boundaries, populated by potential slaves, allies and enemies (when for instance allied with the Oyo Empire). This indeterminacy between ethnic and geographical meanings is significant in an area mostly defined by its geopolitical situation and made of a mosaic of micro-polities founded by groups claiming various origins and itineraries and whose names cross so-called 'ethnic boundaries'.[11] Entering the debate

10. Named Gedevi in the first travellers' accounts: Yoruba ethnogenesis is itself a later process and the term Yoruba applied only to Oyo population in the nineteenth century (Peel, 1989).
11. For instance, one finds Ayato (originally blacksmiths) and Ajanu lineages among the Idasa and Mahi populations and Ayinon can be found in Fon as well as in Mahi villages. Roch Mongbo (1995: 141 ff.) illustrates this trans-ethnic feature in the case of Mahi 'landholders' receiving Idasa newcomers bearing the same clan name. One clan of warriors (Kajanu), member of a typically Mahi network of five clans (*akôta atôon*), is known for its Ile Ife origin (Celestin Chokpon, personal communication, 21 January 2004). Other localities in central Benin that eventually became 'Yoruba' (such as Dasse-Zoumé) had a very similar history of political encounter and cultural sedimentation of ethnic groups from diverse origins (see Adediran, 1984).

on pre-colonial ethnicity would bring us beyond the scope of this text. Let us follow Sandra Greene (1996: 14) when she includes kinship, time of arrival and original homeland as structuring ethnic belonging as much as the idea of an identity based on invented cultural, linguistic and/or regional groupings. Such a perspective stands closer to the narratives I have collected.[12]

Oral tradition (with a few variations; interviews carried out in 1995, 2002, 2004) stresses Gbanlin Hansoue as a starting point for the current village foundation, although informants know that the history of escape and resettlement is much older. The Devo people — or Gbanlinu, the founders of the village — would have come from the Za region (somewhere between Zagnanado and Agonli-Cové, 50 km east of Abomey, around 200 km south of the present village), via the Fitta kingdom (region of Dassa).[13] The narrative of Gbanlin foundation by the Devo is not independent from key relations to other clans, mainly the Ayinon and the Awooyi, stemming from encounters in Gbanlin Hansoué or later in Adjowini (the name of a hill, like Anyao). These are based on matrimonial alliances — the Ayinon as Devo kings' wives or mothers (*axôsunô* or *axôsusi*) — or political alliances — the Awooyi as *to-nukun* of the *axôsu* (the 'eyes' within the community of the king/chief). Interestingly, both clans also have a 'geographical' denomination, respectively Za and Houin (located south of Asanté, not far from Gbanlin Hansoué), referring to a key moment in their history of displacement. Most of the localities in the Gbanlin area were founded according to the same pattern, linking a founding clan and privileged allies, resulting in the multi-lineage village structure.[14] But each of them has developed its own history of alliances, which may be reflected in the great variety of political positions, naming and hierarchies in Mahi villages, also stressed by Mulira (1984: 60–67).

This complex history of mobility — expressed through a sort of segmentary oral history punctuated by pivotal events — explains the weak emic differentiation between the two levels of social organization of *akô* (clan) and *hɛnnu* (lineage). The former is characterized by a specific narrative (*mlan mlan* corresponding to the Yoruba *oriki*), referring to a historico-mythical ancestor. It is a non-localized entity, while the latter appears to be its localized

---

12. Also see Lindgren (2004) for a focus on the internal dynamics of ethnicity in Zimbabwe, paying attention to the forms of differentiation and hierarchy within ethnic groups, related to clan belongings, origins and castes.
13. According to Anignikin (2001: 256), 'since its first installation in Gbowelè, the village of Gbanlin has been rebuilt successively in Ifita, Savalou and Ouèssè-Wogoudo' (he does not quote any source). He further adds that one finds several wards called Gbanlin in north Zou localities, where Gbanlinu live together with Dovi, Ajanu, Gbeto, Hwegbonu and Nago people.
14. Through marriages and later settlements, the founding clan of a locality was a secondary clan in the nearby village. The Daavi, one of the main clans in Vossa (west of Gbanlin) with the Ouegbonu (or Hoko) and the Ahantun Dakpanu (founders) are present in Gbanlin, as well as the Agnanmè, coming from Savalou, and one of the main clans in Tosso (located between Vossa and Gbanlin), together with the Ajanu and the Ayato (founders and also called Tossonu, 'originally' coming from Porto Novo area in southwestern Benin).

expression (at the village level). As mentioned above, the clan/lineage naming of the Devo (and of other groups) is geographically specified according to the history of its members' mobility. Clan/lineage is spontaneously referred to as a primary level of belonging. Religious mediations played a key role in decision-making processes regarding mobility and resource use. Settlement place was chosen through Fa consultation and the *hɛnnu vodun* (Sakpata in the Devo case) warranting that the wealth and growth of the community was transported from place to place.[15] At a more individual level, the opening of a new field was preceded by Fa consultation in order to know more about local field divinity (*glevodun* or *danvodun*) preferences and taboos. The trans-local and trans-ethnic circulation of vodun cults can be seen as a building block of cultural continuity between polities in this frontier zone. What was thus emerging locally was 'moral communities' consisting of social groupings linked by common elements of history and trajectories expressed in shared narrative canvas (despite factual and interpretative divergences) and functional complementarity (fictitious labour division in ritual and political matters) between founding groups (often expressing a specific chronology of arrival).

The Colonial Reshaping of Mobility and Boundaries

The effects of colonization were ambivalent: on the one hand, it resulted in a territorialization of domination and in a stabilization of localities and boundaries, while on the other hand, it entailed renewed and diversified frontier dynamics.

The colonial conquest of the Danhomè kingdom was achieved in 1894 and northern territories were eventually included in the new colony of *Dahomey et Dépendances* in 1898. In Central Benin, the French had concluded protectorate treaties with the kings of the so-called confederacy of the Dassa and confederacy of the Mahi (with Savalou as the capital city) as well as with minor chiefs of the region (Mulira, 1984: 154–7) by 1894. Through the protectorate policy, the colonial administration tended to conflate territorial notion, ethnic denomination and political authority, as regards areas that were ethnically heterogeneous and populations that defined themselves mostly according to a clan denomination reflecting both lineage and locality dimensions. The indirect rule through protectorates was replaced by more direct administration in the following decades and the new power structure was in place by the 1910s. The *cercle*, *subdivision* and *poste* were ruled by a French administrator and the lower levels of the *canton* and the *village* by indigenous chiefs. Several reorganizations happened during the colonial era, a sign of hesitations on the French side about the compromise they had to

15. *Xwlegbe* (a palmist squirrel), Devo's totem, is known for its fecundity; it is the symbol of the growth wealth of the community.

reach between indigenous chiefs' legitimacy (anchored in so-called customs and traditions) and docility (for central Benin, see Asiwaju, 1976: 57 ff.; Mulira, 1984: 159 ff.).[16]

> In Gbanlin, Dossou Ode, the son of the village founder, famous for his wealth — as a big farmer, based on wealth-in-people — would have refused to succeed him, pressing a younger brother, Amoussou, a hunter, to accept the position. He assured him of his material help, if needed. Informants speak of the event in terms of 'bridewealth', which would have been Ode's words. This was done against the opinion of the Ouessè canton chief, Ganglozoun, and of the French *commandant de cercle*. A few years later, Ganglozoun, the Ouessè canton chief died and his brother was chosen 'according to tradition and the unanimous opinion that he was the most worthy to fulfil these functions'. (ANB, Carton 1E17$_2$, 'political situation', March 1905)

The creation of canton and village chiefships implied a new hierarchy between localities (that is, the supremacy of Ouessè over the neighbouring Mahi villages). The development of infrastructures (roads and railway) re-oriented the geography of villages along a West/East direction in the canton of Ouessè (whereas the trajectories of lineages and localities had followed a South/North axis in pre-colonial times). The road linking Idadjo to the North/South axis (road and railway between Cotonou and Parakou via Savè) was built with forced labour. Each village had to construct a set portion of the road, contributing to the delineation of village limits. Moreover, the colonial administration also produced many regulations (such as identity books) and taxes aimed simultaneously at constraining populations' movements (in order to avoid exit options *vis-à-vis* the poll tax) and at securing trade between the northern and southern part of the colony (and also, from 1914 on, at supporting the French economy in wartime).[17]

---

16. We find a nice expression of this tension in the monthly report of the Savè *commandant de cercle*: 'Mamadou, the chief of Savè-Kilibo Region, followed by a few people, also crossed the country to facilitate the work of his subordinates. We enjoined this provincial chief, who tended to revive ancient customs by only travelling with a large cortege, to reduce the number of his servants to the bare minimum. It is true that a too numerous escort has the advantage of raising prestige; but it also has the same inconvenience as the passage of locusts — weighing too heavily on the regions crossed' (ANB, Carton 1E18, monthly reports, *cercle de Savè*, November 1917; my translation). Another significant (and somehow contradictory) manifestation of this dilemma (February 1919) is: 'Village chiefs are, however, little obeyed; this lack of authority is due in large part to a defective social organization that we can hardly modify without harming secular customs' (my translation).
17. 'In addition to being a trading license, the *carte de circulation transportant* was also a means of regulating and deterring local migrations. The French felt that a tax on circulation or the movements of traders from region to region would serve to restrict the migrations of manpower out of the French colonies into the nearby British and German colonies' (Mulira, 1984: 218). 'The co-operation of the local Mahi in areas of commerce and agriculture had been made obligatory by Articles 4 and 5 of the treaties contracted with the Mahi chiefs of Savalou, Paouignan, Dassa, Ouessè, and Djalloukou between 24 April 1894 and December 1895. These articles stated clearly that people of Mahiland were to continue in their agricultural and commercial pursuits in conjunction with making sure that all trade routes passing through their villages and regions were kept open' (ibid.: 224).

However, one must not overestimate the efficiency of this bureaucracy. Complaints about lack of staff, flourishing smuggling and arduous transports are recurrent in colonial reports, as shown by the following quotations:

> 'Taxes of all sorts should return much but the staff is insufficient. Smuggling flourishes, caravaneers do not pay the taxes, alcohol merchants are not inspected, fines are derisory' (ANB, Carton $1E17_2$, 'political situation', April 1907).

> 'All the *poste* chiefs complain about the state of bridges and roads, a large number of which are in very poor condition. They say that communications will be interrupted within a month, resulting in the suppression of civil servant transport and considerable slowing in delivery' (ANB, Carton $1E17_2$, 'political situation', June 1907).

> 'A visit to the canton of Ouécé is necessary. This canton has not been visited by the circle commander for three years' (ANB, Carton 1E32, 3rd Term 1922).

Furthermore — and against the territorializing influences mentioned above — colonial 'pacification', by reducing demographic and land pressure in refuge areas, generated a movement of agrarian colonization. This reshaped local positions on and debates about autochthony[18] and access to land and natural resources, in the form of a new frontier dynamic. Colonial reports collected in the National Archives clearly show that the Ouessè region, though remote and not easily accessible, was an important agricultural area. The commercialization of food crops (mainly maize, groundnuts, cassava and yams), began at regional level (*cercle*) at least by the 1920s, and beyond the local markets, towards Malanville, Bohicon and Cotonou, in the 1940s, if not earlier. Women played a decisive role in the start of the food crop trade (Le Meur and Adjinacou, 1997: 14–15).

These new movements no longer resulted from a slave raider escape strategy. As a result of this, places too difficult for cultivation or too remote for commercializing products were abandoned. This seems to be what happened to the Gbandjandji area north of Gbanlin: it used to be a hunting area and a refuge in times of Abomean intrusions, and it would become the most active agrarian frontier in the 1990s. In the region of Ouessè, access to land was 'free' (in the sense that the land was seen as a common good) and people cleared new land near the village and also further to the south, toward the former Gbanlin settlements of Anyao and Adjawini. One should not see this movement as an exploitation of lineage domains. Such a notion seems irrelevant in this context. It is much more the affair of small corporate groups, made of kinsmen and allies, expressing themselves in the idiom of lineage (Lonsdale, 1992: 335–6), sometimes progressing parallel to one another, but without any binding collective decision regarding areas to be cleared. The process has basically worked (up to now) on the basis of friendship or kin-

---

18. Between 'autochthonous' Mahi, Sabe and Idasa populations, when for instance Idatcha asked Mahi people for land, in areas where Mahi groups had arrived in the late pre-colonial times (Mongbo, 1995; Anignikin, personal communication, 21 January 2004).

ship ties:[19] 'If you are the first on a good fallow land, you invite a brother or a friend' (Abel Danvide, son of the deceased *axôsu* Ode Danvide, interview, 7 September 2002). This loose strategy is seen as a good way to avoid neighbourhood problems. Some informants see the process as even more basic: 'Avoa Dejgbé was the first on the spot. I came later with a friend and we just had to ask him in which direction he used to clear land; he had not informed us about the place' (Koffi Tchomakou, interview, 9 September 2002).

Agrarian colonization was not the only form of mobility entailed by the colonial intrusion. In a situation of broad land availability, the scarce resource is labour. Resorting to family manpower was usual and the frequent polygynous matrimonial strategies can be seen as reflecting the necessity of controlling a labour force.[20] Age groups also functioned as labour teams. But at the same time, fuelled by forced labour and, to a lesser extent, poll taxes, a phenomenon grew which was to have a dramatic impact on the local political economy, namely out-migration to Gold Coast through Togo (the *accramen*; see Adassan, 1977), and later to Côte d'Ivoire (Igué, 1990; Le Meur and Adjinacou, 1998; Zanou, 1986).[21]

Out-migrations of course raised — or aggravated — the labour question. One could say that these migrations of workers' groups, the membership of which was based on kinship and neighbourhood criteria, also contributed — though somewhat paradoxically — to reinforcing the emerging feeling of belonging (more precisely of autochthony) in central Benin localities, but also at a supra-village level. At the same time, struggles for the chieftaincy in Gbanlin were extremely acute. This is another paradox: several members of the chief lineage segment (Katisso *xwe*) refused to return from the Ivory Cost to take over the position: they seemed more interested in the possibilities offered there by the plantation economy. However, the position as village chief (until the 1970s, *togan*, chosen in the *axôsu* lineage segment[22]) was strategic for controlling — or at least having an eye on — matrimonial conflicts and therefore a labour force. Land was obviously not at stake in the 1940s to 1960s.

---

19. Doevenspeck (2005) presents similar material on agrarian colonization ideology in Wari-Maro region, located north to Ouessè.
20. Pawnship and debts were another way of accessing a labour force. See den Ouden (1995) on labour force mobilization strategies in southwestern Benin, and Guyer (1993) for a discussion on the significance of wealth-in-people in central Africa.
21. As early as the 1900s, colonial reports mention migrations of young Mahi people to Atakpamè region in German Togo (ANB, Carton $1E17_4$, monthly reports, 1905, 1907). Interestingly, this region was already a refuge for the Mahi people escaping Abomean razzias (see Anignikin, 2001).
22. Also called *yovogan* (chief of/for the Whites) to stress the difference of legitimacy *vis-à-vis* 'real' *axôsu*.

GOVERNING LAND AND PRODUCING 'STRANGERS': THE *TUTORAT* AS A FRONTIER INSTITUTION

The 1960s saw the emergence of a new modality of land and labour governance. The first migrant workers arrived at that time from the Atakora mountains in northwestern Benin, mainly Natemba and Berba coming from the *sous-préfectures* of Tanguieta and Materi (they are still locally called 'Tanguieta'). For at least ten years, they only came as seasonal workers, having heard 'there was money to earn in Ouessè'.[23] They already had long experience as migrant workers in other parts of Benin and neighbouring countries (Togo, Ghana, Nigeria). The story of the first migrant workers, gleaned from fieldwork, is revealing.

> Pascal Montango (interview, Natemba, 31 August 2002), left Tanguiéta to go to southwestern Nigeria where he worked three years in tomato fields. He then moved to Ouessè in search of work, because he remembered a visit to a relative in Odougba, near Gbanlin, when he was younger. He met a Mahi man, became his friend and the latter introduced him to Sossou Houngbade alias 'Fyossi'. He worked three years on his farm with other people from Atakora, and then Fyossi gave him a piece of land not far from the village of Gbanlin. He stayed there for three years, worked for Fyossi (mainly weeding) without being paid, and as wage labourer on other farms, but the soil was not fertile enough, and he had to move. In the meantime, he used to return to his home region every year and returned to Gbanlin with brothers and friends. They worked for him and he presented them to Fyossi for whom they also would do agricultural work. His brother Albert Montango (interview, Natemba, 8 September 2002) arrived only two years after him (he was still a labourer for Fyossi), after a long migration as wage labourer in Ghana, clearing land for cocoa plantation, Savalou on cotton fields, and Nigeria for yam cultivation. He met Fyossi through his brother and worked for ten years as agricultural labourer for him and on other farms (in that case always 'after he had finished working on Fyossi's farm'; Fyossi was in charge of accommodations). He was then settled by Fyossi on a spot never before cultivated (*agbovɛ*) in the newly (at that time, in the 1970s) opened area of Saagoudji, located south of Gbanlin in the direction of Ouemè river. For Pascal as well as for Albert Montango, Fyossi was a lodger and a tutor (*xwetô*, translated as 'his owner' — *propriétaire* — in local French). The landholding content of the relation was not clearly defined: the new settlers did not know how far the land belonged to Fyossi or if he was speaking on behalf of a household, lineage or lineage segment. The terms of the agreement were extremely thin: there was no entrance fee (but one could say the previous years as a wage labourer acted as an entrance fee), no time limit, and the ban on planting did not need to be said. Fyossi did not control the direction of land clearing, nor did he set limits to the fields to be cultivated. There was no rent, but from time to time, settlers 'spontaneously' helped Fyossi. In short it was not a classical 'contract' with defined rights and duties.

This case[24] gives us the constitutive elements of the *tutorat* relation (Chauveau, 2006), basically a dyadic clientelistic relation between a migrant and a landowner embedded in the local moral economy (Scott, 1976). This institution fulfils different functions dealing simultaneously with the government

---

23. Albert Montango, brother of the first migrant farmer in Gbanlin (interview, Natemba, 8 September 2002).
24. For more empirical material and a discussion of the history and recent evolutions of *tutorat* in this area, see Le Meur (2004).

of land and people. First, migrants get access to farmland. The allocation of a piece of land occurs mostly after a period of time as a wage labourer for the lodger (*xwetô*), which does not exclude the possibility of working on other farms. One can interpret this phase as an entrance fee for access to land use rights. The migrant could be settled on new lands (*agbovɛ*), although a first settlement on fallow land (*gbexô*) near the village seems to have been frequent. It was not an absolute rule, but much more the result of the tutor's landholding strategy.[25] That is where access to farmland on the migrant's side meets a strategy of land appropriation on the tutor's side. It is an enactment of two principles of peasant moral economy: the migrant is welcome in the name of a universal right to subsistence, and appropriation is created through labour (Jacob, 2004). The conflictive subject matter is the link between land property and the right to let someone settle on a piece of land, in areas where territorial sovereignty and land property remain uncertain. There was no land rent but a gift or service of labour, experienced as 'spontaneous' by both parties to the interaction. From the *xweto*'s point of view, the good stranger is the one who gives without being asked. There were seemingly no time and space limits, but planting trees was forbidden.[26]

Tutorat is thus about access to natural resources and land appropriation, but it is also more than that: it is a way of transforming migrants into strangers (*jônôn*) (Shack and Skinner, 1979; see Chauveau et al., 2004: 8–11), that is, giving people who have come to sell their labour force an institutional status within a moral community. This implies a tension between social integration (which is also the tutor's duty) and the maintenance of distance (the good stranger's attitude must be embodied through a sound understanding of social codes allowing him to find his rightful place). In this sense, *tutorat* is not a mere dyadic tie but a social institution and an element of governmentality involving a third party, namely the moral community within which the migrant is integrated.[27]

Immigration is part and parcel of a longer-run dynamic of settlement, narrowly related to the dynamic — or the sequence — of out-migration described above. The dyadic nature of the *tutorat* relationship was also complicated by the arrival of the migrants' 'brothers'. This movement reflected the interests of both tutors and clients (the first migrants), the latter getting a position

25. For instance, a strategy of expansion towards Saagoudji in the case of Fyossi in the 1970s (interviews 20 March 1995, 31 August 2002, 2 September 2002); towards Gbandjandji in the case of Sossou Mathieu (village headman in the 1980s; interviews 11 September 2002, JB 6 and 17 February 2004). A close examination of their biographies shows that the balance between concerns about territorial expansion and control over a labour force evolves according to their strategies and resources.
26. On this point, it is not clear whether this was so obvious to all that there was no need to be explicit, or whether trees were not at stake for the landowners, in a context of broad land availability.
27. See Foucault (2004: 124 ff.) on government and governmentality viewed as the 'conduct of conduct' entailing various disciplining practices and ways of problematizing social domains of life as a matter of government.

of tutor *vis-à-vis* the newcomers, thus creating a second, embedded level of *tutorat*. What was at stake in the 1970s and 1980s was not really land, but much more the labour force. The flow of out-migration had re-oriented toward Nigeria during the oil boom, and it remained significant at least until the expulsion of foreigners in 1983. The growth of agricultural trade (with the purchase of the first cars and later trucks in the 1970s and 1980s) also required labour (substituting those directly engaged in trading activities).

In this context, the power of settling migrants became increasingly central. Strategic bargaining between migrants, tutors and landowners was not merely a matter of who actually held land rights. Controlling knowledge about land availability and migrants' flows was equally crucial. First migrants and *xweto* worked as brokers by trying to maintain a monopoly on information and thus contributing to the constitution of a chain of dyadic ties of *tutorat*.[28] Through this, the distinction between strangers and autochthons was maintained but made more complex, and migrants' communities developed mainly according to their place of origin. Migrants have continued to arrive from Atakora, but newcomers now came from the Adja plateau — since the arrival of Marcellin Glodjo in the early 1970s as *sodabi* (oil palm alcohol) seller[29] — and Fon came from Abomey region from the 1980s onward, following a similar sequence of installation. Their origin was often extremely localized (a village or a group of nearby villages linked by kinship ties), contributing to strengthen the position of the first migrants as intermediaries in the chain of *tutorat* and as legitimate representatives of their own community (see Juul and Lentz, this issue).

CHIEFS AND MIGRANTS IN THE 1990S

Land relations, rural migration and territorial expansion evolved relatively uninfluenced by the political changes of the 1970–80s, namely the 1972 military coup and the turn towards a Marxist-Leninist ideology in 1974 and a one party central state in 1975. One could say, however, that the official slogan 'the land belongs to the tiller' produced a favourable context for rural migrations,[30] although it was not backed by an active policy as it was in Côte

---

28. It must be noted that when a tutor successfully plays his role of mediation between a new migrant and a landowner, this will not necessarily end his relation with the migrant, especially as regards social life, integration, and labour services.
29. The history of his arrival and settlement is still controversial as regards who was tutor, lodger and landowner (see especially interviews with Vigue Glodjo, his widow who married his second wife's son after he deceased, 7 September 2002; Fyossi, who claims landowning on a large part of Saagoudji area, 31 August 2002, 2 September 2002; Yelinmon Housavi, who contests Fyossi's claim, 30 August 2002).
30. According to interviews with Adoba, former *délégué* (elected village headman) in Gbanlin 1974–82 (various interviews in 1995, 2002, 2004).

d'Ivoire (Chauveau, 2000).[31] Furthermore, systematic elections at village and communal level from 1974 onward had a strong impact by widening the local political arena and opening it to new actors (see Le Meur and Adjinacou, 1998: 127–38 for Gbanlin). The democratic transition of 1989–91 exerted contrasted effects at the local level (Bierschenk and Olivier de Sardan, 1998; see Buur and Kyed, this issue, for a not dissimilar analysis of Mozambique). Local elections of village chiefs (former *délégués* under the Kérékou regime) and mayors were organized in 1991 in a somewhat chaotic and improvised manner. Their mandate was supposed to be provisional because of the forthcoming decentralization (inscribed in the 1990 Constitution). Whilst the newly elected bodies had democratic legitimacy, delayed decentralization (due to political hesitations and manoeuvres) contributed to weaken their position. This fragile situation was further undermined by deeply entrenched political and religious conflicts in the case of Gbanlin (Le Meur and Adjinacou, 1998: 138 ff.). Communal elections eventually took place in December 2002 and January 2003, but have not yet happened at village level.

Migrants' Taxation or Land Rent: The Chieftaincy as Public Authority?

The incomplete democratization at the local level gave room for alternative political bodies. The customary chieftaincy achieved an ambiguous comeback on the political scene, partially backed by the clientelistic interests of political forces, playing its own score by internalizing the developmentalist participatory rhetoric (Banégas, 2003: 336 ff.), participating in the decentralization debates,[32] and claiming a jurisdiction over land issues (Bako-Arifari and Le Meur, 2003: 139–40).

When the PGRN arrived in Gbanlin in 1994, its agents did feel it necessary to meet the newly enthroned king (although he was one of the few local 'big men' of the area, a former migrant in Ghana and one of the first to buy a truck for trade). A few years later, however, the central role of *axôsu* in land affairs at village level in Gbanlin and regional level in Ouessè[33] was widely recognized by local actors and state and project instances, even though their methods

31. Two things are worth mentioning here: (1) Fulbe pastoralists' settlement strategy under the Kérékou regime, resorting to state representatives at the district (now *sous-préfecture*) level (district head, rural development services head or RDR) to get an authorization; and (2) the production co-operative policy (GRVC: *groupement révolutionnaire à vocation coopérative*) locally instrumentalized to get access to pioneer areas.
32. In this respect, strongly — though implicitly — inspired by the indirect colonial rule.
33. In Ouessè, the new king, Sounkpe Ganhou, was enthroned on 21 February 1992. He was at that time in Côte d'Ivoire (and not really eager to return home). Gbanlin *axôsu*, Ode Danvide (known as Daa Tchnigbé) followed in the same year.

were overtly criticized. Furthermore, all my informants now see Gbanlin and Ouessé *axôsu* as *ayìkúngbannôn* (literally, landowner/master), linked by a hierarchical relation (actually originating in the colonial configuration of canton and village administrative chieftaincy). How can such a dramatic change be explained?

To begin with, it is noteworthy that Mahi *axôsu* were never attributed jurisdiction over land affairs, either in terms of allocation, or religious and ritual matters.[34] What then is the nature of the chieftaincy and the roots of its claimed legitimacy over land issues? First of all, the *axôsu* represents the first occupant (as his descendant), whose legitimacy results from the justifying principle according to which land appropriation is based on labour investment: the idea that 'labour creates right'. However, this is a kind of *propriété éminente* turned into political sovereignty rather than concrete land appropriation, which would result from the work of opening land, and which must be defended against competing claims by re-cultivating abandoned fields or by settling migrants. Even though the *axôsu*'s claim is originally rooted in an initial investment of labour (through hunting, ritual, clearing), it comes to function at a higher level of abstraction. It expresses a territorialized history of mobility, made of ancient hunting areas, refuge sites to escape slaves raiders (like Gbandjandji), and former village locations (like Adjowini or Anyao).

The king does not actually hold knowledge on cultivated fields, fallow lands (*gbexo*), new lands (*agbovɛ*), hunting domains, and, resulting from all this — but on the basis of often contested interpretations — on the possible village or *terroir* limits. He is the depository of a collective knowledge of land shared by the elders (*mexô lɛ*), actually fragmented according to cropping areas, clearing fronts and the movements of different lineage segments and networks (*akôta atôôn*), and also of specific domains of knowledge (for instance held by the hunters, *gbeto*).[35] Furthermore, this competence, which is basically a knowledge of the past (of course made of ambiguities and interpretations; see Appadurai, 1981; Berry 2001; Peel, 1984), is contested by other types of knowledge, contributing together to define a field of power over land. The latter are centred on the recent history of intervention (PFR,

34. Sakpata *vodun*, orginally Mahi (or Yoruba but adopted in the Dahomey kindgom via Mahi-land) is the smallpox and earth god (or more precisely pantheon or group of gods; *ayìxôsú*; lit. earth king or *ayìnô*; lit. earth owner/master; see also Herskovits, 1938: 129–49). It is also the lineage *vodun* of the Devo and works rather as a guarantor for the community's welfare than specifically as an earth divinity. The opening of new land is an individual affair that does not take place under the aegis of Sakpata.

35. The accumulated knowledge about the past and the present of land defines the latter as a common good that remains virtual as long as knowledge is fragmented and monopolized by various actors and public authorities are contested. Diverging interpretations between tutors and chiefs over the right to extract rents from the migrants reproduce (often inconclusively) this polarity between land as a private or common good (see below).

PGTRN), settlement and land clearing, requiring permanent actualization (as long as migrants flows and land clearing continue).

The debate over knowledge and justifying principles of land property and use is of course an institutional and political one as well. The position of the chieftaincy as regards land issues (conceived as building a semi-autonomous social field in Sally Falk Moore's sense, 1978) rests upon its capacity to produce or control rules, and arbitrate and eventually solve land conflicts, along a dialectic according to which 'the process of recognition of property rights by a politico-legal institution simultaneously constitutes a process of recognition of the legitimacy of this institution' (Lund, 2002: 14). The chief constitutes an authority in land affairs only as long as individuals resort to him in case of dispute. In Gbanlin (and all of the Ouessè region), one may assume this to be the case, particularly because other bodies have a legitimacy deficit in this respect, in a context of increasing tensions around land over the last decade.

The recent conflicts I studied in Gbanlin (some of them involving neighbouring villagers; see below) show first of all the diversity of politico-legal instances engaged in the arena — elected village chiefs, Gbanlin and Ouessè *axôsu*, *notables* and elders, *sous-préfet*, Ouessè *tribunal de conciliation*, village development association, CVGTF, COGEF, UIGREN, and, to a lesser extent, *akôta atôôn* networks. Whilst institutional pathways are not defined in advance (between traditional and modern powers, local and supra-local, formally administrative, judicial, political or emanating from the so-called civil society), one notes the relative centrality of the chieftaincy. Different factors contribute to this situation:

- The explicit articulation between village and regional customary chiefs (reproducing the colonial pattern), which has an effect of 'locking up' the system. Following Ouessè, several villages in the *sous-préfecture* got new traditional leaders, often after a long phase of vacancy (Ouessè, 1988–92; Gbanlin, 1975–92; Idadjo, 1982–2001). Idadjo's new chief (*balɛ*) was chosen in February 2001 after twenty years, with the support of Gbanlin *axôsu* (see below).
- The recognition of chieftaincy land competencies at local level, but also by regional actors such as the *sous-préfet* and the PGTRN in its various instances.
- A form of bureaucratization of the chieftaincy,[36] with the constitution of a board (like in any classical association), the secretary of which is, in this case, the rent collector. The board composition contributes to strengthen the hegemony of the Devo founding lineage, through

36. It is not the case everywhere in Ouessè area, but it exists in other parts of central Benin; cf. Edja (1999: 177 ff.).

co-opting influential younger people and members of other Mahi clans (Ayinon, Za, Agnamè).[37]

Bureaucratization can first be seen as a 'strategy' (how far is it intentional?) to control the knowledge required to solve conflicts. These are mainly related to the relation to the migrants (rent payment, forbidden plantation, migrant settlement on a contested piece of land), and to inheritance and boundary disputes, involving different arguments about the past (anteriority, invested labour, migrants' settlement). Disputes can also concern how land opening actually works: many conflicts are based on the encounter of farmers moving forward by clearing fallow land and planting yams, either parallel to one another (one having changed paths to block the other) or perpendicular. What must be assessed is the degree of 'legitimacy' of the blockage: was it legitimate to invest more in wage labour in order to win the 'clearing race'; did one of the parties really and consciously go out of his clearing track to block his neighbour? (see Doevenspeck, 2004). Furthermore, this bureaucratization expresses a willingness to play a key political role in the mobilization and reallocation of local and external resources, in the form of public investments.

On 15 December 1996, a meeting was held at Ouessè under the aegis of the *axôsu* who argued that conflicts happened mainly with strangers whereas strangers contributed to local development. For him, implementing land rent among migrants would secure their access to land.[38] The main purpose of the meeting was to organize rent collection at village level, by associating customary chiefs, elected village headmen and mayors and hometown association (UDESCO) representatives.[39] It was agreed that all the foreign farmers (that is, those from outside Ouessè *sous-préfecture*) would have to pay 5,000 FCFA and one basin of maize every year. A bank account should be opened and a meeting held (with the same participants) to decide on the use of the money and maize collected. The banning of migrants from planting trees, opening *agbovɛ* land and giving land to their brothers or friends constituted

37. The constitution of a new board (at the beginning of the year after the death of the *axôsu*) is highly conflictive, because of Devo hegemonic claims facing the resistance of a few non-Devo *notables*, playing on the fact that they possess information about the misuse of land rents. The biographical features of these persons are significant: Adoba, Agnamè clan, former *délégué*, CVGTF president, and influential person in the local political landscape; Ogan Bloh, Agnanmè, former member of the armed forces, came back to the village in the early 1990s; Fyossi, Ayinon, Bruno Sossou's uncle and important migrant settlers (his claims on landownership caused a conflict among autochthones and a blockade of the PFR in Saagoudji); Victorin Gnintchédé, former mayor; like Ogan Bloh, he has a strategic position from a generational and political point of view, between elders and younger people. See Le Meur and Adjinacou (1997: 19 ff., 20n, 36n) for elements of their social biographies.
38. Interview with Sounkpeganhou and three of his counsellors (31 January 2004).
39. The process of bureaucratization mentioned above is at work here too, with the creation of village committees and the use of paper (meeting minutes).

a second body of rules (sanctions were formulated as well, in the form of seizure of the trees or of the piece of land by the landowners).

The first attempts made by customary chiefs of Ouessè *sous-préfecture* in 1995/96 to collect a centralized land rent from migrants failed because of resistance by migrants, and also because this was seen by the *sous-préfet* as a discriminatory taxation of Beninese citizens on the basis of regional and ethnic criteria.[40] By 1997/1998, however, land rents were collected in Gbanlin by a representative of the *axôsu*, without any trouble from the *sous-préfet* or the PGRN. Nonetheless, Ouessè *axôsu* never managed to obtain a dominant position within a process that remained localized at the village level.

Officially, the income should have been invested in public infrastructure, according to the model developed in cotton growing areas (Bako-Arifari, 1997; Le Meur, 1999; Sommer, 2000). In fact, no public service was implemented (the money mainly served to finance chiefs' official trips or invitations). Accusations of corruption and embezzlement were made, but the target of the criticism was mismanagement rather than the very idea of this centralized land rent (actually closer to a poll tax). This was, for instance, the position of a new development association created in December 2001, whose board tried to get control over the rent (with the same objectives), but was in turn criticized for its inability to negotiate boundary conflicts with neighbouring villages (see below). From the chieftaincy point of view, negotiation and compromise among autochthons (namely among chiefs) *vis-à-vis* 'their' migrants was more important than defining territorial limits.

Behind the apparent recovery of the customary chieftaincy, what is at stake is both a kind of 'parastatal' taxation and a redefinition of local citizenship. The link between taxation and citizenship is paradoxical: migrants, by paying the tax, are actually excluded from the public sphere. Moreover, the set of rules accompanying the process is devoid of the embedding of migrants' rights in social ties that has characterized the *tutorat* relationship as a 'mode of producing strangers'. Furthermore, the face-to-face relationship between chiefs and migrants cannot be analysed without taking account of the whole set of discourses and strategies that together build the local political arena. The following case study will illustrate the point.

Migration, Locality and Autochthony: A Case-Study

Idadjo is a Sabe village located west of Gbanlin on the Oueme left bank. It constitutes the largest reserve of forested and agricultural land of Ouessè. Since roughly the mid-1990s, there have been encroachments by Mahi farmers from Gbanlin as well as by Atakora migrants. Until 1995, there had been no conflict and no attempt by the Idadjo to extract rent or tribute from them.

---

40. The *sous-préfet* was at the same time accused of partiality based on alleged political alliances.

In 1996, Idadjo hunters brought a migrant from Atakora to the village, who said he had been installed by Gbanlin villagers and that he had to pay a rent to Gbanlin *axôsu*. A village meeting was held under the leadership of the *gobi* (deputy chief) during which it was decided to get control over migrants and rents at the village level. Gbanlin *axôsu* was informed and came to Idadjo to plead the case, acknowledging the facts and taking responsibility for migrants' settlement. Thereafter, an Idadjo delegation went to meet Ouessè *axôsu* who recognized the Sinlinyin river as the border between Idadjo and Gbanlin.[41] He then organized a meeting with Idadjo and Gbanlin representatives and a written agreement was issued. Beside the delimitation, it was agreed that the rent would be paid by the migrants according to their place of settlement, whoever the *xweto*. Autochthonous farmers (those from Idadjo and Gbanlin) can cultivate fields wherever they want.[42]

In November 2003, Atakora migrants arrived at Idadjo, led by Michel Yarigo (their usual speaker was absent). Obviously panic-stricken, they explained that Gbanlin people had come to collect land rents and had threatened them with expulsion.[43] Idadjo *balɛ* sent investigators to the spot. One house had been burnt and a few young goats had been killed. Parallel to the Idadjo elders' meeting and the sending of a delegation to Ouessè *sous-préfecture*, Idadjo young men surprised Gbanlinu in a migrant farm beyond Sinlinyin. After a violent fight, they took Gbanlinu hostages to Idadjo (among them Fyossi, a big landowner and migrants' *xweto*, and Adoba, former *délégué* and influential elder).[44] In the meantime, the *sous-préfet* had come to calm down the situation. After an uneasy negotiation with Idadjo *balɛ*, he obtained the hostages' release. The migrants had taken refuge in Idadjo school buildings.

In the following days, the *sous-préfet* convened a reconciliation meeting.[45] He tried to avoid sanctions and went to the field to record the damage done with Prosper Assogba, the president of the Gbanlin hometown association. A quarrel broke out between the two men (the latter is said to have tried to bribe the former). The *sous-préfet* told the migrants they could go back to

---

41. Interestingly, the villages of Tosso and Vossa, stuck between Idadjo and Gbanlin, do not appear at that stage of the story.
42. This version relies mainly on the narratives of Ferdinand Tchakin and Paul Davokan, both of Idadjo (interview JB, 2 February 2004). Interviews carried out with Gbanlin informants basically confirm the events sequence (amongst others, Benoît Ahodégnon, village headman, interview, 28 January 2004; Alphonse Gnanhoui, COGEF member, interview, 3 February 2004; Victorin Gnitchédé, former mayor, interview JB, 24 January 2004).
43. Other informants speak of surface reduction instead of expulsion.
44. According to an alternative version, they locked up Gbanlinu in a house and beat them, which would be reminiscent of the practice of 'rodeo' in vogue during Kerekou's regime (see cases in Bierchenk and Olivier de Sardan, 1998).
45. For Idadjo: Paul Davokan, Gaston Boni (youth representative), Alphonse Worou (Boni), Atachade Antoine and Worou Alfred (*balɛ* court member). For Gbanlin, around twenty people, among them the seven hostages (Fyossi, Adoba, Cyriaque Molonki, village council member, Benoît Ahodégnon, the current village chief, Bloh Victor, member of the communal council, Assogba Prosper, president of Gbanlin hometown association).

their farms. Thereafter, another meeting was set up in the farming area and attended by the *sous-préfet*, the head of *sous-préfecture* development services (RDR), the head of the brigade (*gendarmerie*) and the main PGTRN agent (Clément Dossou-Yovo, lawyer and NGO agent). Gbanlin young people hid in the bush with weapons they refused to give up. The official delegation had to run away under the threat (the RDR is said to have tried unsuccessfully to disarm them; some say there was a fight after their departure).

After the communal poll (December 2002/January 2003), tensions were renewed. Assogba and other members of the Gbanlin hometown association tried again to collect rents on the Idadjo side. A young migrant was surprised while pumping water at an 'illegal' well on Idadjo territory and was mauled by Gbanlinu (according to other informants, this event took place during the election campaign).

For Benoît Ahodégnon (Gbanlin village chief, interview, 28 January 2004), the conflict has now been solved (see Alphonse Gnanhoui, PGTRN local agent, interview, 3 February 2004). A delegation was twice sent to Idadjo in December 2003 in order to set aside the old quarrels and propose renewed relations, around the project of building a bridge over the Gbeffa river which would secure access to the Gbanlin and Idadjo agrarian frontier. The rent — this time paid by both strangers and autochthons — is now collected by Gbanlinu[46] under the supervision of Idadjo representatives. Benoît Ahodégnon asserts that the negotiation between the two villages has been an open process involving the notables (*cadres*) of both localities. Ouessè *axôsu* was not directly involved but 'he should have known about it' (and Victor Bloh, the vice-president of Gbanlin association, stands as communal council 'speaker'). The bridge project has nevertheless generated new tensions with another neighbouring village Tosso, whose inhabitants see this initiative as a deliberate strategy to bypass their market.

This story tells us things about how the government of resources and people contributes to the making and the unmaking of public authority. On the one hand, the *sous-préfet*, representing the state authority, should protect all the citizens and re-assert the rule of law. We can observe that he resorts to negotiation in conflict-solving processes rather than to force and law enforcement (see Le Meur, 2002 for a similar case). It is noteworthy that the PGTRN agent stands here beside — not to say among — the state representatives and thus contributes to blurring state limits (as we will see below). On the other hand, the chiefs' strategy is based on a discourse of autochthony and tradition: ethnic belonging is not at stake, nor village boundaries. They build a new legitimacy as an authority in land affairs by controlling the migrants through the rent they extract from them. And they do this partly against

46. Jules Gnanhoui and Adre Salomon, amongst others. The former occupies a strategic position on the pioneer front beyond Gbandjandji and close to Idadjo, by developing various commercial activities and acting as the speaker — if not the tutor — and development broker (regarding access to water) for the migrants' local community (interview JB, 31 January 2004). The latter used to work for the PFR (interview, 31 August 2002).

individual landholders and tutors, trying to subvert the dyadic tie linking *xweto* and *jonon* into a form of public patronage.[47] In contrast, the hometown association members relate autochthony to locality, reproducing village administrative boundaries originating in colonization and taken over by the post-colonial state. Nonetheless, both institutions see local citizenship as an attribute of autochthony and state officials do not really question this form of discrimination.[48] The migrants' situation remains fragile as regards land tenure security; Adja families were evicted by landowners in 2002 without recourse — except to try to go further into the bush and to look for a new *xweto*, thus combining the exit option with the search for a new loyalty.

LOCAL POLITICS, RESOURCE MANAGEMENT AND STATE MAKING

Competing discourses irrigate local political life: discourses of locality, of autochthony, of state authority, of religious belonging, of frontier and segmentarity. These discourses function as justifying principles and contribute to the permanent reshaping of moral communities and public authorities. As we have seen, political institutions resort to these discourses according to the context and the stake.

The context of democratization also plays a role. Hometown association leaders have engaged in electoral politics and attempted to capture the migrants' vote through a new form of political patronage during the decentralization polls in 2002/2003 (promising school and pumps or even joining the political party dominant in the migrants' home region).[49] At the village level, the delayed decentralization has made things tricky for the village council. Members were elected in 1991 in a rather chaotic fashion, in a context of strong religious and political tensions between Catholic and *vodun* adepts on the one hand and, on the other hand, the Protestant members of the Beninese independent church *Union Renaissance de l'Homme en Christ* (URHC).[50] The elected council was 100 per cent URHC. Accusations of embezzlement were raised against the village chief, Bruno Sossou, who was eventually suspended in 1997. Benoît Ahodégnon was chosen as interim village chief but the influence of the council declined steadily and in 2003 the three remaining members (of the original seven) were convoked by the *sous-préfet* to try to remedy to this decay.

Two solutions were discussed, both reflecting the segmentary logic of fission and fusion characterizing village politics in Gbanlin. The first idea,

47. Without really taking over the set of obligations inherent in the *tutorat* tie: the *axôsu* merely warrants land tenure security for migrants (if they behave well).
48. See, for instance, interview JB, 3 September 2003 with Justin Awonou, rural development head, RDR, in Ouessè.
49. The interplay in decentralization polls between village, party, ethnic and historical affiliations would in itself deserve a careful study.
50. See Le Meur and Adjinacou (1998: 147–9); the lines of cleavage were actually more complex with a strong intergenerational component and points of conflict between local big men.

which had been discussed and pushed forward since the mid-1990s (Le Meur and Adjinacou, 1998: 165–6) was the partitioning of the village into three autonomous administrative entities: the smaller the village, the easier it is to control undisciplined youths. The second plan, achieved in 2003, was to form a new village council on the basis of religious balance. This was already done during the democratic transition (before the 1991 local poll) with two Catholic counsellors, two *vodun* and two *renaissants*, each chosen in their own 'community' (ibid: 147–8). In the meantime, URHC had split up at the national level and the idea had emerged that two members could be chosen outside religious allegiances. The new village council formed in 2003 was thus made up of ten members — two Catholic, two *vodun*, two of each URHC branch and two 'elders'. It should be noted here that the elders eventually delegated two young men as council members (there are no women in this arena) and the latter present themselves as 'civil society representatives'. One should rather say 'autochthonous civil society' as migrants are strikingly absent from these political schemes. When asked, local political leaders do not see any problem: migrants are specifically followers of their patron; their social position depends on political choices made among and about autochthonous factions. The chieftaincy and the hometown association partake in these cycles of fission and fusion: the former by alternately stressing the locality or the lineage nature of Gbanlin (as representing the founding lineage),[51] the latter by hardening village boundaries and slipping toward ethnic politics. Both institutions resort to a discourse of modernization and community development and try to show their (at least rhetorical) ability to mobilize local resources, namely migrants' rent, for social investments.

As K. Sivaramakrishnan states (2000: 448):

> Governmental procedures that nominate one form of community as relevant to the government's vision of development promptly move villagers and political representatives to reveal the existence of numerous other forms of community. The denial of other forms of community, implicit in the imposition of one form, threatens certain interests and identities [see Buur and Kyed, and Pratten, this issue]. These are then asserted in the ensuing contest to give shape to public order institutions.

Local politics, as the interplay between endogenous and external forces and discourses, contributes to the permanent reshaping of plural moral communities. In this respect, the natural resource management project (PGRN 1993/1998, PGTRN 1999/2003) has played a key, athough ambiguous, role. This project, funded by French and German technical co-operation and, until 1998, by the World Bank, selected five (later six) pilot sites at *sous-préfectures* level, among which was Ouessè. It began to work in 1993 in

51. Ouessè *axôsu* discourse has evolved over the last ten years as regards the public nature of his leadership. The traditionalization of political arenas seems more fragile than expected and he tends now to present migrants and land rent issues — and even elected village chiefs' positions — as private/lineage affairs (interviews, 21 March 1995, 9 September 2002, 31 January 2004).

Gbanlin. After preliminary studies (in the form of participatory/rapid rural appraisals), various actions were launched in the domain of soil conservation. In 1997 the Rural Land Plan (PFR) started, aiming at registering all land use and property rights, including customary rights (along the model already implemented in Ivory Coast and later diffused in Burkina Faso and Guinea; Chauveau, 2003). PFR contributes to the production of the village — to a renewed form of villagization — by superimposing different dimensions of the locality: administrative units, residential units of farmers exploiting a space made of one block (a *terroir*) or communities of landowners. It proceeds by defining village boundaries that were never specified before from an administrative point of view.

One aspect of its implementation needs to be evoked here (see Le Meur, 2006 for an in-depth analysis of PFR in Benin) in relation to my argument about the dialectic between frontier and territorialization. PFR agents never completed the PFR in Gbanlin. They did the job in the core area, where land rights and occupation had been more or less stable for quite a long time. In the areas of agrarian colonization, the process was blocked, either because of conflicts about the reality of the property rights claimed by some *xweto* (including Fyossi in the southern part of Gbanlin), or simply because it was impossible to draw any limits between villages in highly unstable pioneer areas (such as Gbandjandji, north of Gbanlin). It was as if the frontier logic had successfully resisted the territorializing trend implied by the PFR implementation. PFR agents reasonably acted as if the *terroir* to be registered was the stabilized part actually registered and they closed this unachieved rural land plan without trying to explore the pioneer fronts (actually about two-thirds of Gbanlin lands). PFR rendered land tenure reality legible not only by simplifying its features, as Scott asserts (1998: 37 ff.), but also by excluding entire sections of it.

Besides PFR, various bodies were created (COGEF, land management commissions institutionalizing the PFR, CVGTF for natural resources management at village level) and, at the regional level, natural resource management unions (UIGREN in the Mahi part of Ouessè *sous-préfecture*, AGEDREN in the Sabe part). These two were brought together as a communal union (UCGRN) in 2003 out of a concern for consistency with decentralization (actually a façade). As we have seen, both the chieftaincy and the hometown association bore a discourse of autochthony within the political arena. This discourse is widely shared — at least pragmatically exploited, sometimes more cynically instrumentalized — by so-called modern institutions, and to a certain extent institutionalized through participatory *programmes de gestion de terroir*. This fact must invite us to be cautious with the hypothesis of re-traditionalization of political arenas or local societies (Bako-Arifari and Le Meur, 2003; Banégas, 2003). Gbanlin PGT, implemented under the aegis of the CVGTF, forbids migrants the right to open new lands (*agbovɛ*); an autochthon cannot lend a migrant more than two hectares of fallow land (*gbexo*) whereas he can open up to six hectares. At the same time, migrants and autochthons must contribute equally to community work (one must add here that the PGTRN has also organized meetings and negotiations between autochthons and migrants, as well as between farmers and pastoralists, in order to secure both land use and property rights and to solve boundary conflicts).

Another sensitive point in PGTRN action regards forest management. Forest reserves, dating back to the late colonial environmental policy, are managed by the forest state department (*Eaux & forêts*). The other forested areas of the state domain are classified as 'protected forests' (*forêts protégées*) by the 1993 forest law. The management of these areas became highly conflictive when unions (UIGREN/AGEDREN) emanating from PGTRN undertook to arrest and fine illegal woodcutters. This was seen as a scandalous provocation on the forest agents' side: 'How could an NGO [here UIGREN] take on state responsibilities?', as one forest agent said in 2002 — and incidentally cut them from their main source of income. The last point — rents that can be extracted from forest exploitation — is of course crucial. However, it is not merely a matter of sharing economic resources. It relies on ways of representing, and thus building, the legitimacy of institutions to fulfil state functions: maintaining public order, sanctioning illegal actions, collecting taxes and delivering public services (see Blundo, Pratten, this issue).

This is not the place for details of the negotiations that took place between PGTRN agents, UCGRN and forest services (and later the communal council elected with the decentralization) in order to craft an unstable compromise in this field, but two points need to be mentioned briefly. The first regards the interpretation of the CVGTF/UCGRN's institutional status. As a simple NGO it cannot claim to sanction fraud, fine people or seize material, according to the forest agent quoted above. During the latest fieldwork in 2004, the forest department views had changed (partly due to decentralization): UCGRN was now seen as subordinate to the state apparatus since it was created within a project, the PGTRN, itself placed under the aegis of the Ministry of Agriculture to which the Forest department belongs (a somewhat specious argumentation). Forest services now see UCGRN agents as legitimate auxiliary forces. It is worth mentioning here that forest services are widely seen as deeply corrupt and are thus discredited as public authorities. They could gain some legitimacy from an alliance with an institution seemingly originating within civil society.

The second point is that the everyday work of forest control is carried out at village level by CVGTF members. In Gbanlin, there is a broad overlap between CVGTF membership and other bodies involved in land issues (and especially in rent collection). However, due to the delayed decentralization (at village level) and to the 'remoteness' of the commune, the linkage between both levels is highly problematic. This means that the compromise elaborated in Ouessè between PGTRN, UCGRN, the commune and the forest department does not solve the problem of access by communal bodies to resources collected at village level. One could argue that one of the main challenges democratic decentralization faces today in rural Benin concerns the integration of village governmentality into a decentralized state design.

CONCLUSION: GOVERNMENTALITY ON THE FRONTIER

In central Benin, mobility and locality are inherently interacting through processes of community building and state making. A village like Gbanlin does not correspond to any bounded or corporate community. It is rather the locus of competing and overlapping moral and epistemic communities claiming forms of legitimacy deriving from diverse discourses — in the Foucaldian sense of a set of intertwining representations and practices — of autochthony, locality and territory, ethnic or religious belonging, state power, frontier ideology.[52] Placing mobility at centre stage, as Kopytoff invites us to do, helps capture the essence of Gbanlin's trajectory as a frontier society. Mobility rimes with encounter and otherness, and communities have to deal with this fact. Giving newcomers and migrants a social status constitutes a central way of integrating them as allies or strangers, endowed with specific economic and civic rights as well as social obligations within a shared moral community. In this respect, the *tutorat* institution constitutes a core institution and an element of governmentality that links hosts and strangers in a dense web of rights and duties. It crystallizes the paradoxical relation between locality and mobility and has been structuring a long-term process of land clearing and agrarian colonization.

In this context, the penetration of the state could be seen as contradicting the frontier logic by trying to establish and territorialize an exogenous domination. In fact, historical and ethnographical evidence shows how the colonial intrusion and its post-colonial avatars actually gave way to renewed relations between mobility and locality, in particular in the form of a complex articulation between control over labour force, access to land and natural resources, and out- and in-migrations. Local governmentality has been strongly influenced by a frontier ideology combining a discourse of autochthony (historically anchored in a principle of anteriority) with a capacity to integrate and reshape exogenous parameters, be they migrants or development interventions. Within a strongly polycentric political landscape, state intervention is itself plural. Beside territorial and development services and political

52. Here I follow Sivaramakrishnan (1999: 36) who distinguishes the two connotations of 'community', as 'morally valued ways of life and the constitution of social relations in a discrete geographical setting' (see also Londsale, 1992 on moral ethnicity). However, the second meaning can be extended to multi-localized communities (diasporas for instance, see Akyeampong, 2000), though often focused on a 'locus', as shown for instance by Lilian Trager in the example of Yoruba hometown associations (2001: 236–45). Moral communities can in fact represent themselves as strictly bounded communities, although inserted in a broader network, like the Gbanlin *renaissants*' 'counter-society' (Le Meur and Adjinacou, 1998: 144–7).

decentralization, it takes the ambiguous form of a natural resource management project funded by foreign donors and bearing a discourse of democratic participation, community building, and territorialized empowerment. At stake is a kind of new 'villagization' in the guise of the Rural Land Plan (PFR) and the *gestion de terroir* policy. This production of villages is, however, restricted by the resilience of the frontier logic and the state's inability to capture the village society within the decentralization framework. State making in this context is much more a product of this blurring of discursive and institutional boundaries — and a process of continuously reshaping them — than it is an evolutionary process of state construction.

REFERENCES

Adassan, F. (1977) 'Être chef migrant: Un témoignage', *Revue Tiers-Monde* XVIII(69): 151–4.

Adediran, B. (1984) 'Idaisa: The Making of a Frontier Yoruba State', *Cahiers d'études africaines* XXIV(1): 71–85.

Adjinacou, C. (1995) '"Vous avez dit Démocratie? Alors tous les acteurs du village doivent être associés à la prise de décision, élus ou non". Monographie sociopolitique desociopolitical monograph of Gbanlin', in T. Bierschenk (ed.) *Les effets socio-politiques de la démocratisation en milieu rural au Bénin*, vol. 2. Unpublished research report, 2 volumes. Stuttgart: Hohenheim University.

Akyeampong, E. (2000) 'Africans in the Diaspora: The Diaspora in Africa', *African Affairs* 99: 183–215.

ANB (various documents) National Archives of Benin, Porto-Novo.

Anignikin, S. (2001) 'Histoire des populations mahi. À propos d'une controverse sur l'ethnonyme et le toponyme "Mahi"', *Cahiers d'études africaines* 162(2): 243–65.

Appadurai, A. (1981) 'The Past as a Scarce Resource', *Man* (N.S.) 16: 201–19.

Appadurai, A. (1996) *Modernity at Large. Cultural Dimension of Globalizations*. Minneapolis, MN: University of Minnesota Press.

Asiwaju, A. I. (1976) *Western Yorubaland under European Rule, 1889–1945: A Comparative Analysis of French and British Colonialism*. London: Longman.

Bako-Arifari, N. (1997) 'Financement sans budget: rétribution des fonctions politiques locales et corruption'. Paper presented at the seminar 'Sozialanthropologie und Entwicklungssoziologie', Université de Hohenheim, Stuttgart.

Bako-Arifari, N. (1998) 'La démocratie à Founougo (Borgou): paysans et 'déscolarisés' en compétitition pour le pouvoir local', in T. Bierschenk and J. P. Olivier de Sardan (eds) *Les pouvoirs au village. Le Bénin rural entre démocratisation et décentralisation*, pp. 57–99. Paris: Karthala.

Bako-Arifari, N. and P. Y. Le Meur (2003) 'La chefferie au Bénin: une résurgence ambiguë', in C. H. Perrot and F. X. Fauvelle-Aymar (eds) *Le retour des rois. Les autorités traditionnelles et l'État en Afrique contemporaine*, pp. 125–43. Paris: Karthala.

Banégas, R. (2003) *La démocratie à pas de caméléon. Transition et imaginaires politiques au Bénin*. Paris: Karthala.

Barbier, J. (2005) *Accès à la terre et gestion des ressources naturelles dans une localité du centre du Bénin*. MSc dissertation. Montpellier: CNEARC-CLAIMS Project.

Bergé, J. A. M. A. R. (1928) 'Étude sur le pays Mahi', *Bulletin du Comité d'Études Historiques et Scientifiques de l'AOF* 11: 708–55.

Berman, Bruce and John Lonsdale (1992) 'Introduction: An Encounter in Unhappy Valley', in B. Berman and J. Lonsdale (eds) *Conflict in Kenya and Africa (Book 1: State & Class)*, pp. 1–10. Athens, OH: Ohio University Press; Oxford: James Currey.

Berry, S. (2001) *Chiefs Know their Boundaries: Essays on Property, Power, and the Past in Asante, 1896–1996*. Portsmouth, NH: Heinemann; Oxford: James Currey.

Bierschenk, T. (1988) 'Development Projects as Arenas of Negotiation for Strategic Groups: A Case Study from Benin', *Sociologia Ruralis* XXVIII(2–3): 146–60.

Bierschenk, T. (1993) 'Außenabhängigkeit und Intermediarität: Merkmale des Staates in Bénin vor 1989'. Soziolanthropologische Arbeitspapiere 52. Berlin: Freie Universität Berlin, Das Arabische Buch.

Bierschenk, T. and J. P. Olivier de Sardan (eds) (1998) *Les pouvoirs au village. Le Bénin rural entre démocratisation et décentralisation*. Paris: Karthala.

Bierschenk, T. and J. P. Olivier de Sardan (2003) 'Powers in the Village: Rural Benin between Democratisation and Decentralisation', *Africa* 73(2): 145–73.

Chauveau, J. P. (2000) 'La question foncière en Côte d'Ivoire et le coup d'État', *Politique Africaine* 78: 95–125.

Chauveau, J. P. (2003) 'Plans fonciers ruraux: conditions de pertinence des systèmes d'identification et d'enregistrement des droits', in P. L. Delville, H. Ouédraogo, C. Toulmin and P. Y. Le Meur (eds) *Pour une sécurisation foncière des producteurs ruraux*, pp. 35–48. London: IIED-GRET-GRAAF.

Chauveau, J. P. (2006) 'How Does an Institution Evolve? Land, Politics, Intra-household Relations and the Institution of the '*Tutorat*' between Autochthons and Migrant Farmers in the Gban Region (Côte d'Ivoire)', in R. Kuba and C. Lentz (eds) *Landrights and the Politics of Belonging in West Africa*, pp. 213–40. Leiden: Brill.

Chauveau, J. P., J. P. Jacob and P. Y. Le Meur (2004) 'L'organisation de la mobilité dans les sociétés rurales du Sud', in J. P. Chauveau, J. P. Jacob and P. Y. Le Meur (eds) *Gouverner les hommes et les ressources: dynamiques de la frontière interne*, special issue of *Autrepart* 30: 3–23.

Colin, J. P., P. Y. Le Meur and E. Léonard (eds) (forthcoming) *Les politiques d'enregistrement des droits fonciers. Du cadre légal aux pratiques locales*. Paris: IRD-Karthala.

Doevenspeck, M. (2004) 'Migrations rurales, accès au foncier et rapports interethniques au sud du Borgou (Bénin). Une approche méthodologique plurielle', *Afrika Spectrum* 39(3): 359–80.

Doevenspeck, M. (2005) *Migration im ländlichen Benin. Sozialgeographische Untersuchungen an einer afrikanischen Frontier*. Saarbrücken: Verlag für Entwicklungspolitik.

Dunglas, E. (1957/1958) 'Contribution à l'étude du moyen-Dahomey', *Études dahoméennes* XIX: 5–185, XX: 3–151, XXI: 7–118.

Edja, H. (1999) *Colonisation agricole spontanée et milieux sociaux nouveaux: la migration rurale dans le Zou-Nord au Bénin*. Kiel: Wissenschaftsverlag Vauk Kiel KG.

Foucault, M. (2004) *Sécurité, territoire, population. Cours au Collège de France, 1977–1978*. Paris: Seuil-Gallimard.

Greene, S. (1996) *Gender, Ethnicity, and Social Change on the Upper Slave Coast. A History of the Anlo-Ewe*. London: James Currey; Portsmouth, NH: Heinemann.

Guyer, J. (1993) 'Wealth-in-People and Self-Realization in Equatorial Africa', *Man* (N.S.) 28: 243–65.

Herskovits, M. (1938) *Dahomey. An Ancient West African Kingdom* (2 volumes). New York: J. J. Augustin Publisher.

Igué, J. (1990) *Migrations des populations dans le département du Zou au Bénin. Cas des sous-préfectures de Djidja, Zakpota, Glazoué, Savalou, Ouessè et Savè*. Unpublished research report. Aborney Calavi: National University of Benin.

Ingold, T. (ed.) (1996) *Key Debates in Anthropology*. London: Routledge.

Jacob, J. P. (2004) 'Gouvernement de la nature et gouvernement des hommes dans le Gwendégué (centre-ouest du Burkina Faso)', in J. P. Chauveau, J. P. Jacob and P. Y. Le Meur (eds) *Dynamiques de la frontière interne: gouverner les hommes et les ressource*, special issue of *Autrepart* 30: 25–43.

Kopytoff, I. (ed.) (1987) *The African Frontier. The Reproduction of Traditional African Societies*. Bloomington and Indianapolis, IN: Indiana University Press.

Kopytoff, I. (1999) 'The Internal African Frontier: Cultural Conservatism and Ethnic Innovation', in M. Rösler and T. Wendl (eds) *Frontiers and Borderlands: Anthropological Perspectives*, pp. 31–44. Bern: Peter Lang.

Law, R. (1991) *The Slave Coast of West Africa 1550–1750. The Impact of the Atlantic Slave Trade on an African Society*. Oxford: Clarendon Press.

Le Meur, P. Y. (1998) 'Décentralisation par le bas et participation clientéliste au Bénin', *Bulletin de l'APAD* 15: 49–63.

Le Meur, P. Y. (1999) 'Coping with Institutional Uncertainty: Contested Local Public Spaces and Power in Rural Benin', *Afrika Spectrum* 34(2): 187–211.

Le Meur, P. Y. (2000) 'Logiques paysannes au Bénin: courtage, associations, réseaux et marchés', *Autrepart* (IRD) 13: 91–108.

Le Meur, P. Y. (2002) 'Trajectories of the Politicisation of Land Issues. Case Studies from Benin', in K. Juul and C. Lund (eds) *Negotiating Property in Africa*, pp. 135–55. Portsmouth, NH: Heinemann.

Le Meur, P. Y. (2004) 'Le tutorat comme institution et relation. Etude de cas béninoise'. Paper presented at Research Seminar, 'Ethnographie des droits et dynamiques foncières', EHESS, Marseilles (16–19 November).

Le Meur, P. Y. (2006) 'Governing Land, Translating Rights. The Rural Land Plan in Benin', in D. Lewis and D. Mosse (eds) *Development Brokers & Translators: The Ethnography of Aid and Agencies*, pp. 75–100. Bloomfield, CT: Kumarian Press.

Le Meur, P. Y. (forthcoming) 'Gérer l'attente. Le Bénin rural entre démocratisation et décentralisation', in C. Fay, F. Koné and C. Quiminal (eds) *Pouvoirs et décentralisations en Afrique et en France*. Paris: IRD.

Le Meur, P. Y. and C. Adjinacou (1997) 'Le politique dans tous ses états. Dynamique et formes du pouvoir dans la commune de Gbanlin (Bénin, Département du Zou)'. Working Papers on African Societies 7. Berlin: Das Arabische Buch.

Le Meur, P. Y. and C. Adjinacou (1998) 'Les pouvoirs locaux à Gbanlin (Zou) entre migration, commerce et religion', in T. Bierschenk and J. P. Olivier de Sardan (eds) *Les pouvoirs au village. Le Bénin rural entre démocratisation et décentralisation*, pp. 121–69. Paris: Karthala.

Lespinay, C. (1994) 'Le Sud Bénin: Kétu et la question des origines', *Cahiers du CRA* 8: 121–47.

Lindgren, B. (2004) 'The Internal Dynamics of Ethnicity: Clan Names, Origins and Castes in Southern Zimbabwe', *Africa* 74(2): 173–93.

Lonsdale, J. (1992) 'The Moral Economy of Mau Mau. Wealth, Power and Civic Virtue in Kikuyu Political Thought', in B. Berman and J. Lonsdale (eds) *Conflict in Kenya and Africa* (Book 2: *Violence & Ethnicity*), pp. 315–504. Athens, OH: Ohio University Press; Oxford: James Currey.

Lund, C. (2002) 'Negotiating Property Institutions: On the Symbiosis of Property and Authority in Africa', in K. Juul and C. Lund (eds) *Negotiating Property in Africa*, pp. 11–43. Portsmouth, NH: Heinemann.

Mongbo, R. (1995) 'The Appropriation and Dismembering of Development Intervention. Policy, Discourse and Practice in the Field of Rural Development in Benin'. Doctoral dissertation, Agricultural University of Wageningen.

Moore, D. S. (2000) 'The Crucible of Cultural Politics: Reworking "Development" in Zimbabwe's Eastern Highlands', *American Ethnologist* 26(3): 654–89.

Moore, S. F. (1978) *Law as Social Process*. London: Routledge.

Mulira, J. G. (1984) 'A History of Mahi Peoples from 1874 to 1920'. PhD dissertation. Los Angeles, CA: University of California.

Nuijten, M. (2003) *Power, Community and the State: Political Anthropology of Organisation in Mexico*. London: Pluto Press.

von Oppen, A. (1999) 'Die Territorialisierung des Dorfes (Nordwest-Zambia, seit ca. 1945)', in R. Kössler, N. Dieter and A. von Oppen (eds) *Gemeinschaften in einer entgrenzten Welt*, pp. 35–54. Berlin: Das Arabische Buch.

von Oppen, A. (2002) 'Jenseits von *ujamaa*: Zur Soziologie der Dekommunalisierung', in A. Brandstetter and D. Neubert (eds) *Postkoloniale Transformationen in Afrika. Zur Neubestimmung der Soziologie der Dekolonisation*, pp. 93–111. Hamburg: Lit Verlag.

den Ouden, J. H. B. (1995) 'Who's for Work? The Management of Labour in the Process of Accumulation in Three Adja Villages, Benin', *Africa* 65(1): 1–35.

Peel, J. D. Y. (1984) 'Making History: The Past in the Ijesha Present', *Man* (N.S.) 19: 111–32.

Peel, J. D. Y. (1989) 'The Cultural Work of Yoruba Ethnogenesis', in E. Tonkin, M. McDonald and M. Chapman (eds) *History and Ethnicity*, pp. 198–215. London: Routledge.

Pels, P. (1997) 'The Anthropology of Colonialism: Culture, History, and the Emergence of Western Governmentality', *Annual Review of Anthropology* 26: 163–83.

van der Ploeg, J. D. (1993) 'Potatoes and Knowledge', in M. Hobart (ed.) *An Anthropological Critique of Development. The Growth of Ignorance*, pp. 209–27. London: Routledge.

Rose, N. (1999) *Powers of Freedom: Reframing Political Thought*. Cambridge: Cambridge University Press.

Shack, W. A. and E. P. Skinner (eds) (1979) *Strangers in African Societies*. Berkeley and Los Angeles, CA: University of California Press.

Scott, J. (1976) *The Moral Economy of the Peasant. Rebellion and Subsistence in Southeast Asia*. New Haven, CT: Yale University Press.

Scott, J. (1998) *Seeing like a State. How Certain Schemes to Improve the Human Condition Have Failed*. New Haven, CT, and London: Yale University Press.

Sivaramakrishnan, K. (1999) *Modern Forest: Statemaking and Environmental Change in Colonial Eastern India*. Stanford, CA: Stanford University Press.

Sivaramakrishnan, K. (2000) 'Crafting the Public Sphere in the Forests of West Bengal', *American Ethnologist* 27(2): 431–61.

Sommer, J. (2000) 'Korrupte Zivilgesellschaft. Unterschlagungen und die Kontrolle dörflicher Eliten bei den Bauern im Borgu (Benin)'. Doktorarbeit, Berlin: Freie Universität, Institut für Ethnologie.

Trager, L. (2001) *Yoruba Hometowns: Community, Identity, and Development in Nigeria*. Boulder, CO: Lynne Rienner Publishers.

Woost, M. (1994) 'Developing a Nation of Villages: Rural Community as State Formation in Sri Lanka', *Critique of Anthropology* 14(1): 77–95.

Zanou, C. (1986) *Les migrations de population et leur impact socio-économique en pays maxi dans le Zou-Nord*. Abomey Calavi: FLASH-UNG.

11

Decentralization, the State and Conflicts over Local Boundaries in Northern Ghana

Carola Lentz

INTRODUCTION

With the slogan 'bring the government to the people' the Rawlings government in Ghana announced, at the end of the 1980s, the creation of new districts. Throughout the country, this announcement set in motion intense lobby politics and political mobilization at the local level. Population and economic viability were the most important official criteria in deciding which areas qualified for district status, but respect for the integrity of chiefdoms and ethnic groups became equally influential arguments in the struggles over the boundaries of the new districts.

Decentralization projects such as this create a political space in which the relations between local political communities and the state are re-negotiated and re-ordered. The state claims to devolve part of its powers to local groups. Usually, however, this devolution does not motivate more local 'self-help', as the government hopes, but rather intensifies special-interest politics and political mobilization which is aimed at securing a 'larger share of the national cake', in the form of more state funds, infrastructure and posts for the locality (cf. Crook, 1994; Harneit-Sievers, 2002). When presenting their claims *vis-à-vis* the state, civic associations such as 'hometown' unions, as well as traditional rulers and other non-state institutions often invoke some form of 'natural' solidarity that binds the local community together and legitimates its quest for a separate administrative entity (with its material benefits). Decentralization projects therefore become arenas of debate over the boundaries of community and the relationship between 'local' and national citizenship.

This article analyses one such debate, in the former Lawra District of Ghana's Upper West Region, where the creation of new districts provoked protracted discussions among the local political elite as well as the peasants and labour migrants, concerning the political history and future of the area.[1] There was consensus that the Lawra District was to be divided into two, or perhaps three, new districts whose boundaries were to be drawn in accordance with existing paramount chiefdoms, but there was heated debate over who

1. The paper is based on extended fieldwork as well as archival studies which I have carried out on Lawra District and the neighbouring areas in Burkina Faso since 1987. For more details on the history of the area and full references to interviews and archival sources used, see Lentz (2006).

should join the Lambussie Traditional Area which was too small to stand alone. The debate focused on the connections between land ownership and political authority, including the right of taxation, on the relations between the local ethnic groups (Dagara and Sisala), and on the relevance of ethnic versus territorial criteria in defining local citizenship. The Lawra District case suggests that using the concept of 'traditional' local communities as the quasi-natural basis of grassroots democracy, as the Ghanaian decentralization project implicitly did, is highly problematic. It is a Pandora's box rather than a panacea for curing the evils of a distant state.

This article will discuss two issues which were central to the conflicts and which allow us to explore more general questions of governance and the relation between the state and 'civil society' at the local level: the spatial delimitation of administrative units and the social delimitation of local political communities. On which existing boundaries should the territorial delimitation of the new districts be based — on the pre-colonial earth shrine territories that are connected with property rights in land, on the colonial chiefdoms, or on the post-colonial electoral constituencies? In Lawra District, as in many other localities of Northern Ghana, these different boundaries do not coincide, but intersect and cross-cut each other. Any decision on the spatial delimitation of the new administrative units has important implications for their social and ethnic composition and raises delicate questions with respect to the political rights of land-owning 'natives' versus immigrant farmers. Should the traditional ritual prerogatives and property rights of the 'first-comers' be in any way translated into a privileged position in modern political decision making? Or should the immigrants, particularly if they constitute a sizeable majority, enjoy the same influence as these 'first-comers', because all are citizens of the same nation state? After how many generations of residence does an immigrant transform into a 'native'? These are some of the difficult questions that the recent decentralization project brought up and that, at the time of writing, have not yet found a solution.

These questions are hotly contested, not only in Northwestern Ghana but also in many other localities. The debates on autochthony that presently flourish in many parts of West Africa (Chauveau, 2000; Geschiere and Gugler, 1998; Geschiere and Nyamnjoh, 2000; see also Buur and Kyed, Juul, Le Meur, this issue) point to the problematic connections between migration, landed property, local belonging and political participation in the modern state. However, in order to understand these debates and the conflicts triggered by recent decentralization projects, one has to look at the long colonial and early post-colonial history of defining the territorial and socio-political boundaries of viable political communities — a history during which local models of host–stranger relations were articulated with European ideas of autochthony, and later superseded by notions of an egalitarian, supra-ethnic citizenship that ties political participation to membership in a modern nation state, not a locally anchored 'native' community. In what follows, I will therefore first present a historical perspective on the relations between first-comers and late-comers, ethnic boundaries and political allegiances in Lawra District, before turning to the recent conflicts over district boundaries, land and political participation.

DIFFICULT NEIGHBOURHOOD: A BRIEF HISTORY OF THE LAWRA DISTRICT

The conflicts provoked by the district delimitation exercise in Lawra District were foreseeable for anyone familiar with the history of the area. History mattered because the different parties brought it to bear on the current conflict, through their historically informed interpretations of what was at stake. But more importantly, history mattered because the problems of defining the spatial and social boundaries of the local political communities persisted.

First-comers and Late-comers

In order to understand the roots of the issue of land ownership raked up by the district conflict, one has to go back to the nineteenth century. What came to be the Lawra District in colonial times was then an agricultural and, in some senses, ethnic frontier. When small groups of Sisala-speaking farmers first settled in the area is difficult to ascertain. There is agreement, however, that in many parts of the district the expansionist Dagara-speaking agriculturalists who arrived on the scene probably from the eighteenth century onwards had to come to terms with Sisala first-comers. They did so by ethnic assimilation (thus becoming members of the first-comer community), by the purchase of land and earth shrines from the Sisala, or by their forceful expulsion. In any case the Dagara transformed themselves into allodial land owners, in full control of the land and the earth shrines.[2]

This process of 'autochthonization' came to a halt with colonial pacification when property rights and ethnic boundaries were 'frozen'. The Dagara continued to establish new settlements on Sisala land, but they were no longer given earth shrines and were thus unable to become allodial land owners. The precise nature of rights and duties of the Dagara 'settlers' or 'strangers', as the Sisala came to call them, towards their Sisala hosts, on whose land they farmed, depend on the specific circumstances of the original land grant. In some cases, bonds of friendship between the settler and his landlord make the actual burden of regular gifts very light (or even non-existent), and the settler's sons can expect to inherit the land (or, more precisely, the rights of usufruct). In other cases, the land owners exercise much stricter control by insisting, for instance, on their right to harvest commercial trees on a settler's farm or by allocating fallow land to other clients.

---

2. For an overview of Sisala–Dagara relations with respect to settlement, land tenure and earth shrines, see Kuba and Lentz (2002); for case studies see Lentz (2000a, 2001).

Landlord–settler relations usually were, and continue to be, an interpersonal affair. However, they can be affected by tensions between chiefdoms and ethnic groups, as was the case in the recent district conflicts. This is due to the fact that the boundary between first-comers and late-comers was politicized in the colonial period. The British model of indirect rule made allodial land ownership, based on first-comer status, the cornerstone in defining the 'native community' that was to be governed by an indigenous chief. Only 'natives' enjoyed local citizenship, while 'strangers', such as the Dagara on Sisala land, had no right to furnish the village chief. At the same time, the boundary between natives and settlers was defined ethnically. If a newcomer to a village happened to belong to the same ethnic group as the land owners, he was integrated into the native community, while ethnic strangers continued to be regarded as non-natives even after more than a generation of residency.[3]

The Creation of Chiefdoms

With the exception of the small urbanized state of Wa, the Northwest was not organized into kingdoms or chiefdoms in the pre-colonial period. Interacting with local actors, who were themselves interested in political centralization and power, the British succeeded in transforming the political landscape. By 1907, the colonial officers had divided the Lawra District into ten 'native states', of which some encompassed up to thirty settlements, while others included only two or three, each native state being subject to a head chief. In the early 1930s, the smaller native states were allocated to the four largest ones (later called 'divisions'), Lawra, Jirapa, Nandom and Lambussie, as subdivisions. The Lawra Confederacy, which was created in this way, survived the administrative reforms of the 1950s and, to date, has marked out the framework within which local political alliances and enmities are sealed and the establishment of new districts and constituencies is disputed (Lentz, 2000b).

The divisions of the Lawra Confederacy were neither congruent with earth shrine areas nor with ethnic groups. The extent of the chiefdoms was defined according to the power networks of the first head chiefs and according to criteria of administrative convenience, but not with respect to the boundaries dictated by allodial land rights. All divisional (paramount) chiefdoms encompass several earth shrine areas which usually do not extend beyond the confines of single villages (Eyre-Smith, 1933). This implies that paramount chiefs, in principle, have no jurisdiction over village land affairs. In practice, however, they may seek to influence land matters, as has happened in the recent district conflicts.

Chiefdoms also stood, and continue to stand, in tense relation to the ethnic criteria of group membership. Up to the 1930s the British tried to make

3. For more detail on this, see Lentz (2006: Chs 4, 9).

chiefdoms and 'tribes' congruent, but all such plans failed. In the end, it was a matter not of 'tribes' organized into chiefdoms but of chiefdoms, whose borders were determined by factors quite different from ethnic ones, being provided with a post-facto ethnic label, according to the ethnic identity of the head chief. This was how Lambussie came to be regarded as a Sisala chiefdom and the other three Lawra Confederacy divisions as Dagara — or, to use the colonial ethnic terms, Nandom came to be seen as Lobi-Dagarti, Lawra as Lobi and Jirapa as Dagarti.

If the British model of native states was targeted towards the erection of small territorial states, chiefly rule in the first decades of the colonial regime was nonetheless based on personal networks with divisional chiefs controlling these networks but no territory. Their area of rule was defined through lists of the sub-chiefs and villages owing them tribute in the form of labour or goods. Only in the 1930s were political membership and rule increasingly territorialized, when a poll tax was introduced and a central treasury for the Lawra Confederacy set up (later supplemented by sub-treasuries in the four divisions). Only then, as part of an effort to draw up taxation lists, did the membership of all men to a compound, all compounds to a village and all villages to a division need to become clearly fixed. This model of a clear territorial–political allocation of all compounds, including their farmlands, to a division cut across local practice characterized by mobility and multi-locality. From the 1930s onwards conflicts, especially in border zones, were sparked off by the question of to which chiefdom particular compounds should bring their political followings, and to whom farmers living in one division but having most of their farm elsewhere owed taxes.

Relations between Nandom and Lambussie

Such conflicts were particularly acute between the Nandom and Lambussie divisions. Due to the shortage of land in their villages of origin, ever-growing numbers of Dagara farmers from the Nandom division moved on to Sisala lands in the Lambussie chiefdom. The Nandom Naa initially attempted to stop this movement because he feared losing control over the labour and taxes of his (former) subjects. Matters were, however, facilitated when in 1935 the Lambussie division came under Nandom control, following succession conflicts in Lambussie, during which the Nandom Naa was invited by the dying Lambussie chief to supervise Lambussie affairs. Out of this temporary arrangement developed a reign lasting more than twelve years, until a group of 'politically conscious' Sisala demanded that the independent status of the Lambussie division be restored.[4] The British finally supported the Sisala claims believing that 'local government is [not] likely to flourish unless the

4. Chief Commissioner Northern Territories to Colonial Secretary, 5 November 1947, Regional Archives Tamale (RAT), NRG 8/2/101.

system we set up makes some appeal to the natural loyalties the people possess'.[5]

The restoration of Lambussie's independence in 1948 triggered off a series of conflicts. The first concerned the political allegiance of Hamile, a market town and border post on the international boundary between the French and the British colonies. Politically, British Hamile had been part of the Nandom Division; it followed the Nandom Naa through the Dagara headman in Hamile and the sub-divisional chief of Kokoligu. Land ownership in Hamile, however, was controlled by Sisala earth priests. When Lambussie regained its political independence from Nandom, the Lambussie Kuoro insisted that Hamile be included in his chiefdom because the land belonged to the earth priests of Happa, a village in the Lambussie division. His attempt to claim Hamile was supported by the majority of traders in Hamile and even by the Dagara headman, who all wished to follow Lambussie instead of Nandom. After a period of conflict and negotiation, Hamile was finally placed under the jurisdiction of the Lambussie Local Council.

Further conflicts between Lambussie and Nandom concerned the political allegiance of Dagara farmers residing in the border zone between the two divisions. The Lawra Confederacy State Council, the district house of chiefs before which the conflicts were brought, decided that Dagara farmers living on Sisala land should pay taxes to the Lambussie Local Council, but those residing within Nandom territory and merely farming on Sisala land should belong to the Nandom Local Council. However, in a number of cases Sisala and Dagara disagreed on the history of land ownership. In Dahile, for instance, the Sisala earth priest insisted that the land under his control continued to reach as far as the Black Volta, that is well into the Nandom Local Council territory, while the Dagara claimed that their fathers had gained allodial rights over this land which *they* now farmed.[6] Ultimately, the Lawra Confederacy State Council decided that the Dagara compounds in question belonged to the Lambussie Local Council.

Yet matters did not end there. The Nandom Naa appealed to the British Government Agent and petitioned to break away from the Lawra Confederacy. This turn of events angered the Lawra Naa, the president of the Lawra Confederacy State Council, who fabricated destoolment charges against the Nandom Naa, availing himself of an initiative by the latter's local opponents. In the mid 1950s, these struggles over land and chieftaincy became deeply enmeshed in party politics.[7] The Nandom Naa sought the support of Kwame Nkrumah's Convention People's Party (CPP) while the Lawra Naa was one of the leading figures of the opposition Northern People's Party (NPP). The Nandom Naa died in 1957 and did not live to see his secessionist plans

---

5. District Commissioner Lawra-Tumu to District Commissioner Wa, 1 October 1947, RAT, NRG 8/2/101.
6. Lawra Conf. State Council, 4 May 1956, RAT, NRG 7/4/5.
7. For more details on early party politics in the Lawra District, see Lentz (2002).

fulfilled. His successor, however, struck an alliance with the first African district commissioner in Lawra, a CPP appointee from a Dagara village under Nandom, who saw to it that Lambussie and Nandom were placed together in one district, with headquarters in Nandom (1960–62). The Lambussie chiefly house had initially supported the cause of the NPP, but changed to the CPP in order to win support against Nandom hegemony. In 1962 Lambussie was indeed granted an independent district. The old Lawra Confederacy was now split into four separate districts — a politically expedient, but economically and administratively unsuitable solution to the protracted conflicts. The former Lawra District was restored after Nkrumah's overthrow (1966) and continued to function until the late 1980s when the Rawlings government decided that new districts should be created in order 'to bring the government to the people'.

It is not surprising that many in the area felt that the petition of the Nandom Youth and Development Association (NYDA) for the creation of a Nandom or, 'if the need arises', a joint Nandom–Lambussie District, which the youth association presented to the Upper West Regional Secretary in 1986, was opening old wounds.[8] Fears were aggravated by obvious personal continuities: the new Nandom Naa, in office since 1985, was the son of the chief against whom the Sisala had been forced to fight for their independence; the incumbent Lawra Naa was the son of the chief who had been the erstwhile Nandom Naa's most powerful opponent; and, finally, the incumbent Lambussie Kuoro had once served as secretary to the Lambussie chief who succeeded in restoring Lambussie's independence from Nandom.

THE RECENT CONFLICTS OVER DISTRICTS AND LAND: A CHRONOLOGY OF EVENTS

Three criteria were to guide the demarcation of new districts which the Rawlings government intended to create: population (not below 50,000 in rural districts), economic viability and existing infrastructure. The 1984 population census had counted 67,721 inhabitants in the Nandom–Lambussie and 88,453 in the Lawra–Jirapa Local Councils (the old census units of the early 1960s had been retained). Clearly, the population of the Lawra District was sufficient for the creation of two or even three new districts. However, Nandom did not reach the 50,000 inhabitants mark by itself and was therefore in need of a partner if it was to become a new district.

Although the NYDA petition mentioned a combined Nandom–Lambussie district only as one of two possible options, this was the one that the NYDA activists actually favoured.[9] A joint Nandom–Lambussie district had

8. NYDA, Petition for the Creation of a District for the Nandom Traditional Area, presented during the NYDA national delegates' conference, December 1986: 6.
9. On the history and agenda of NYDA and other ethno-regional associations, see Lentz (1995, 2000c).

advantages in terms of infrastructure and proximity, but the NYDA also supported it because it would encompass in one politico-administrative unit the numerous Dagara from Nandom who were living on Sisala land in Lambussie villages. The Sisala politicians in Lambussie, on the other hand, preferred the creation of a joint district with Jirapa, despite the greater physical distance and other inconveniences, because they feared the dominance of the Dagara from Nandom and regarded the Dagaba from Jirapa 'as friends or brothers' who 'don't disturb them [the Sisala] like the Nandom people do'.[10]

The disagreement between Nandom and Lambussie about the future district manifested itself openly, for the first time, over the question of where Hamile belonged — the very issue that had triggered the protracted conflicts of the 1940s and 1950s. It was probably the Lambussie Kuoro himself, a member of the National Commission for Democracy (NCD), that was in charge of defining the new districts, who had advised against NYDA's Nandom–Lambussie district project. In any case, the NCD and the regional administration decided in favour of a Lawra–Nandom and a Jirapa–Lambussie district. In March 1987, the Lawra District Secretary went on a tour of inspection in order to explain the demarcation of the new districts to the village chiefs and the local population. In a meeting in Hamile, the Nandom Naa declared that only the territory east of the Hamile–Nandom road was part of the Lambussie Traditional Area and would therefore belong to the new Jirapa–Lambussie District, while the territory west of the road was under the jurisdiction of Nandom. This claim provoked an indignant outcry from various segments of the population of Hamile. They were reminded of the Nandom Naa's father whose severe policies towards the Hamile traders in the 1940s and 1950s had caused the town to break away from Nandom and seek to be placed under Lambussie.

The Nandom Naa's claim to Hamile was almost immediately followed by the massive seizure of farms from Dagara farming on Sisala land, right at the beginning of the new agricultural season. The matter was brought to the attention of the Lawra District Secretary who called the Lambussie Kuoro, the Nandom Naa and the chiefs of Kokoligu and Happa to a meeting in Lawra. Confirming that according to a 'High Court' decision of 1951 Hamile belonged to the Lambussie Traditional Area,[11] the District Secretary exhorted the Nandom Naa and his chiefs to comply with the ruling that 'all of the Hamile township and its environs [were] not to be divided in any way between Lambussie and Nandom'. The Lambussie Kuoro, on the other hand, should 'rescind his decision communicated to all his chiefs to forbid

10. Interview with Jacob Boon, Jirapa-Lambussie District Commissioner, 23 November 1989.
11. The District Secretary obviously followed the Lambussie Kuoro's version who used to speak of a 'High Court decision' on the Hamile affairs; in fact, the case was never brought before the High Court, but decided by a native authority court, namely the Lawra Confederacy Court A. See RAT, NRG 7/2/5 for the Lawra Confederacy Court Book with verbatim extracts of the court case in 1950, and an appeal in 1951.

and prevent Dagartis from Nandom area farming on Sissala land'.[12] After further 'peace talks' between the Lambussie chiefs and land owners and the Nandom Dagara farmers in July 1987, the new Regional Secretary was confident that the 'tenant farmers' from Nandom would be allowed to 'return to their farms without fear of molestation'.[13]

However, this proved to be a premature hope. The land conflicts were propelled by the anger of the Lambussie Kuoro over renewed attempts of the NYDA and its self-declared 'think tank' ANSOC (Accra Nandom Social Club), to revise the demarcated districts. In July 1987 ANSOC sent a new petition for a joint Nandom–Lambussie district, this time directly to the NCD and not to the regional administration which they believed to be biased against Nandom. The Lambussie Kuoro, assisted by the Issaw West Development Union, an almost defunct but now revived Sisala youth association, reacted promptly. In a counter petition he declared his acceptance of government's decision for a Jirapa–Lambussie District and criticized Nandom for making 'false claims to parts of Lambussie' and 'false allegations' which created 'a state of suspicion and mistrust ... between the people of the two areas'.[14] Such 'mistrust' made it impossible to imagine a joint district.

The NYDA executive, who had been informed of the Lambussie Kuoro's letter, insisted that there was generally no tension between the Sisala from Lambussie and the Dagara from Nandom, but only 'isolated cases' of 'occasional quarrels between individual land owners in Lambussie and some farmers from Nandom farming on Sisala land'.[15] The exchange of letters was followed in January 1988 by a series of confidential meetings between members of the NYDA and ANSOC on the one hand and the Regional Secretary in Wa and the NCD in Accra on the other. The NCD even seems to have offered to create an autonomous district for Nandom alone, but ANSOC declined, fearing that the Dagara living in the Lambussie Traditional Area would suffer as a result of their administrative separation from Nandom. But all the letters and lobby politics did not change the original decision with regard to the district. In July 1988, Jacob Boon, a lawyer from Lambussie who had helped revive the Sisala youth association, took up his position in Jirapa as the new district secretary of the Jirapa–Lambussie District.

The dispute over the district was closed, but the land conflicts continued. At the beginning of the new farming season of 1988, a sizeable number of Dagara farmers on Sisala land were again not allowed to work on their farms. In other cases, Sisala land owners requested much higher 'gifts' from their Dagara clients than before, and insisted on their rights to harvest sheanut (*karité*) and *dawadawa* (*néré*) trees on the fields of their 'tenant farmers'. One conflict, in Taalipuo, a village on the border between the Nandom and Lambussie

12. Lawra District Secretary to Lambussie Kuoro, Nandom Naa and others, 5 May 1987.
13. *People's Daily Graphic*, 11 July 1987.
14. Lambussie Kuoro, K.Y. Baloro, and Secretary Issaw West Development Union, Jacob Boon, to NCD, PNDC Regional Secretary, Wa, and District Secretary, Lawra, August 1987.
15. NYDA National Executive to PNDC Regional Secretary, 2 September 1987.

chiefdoms, became particularly prominent and attracted a lot of local and administrative attention. The basic disagreement in Taalipuo revolved around the administrative allegiance of a number of Dagara compounds, much as it did in the land conflicts of the 1950s. Did these houses belong to Lambussie, via Nabaala, the Sisala village which claimed to have given the permission to the Dagara farmers to settle? Or did they belong to Nandom, via the Nandom earth priests who likewise claimed to have established the compounds in question? The Sisala felt that these compounds should pay their taxes to the new Jirapa–Lambussie District and brought pressure to bear on the Dagara farmers by refusing them permission to farm bush fields further inside Sisala territory.

The District Security Committee, alerted by the youth associations and the paramount chiefs, organized a series of local meetings, with the affected Dagara farmers and the Sisala land owners as well as the earth priests from Nandom, Nabaala and Lambussie. However, the agreements reached remained ineffective, not least because they were challenged by competing local dignitaries who denied those present at the meeting any authority. As the earth priests, traditionally responsible for the settlement of land disputes, were not able to resolve the matter, other institutions were brought into play: the paramount chiefs, the political authorities at the district, regional and even national levels, and the ethno-political youth associations that presented themselves as the legitimate spokesmen of the 'grassroots', namely the affected farmers. However, none of these institutions succeeded in resolving the conflict, and the Taalipuo and other Dagara farmers on Sisala land were once again denied access to land during the 1989 agricultural season.

The Gordian knot was finally cut by the Catholic Archbishop of Tamale, Peter Dery, a man from the Nandom Traditional Area, of mixed Dagara and Sisala ancestry, who commands much respect throughout the region. After some preliminary talks with both sides, the Archbishop managed, in January 1990, to summon the Nandom and Lambussie paramount chiefs to a meeting in Hamile, on the 'neutral grounds' of the Catholic mission but precisely in the town where the dispute over the district boundaries had begun. Dery drastically reduced the complexity of the conflict by focusing on the Taalipuo issue. He treated the district matter as closed and avoided entering into any of the intricate debates on the settlement history and ethnic relations, but reminded the chiefs and others present that 'land is the creation of God for the use of human beings'. The chiefs eventually agreed that three of the disputed Taalipuo compounds were to be placed under the jurisdiction of the Lambussie District and that, in turn, 'the Lambussie Traditional Area will revoke all existing seizures of farm lands of immigrant and settler farmers'.[16]

Up to the present, no further large-scale land conflicts have erupted in the area. On the other hand, Nandom's aspirations for its own district, separate

16. 'Summary of decisions taken at a meeting of Lambussie Kuoro, Nandom Naa and their respective Tindanas with His Grace Archbishop P.P. Dery', Hamile, 23 January 1990.

from Lawra, continue to be frustrated. And what was particularly bitter for the NYDA and ANSOC activists, was that when new constituencies were drawn up for the parliamentary elections of 1992, it was Lambussie, but not Nandom which was granted a separate constituency.

EARTH SHRINES, CHIEFDOMS AND DISTRICTS: DEFINING THE SPATIAL BOUNDARIES OF ADMINISTRATIVE UNITS

One of the issues at stake in the Taalipuo conflict was the spatial delimitation of the new districts and the nature of administrative boundaries. Local administration must necessarily define the extent of its territorial reach. Administrative boundaries are relevant, among other reasons, for matters of taxation and for the creation of infrastructure. In the conflicts between Nandom and Lambussie one of the questions that was controversial concerned the precise course of the new district boundary. I shall briefly explain why this question is so thorny.

As already mentioned, chiefly rule in the first decades of colonial regime was personal rather than territorial. It is no coincidence that the British officers never attempted to draw up a map with the precise boundaries of the chiefdoms. Chiefdoms were defined through lists of the sub-chiefs and villages subordinate to them. This practice continued into the 1950s, when local and district councils were defined on the basis of the existing chiefdoms. Again, I have never come across a map for that period which shows precise local council and district boundaries. Today such maps exist, but it seems that the administrative boundaries are drawn in a rather off-hand fashion, using, wherever possible, natural features such as small streams, and making sure that the villages in border zones are included in the 'correct' district. District boundaries have never been demarcated on the ground. Any such exercise would undoubtedly cause unending discussions, as can be gleaned from the conflicts that often develop over the placement of signposts with village or district names along the roads.

In colonial times, the boundaries of chiefdoms and districts were defined pragmatically. For the maintenance of the roads, for instance, neighbouring villages were made to agree on a specific spot on the road, easily recognizable by some landmark such as a stream or a big tree, up to which each side would work. Such places came to be regarded as indicators of the relevant administrative boundaries. In the Taalipuo conflict, the Dagara invoked such a spot on the road between Taalipuo and Nabaala as proof that their forefathers actually owned the disputed land and that the village belonged to Nandom. However, the Sisala did not accept this claim, and insisted on their status as first-comers. They reminded the Dagara that it was the Lambussie earth priests who had once given Nandom its earth shrine and that therefore no substantial boundary existed between these two areas and, consequently, between Taalipuo and Nabaala. What counted, in their eyes, was that the

Sisala from Nabaala and Billaw had given the Dagara permission to settle in Taalipuo.[17]

This argument points to an alternative basis for demarcating administrative units, namely in accordance with those boundaries set out by allodial land ownership. The idea that specific political rights ensue from first-comer status and property ownership was central to the British model of native authorities. In practice, however, various historical circumstances led to situations in which the chieftaincy was not always in the hands of land owners. But as we have seen in the case of Hamile, first-comer groups used this model in order to bolster claims to political power. This indeed is what subsequently came to bear in the district conflict, in which the Lambussie Kuoro was convinced that the Taalipuo compounds located on Sisala land belonged to the newly created Jirapa–Lambussie District. It was thus argued that district boundaries should be drawn in accordance with those boundaries dictated by property rights.

Yet these property boundaries are by no means straightforward and uncontested. For one, debate may arise over the assignment of first-comer status and the legitimacy of subsequent property transfers. If, for example, the Sisala claim that the land up to the Black Volta belongs to them, then it is for one of two reasons. First, they claim that even after an earth shrine has been transferred to the Dagara, the shrine-giver ultimately retains some rights over the territory. Second, they may claim that the appropriation of land by Dagara was not legitimate. While it is true that in the last quarter of the nineteenth century violence played an increasingly important role in Dagara expansion, does this justify demands to revise property rights in times of peace? A member of the NYDA executive compared the situation to that in the Middle East:

> They [the Sisala] were kind of the original settlers in the area. When our people [the Dagara] came, they drove them farther and farther away... That is the story with the Israelites and the Arabs now, you conquer, you fight somebody and get his land, and then later on the man comes back and says that because there is peace now, just give me back my land. This is the problem.[18]

The disagreement between Sisala and Dagara regarding the history of land ownership had little effect on day-to-day access to farmland. The issue did, however, become virulently contested in the context of discussions over district boundaries as these fuelled fears of expulsion and loss on both sides.

Furthermore, as the Taalipuo conflict has shown, the actual village boundary demarcations, along which district boundaries were to be oriented, are often contested. In most agricultural societies, including those in the Black Volta region, field boundaries are held to be linear. Often they are marked

17. See the minutes of the District Security Committee visit to Taalipuo, 5 May 1988.
18. Interview with the NYDA executive, Wa, 15 November 1990.

either by notches on trees, by paths or by shrubs. In contrast, the boundaries of village — or, to be more precise, earth shrine — territories were seldom, if ever, imagined as linear, but as a series of 'meeting points' in the bush, marked by hills, rivers, rocks, ponds or specific trees. In case of armed conflict between neighbouring settlements, these meeting points could become ritually loaded if the conflict was ended by a peace-making ceremony. As more and more bush was cultivated, the boundaries between earth shrine areas had to be defined more precisely. Near the border, the ritual allegiance — and village membership — of houses and fields was usually defined according to which earth priest had originally given permission to cultivate or build. The social networks of these spiritual services were, and still are, interpreted territorially. That is why, in the Taalipuo conflict, debate was so intense as to which earth priest — the one from Nabaala or the one from Nandomkpee — had given the compounds in question the right to settle. Because these service relationships often encompass numerous aspects (including the right to build houses, to farm and to bury the dead) and are by no means unambiguous or unchangeable, the spatial allegiance of a compound is not always unequivocal. The inhabitants can, depending on the context and interests, refer to different services as evidence for property rights.

Each of the interested parties attempts to present their criteria of boundary making as 'natural', resulting automatically from undisputed property rights or colonial political hierarchies. However, all criteria are potentially controversial and subject to negotiation which, in turn, is influenced by local power relationships as well as the mobilization of regional and national political contacts. They have important consequences for the inclusion or exclusion of local citizens, as I will discuss below.

'NATIVES' AND 'STRANGERS' OR GHANAIAN CITIZENS? THE SOCIAL DELIMITATION OF LOCAL POLITICAL COMMUNITIES

The question of the spatial demarcation of districts cannot be addressed without looking at the social and ethnic composition of the local political community. In the district assemblies which the NCD wanted to establish, district inhabitants — as citizens of Ghana — all have the same fundamental rights and duties. Differences in ethnic identity and questions of autochthony — the distinction between 'natives' and 'strangers', constructed by the British model of native authorities — are systematically ignored. It is exactly this model of political participation by citizens with equal rights, to which NYDA and the Dagara generally referred. Sisala politicians, on the other hand, emphasized specific rights, which arose out of their status as property owners and first-comers to the region. Furthermore, they used their control over land to emphasize their position with regard to the question of the district, this being the most powerful means of exerting pressure on the Dagara, who tend to be less well-endowed with land. The Sisala fear that equal participation of Dagara and Sisala in a common district would ultimately only buttress Nandom's superiority. At the heart of these powerful sentiments are tensions arising from the unequal development of Nandom and Lambussie. The Dagara of Nandom are not just more numerous than the Sisala, but also have — due to massive conversion to Catholicism — enjoyed earlier and more extensive access to education than the Sisala. They have, therefore, had more success than their Sisala counterparts in securing a wider variety of employment opportunities as well as bringing more infrastructure into their villages and into Nandom. Sisala politicians also view the Dagara as being more skilled at lobby politics and as using this advantage to 'take land away' from the Sisala. This is why they wish to block the establishment of a common district at all costs, as well as institute a system under which the Dagara are forced to pay for the land in Lambussie which they cultivate — taxes, if they live in the Lambussie Traditional Area, or a kind of rent should they only cultivate fields there.

In a letter to the government in Accra laying out the arguments against a Nandom–Lambussie district, the Regional Secretary summarized the Sisala position as follows:

> [T]he Sissalas of the Lambussie Traditional Area are totally opposed to being in the same District with the Dagaaba [Dagara] of the Nandom Traditional Area. They foresee . . . the loss of their lands which the Dagaaba covet, and of their identity because of the numerical advantage of the Dagaaba.
> The Dagaaba are more politically conscious. The Dagaaba are better educated. The Dagaaba are in more dispersed, prestigious employment and in influential positions, have numerous country-wide contacts and are thus formidable lobbyists. Even in the Lambussie Traditional area itself the Dagaaba outnumber the Sissala. The one trump card held by the Sissala is that the Sissala are the traditional landowners of the Lambussie Traditional Area and even claim ownership of most land in the Nandom Traditional area. A number of prominent Sisala have seen the move for the two Traditional Areas to belong to one District as an attempt by the Dagaaba to colonise them and take over Sissala land. . . . The Sissala are in the minority, but a significant minority whose aspirations cannot be brushed aside without dire consequences for the peace and progress of the area. . . The Sissala should be coaxed and not coerced to accept the creation of a Nandom–Lambussie District.[19]

For the NYDA activists the Regional Secretary's reference to the first-comer status of the Sisala was unacceptable, or, at the very least, one-sided. They insisted that it was unjust to continue classifying someone as a 'settler' after more than sixty years of settlement, effectively excluding them from full political participation. Furthermore, they claimed that ownership rights, and therefore rights to political participation, ensue from the active cultivation of the land. Finally, they saw the emphasis on ethnic difference as a political strategy on the part of only a small Sisala elite, while 'the vast majority of

19. Upper West Regional Secretary to Ag Director Castle Information Bureau, Accra, 10 May 1989.

ordinary people are quite capable of making up their minds without resorting to ethnic identities'. In their comments on the Regional Secretary's letter they wrote:

> How really distinct are the two ethnic groups... [Dagara and Sisala]...? These are people who have lived together for more than a century. There have been inter-marriages between the two... Also the two communities have always shared common social and economic infrastructure such as a daily market, a rural bank, health care, educational facilities etc. Our suspicion therefore is that the animosity between the two areas [Nandom and Lambussie] is being deliberately fanned by some individuals who think that their personal ambitions are best served that way...
>
> If anything, at all, it is the Dagaaba in the Nandom–Lambussie area who stand in the danger of having their land rights undermined. ... Most of the Dagaaba in the Nandom–Lambussie area have made the place their home since the early part of the 19th century. The Sissaala are themselves people who migrated into the area from somewhere else. They did not germinate from the ground in the area. The fact that they arrived before us and established a few communities in the wild bush that the area was at that time does not justify the landowner–tenant relations that some would like to see existing between the two areas. In fact, the pioneer Sissala settlers could not have tamed and put under cultivation the wild bush that the area was without the Dagaabas. Descendants of these intrepid conquerors of the land cannot now be dismissed, generations later as mere settlers, as is now currently happening in Taalipuo.[20]

In an unsent letter, the NYDA cited the Ga in Accra as a positive example of how both the 'autochthonous' rights of cultural self-determination as well as immigrants' rights to political participation could be upheld: 'When the Gas have their purely traditional performances, customs and cultures they do it alone, but when it concerns Government and other issues emanating from Government for the general concern of the people in Accra, all residents in Accra decide on it'.[21] Whether the situation in Accra really developed as idyllically as NYDA would like us to believe is a matter of serious doubt. The reality is that everywhere — in Accra as well as in rural areas with large immigrant populations — debates are becoming increasingly important as to which economic and political rights are to be derived from the status of an autochthone or a first-comer. In case after case we see that one of the main issues at stake is land control.

The NYDA activists accused the Sisala of using land for political leverage. The Lambussie Kuoro, on the other hand, insisted that Sisala land owners would have real concerns regarding future access to land:

> The land is becoming short. ... Our people have realized that they can make a lot more income from farming instead of going down south to burn charcoal. So people who were down south have now moved up here to farm. Now secondly, people feel that they have to reserve their land because the cost of inputs are now very very high. So if you give up all your land and it is exhausted, you yourself will have nowhere to go.[22]

20. NYDA National Chairman to Ag. Director, Castle Information Bureau, 26 May 1989.
21. NYDA National Chairman to Upper West Regional Secretary, 8 February 1988.
22. Interview, 28 November 1989, Lambussie.

Archbishop Peter Dery argued similarly, but also agreed with the NYDA that land was not the only issue being debated, and that political relations as well as ethnic discrimination were also central concerns:

> Recently, the Sisala are trying to punish the Dagara for the discrimination they suffer, by taking away the land from Dagara farmers who are farming on Sisala land. It is very clear that all the land between the Kambah and Hamile belonged to the Sisala when the Dagara moved into the area. The Dagara were fighters and pushed the Sisala further and further eastward until at a certain point, a boundary needed to be established to stop the fighting. This boundary gave the more plentiful and better lands to the Sisala, and when the Dagara had filled their place between the Black Volta and this boundary and were lacking land to farm, they asked the Sisala for land to farm. They were given land to farm and in return had to give some produce to the Sisala. In most cases, apparently this was done only once, at the beginning of the contract… At a certain point, however, Dagara farmers were complaining about Sisala landowners that they were lazy and demanded too much from them, and they no longer wanted to give the Sisala any produce. The Sisala reacted by seizing their lands, and the political problem developed. … The root of the problem really is the discriminatory attitude of the Dagara towards the Sisala. The NYDA 'young men' have had their second thoughts and planned to pull Bussie [Lambussie] under Nandom, and since Nandom is numerically much stronger than Bussie, Bussie would have been swallowed. They are trying to revise history, for instance in the Hamile case.[23]

The central point that was, and still is, up for debate in all these exchanges, is the following: does a political community, which exercises effective political control in a given district, define itself historically or does it constitute itself through the idea of fundamental equality, regardless of the historic development of land ownership, and through a shared vision of the future?

CONCLUSION

Mahmood Mamdani (1996) declared the difference between 'citizen' and 'subject', which he views as the most important legacy of the colonial 'bifurcated state' and the decentralized despotism of the 'native authorities', as the defining characteristic of the African organization of power. But as demonstrated in the case presented here, Mamdani's view of colonial political organization as one based on 'tribes' is too simplistic. His association of the citizen–subject binary with the rural–urban dichotomy is inaccurate. Furthermore, there is nothing intrinsically 'African' about it. Analogous debates regarding the legitimate basis of political participation took place in seventeenth and eighteenth century England. The idea that voting rights needed to be tied to property ownership, because migrants and non-land owners are subject to a multiplicity of loyalties and therefore regarded as unreliable and potentially irresponsible, was a topos common well into the twentieth century. Ultimately up for debate was, and continues to be, the question of which forms of political community could be established on the basis

23. Interview, 17 November 1990, Tamale.

of mobility and multi-locality — a question not even raised in the current decentralization-mania in Africa, but one which will inevitably impose itself by way of conflict such as the one analysed here.

Closely linked to this question is the issue of the role of (neo)traditional institutions such as chieftaincy *vis-à-vis* elected district assemblies or youth associations in local government and mechanisms of conflict resolution (see also Le Meur, this issue). The conflicts between Lambussie and Nandom in particular make clear the problematic nature of the idealistic support voiced by numerous politicians of decentralization as a strategy for the strengthening of local 'traditional' authorities. The institution of the chieftaincy links political rights to the status of 'natives', which leaves the Dagara settlers on Sisala land represented — if at all — only by a subordinate headman. But even the modern democratic majority vote to select assembly men and women can be influenced by informal pressure exerted by land owners in the context of candidate selection. In quite a few villages, settlers are openly pressured into not running for the assembly under threats to impede their access to land. The idea that close co-operation with 'traditional authorities' guarantees grassroots democracy is naive. But hopes for easy alternatives are unwarranted.

The policy of decentralization has not caused the conflicts I presented above. The underlying problems — the connections between land ownership and political authority, and the tension between ethnic and territorial criteria in defining local citizenship — are much older. However, the more narrowly the boundaries of the administrative units are drawn, the more acute the problems become of spatially and socially demarcating political communities.

REFERENCES

Chauveau, J. P. (2000) 'Question foncière et construction nationale en Côte d'Ivoire', *Politique Africaine* 78: 94–125.

Crook, R. (1994) 'Four Years of the Ghana District Assemblies in Operation: Decentralisation, Democratisation and Administrative Performance', *Public Administration and Development* 14: 339–64.

Eyre-Smith, R. St. J. (1933) *A Brief Review of the History and Social Organisation of the Peoples of the Northern Territories of the Gold Coast*. Accra: Government Printer.

Geschiere, P. and J. Gugler (eds) (1998) 'The Politics of Primary Patriotism', *Africa* 68(special issue).

Geschiere, P. and F. Nyamnjoh (2000) 'Capitalism and Autochthony: The Seesaw of Mobility and Belonging', *Public Culture* 12: 423–52.

Harneit-Sievers, A. (2002) 'Federalism to the Bitter End: Politics and History in South-Eastern Nigeria's "Autonomous Communities"', *Sociologus* 52: 47–76.

Kuba, R. and C. Lentz (2002) 'Arrows and Earth Shrines: Towards a History of Dagara Expansion in Southwestern Burkina Faso', *Journal of African History* 43: 377–406.

Lentz, C. (1995) '"Unity for Development": Youth Associations in North-western Ghana', *Africa* 65: 395–429.

Lentz, C. (2000a) 'Of Hunters, Goats and Earth-shrines: Settlement Histories and the Politics of Oral Tradition in Northern Ghana', *History in Africa* 27: 193–214.
Lentz, C. (2000b) '"Chieftaincy has Come to Stay". La chefferie dans les sociétés acéphales du Nord-Ouest Ghana', *Cahiers d'Etudes Africaines* 159: 593–613.
Lentz, C. (2000c) '"Youth Associations" et ethnicité au Nord-Ghana', in C. Toulabor (ed.) *Le Ghana de J. J. Rawlings. Restauration de l'État et renaissance du politique*, pp. 126–44. Paris: Karthala.
Lentz, C. (2001) 'Ouessa. Débats sur l'histoire du peuplement', in R. Kuba, C. Lentz and K. Werthmann (eds) *Les Dagara et leurs voisins. Histoire du peuplement et relations interethniques au sud-ouest du Burkina Faso*, pp. 29–61. Frankfurt: Berichte des Sonderforschungsbereichs 268 'Westafrikanische Savanne', 15.
Lentz, C. (2002) '"The Time when Politics Came": Ghana's Decolonisation from the Perspective of a Rural Periphery', *Journal of Contemporary African Studies* 20: 245–74.
Lentz, C. (2006) *Ethnicity and the Making of History in Northern Ghana*. Edinburgh: Edinburgh University Press (International African Library).
Mamdani, M. (1996) *Citizen and Subject: Contemporary Africa and the Legacy of Late Colonialism*. Princeton, NJ: Princeton University Press.

12

Strong Bar, Weak State? Lawyers, Liberalism and State Formation in Zambia

Jeremy Gould

BEYOND THE POST-COLONIAL STATE?

> 'To endeavor to think the state is to take the risk of taking over (or being taken over by) a thought of the state, that is, of applying to the state categories of thought produced and guaranteed by the state and hence to misrecognize its most profound truth'. (Pierre Bourdieu, 1999: 53)

For Africa, writes Crawford Young (2004: 49), 'the post-colonial moment appears to have passed'. Post-coloniality — which Young associates with 'the wholesale importation of the routines, practices, and mentalities of the African colonial state into its post-colonial successor' (ibid.: 23–4), and which laid the foundations for state-driven developmentalism — no longer holds sway over political institutions and processes. As once robust political monopolies are usurped by what Mbembe (2001) has termed 'private indirect government', Young invites us to reflect on the extent to which 'new elements in the contemporary political equation' might not 'add up to a basic alteration in the parameters of stateness' (Young, 2004: 24). African states appear cut loose from their colonial moorings and anything seems possible. And yet, while 'the tug of liberal democracy and a market economy is strong', it is far from certain, Young suggests, that these liberal ideals 'represent the eventual destinations' for African state formation (ibid.: 48).

One need not underwrite Young's dismissal of the colonial legacy to agree that the implicit teleology of late/post-colonial liberalism no longer conveys the dynamics of contemporary African politics. It seems rather uncontroversial, but accepting this premise opens a Pandora's box of theoretical dilemmas. If not in terms of liberalism, how then should one frame emerging post-postcolonial states and their concomitant political dispensations? How indeed is one to theorize the trajectory of African state formation since the end of the Cold War?[1] Young offers no answers, but points approvingly in

1. My use of 'state formation' draws, among others, on the work of Abrams (1988), Corrigan and Sayers (1985), Hansen and Stepputat (2001), Joseph and Nugent (1994) and Steinmetz (1999). In contrast with incidents of 'state building', such as the US and its allies currently seek to engineer in Afghanistan and Iraq, state formation, as understood here, refers to the long-term changes in the ideas and practices of stateness in a particular context, and to the implications of these changes for concomitant shifts in the relationship between rulers and ruled.

the direction of authors working from a neo-Weberian notion of patrimonialism to characterize contemporary African politics (such as Bayart, 1991; Bayart et al., 1999; Chabal and Daloz, 1999; also Médard, 1982). What unites these authors, besides their largely Francophone pedigree, is the premise that liberalism dressed up as democratization was a feckless façade for persistent and often kleptocratic autocracy. The patrimonial genre illustrates this premise with a rich array of anecdotes demonstrating how a culture of liberalism has failed to institutionalize itself in most of Africa. As the 'third wave of democratization' dissipated under the weight of recalcitrant despotism, it is claimed, personalized rule by prerogative has prevailed, albeit over an increasingly hollowed-out state.

This illiberal view dominates the contemporary literature on African politics. Its popularity and persistence can partly be explained by the way that its dismal narratives are reinforced by routine dispatches of Western journalists on their way from one complex African emergency to another. (Indeed, writers in the patrimonial genre draw copiously on journalism for empirical data.) Over the past decade, this perspective has also provided impetus to and justification for the livelihoods of a growing professional fraternity of transnational democratizers and international human rights specialists. These liberal evangelists comprise a growing guild based in public and private aid agencies, mandated by Northern taxpayers and philanthropists to build the capacity of civil society and promote governance reforms in the semi-authoritarian polities of the global South (Carothers, 1999). Much of the growing literature on the failures of the African state (corruption, electoral fraud, human rights abuses, constitutional lapses, and so forth) is funded or commissioned by these democracy engineers and their agencies.

There are other views, including those that uphold the contemporary relevance of liberalism for African statehood. Many of these emanate from South Africa, where the celebration of the nation's liberation from apartheid, and the popular enactment of a quintessentially liberal constitution, resonate in scholarly literature and political commentary. Although fewer, one can also find similarly buoyant analyses set elsewhere. To cite two recent offerings: Richard Werbner's sojourn into public anthropology (2004) commemorates the contemporary history of political liberalism in Botswana. Werbner singles out the contribution of elite members of an influential minority group whose assertive commitment to liberal values is said to have kept authoritarian tendencies in check. Jennifer Widner's book-length analysis of the Tanzanian legal system (2001), focusing on that country's former Chief Justice, portrays a judiciary comprised of dedicated liberals devoted to 'building the rule of law'.

Opposing liberal and patrimonial views capture partial truths but are each problematic, for different reasons. The patrimonial perspective is analytically unsatisfying because it only succeeds in identifying what the 'post-postcolonial' state is *not*. Weber's initial formulation of a patrimonial political order (1968: Vol. 2, Ch. XII) was predicated on the generalization of domestic ('patriarchical') relationships of *Herrschaft* (authority, domination), legitimized through 'habituation' and custom rooted in 'time out of mind' (ibid.: 1006). Patrimonial tendencies in post-colonial African states were initially identified by political analysts nursed on neo-Weberian modernization theory in the 1960s (cf. Roth, 1968). These characterizations sought to highlight the discrepancies between theoretical predictions of how modernized elites should behave, and their empirical dependence on traditionalist mechanisms of legitimation (cf. Geertz, 1963). As the social scientific understanding of the relationship between modernity and tradition has subsequently moved beyond their simple juxtaposition as opposing and mutually exclusive modes of sociality, the theoretical basis for a model of the patrimonial state has eroded. What remains are persistent performances of the patrimonialist narrative as a form of static normative labelling. Especially in the wake of the 'third wave of democratization' — an attempt to resuscitate modernization theory for the post-Cold War context (witness Barkan, 1994) — descriptions of African politics based on the premise of patrimonial failings have become devoid of theoretical content.

In effect, then, to assert that African states are autocratic, neo-patrimonial or kleptocratic is simply to say that they have not achieved standards of an idealized model liberal democracy. These claims may well be valid, but they do not deepen our theoretical understanding of state formation over time. More upbeat affirmations of Africa's liberal potential, in contrast, err in the opposite direction. Indeed, even Botswana, with its exceptional legacy of stability and democratic elections can only be subsumed under a model of liberalism borrowed from occidental political theory by ignoring much that is essential about its state and its politics. Tellingly, both Botswana and Tanzania have their patrimonialist raconteurs.[2]

Seen in this light, mainstream debates offer meagre nourishment for rethinking the African state (and its twilight institutions) in diachronic terms. I suspect that this dead end hinges on the way liberalism is theorized in current debates.[3] For all their differences, this is what the liberals and the patrimonialists have in common: the notion that the 'proper' trajectory of post-colonial state formation implies approximating some variant of the modern liberal state form.[4] Liberalism haunts diachronic thinking about the state in the form of a foundational, and static, normative abstraction. Liberalism functions in these debates as an ever-present, but often implicit set of abstract, universal ideals that are not grounded in concrete social practices. Debates about post-colonial state formation seek to apply idealized evaluative standards

2. For Botswana, see Good (1994, 2002); for Tanzania, Kelsall (2002) comes close.
3. A number of authors seek to push the limits of this dichotomy. For very different reasons, works like Mbembe (2001) and Schatzberg (2001) would deserve greater attention than is possible in this connection.
4. Naturally some Africanist studies take a reflexive stance with respect to the theoretical status of liberalism. For a complementary meditation on liberalism see the valuable collection on the rhetoric of rights edited by Englund and Nyamjoh (2003).

(regarding democracy, pluralism, individual rights and liberties) which lack a real-world empirical referent in most African contexts. With no repertoire of concrete experiences of 'the modern democratic African state' to frame one's understanding, imaginings of post-colonial stateness that take liberal ideals as their reference point must revert to decontextualized abstractions for a critical fulcrum. As a result, the discussion swirls around in a normative cul-de-sac. The purpose of this essay is to challenge this impasse by attempting to chart out theoretical space within which to think about African politics outside of the tyrannical dichotomy of liberal democracy contra patrimonial autocracy.

This article argues for the need to give more nuanced attention to the empirical nature and political consequences of liberalism in post-colonial Africa. Liberal sentiments have a tangible presence in contemporary African politics — as rhetoric, as political self-identification and as a basis for social networks and collective action — but these localized elements of liberalism do not form an integrated system of ideas and actions. Set in motion by the (post)colonial liberal project[5] via its many agencies and manifestations, 'liberal' identities, relations and modes of political engagement have taken on a life of their own. They do not necessarily contribute to liberal political outcomes ('democratization'), yet this does not render them any less circumstantial with regard to the form and substance of state formation. By concrete illustration, this essay attempts to show how localized modes of liberalism have, in different and often unanticipated ways, been crucial to the trajectories of post-Cold War Zambian politics. The intent here is not to judge or celebrate liberal ideals, or assess their worth as abstract models for political development. Rather, this essay seeks to make visible some of the practical 'work' that liberal sentiments achieve in empirical settings.

LIBERALISM IN CONTEXT: ZAMBIA'S THIRD REPUBLIC

In 1991, Zambia effected an orderly transition from single-party rule (the Second Republic) to a constitutional order based on a multi-party electoral system (the Third Republic). In the subsequent 1991 elections, power transferred from founding president Kenneth Kaunda and his United National Independence Party (UNIP) to the Movement for Multiparty Democracy (MMD) fronted by trade unionist Frederick Chiluba. Chiluba's administration, strongly influence by neo-liberal policy rhetoric (and kept afloat with

5. The 'liberal project' (cf. Hindess, 2002) is conceptual shorthand that refers to the intrinsic evangelism of the European enlightenment — the nearly universal effort to export values, practices and institutions of Western liberal democracy to non-Western societies. An underlying assumption of this analysis, which I will not elaborate upon further at this point, is that liberalism 'considered as a rationality and technology of government rather than as a political philosophy' (Dean, 1999: 173) is innately predisposed to colonize political space with its rationality and techniques.

loans from Washington and its allies) set about deregulating, or 'liberalizing' the Zambian political economy. Deregulation took place in the market (fiscal liberalization, deregulation of commodity markets), in politics (multipartyism, 'decentralization by default', a grassroots power vacuum), in the media and in socio-linguistic and ethnic relations (the resurgence of traditional leaders as political players, a revival of micro-regionalist nationalism), and so on.

Deregulation, in various forms, has had a huge impact on Zambian society; among these has been the abrupt emergence of new arenas of political activity. These novel political emanations encompass the mobilization of new social forces, new organizational forms and alliances, new sites and procedures for negotiating disputes and interests, and new fora for the enunciation of political claims and agendas. Still, deregulation and political pluralism have far from vanquished counter-tendencies toward centralism fuelled by MMD's determination to stay in power. Liberal ideals of democratic rule, with which pluralism was initially equated in the neo-liberal social engineering rhetoric of the late Cold War, have not come to dominate Zambian political culture. And yet, the reconfiguration of the state and politics in Zambia in the Third Republic cannot be understood without reference to liberal principles.

As the story of the Oasis Forum, recounted below, will demonstrate, legalism has a strong foothold in the political imagination of Zambia's professional middle class. The vitality of legalism is fed by numerous factors, some indigenous to the culture of Zambian politics, others grounded in exogenous forces. These latter forces, through which transnational actors and discourses provide ideological and material support for legalist models of government, are both powerful and diffuse. The rhetoric of human rights — institutionalized in the relatively toothless Permanent Human Rights Commission — permeates interactions between Zambians and foreign donors. The currently fashionable 'rights-based approach to development' finds expression in a thriving market for human rights projects among local NGOs. In a devastatingly debt-ridden and aid-dependent country like Zambia, the rhetorical fashions of the donor community are substantive social facts. Sometimes, these fashions have been embraced more out of opportunism than authentic enthusiasm. The ongoing donor crusade for more rights and better governance, however, finds some degree of genuine resonance among the middle classes.

This proliferation of liberal sentiments relates to two features of the political landscape which have seriously undermined the legitimacy of contemporary political institutions. On the one hand is the incumbent president's minority mandate. President Mwanawasa was elected in 2001 with less than 30 per cent of the ballot, in a situation where less than half of the entitled electorate cast a vote. The second fact is the prevailing 'moral crisis' of the post-Chiluba era. The widespread perception of Chiluba's administration as a gang of kleptocratic 'plunderers' has seriously shaken the faith of the

Zambian electorate — that supported his reformist agenda so enthusiastically in 1991 — in the integrity of 'the system'. There are strong grounds for arguing that liberal ideals of modern government have great allure as an antidote to the current crisis.

In one form or another, with different ideological and social groundings, the language and normative imagery of liberalism is an inescapable aspect of deregulated state formation in the Third Republic. This rhetoric takes a multiplicity of forms. The predominant expression of liberalism in the Third Republic comes in the shape of neoliberal free-marketism. This emanates most commonly from government spokesmen and donor overseers who invoke a positivist version of liberalism (as political pluralism and economic liberty) to frame the overall process of social change. Such discourse has the function of limiting respectable policy options to those which make sense within this particular liberal normativity. A *welfarist* version of liberalism also has considerable currency, especially among trade union leaders and social activists. This version commonly calls for greater state regulation based on liberal ideals of equity, human rights and justice.

Liberalism is also invoked in the negative, as self-styled anti-imperialist labelling meant to identify and stigmatize (neo)liberal policies of structural adjustment and associated external intervention. Commonly, but not always, such critiques of neoliberalism are grounded in classical liberal values of equity and justice. Increasingly, liberal ideals also resonate in the constructive critique that motivates and legitimizes the strategies of civic activists and state reformers. Such rhetoric is usually directed at specific government policies and actions and, depending on the context, can take either a free-market or welfarist bearing. Activist lawyers, clergy and social movement leaders are the primary vehicles for the constructive deployment of liberal critique. Finally, in a country currently obsessed with the alleged 'plunder of national resources' by the Chiluba regime it is evident that liberalism also had its cynical variant. In retrospect, many will read duplicity into the eloquent proclamations of liberal principles which became Mr Chiluba's public trademark.

LIBERALISM AS AGENCY

Rhetorical manifestations of liberalism are important social facts, yet these ideas are empty structures without the actions of interested actors to ground them in social experience. Unravelling the nature of localized liberalisms, then, demands careful attention to agency. Actors are naturally constrained by structural features of their social environments: material imperatives, established moral and epistemological dispositions, as well as structures of political opportunity — all enable and constrain both thought and action. Yet the appropriation and instantiation of ideas and sensibilities — such as those that actors themselves perceive to be 'liberal', or those so classified by a participant observer — is an accomplishment of the agency of individual and collective actors in which necessity, intent, and habitus[6] are inextricably present.

Juridically trained and professionally socialized lawyers, in Zambia no less than anywhere else, are stalwart defenders of liberal principles; if asked, Zambian lawyers will uniformly swear in the name of individual liberty, inalienable rights, human equality, and so on. Lawyerly liberalism, however, is of a very specific kind. As Halliday and Karpik (1997: 17) point out, 'If [lawyers] are ever to take a concerted stand, it must be on lawyers' distinctive conception of liberalism, a conception much narrower than broad political definitions, and one that is closely tied to the rule of law'. The liberalism of Zambian lawyers resembles that of lawyers throughout the common law world. It is clearly a species of what American legal scholar Judith Shklar (1986) has portrayed in rich and suggestive detail as *legalism*. For Shklar, legalism is more than a professional disposition, it is a holistic 'social outlook' that permeates a lawyer's moral and political personhood. More precisely, Shklar defines legalism as 'the ethical attitude that holds moral conduct to be a matter of rule following, and moral relationships to consist of duties and rights determined by rules... [Legalism] expresses itself in philosophical thought, in political ideologies, and in social institutions' (ibid.: 1).[7]

Legalism, then, should be understood as a specific manifestation of liberalism. Derived from the core ideas and practices of liberal government — rights and liberties — legalism is in a sense a distillation of a broader constellation of liberal ideals. As embodied in the agency of the legal profession, who are collectively entrusted with the everyday reproduction of the law system, legalism has a special relationship to the state. No matter how one seeks to theorize modern state forms, law is an inescapable element, a cornerstone. This intimate trinity of lawyers, state and law can be a further argument for taking the constitution and consequences of lawyerly agency as a window on state formation. It is also a cautionary reminder of the limitations of viewing complex social processes — including state formation — from a social perspective too closely bound to the state (cf. Bourdieu, in epigraph).

6. The notion of *habitus* is used here in Bourdieu's (1990) sense of the cumulative experience of past socializations (cf. Mouzelis, 1995 for a discussion).
7. This formulation is originally from 1964. In 1986, on the occasion of a reprint of her book, Shklar notes that she used legalism in 'two different senses': first, 'as an ideology' (also: 'belief system') 'internal to the legal profession as a social whole'; and second, as something 'projected into the greater political environment of multiple and competing ideologies' (Shklar, 1986: vii–viii). In this latter sense, legalism is 'not at all restricted to lawyers, although the court of law remains of necessity the most legalistic of all public agencies'. Rather, it competes with 'a considerable number of ethical and political alternatives'.

Table 1. Factors Affecting the Choice to Study Law[8]

Factor	Percentage
Influence of family or friends	22
Making a contribution to society	22
Compatibility of law studies with personal skills and traits	17
Status	11
Other options failed or were less desirable	11
Love of law	8
Money	6
Influence of employer	3
	100 (n = 36)

The Constitution of Legalist Agency

A lawyer's social outlook develops over time, but the critical impact of one's initial professional socialization over the course of law school, internship and studying for the Bar exam is widely acknowledged. As noted by LSE law professor J. A. G. Griffith (1959: 117–19),

> A man who has had legal training is never quite the same again . . . is never able to look at institutions or administrative practices or even social or political policies, free from his legal habits or beliefs . . . He is interested in relationships, in rights in something and against somebody, in relations to others . . . [A lawyer] will fight to the death to defend legal rights against persuasive arguments based on expediency or the public interest or the social good . . . He distrusts them . . . He believes, as part of his mental habits, that they are dangerous and too easily used as cloaks for arbitrary action.

Following these insights, a random selection of students at the Zambia Institute for Advanced Legal Education (ZIALE) was asked 'What factors affected your choice to study law?'. The open-ended responses of these LLB students, two months shy of their Bar exam, are summarized in Table 1. The methodological limitations of the standardized interview format notwithstanding, these responses convey a fair idea of the aims and motives of young Zambian lawyers. Clearly, the students' burgeoning legalist perspective is socially constituted. As a social outlook, it reflects the push and pull of the more immediate features of one's social, economic and political environment. On a personal level and in terms of a corporate professional identity, legalism is linked to a certain mode of engagement with society. Above all, it promises an effective, empowered type of personhood, a capacity to influence and have an impact.

A legalist world view is commonly portrayed as a function of ideas, a function of one's 'habits and beliefs'. Yet these data suggest that the intellectual compellingness of jurisprudence is only one of many factors which draw people to the law, and a relatively minor one at that. For some, the law's perceived neutrality, symmetry and pragmatism are decisive selling points. For the majority, however, less intellectual elements — such as living up to family expectations, being respected by one's peers, a will to do good, or the desire to look good — outstrip the alleged pull of liberal ideals.

To recap: a conceptual cul de sac obstructs innovative theorization of the trajectory of African state formation. This blockage hinges on a misunderstanding of how liberal ideals relate to the exercise and contestation of post-colonial government. A close empirical look at the political agency of Zambian lawyers provides a window onto the ways that elements of liberalism have insinuated themselves into the lives and experience of consequential actors in one scenario. In what follows, the agency of these lawyers, taken as a workable proxy for a more generic constellation of liberal sentiments, is examined as an expression of legalism. The essay ends with a theorized reading of these events and discussion of the consequences of the particular forms of liberal agency encountered for the trajectory of Zambian state formation.

THE POLITICAL AGENCY OF ZAMBIAN LAWYERS: A CASE STUDY

At the core of the story is the Law Association of Zambia (LAZ), the national bar association which has the statutory mandate to regulate the right to practice law in Zambia. LAZ has achieved great visibility in the national awareness and in practical politics in recent years, largely (as discussed below) by virtue of its role in the Oasis Forum. The Association has about 600 members; in other words, there are about 600 practising lawyers in Zambia, mostly based in Lusaka, the capital city.[9] About half of these are relatively prosperous, members of the thin elite stratum of well-to-do Zambians whose lifestyles and consumption patterns are distinctively cosmopolitan. The Zambian legal profession has strong attachments to the British/colonial legal system, and exhibits many of the iconographic trappings of English law (court procedure, wigs and gowns, legal Latin). While Zambia diverges from Britain in that it has a written Constitution, it remains a Common Law jurisdiction and English law can still be cited in precedent, forty years after Independence.

During the First and Second Republics (1964–72 and 1973–91 respectively), lawyers were tightly bound to the UNIP Party/State. In the Third Republic (from 1991), lawyers were initially harnessed to create a framework for political and economic liberalism, the political ideology of the new state party of the Movement for Multiparty Democracy. Though MMD came

---

8. These data were collected in October 2004. Thanks to the Director of Ziale, the Dean of the School of Law at the University of Zambia and to Ian Mabbolobbolo and Tinana Wonani for their assistance. A fuller analysis based on a comprehensive survey of the socio-political views of Zambian law students is forthcoming.
9. LAZ's membership comprises private practitioners and corporate (in-house) lawyers. State advocates are not automatically members of the bar association.

to power through the ballot box, and on a platform of political pluralism, it has demonstrated little tolerance for political opposition. During the 1990s, MMD used the legal profession to prosecute (and persecute) the ousted UNIP leadership, viewed as MMD's main political enemy.[10] At other junctures, for example, in connection with the adoption of the 1996 Constitutional Amendment Act (see below), the Chiluba administration superciliously sidelined the views of the legal community.

After the economic austerity of the 'socialist' 1980s, with endemic shortages of basic commodities, the 1990s were a time of unprecedented prosperity, but only for a small elite largely based in Lusaka. The nouveau riche was made up of three relatively distinct groups with direct access to the dollar economy: the business elite, under a squeeze because trade liberalization opened the floodgates for cheap imports; the formal political elite, often with intimate links to business, consisting of MMD's inner circle, who benefited from economic deregulation by managing the privatization of public assets; and the leadership of externally linked private organizations supported by development aid agencies. The Third Republic heralded in political pluralization and saw the emergence of a much freer (private) information media, but the economic transformation promised by neoliberal ideologues did not materialize. (The copper industry was not revived and there have been only narrow and enclavic developments in export agriculture.) Meanwhile, the vast majority, both rural and urban (more than half of the Zambian population live in cities), have slid into deepening poverty. Throughout the 1990s, public spending was minimal and, apart from some showcase donor investments in road infrastructure, 'development' ground to a halt and virtually stopped toward the end of the Chiluba era as donors curtailed grants and credits in an attempt to leverage better governance. As a result, public services have shrivelled and levels of vulnerability have grown across Zambian society; the HIV epidemic especially has left no family untouched.

These contradictions have had severe consequences for the exercise of government. As the MMD leadership grew increasingly wealthy amidst deepening impoverishment and deprivation, it seemed to abandon its already tenuous respect for state law. Chiluba's second term (1996–2001) is widely viewed as a period of widespread corruption on the part of senior office holders, including the President. The MMD inner circle — Chiluba, the MMD national secretariat, his Minister of Finance, his chief of Intelligence and a number of other 'plunderers' — are widely believed to have dug deep into the public coffers through diverse schemes and scams.[11] As the 2001 elections approached the Chiluba government was widely and openly disliked. For ten years MMD had held the presidency, all cabinet portfolios, and more than 75 per cent of the parliamentary seats, but its prospects looked dim for holding

10. Opposition leaders were targeted for two treason trials in the mid-1990s: the so-called Zero Option and Black Mamba incidents. For more on this period see Rakner (2003).
11. These cases are still in court.

onto power in the 2001 elections. Chiluba's dilemma was further confounded by factors of his own device, relating to the Constitution.

A Private Constitution?

The Zambian Constitution plays a pivotal role in the story of legalist agency, and it is worth recounting Chiluba's 2001 constitutional dilemma in more detail. In 1991, then President Kaunda bowed to intense anti-UNIP sentiments and instigated a Constitutional revision that removed a 1972 clause that guaranteed UNIP's political monopoly. One of the MMD's more popular themes in the 1991 election campaign was the promise of thorough Constitutional reform, aimed at weeding out all elements of one-party authoritarianism from the Constitution.

In 1993, after some procrastination, Chiluba invoked the Inquiries Act (Cap 41 of the Laws of Zambia) to set up a Constitutional Reform Commission under the leadership of John Mwanakatwe, a widely respected legal expert and ex-Minister.[12] Under the terms of its mandate, the Mwanakatwe Commission was to conduct thorough consultations with the Zambian people and to make proposals for fundamental constitutional reform. Based on the provisions of the Inquiries Act, Mwanakatwe's recommendations had to be submitted to the President for consideration, after which Cabinet could table a new draft constitution before Parliament.

Between 1993 and 1995 the Mwanakatwe Commission toured the country and collected reams of public testimony concerning the sort of constitution the Zambians desired. After receiving the Constitutional Review Commission's report and draft constitution, however, Chiluba used his prerogative under the Inquiries Act to throw out the bulk of its recommendations (including many delimiting executive powers), while making a number of strategic insertions of his own. The most controversial of these related to eligibility for Presidential candidature. According to the Constitutional Amendment Act approved by the National Assembly just prior to the 1996 elections, a candidate cannot have already served for two terms as republican president and his or her parents must have been born in Zambia. Chiluba also took advantage of this opportunity to overturn the requirement that the winner of a presidential poll must receive more than half of the votes cast (the '50 per cent + 1' rule). Reverting to a simply majority rule gave a strong advantage to the incumbent party's candidate in a situation characterized by a large number of opposition aspirants.

Regardless of any legal or moral principles that might be invoked for or against such revisions, it was obvious that these qualifications were targeted at ex-President Kenneth Kaunda. Kaunda had already served seven terms as

12. John Mwanakatwe was the first Zambian to earn a university degree (see Mwanakatwe, 2003).

Republican President and his parents were commonly known to have been missionaries of Malawian origin. There was an uproar at the time among human rights and election monitoring NGOs (NGOCC, Fodep, Afronet) about Chiluba's personalization of the constitutional reform process. Significantly, however, LAZ and the legal profession was relatively quiet, despite the fact that this perversion of the MMD's democratic rhetoric occurred at the core of the constitutional order, of which LAZ considers itself to be a publicly consecrated gatekeeper.

In any event, come 2001 Chiluba had a problem. Given the widespread conviction that he was corrupt, and the deep public sentiments against him, leaving office was a risky option. Who would protect him if he stepped down? Despite MMD's overwhelming nominal majority in Parliament it was far from certain, this being an election year, that Chiluba could command the necessary three-quarter's support needed to change the Constitution yet again, removing the two-term limitation on his eligibility. The paradox proved paralysing and Chiluba seemed incapable of making a decision about his next move. Elections had to be held before the end of the year, and yet for the first 220 or more days of 2001 there was no action in parliament to change the constitution and no public announcement of MMD's presidential candidate for the approaching elections.

The Oasis Forum

Chiluba's moment of indecision opened a window of political opportunity, and it was recognized by a number of actors. On the one hand, there was a substantial exodus from MMD of frustrated senior politicians, many of whom had hoped to be anointed as Chiluba's successor. Sixty MPs signed a petition opposing Chiluba's candidacy, and a third of parliament (including fifty MMD Members) petitioned the Speaker to initiate impeachment proceedings against the president (Rakner, 2003: 114). Meanwhile a number of MMD stalwarts grew impatient and decided, based on their reading of the political atmosphere, that they might have better chances in the upcoming elections if they distanced themselves from MMD. These renegades formed a splinter party called the Forum for Democracy and Development (FDD) hoping that a reformist movement could harness the deep popular discontent towards MMD.

Outside the political arena proper, there was much foreboding of impending political crisis were Chiluba to try and hang onto the presidency. Two civic groups were particularly vocal. One group comprised the so-called civil society organizations, which in this context means a diverse range of governance and human rights advocacy groups. Among the most prominent spokespersons for this group were leaders in the Zambian women's movement (like Women for Change's Emily Sikazwe and Grace Kanyanga of the NGO Co-ordinating Committee). The second group, the main Church bodies, with the Catholics in the forefront, openly accused the president of harbouring unconstitutional intentions. Quite remarkably, as popular pressure began to mount in early 2001 a third group, representatives of the Law Association, joined in and began to speak out against the ethical and legal implications of revising the constitution to allow for Chiluba's candidacy.

Under the mediation of Mark Chona, an influential behind-the-scenes political broker in the Kaunda period and a confident of the Catholic bishops, the leaderships of the women's movement (the NGOCC), the three main Christian bodies (the Catholics, Protestants and Evangelicals) and LAZ met quietly and agreed to work together to thwart any designs Chiluba might have on a third term of office. Echoing a precedent set by the emerging MMD a decade earlier,[13] the five organizations convened a workshop in February 2001 at the Oasis Restaurant in Lusaka to agree on a joint communiqué about Chiluba's apparent Third Term bid, which subsequently became known as the Oasis Declaration.

The Oasis Declaration

The Oasis Declaration is a unique document in Zambia's political history and is widely seen among the progressive and professional middle class (of which the legal profession is a social pillar) as a watershed in the consolidation of a broadly-based civic movement for what many would term a genuinely modern form of government. The following excerpt conveys a sense of the language:

> The Law Association of Zambia *in conjunction with* the Church, that is to say the Zambia Episcopal Conference (ZEC), the Christian Council of Zambia (CCZ), the Evangelical Fellowship of Zambia (EFZ) and the Non-Governmental Organisations Co-ordinating Committee (NGOCC) and the People gathered here, having deemed it necessary, expedient, imperative and desirable to promote and conduct a debate in relation to the intimation by the ruling party, the Movement for Multi-Party Democracy (MMD) to amend the Republican Constitution to provide a third term of office in order to facilitate the eligibility of the incumbent President FTJ Chiluba in the forthcoming Presidential and Parliamentary Elections...
>
> [And whereas] ... the Constitution of Zambia as amended in 1996 declares that 'Not withstanding anything to the contrary contained in this Constitution or any other Law, no person who has twice been elected as President shall be eligible for re-election to that office'.
>
> Now this Forum declares as follows:
>
> 1. that the Forum calls upon the incumbent Republican President to exercise statesmanship by unambiguously pledging to Uphold, protect and defend the Constitution of Zambia and not contest the 2001 Presidential Elections...

The Declaration goes on, in §14, to further call 'upon the women, men and the youth of this country to close ranks and resist ever again from being

13. The MMD was launched at a heterogeneous gathering of anti-UNIP activists at the Garden Motel in 1991.

used and abused in any political process for selfish political ends that may threaten our nation's peace and security'.[14]

There are a number of things going on here, and many readings of this text are possible. Even at first blush, however, it is evident that this is a *legalist* attempt to harness the legitimacy of 'the People' to launch an intervention into the arena of state politics. LAZ takes the active voice and assumes a stance of organizational, moral and political leadership in the face of impending crisis. The Oasis Declaration expresses, in its language and its substantive intent, a specifically *lawyerly* imagining of the state, and a specifically *legalist* mode of authority, of politics and political morality. To anticipate a later argument, one can see here the appropriation and promotion of juridical capital as a political tool.

The Oasis Declaration along with subsequent Oasis Forum communiqués, articles and speeches articulate a decisive and vigorously imagined vision of 'modern government'. Note also that this lawyerly imagining is not meant to guide *legal* action — it is not a reflexive meditation on the 'rule of law' or on substantive constitutional issues — rather it is an expression, both in form and content, of a judicialized mode of politics, one in which the authority of the Law transcends and arbitrates between the self-serving interests of given social and political forces. It is meant to guide civic, popular political action, as evidenced in §14.

A Success Story

The Oasis Forum (OF) is a fascinating socio-political project. It represents an unprecedented coalition of diverse social forces — urban professionals alongside rural politicians, community leaders and traditional chiefs. In Bourdieu's terms, OF might be seen as the unlikely alliance of three different species of symbolic capital legal. In the words of one of the main Catholic activists in the OF:

> [T]he Church played a big role in the initiation of the Oasis Forum, because it was the churches that invited the other organisations, to say 'let's work together to stop this business of the third term' and defended the constitution. And we are lucky that the Law Association of Zambia was quickly, you know, excited about it. And they also said they are founded on the protection of the law . . . [T]he Law Association of Zambia which was a very professional organisation, not really involved in these social issues in the manner in which they are now, but from the experience of the third term debate, started taking that public role. Before that we had individual lawyers who were very active in this, like even in 1995–6 we had a good number of lawyers who were very active as individuals in the constitutional process, but not the Law Association of Zambia as an organisation, until 1999–2000 when the third term issue came up. Then the Law Association took a very clear stand and . . . if you look at the Memorandum

14. Emphasis added. The Oasis Declaration is a permanent fixture on the website of Zambia's largest private newspaper, and defender of liberal modernity, *The Post*. Available at http://www.zamnet.zm/zamnet/post/oasisdec.html.

> of Understanding, it was clearly seen that ... the church has this reputation of integrity, of moral authority. And then the Law Association of Zambia came with their authority on the law, their legal authority. And then the NGOCC came with their capacity to mobilise and to inspire, so now when you bring those strengths together, capacity to mobilise, legal authority and moral authority, you have a very formidable [alliance].[15]

The patrimonial perspective suggests a more cynical view, that is, that the OF represents the co-option of the democratic mandates of the church and the women's movement in the technocratic/patrimonial interests of the legal profession. Such a reading is not immediately compelling. Like many earlier civil society coalitions,[16] OF could have been a flash in the pan, dissolving quickly into distrust and competing claims to leadership and authority. Quite unexpectedly, for everyone I think, OF persevered, despite a decade of inter-denominational tensions within the Christian community and initial mutual suspicion between the women activists and the 'men in suits' of LAZ. It is a remarkable story, punctuated by landmark political events. I would like to call attention to three major features of the OF chronicle thus far.

First, the OF campaign against Chiluba's third term bid was hugely successful in both its means and its ends. It spearheaded a mass popular movement that blocked Chiluba's candidacy and secured the integrity of the constitution. Stymied by a mass campaign of passive resistance that cleverly visualized deep popular opposition to his administration rule, Chiluba was forced to anoint former vice-President Levy Mwanawasa as his successor only months before the election. Mwanawasa is himself a lawyer, and though he carried MMD to victory he was voted into office with a margin of just 12,000 in circumstances very conducive to electoral fraud. He subsequently consolidated his position by turning his back on Chiluba, and getting parliament to lift Chiluba's judicial immunity. This is a pertinent story in itself that unfortunately can't be pursued here. The main point is that the OF victory restored a semblance of political agency to 'the people' of Zambia, and instilled a sense of trust in 'the system'.

Second, OF revolutionized the organization of Zambian social movement politics. Its leadership evolved an innovative mechanism of collective/rotating leadership that succeeded in keeping the Forum together and in maintaining a unified rhetorical front for the duration of the anti-Third Term campaign. As the arbiters of the legal expertise central to all communiqués and declarations, LAZ has a special role in the coalition. Yet the spokesperson rotates from one member organization to another (from lawyer to bishop to feminist activist), requiring considerable trust and self-discipline on all sides.

Third, most remarkably perhaps, OF has maintained its unity. After a period of relative post-election dormancy, OF regrouped in early 2003 to challenge

15. Joe Komakoma, Lusaka 8 July 2004; interviewed by Noora Rikalainen.
16. For example, Coalition 2001 of human rights organizations formed to pool election monitoring resources and recruit donor support for the defence of 'free and fair elections' dissolved amidst in-fighting soon after the elections.

the government on its plans for a new Constitutional Review. This revitalization of the Forum around constitutional reform has also accentuated the legalist undercurrent in its activities. LAZ has moved to the forefront of this new OF campaign which is pitted against the President's decision to appoint a Constitutional Review Commission based on the Inquires Act — thus rendering its recommendations susceptible to presidential manipulation, as was the case with the Mwanakatwe Commission's recommendations in 1996. The new OF campaign advocates on behalf of drafting and adopting the new constitution by a Constituent Assembly along the South African model, in explicit opposition to allowing the president to table a constitutional draft for parliamentary ratification that reflects the executive's discretionary powers.[17]

Localized Liberalism

The story of the Oasis Forum reveals legalist agency in action. The agency of lawyers has many outlets, though, and one could cite a number of very different accounts of localized liberalism.[18] In many respects, this particular example of lawyers' political activism through the Law Association is quite exceptional. As an expression of a lawyerly social outlook, however, there is nothing *a*typical about the sentiments expressed in the OF's rhetoric and actions. Taken as an affirmation of certain ideal typical features of legal agency in the Zambia context, the lessons of the OF offer an opportunity to think about the consequences of legalism in practice for the contours of politics and for alternative paths of state formation.

The OF narrative manifests a series of events by which a novel form of political agency grounded in an ideology of legalism and organized around the legal profession and allied social actors grew to surprising dimensions. These developments corroborate the premise that the practices and relations of government in Zambia are undergoing, to borrow a term from the Comaroffs (2003), a process of 'legalization'. This refers not so much to the 'colonization' by law of life-worlds that Habermas (1984) bemoans; nor to the 'judicialization' of politics (Shapiro and Stone Sweet, 2002), whereby judges undertake to regulate politicians and their agendas. Rather, the legalization of politics indicates a tendency for social networks, ideas and

17. An earlier wave of civic activism on behalf of a Constituent Assembly mode of adoption of the constitution occurred in 1995/6 when a Civil Society Action Committee comprising twenty-seven member organizations convened a Citizens' Convention in protest at Chiluba's 1996 Constituional Amendment Act. The Law Association was not party to the CSAC, although a few individual lawyers were active in the campaign (*The Citizens' Convention Report*, mimeo, nd).
18. Examples I have been working on include the constructive engagement of lawyers with customary law and traditional leaders; their involvement in the 'war against corruption'; and political uses of judicial review.

procedures grounded in an ideology of legalism to subsume social spaces earlier organized by other political logics.

As we have seen, unfolding and heavily contingent political processes in Zambia have led lawyers into a number of sites and processes whereby the professional agency of legal practitioners has become intimately engaged with the state, and in doing so has become a form of politics. Reflecting on these sites and confrontations, of which the Oasis Forum saga is a prime example, suggests that the relationship between 'law' and 'politics' is undergoing a major transformation in contemporary Zambia. To understand this transformation, as Bourdieu (1999: 72) suggests, 'one must focus in particular on the structure of the juridical field and uncover both the generic interests of the holders of [a] particular form of . . . symbolic capital, that is, juridical competence, as well as the specific interests imposed on each of them by virtue of their position in a still weakly autonomous juridical field'.

What does this imply? Bourdieu's dense terminology begs unpacking. For these purposes, the legal field (Bourdieu, 1987) can be understood as the social and political space occupied by differently constituted, situated and competing claimants to 'juridical capital'. Bourdieu identifies four species of capital representing the resources wielded by social actors acting politically, in their struggles among themselves for social dominance. For the purposes of this discussion, it is useful to think of 'the state' as an outcome of these processes of political contestation. Or, as Bourdieu (1999: 58) puts it: 'It follows that the construction of the state proceeds apace with the construction of a field of power, defined as the space of play within which the holders of capital (of different species) struggle in particular for power over the state, i.e., over the statist capital [capital étatique] granting power over the species of capital and over their reproduction'.

The main forms of capital are the capital of physical force; economic capital; informational capital and symbolic capital. Symbolic capital is especially potent in that its arbiters have significant leverage over defining what constitutes socially recognized forms of legitimate authority. The educational system is generally seen as the primary site of the formation and deployment of symbolic capital. Bourdieu's reading of early modern French political history, however, singles out juridical capital, a subspecies of symbolic capital, as having a privileged historical role in the process of state formation.

The fit between Bourdieu's abstract construct and Zambian empiria is striking. Participation in the Oasis Forum provided Zambian lawyers with a unique opportunity to both appropriate symbolic capital and to enhance the political value of the juridical capital they embody as a profession. One might think of symbolic/juridical capital in this connection as a kind of stock which one can own more or less of, and which fluctuates in value depending on the vagaries of the market. If juridical capital is seen to proffer special privileges *vis-à-vis* the state, it is reasonable to assume that lawyers with ambitions in that direction (whatever these might be) would seek to accumulate stock of juridical capital and boost its share value. A situation in which the state's propriety — in the dual sense of both ownership and decency — is less than certain might be assumed to encourage actions oriented toward the accumulation and value-enhancement of juridical stock.

This is certainly the case in Zambia. The country is not embroiled in a political crisis, but one can definitely sense a 'crisis of politics', public suspicion that no one is fully in control of the regulatory tools of government. The weak mandate of the incumbent executive, and his government's enduring indecisiveness in all areas of leadership has activated a great many novel forms of politics. Law has become such a 'field of power', a site of intense contestation within and through which the legal profession and its select allies are waging campaigns for a redefinition of the contours of the state and the substance of politics. At the same time, state propriety over law is diminishing. Not only are lawyers and their activist allies trying to wrest the constitutional reform process from the control of the government, the legitimacy of state actions are increasingly challenged through public petition and judicial review.[19] It would seem that the weight of juridical capital is increasing relative to that wielded by other species of symbolic capital, including those of professional politicians and other core state actors.

Because the legal-political field is defined by an ideology of legalism, it has its own special rules; by the same token, the politics of this arena are of a very specific kind — specific kinds of issues become political in specific ways and are dealt with in a specifically legalist manner. Within this semi-autonomous legal-political field, law itself becomes a special political object, legal authority takes on enhanced political capital and legal processes substitute for the resolution of political disputes and competition.

Legalization and State Formation

The substance of 'legalism' is both ambiguous and intensely contested. Among contesting notions of legalism only a minority advocate 'political liberalism' in the sense of a moderate state and a respect for citizenship (cf. Halliday and Karpik, 1997: 16). One must also contend with 'natural law' legalism (which seeks to harness legal authority to the defense of 'custom'); with legalism as formal proceduralism (driven by a will to exploit the authority of a very conservative legal system); with legalism as political instrumentalism (drawing on legalistic arguments to attain short-term political benefits, such as expelling a competitor from one's party), and so on.

---

19. A good example is the attempted deportation, in early 2004, of outspoken *Post* columnist Roy Clarke. Clarke, a British citizen and long-term Zambian resident, published a satire which likened the wild animal population of a national park to the president and his cabinet. The next day, the Minister of Home Affairs issued a deportation order. Through his attorney, LAZ stalwart Patrick Matibini, Clarke's application for judicial review blocked the deportation order. Overturning the Minister's direct decree in court constituted yet another victory over the government for LAZ, the *Post* and liberal legalism. Such things didn't happen under Kaunda or Chiluba.

Perhaps more important than the substantive ideas or principles with which legalism is advanced are the social relations and modes of co-ordinated action that emerge around legalistic contestation: the promotion of a legalist agenda can draw the support of important political allies (including those in the transnational realm) and thus (inadvertently) empower very 'illiberal' agendas (see Pratten, this issue). Certain instantiations of legalism, when bound to exclusive and asymmetrical power relationships, can be anything but 'liberating'.

The normative assessment of legalization should be based on outcomes, not ideal intentions. Thus far, the marked hike in the share-value of juridical capital has largely contributed to the trajectory of intra-elite contestation. It may, in the long run — say, if demands for a new Bill of Rights succeed in bolstering the statutory rights of vulnerable groups — imply tangible outcomes for the common citizen. For the time being, this is merely a promise. The final assessment of legalist agency's prime achievement — blocking Chiluba's third term designs — is generally seen as positive. Yet here too, one can harbour reasonable doubts. In the longer term, democracy might have been better served if Chiluba had stood and met with a resounding defeat at the polls, dislodging the dysfunctional MMD from power, and returning a majority president. This is pure speculative hindsight, but the evident credibility of such a scenario suggests that civic mobilization, especially when driven by elite aims and values, should not be embraced as an end in itself.

Does the advance of legalism, and the concomitant empowerment of the legal fraternity, auger well for liberal democracy? It's far too early to draw clear conclusions on this. It is not impossible that a future administration could break the back of the Law Association and kowtow the profession into the sort of compliance that prevailed until the mid-1990s. From the perspective of state formation, a more interesting question concerns the fate of the law as a regulatory mechanism capable of mediating between political interests. To the extent that 'the law' is a product (construction) of the discourse, practices and social relations of legalism, it appears to be increasingly up for grabs. Analyses of extant legal processes indicate that the most resourceful, aggressive, skillful, strategic, charismatic, scale-jumping players can succeed in playing the law to their own advantage. For the time being, no clear political interests or agendas have demonstrated a systematic capacity to dominate the legal-political field. One can rather confidently predict, however, that legal processes will become increasingly important sites of political contestation (further enhancing the position of the legal profession as a political broker).

The trend is clear: 'the law' is diminishingly an arm of 'the state' in any but a rhetorical and romanticized sense. The liberal language of 'stateness' (Hansen and Stepputat, 2001) is a constant corollary of legal rhetoric, and the liberal aesthetic of the legal field continues to evoke memories of a once-hegemonic post-colonial state. But while 'rule of law' appears to be in the ascendant, a Zambian *rechtsstaat* does not.

REFERENCES

Abrams, P. (1988) 'Difficulties of Studying the State', *Historical Sociology* 1(1): 58–89.
Barkan, J. D. (1994) 'Resurrecting Modernization Theory and the Emergence of Civil Society in Kenya and Nigeria', in D. Apter and C. Rosberg (eds) *Political Development and the New Realism in Sub-Saharan Africa*, pp. 87–116. Charlottesville, VA: University of Virginia Press.
Bayart, J. F. (1991) *The State in Africa: The Politics of the Belly*. London: Longman.
Bayart, J. F., S. Ellis and B. Hibou (1999) *The Criminalization of the State in Africa*. Oxford: James Currey.
Bourdieu, P. (1987) 'The Force of Law: Toward a Sociology of the Juridical Field', *Hastings Law Journal* 38(5): 814–53.
Bourdieu, P. (1990) *The Logic of Practice*. Cambridge: Polity Press.
Bourdieu, P. (1999) 'Rethinking the State: Genesis and Structure of the Bureaucratic Field', in W. Steinmetz (ed.) *State/Culture: State Formatino after the Colonial Turn*, pp. 53–75. Ithaca, NY: Cornell University Press.
Carothers, T. (1999) *Aiding Democracy Abroad. The Learning Curve*. Washington, DC: The Carnegie Endowment.
Chabal, P. and J. P. Daloz (1999) *Africa Works: Disorder as a Political Instrument*. Oxford: James Currey.
Comaroff, J. and J. Comaroff (2003) 'Law and Disorder in the Post-colony'. Harvard, MA: Radcliffe Institute for Advanced Study (mimeo).
Corrigan, P. and D. Sayers (1985) *The Great Arch: English State Formation as Cultural Revolution*. Oxford: Basil Blackwell.
Dean, M. (1999) *Governmentality: Power and Rule in Modern Society*. London: Sage.
Englund, H. and F. Nyamjoh (2003) *Rights and the Politics of Recognition*. London: Zed Books.
Geertz, C. (ed.) (1963) *Old Societies and New States: The Quest for Modernity in Asia and Africa*. London: The Free Press of Glencoe.
Good, K. (1994) 'Corruption and Mismanagement in Botswana: A Best Case Example', *Journal of Modern African Studies* 32(3): 499–521.
Good, K. (2002) 'Rethinking Non-accountability and Corruption in Botswana', *Africa Insight* 32(3): 11–18.
Griffith, J. A. G. (1959) 'The Law of Property', in M. Ginsberg (ed.) *Law and Opinion in England in the 20th Century*, pp. 117–19 Westport, CT: Greenwood Publishing.
Habermas, J. (1984) *The Theory of Communicative Action*. Vol. 1: *Reason and the Rationalization of Society*. London: Heinemann.
Halliday, T. C. and L. Karpik (1997) *Lawyers and the Rise of Western Political Liberalism*. Oxford: Clarendon Press.
Hansen, T. B. and F. Stepputat (eds) (2001) *States of Imagination: Ethnographic Explorations of the Postcolonial State*. Durham, NC: Duke University Press.
Hindess, B. (2002) 'Neo-liberal Citizenship', *Citizenship Studies* 6(2): 127–43.
Joseph, G. M. and D. Nugent (eds) (1994) *Everyday Forms of State Formation. Revolution and the Negotiation of Rule in Modern Mexico*. Durham, NC: Duke University Press.
Kelsall, T. (2002) 'Shop Windows and Smoke-filled Rooms: Governance and the Re-politicisation of Tanzania', *Journal of Modern African Studies* 40(4): 597–619.
Mbembe, A. (2001) *On the Postcolony*. Berkeley, CA: University of California Press.
Medard, J. F. (1982) 'The Underdeveloped State in Tropical Africa: Political Clientelism or Neo-patrimonialism', in C. Clapham (ed.) *Private Patronage and Public Power: Political Clientelism in Modern State*, pp 162–92. London: Macmillan.
Mouzelis, N. (1995) *Sociological Theory: What Went Wrong?* London: Routledge.
Mwanakatwe, J. (2003) *Teacher Politician Lawyer: My Autobiography*. Lusaka: Bookworld.
Rakner, L. (2003) *Political and Economic Liberalisation in Zambia 1991–2001*. Uppsala: Nordic Africa Institute.

Republic of Zambia (1996) *Constitution of the Republic of Zambia*. Lusaka: Government Printers.
Roth, G. (1968) 'Personal Rulership, Patrimonialism and Empire-building in New States', *World Politics* 20(2): 194–206.
Schatzberg, M. (2001) *Political Legitimacy in Middle Africa: Father, Family, Food*. Bloomington, IN: Indiana University Press.
Shapiro, M. and A. Stone Sweet (2002) *On Law, Politics & Judicialization*. Oxford: Oxford University Press.
Shklar, J. N. (1986) *Legalism. Law, Morals and Political Trials* (reprint). Cambridge: Harvard University Press.
Steinmetz, G. (ed.) (1999) *State/Culture: State-formation after the Cultural Turn*. Ithaca, NY: Cornell University Press.
Weber, M. (1968) *Economy and Society: An Outline of Interpretive Sociology*, eds G. Roth and C. Wittich. New York: Bedminster Press.
Werbner, R. (2004) *Reasonable Radicals and Citizenship in Botswana*. Bloomington, IN: Indiana University Press.
Widner, J. (2001) *Building the Rule of Law: Francis Nyalali and the Road to Judicial Independence in Africa*. New York: Norton and Co.
Young, C. (2004) 'The End of the Post-colonial State in Africa? Reflections on Changing African Political Dynamics', *African Affairs* 103: 23–49.

Index